Decolonizing Nature

T. J. Demos

Decolonizing Nature

Contemporary Art and the Politics of Ecology

Sternberg Press

Contents

Introduction

This book investigates the intersection of contemporary art, environmental activism, and political ecology. While ecology—in particular, its political dimensions—has received limited attention within academic studies of the visual (and particularly the art historical), in recent years the looming threat of manifold environmental crises, exacerbating sociopolitical and economic ones, has grown ever more evident worldwide. Indeed, there is an increasing sense of urgency within multiple realms of visual culture, including art exhibitions, social movements, and mainstream and independent media, as ecological concerns have been taken up in video, documentary photography, creative activism, architecture, and socially engaged art.[1] The term "political ecology," as used herein, acknowledges approaches to the environment that, although potentially divergent, nevertheless insist on environmental matters of concern as inextricable from social, political, and economic forces. Since environmental stresses can be both a driver and consequence of injustice and inequality—including

1 A selection of recent publications in art history, visual culture, and architectural and curatorial studies that addresses art and ecology includes: James Brady, ed., *Elemental: An Arts and Ecology Reader* (Manchester: Cornerhouse Publications, 2016); Emily Eliza Scott and Kirsten Swenson, eds., *Critical Landscapes: Art, Space, Politics* (Oakland: University of California Press, 2015); Maja Fowkes, *The Green Bloc: Neo-avant-garde Art and Ecology under Socialism* (Budapest: Central European Press, 2015); Lucy R. Lippard, *Undermining: A Wild Ride through Land Use, Politics, and Art in the Changing West* (New York: The New Press, 2014); Forensic Architecture, eds., *Forensis: The Architecture of Public Truth* (Berlin: Sternberg Press, 2014) Also see "Contemporary Art and the Politics of Ecology," ed. T. J. Demos, special issue, *Third Text*, no. 120 (January 2013); and the "Anthropocene Project" (2013–14) at the Haus der Kulturen der Welt, Berlin. I examine the longer history of environmental art in chapter 1.

poverty, racism, and neocolonial violence—political ecology recognizes that the ways we regard nature carry deep implications and often unacknowledged ramifications for how we organize society, assign responsibility for environmental change, and assess social impact. At the same time, as I work out of my own intellectual formation in art history, analyses in this book draw on interdisciplinary science and cultural studies as well as critical philosophy that artists have also engaged with—speculative realism and new materialism as much as Indigenous cosmologies and climate justice activism.[2] My conviction is that environmentally engaged art bears the potential to both rethink politics and politicize art's relation to ecology, and its thoughtful consideration proves nature's inextricable binds to economics, technology, culture, and law at every turn.[3] Addressing that convergence, and its political effects, cultural translations, and artistic mobilizations, is this book's central concern.

As we know, the ongoing destruction of our environment by anthropogenic pollution is pushing us toward catastrophic circumstances. This situation promises only to worsen as we advance toward a series of climate-change tipping points.[4] Amounting to the most momentous experimentation with the earth's living systems in human history, this environmental alteration, put into place by industrial modernity (with roots in the formation of capitalism centuries before), threatens increased temperatures, plummeting agricultural yields, wide-ranging droughts and consequent raging wildfires, massive flooding, extreme weather events, the collapse of fisheries, and public health breakdowns

2 By capitalizing Indigenous throughout this book, I'm following recent critical scholarship—for instance, Glen Coulthard, *Red Skin, White Masks: Rejecting the Colonial Politics of Recognition* (Minneapolis: University of Minnesota Press, 2014)—that employs this style as a mode of cultural respect for, and political affirmation of, native peoples and their manifold rights struggles.

3 Political ecology has a varied and complex genealogy, articulated at the intersections of cultural geography, human ecology, anthropology, environmental studies, and political economy over the course of the twentieth century. In general, it examines the unequal distribution of costs and benefits of environmental changes according to social, cultural, and economic differences, in relation to their political implications. For overviews, see Raymond L. Bryant and Sinead Bailey, *Third World Political Ecology* (London: Routledge, 1997); and Paul Robbins, *Political Ecology: A Critical Introduction* (Oxford: Blackwell, 2004).

4 For overviews of climate-change science, see James Hansen, *Storms of My Grandchildren: The Truth about the Coming Climate Catastrophe and Our Last Chance to Save Humanity* (New York: Bloomsbury Press, 2009); Naomi Klein, *This Changes Everything: Capitalism vs. the Climate* (New York: Allen Lane, 2014); Elizabeth Kolbert, *The Sixth Extinction: An Unnatural History* (New York: Henry Holt and Company, 2014); Bill McKibbon, *Eaarth: Making a Life on a Tough New Planet* (New York: Henry Holt and Company, 2010); and Rajendra K. Pachauri, Leo Meyer, and the Core Writing Team, eds., *Climate Change 2014: Synthesis Report; Contribution of Working Groups I, II and III to the Fifth Assessment Report of the Intergovernmental Panel on Climate Change* (Geneva: IPCC, 2014), http://www.ipcc.ch/pdf/assessment-report/ar5/syr/SYR_AR5_FINAL_full_wcover.pdf.

with spreading epidemics.[5] While the predictions seem to worsen each year, none should be new. A long-standing subject of peer-reviewed journals and expert research, anthropogenic climate disruption has reached global scientific consensus in the form of the Intergovernmental Panel on Climate Change (IPCC), which issued its fifth synthesis report in 2014, reaffirming—in quite conservative terms, according to some critics—what we have known, at least in part, for decades. Kevin Anderson, deputy director of the Tyndall Centre for Climate Change Research a notable scientist-activist of our day, observes that with the current production of greenhouse gases, we're heading toward global warming of some four degrees Celsius (7.2°F) by the end of this century, which is of a magnitude "incompatible with any reasonable characterization of an organized, equitable and civilized global community."[6]

In the meantime, we have seen more than twenty years of international meetings sponsored by the United Nations (beginning with the Rio Earth Summit in 1992)—our closest approximation of global climate governance—charged with proposing ways to stabilize atmospheric greenhouse gas concentration at safe levels that would not alter the earth's climate. The meetings began a few years after NASA climatologist James Hansen, in 1988, gave his historic presentation in the US Senate explaining that the record temperatures of the year so far were owed *not* to natural variation, but to the increase of human-produced atmospheric pollutants. Since then, emissions have gone up by more than half.[7] The Rio summit agreed with the now-accepted, crucial principle of "common but differing responsibilities" of developing and industrialized countries in addressing climate change, giving rise to a key strand of climate justice that both counters the idea that all humans are equally culpable for environmental change and legitimates the concept of climate debt (the notion that countries burning fossil fuels since the Industrial Revolution have used up their pollution allowance and owe a liability to the others).[8] Yet

5 As the scientific journal *Nature* explains in a recent issue on conservation and extinction, "Thousands of species are disappearing each year. If that trend continues, it could lead to a mass species extinction—defined as a loss of 75% of species—over the next few centuries." Richard Monastersky, "Biodiversity: Life—A Status Report," *Nature* 516 (December 2014): 159. Also see Dahr Jamail, "Climate Disruption's New Record: Carbon Dioxide Levels Reach Highest Point in 15 Million Years," *Truthout*, February 29, 2016, http://www.truth-out.org/news/item/22521-climate-disruption-dispatches-with-dahr-jamail.

6 "It indeed becomes difficult to imagine that a peaceful, ordered society could be sustained (that is, where such a thing exists in the first place)." Kevin Anderson, "Climate Change Going Beyond Dangerous: Brutal Numbers and Tenuous Hope," *Development Dialogue*, no. 61 (September 2012): 29.

7 See the data of the Carbon Dioxide Information Analysis Center, which puts the current global CO_2 atmospheric levels at an alarming 403.94 ppm; accessed March 29, 2016, http://cdiac.ornl.gov.

UN climate meetings to date have not yielded any binding agreements or governmental leadership regarding environmental policy, particularly the annual Conference of the Parties, or COP, including the most recent in 2015.[9] Though agreements at such events are regularly signed to keep temperatures from increasing more than two degrees Celsius (3.6°F) above preindustrial levels (or 1.5°C, agreed at COP21), they are effectively meaningless when voluntary and unenforceable. To low-lying states threatened with sea-level rise and sub-Saharan African countries already suffering drought-stressed heat waves, these non-measures amount to what Nigerian environmental activist Nnimmo Bassey calls a "death sentence."[10] With G8 government representatives continually lobbied by the fossil fuel industry, it has become clear that we are being held hostage to corporate powers that place short-term profits over long-term sustainability, as free-market economics is worshipped at the cost of our planet's very life-supporting capacity.[11] The system of global governance is clearly failing.

At the same time, we are seeing a flourishing of contemporary artistic and activist practices that address and negotiate environmental conflict in other ways. These include cogent analyses of ecological destruction (as carried out by extractivism, oil drilling, and marine industrialization) as well as creative alternatives that model forms of environmental sustainability and egalitarian structures of living. Fields of visual culture wider than institutional art practice are involved here—namely, broadcast media, experimental video and film, Internet-based and independent news, creative activism, NGOs, and collective social movements. The productions of this

8 See Andrew Ross, "Climate Debt Denial," *Dissent* (Summer 2013), http://www.dissentmagazine.org/article/climate-debt-denial.

9 See Subhabrata Bobby Banerjee, "A Climate for Change? Critical Reflections on the Durban United Nations Climate Change Conference," *Organization Studies* 33, no. 12 (2012): 1761–86. For a summary of much of the critical commentary around COP21, see George Monbiot, "Grand Promises of Paris Climate Deal Undermined by Squalid Retrenchments," *Guardian*, December 12, 2015, http://www.theguardian.com/environment/georgemonbiot/2015/dec/12/paris-climate-deal-governments-fossil-fuels.

10 After COP17, Bassey, chair of Friends of the Earth International, claimed, "If countries agree to the text as it stands, they will be passing a death sentence on Africa." Reported in Stephen Leahy, "Draft Climate Deal Dubbed a 'Death Sentence for Africa,'" *Inter Press Service*, December 9, 2011, http://www.ipsnews.net/2011/12/draft-climate-deal-dubbed-a-death-sentence-for-africa. More recently, see Marion Deschamps and Cyril Mychalejko, "Did World Leaders Sign a 'Death Warrant for the Planet' at COP21?," *Truthout*, December 14, 2015, http://www.truth-out.org/opinion/item/34016-world-leaders-signed-a-death-warrant-for-the-planet-at-cop21.

11 See Naomi Klein, "Hot Money: How Free Market Fundamentalism Helped Overheat the Planet," in *This Changes Everything*, 64–95; and John Cavanagh and Jerry Mander, eds., *Alternatives to Economic Globalization: A Better World Is Possible; A Report of the International Forum on Globalization* (San Francisco, CA: Berrett-Koehler, 2002). See also "The COP 21 Guide to Corporate Climate Lobbying," *InfluenceMap*, November 26, 2015, http://influencemap.org/report/The-COP-21-Guide-to-Corporate-Climate-Lobbying.

assemblage form a complex aesthetic field that is also politically organized, contesting the dominant "distribution of the sensible," where, according to Jacques Rancière's useful conceptualization, some voices clearly count and others are relegated to the sensory background, an economically determined, antidemocratic arrangement that activist-artists are continually challenging.[12] This book hopes to further enliven this intersection of art and activism by offering critical analysis of their diverse strategic rhetorics, visual constructions, affective impacts, conceptual maneuvers, political goals, and actual effects, by which people form alliances, create social movements, and make visible publics that counter corporate and governmental positions via creative engagements with media.[13] In this regard, my approach remains attentive to what Meg McLagan and Yates McKee term the "image complex," or "the whole network of financial, institutional, discursive, and technological infrastructures and practices involved in the production, circulation, and reception of [...] visual-cultural materials." That formation calls for a diagnostics not centered solely on the "politics of aesthetics" of the image, but also on the wider channels of image circulation, the institutions of containment, and the legal-political-economic assemblages that frame and in part determine the visual culture of environmentalism.[14]

An additional commitment of this project is to consider ecological formations and conflicts in their global dimension—the convergence of politics and aesthetics in the Global South as well as the North, regions filled with continuities and differences that are economic and geopolitical as much as sociocultural and environmental. In this regard, contemporary positions of environmental artistic practice substantially differ from past varieties in that they tend to avoid the now-inadequate elements of earlier eco-artistic languages, such as those of the 1970s, particularly "the constant elegy for a lost unalienated state, the resort to the aesthetic dimension (experimental/perceptual) rather than ethical-political praxis, [and] the appeal to 'solutions,' often anti-intellectual," as ecology and literature theorist Timothy Morton has put it.[15] Many contemporary practices also go beyond eco-aesthetic forms of parochial environmentalism (such as those exclusively attached to the wilderness

12 Jacques Rancière, *Dissensus: On Politics and Aesthetics*, trans. Steven Corcoran (London: Bloomsbury, 2015).

13 George Marcus, *Connected: Engagements with Media* (Chicago: University of Chicago Press, 1996), 6; and Bruno Latour and Peter Weibel, eds., *Making Things Public: Atmospheres of Democracy*, trans. Robert Bryce (Cambridge, MA: MIT Press, 2005).

14 Meg McLagan and Yates McKee, eds., introduction to *Sensible Politics: The Visual Culture of Nongovernmental Activism* (New York: Zone Books, 2012), 12, 9.

15 Timothy Morton, *Ecology without Nature: Rethinking Environmental Aesthetics* (Cambridge, MA: Harvard University Press, 2007), 23.

landscapes of North America), and take up relational geographies, comparative analyses, and transnational alliances directed against, for instance, the ecocide of corporate globalization or the socioeconomic ramifications of environmental destruction. The most compelling current artistic models, in my view, join the aesthetic dimension of experimental and perceptual engagement with the commitment to postcolonial ethico-political praxis, and do so with sustained attention to how local activities interact with global formations.[16]

War on Nature

My analysis of art and environment extends from the view that climate change is first and foremost a *political* crisis, not one that poses insurmountable technological problems or natural barriers: what is needed most is the will to address ecological concerns systematically and comprehensively. There are, in fact, plenty of solutions for sustainable living today, which, if implemented globally, could protect biodiversity and define a more equitable and inclusive socioeconomic order than today's environmentally destructive corporate-state oligarchy.[17] I agree with a range of environmental and political activists who contend that the threat of climate change is the best motivation for a "Great Transition," which will require a systemic shift in reorganizing social, political, and economic life, in order to bring us into greater harmony with the world around us, including its human and nonhuman life-forms.[18] In other words, we cannot address climate justice adequately without also targeting the corruption of democratic practice by corporate lobbying, or the underfunding and failure of public transportation systems, or Indigenous rights violations by industrial extractivism, or police violence and the militarization of borders. For these areas all link up in one way or another as interconnected strands of political ecology.

16 For a critical discussion of local and global ecologies, see Ursula K. Heise, *Sense of Place and Sense of Planet: The Environmental Imagination of the Global* (Oxford: Oxford University Press, 2008).

17 Klein points to the work of Mark Z. Jacobson, professor of civil and environmental engineering at Stanford University, and Mark A. Delucchi, research scientist at the Institute of Transportation Studies at University of California, Davis, which details "how 100 percent of the world's energy, for *all* purposes, could be supplied by wind, water and solar resources, by as early as 2030"; Mark Z. Jacobson and Mark A. Delucchi, "A Plan to Power 100 Percent of the Planet with Renewables," *Scientific American*, November 2009; cited in Klein, *This Changes Everything*, 101.

18 Paul Raskin, Tariq Banuri, Gilberto Gallopín, Pablo Gutman, Al Hammond, Robert Kates, and Rob Swart, *Great Transition: The Promise and Lure of the Times Ahead* (Boston: Stockholm Environment Institute, 2002), http://www.world-governance.org/IMG/pdf_0090_Great_Transition_-_ENG.pdf; see also Stephen Spratt, Andrew Simms, Eva Neitzert, and Josh Ryan-Collins, *The Great Transition: A Tale of How It Turned Out Right* (London: New Economics Foundation, 2010), http://www.neweconomics.org/publications/entry/the-great-transition.

It is often in civil spheres where we find the most critical and creative energies, the most ambitious and unconventional proposals, in addressing these interlinked crises. While corporate media and the entertainment industry generally rest content (and benefit financially) in presenting an endless stream of apocalyptic scenarios that make it seem as though environmental catastrophe is our ineluctable fate (or they ignore climate change entirely), there are growing numbers of social-movement campaigners, artists, political theorists, and activists intent on thinking outside the enforced narratives of disaster capitalism. They are doing so increasingly both within the institutionalized exhibition areas of the contemporary art system—I examine numerous models of such practices in the chapters that follow—and beyond those walls, in conflicted public spaces, independent media outlets, and in reclaimed zones of autonomy and the commons. Working within and against the thick, heterogeneous histories of conceptualist art, the complex intertwining of aesthetics and politics within documentary moving-image practices, and the socio-spatial politics of environmental sculpture of decades past, contemporary artists are connecting to and building upon past approaches of institutional critique, documentary fictions, and multispecies assemblages.[19] In this respect, the most adventurous practitioners are also pushing beyond those earlier precedents—for instance, analyzing the political ecologies and economies of art institutions (as well as liberating existing institutions or even inventing whole new models, as in the cases of Liberate Tate and the Laboratory of Insurrectionary Imagination); joining the speculative fictions of video-essay making to politico-environmental imaginaries; and growing linkages between permaculture farming, experimental social relationships, and post-anthropocentric modalities of belonging. As these observations indicate, some of the most ambitious artistic engagements, for me, are those that enact an intersectionalist politics of aesthetics, where art no longer prioritizes the gallery-enclosed experience of aesthetic contemplation alone, but rather emerges in close proximity to field research, creative pedagogies, political mobilization, and civil society partnerships and solidarities, whereby interdisciplinary collaboration mirrors the very complex relations of political ecology.[20] A selection of these practices finds extended consideration in these pages.

19 Here I'm building on my own recent work that has explored the aesthetics and politics of documentary art and neo-conceptualist mixed-media practices, as in *The Migrant Image: The Art and Politics of Documentary* (Durham, NC: Duke University Press, 2013); and *Return to the Postcolony: Specters of Colonialism in Contemporary Art* (Berlin: Sternberg Press, 2013).

20 In this regard, this book resonates with recent publications that investigate the vibrant contemporary efflorescence of activist-arts participating in social-movement cultures, including Yates McKee, *Strike Art: Contemporary Art and the Post-Occupy Condition* (London: Verso Books, 2016); Nato Thompson, *Seeing Power: Art and Activism in the 21st Century* (Brooklyn: Melville House, 2015); Catherine Flood and Gavin Grindon, eds., *Disobedient Objects* (London: V&A Publishing, 2014); and Nicolas Lampert, *A People's Art History of the United States* (New York: The New Press, 2013).

Of course, ecology has not always been so defined. In 1866, German biologist Ernst Haeckel coined the term, which designated "the body of knowledge concerning the economy of nature—the investigation of the total relations of the animal both to its organic and inorganic environment."[21] Ecology's disciplinary formation coincided with the height of European colonialism, a regime not limited to the governing of peoples but also the structuring of nature. The colonization of nature, emerging from the Enlightenment principles of Cartesian dualism between human and nonhuman worlds, situated the nonhuman world as objectified, passive, and separate, and "elaborated a rationalizing, extractive, dissociative understanding which overlaid functional experiential relations among people, plants and animals."[22] Destructive and utilitarian, idealized and exoticized nature has been colonized in concept as well as in practice. It entailed a multifarious, complex, and at times contradictory pattern of bureaucratic rationalization, scientific and technological mastery, military domination, integration within the expanding capitalist economy, and legal systematization in order to manage and maximize the possibilities of resource exploitation. In this vein, ecology was far from the innocent discipline Haeckel named; rather, it comprised "the science of empire."[23]

This colonization only continues today. Michel Serres once characterized Western modernity's relation to nature as constituting a "war" based on the "mastery and appropriation" of the earth, against which the French philosopher called for a "natural contract" to inaugurate a new political ecology based on a postcolonial equality between human and nonhuman life.[24] Clearly we are still far from realizing such a contract, even though growing social movements, emerging out of Indigenous philosophy and environmental activism alike, insist on recognizing the "rights of nature," and some nations in Latin America (Ecuador and Bolivia) have recently enshrined those rights in their constitutions and legal systems, albeit with uneven implementation.[25] That said, we

21 Ernst Haeckel, cited in J. Donald Hughes, *An Environmental History of the World: Humankind's Changing Role in the Community of Life* (New York: Routledge, 2009), 7.

22 William M. Adams and Martin Mulligan, *Decolonizing Nature: Strategies for Conservation in a Post-colonial Era* (London: Earthscan, 2003), 24. However, by the 1850s British and French colonial rule amounted "to a highly heterogeneous mixture of Indigenous, romantic, Orientalist and other elements," which defies any single consistent ideology of nature (ibid., 19). See also Richard H. Grove, *Green Imperialism: Colonial Expansion, Tropical Island Edens and the Origins of Environmentalism, 1600–1800* (Cambridge: Cambridge University Press, 1995), 12.

23 See Libby Robin, "Ecology: A Science of Empire?," in *Ecology and Empire: Environmental History of Settler Societies*, ed. Tom Griffiths and Libby Robin (Keele: Keele University Press, 1997), 63–75.

24 See Michel Serres, *The Natural Contract*, trans. Elizabeth MacArthur and William Paulson (Ann Arbor: University of Michigan Press, 1995).

25 For more on this subject see my catalogue essay for the exhibition I cocurated, "Rights of Nature: Art and Ecology

continue to confront what Indian activist Vandana Shiva calls "the corporate control of life," owing to neoliberal globalization, international trade policies, deregulated environmental protections, and the patenting of biological matter (in the form of genetically modified seeds, for instance), all of which have brought ruin and devastation to many tribal and subsistence farming communities worldwide.[26] For sociologist Melinda Cooper, that context is the culmination of biogenetic capitalism's expansion, first surfacing in the 1980s and deployed to overcome an earlier environmentalism gathered around the commitment of "limits to growth." Formulated in the eponymous 1972 report commissioned by the Club of Rome (a group of European industrialists, academics, and scientists founded in 1968), the study used computer modeling to calculate the negative environmental effects of growing population, industrialization, pollution, food production, and resource depletion. Unlike nonrenewable energy and its ecosystem despoilment, biogenetic capitalism transforms life itself into a prospective infinite source of growth via biotechnology and financial speculation, representing further incursions of neoliberalism, now directed at colonizing the primordial genetic elements and temporalities (including financializing the futures) of our material existence.[27]

This corporate-industrial and politico-economic onslaught has not gone unchallenged, however. A growing international formation mobilizing against the continuing plunder is comprised of environmentalists such as Naomi Klein, Bill McKibben, and David Solnit; anti-austerity social movements that emerged from Occupy, and their related recent uneven transformations into anti-neoliberal political parties in Europe, such as Podemos in Spain and Syriza in Greece; NGOs like the African Biodiversity Network and the Gaia Foundation; politically engaged scientists like Kevin Anderson and James Hansen; Indigenous activists, from the Sarayaku region in Ecuador to the Gwich'ins in Alaska; and solidarity networks like Idle No More. As stated in the declaration of the multiple Indigenous groups who participated in the Kari-Oca II Earth Summit in 2012: "We reaffirm our responsibility to speak for the protection

in the Americas," at Nottingham Contemporary, "Rights of Nature: The Art and Politics of Earth Jurisprudence," April 2015, https://creativeecologies.ucsc.edu/wp-content/uploads/sites/196/2015/10/Demos-Rights-of-Nature-2015.compressed.pdf. On the rights of nature, see Cormac Cullinan, *Wild Law: A Manifesto for Earth Justice* (Claremont, South Africa: Siber Ink, 2002); Peter Burdon, ed., *Exploring Wild Law: The Philosophy of Earth Jurisprudence* (Kent Town: Wakefield Press, 2011); and Evo Morales Ayma et al., *The Rights of Nature: The Case for a Universal Declaration of the Rights of Mother Earth* (Ottawa: Council of Canadians, 2011).

26 Vandana Shiva, *The Corporate Control of Life*, dOCUMENTA (13): 100 Notes—100 Thoughts, no. 12 (Ostfildern: Hatje Cantz, 2011).

27 Melinda Cooper, *Life as Surplus: Biotechnology and Capitalism in the Neoliberal Era* (Seattle: University of Washington Press, 2008).

and enhancement of the well-being of Mother Earth, nature and future generations of our Indigenous Peoples and all humanity and life. [...] We, Indigenous Peoples from all regions of the world have defended our Mother Earth from the aggression of unsustainable development and the overexploitation of our natural resources by mining, logging, mega-dams, exploration and extraction of petroleum. Our forests suffer from the production of agro-fuels, bio-mass, plantations and other impositions of false solutions to climate change and unsustainable, damaging development."[28] So how can we reverse this untenable, unjust situation? And what role exists for artists and activists, increasingly brought together under these emergency conditions?

Decolonizing Nature

To decolonize nature represents a doubtlessly ambitious and manifold project, with artists, activists, and creative practitioners (in addition to scientists, policy makers, and politicians) involved at every stage. As Naomi Klein asks, "Can we imagine another way of responding to crisis other than one of deepening inequality, brutal disaster capitalism and mangled techno-fixes"?[29] If so, it will require an immense project of imaginative thinking and practice to rescue nature from corporate control, financialization, and the proprietary exploitations of biogenetic capitalism. For David Harvey, these forces represent the "accumulation by dispossession" that constitutes a new imperialism, the grossly uneven development of the present day. For Jason Moore, such is the result of centuries of interpenetration between capitalism and nature, including "capitalism's internalization of planetary life and processes, through which new life activity is continually brought into the orbit of capital and capitalist power" and "the biosphere's internalization of capitalism, through which human-initiated projects and processes influence and shape the web of life."[30] The resulting inequality it staggering. According to a recent Oxfam report, the world's richest eighty people own as much as the bottom half of the earth's population combined (about 3.5 billion people), just as around ninety corporations are responsible for running the fossil fuel economy, and a much smaller number of governments is accountable for the geopolitical and humanitarian wars that camouflage control of the

28 "Kari-Oca II Declaration," Rio de Janeiro, June 17, 2012, *Climate & Capitalism*, http://climateandcapitalism.com/2012/06/19/kari-oca-2-declaration. The declaration was signed by over five hundred Indigenous representatives from around the world at an alternative meeting that took place alongside the UN's Rio+20 summit on sustainability (Kari-Oca means "White man's house" in the Tupi-Guarani languages).

29 In John Tarleton, "Interview: Naomi Klein Breaks a Taboo," *Indypendent*, September 12, 2014, https://indypendent.org/2014/09/12/interview-naomi-klein-breaks-taboo.

30 Jason W. Moore, *Capitalism in the Web of Life: Ecology and the Accumulation of Capital* (London: Verso Books, 2015), 13.

world's natural resources and energy supplies.[31] Political ecology necessitates engaging with these inequalities of our neocolonial present, just as centuries of colonialism initiated climate change.[32] Accumulation by dispossession occurs when the fossil fuel economy in so-called developed nations creates the atmospheric pollution that, in causing global warming, now threatens the existence of small island nations, such as Kiribati and the Maldives, creates havoc in the Bangladesh's delta, and melts permafrost in Alaska. Or when agents of "green capitalism"—which grants post-1970s corporate practice a cosmetic environmental guise—buy tracts of rainforest in the Brazilian Amazon in order to plant eucalyptus monocultures (green deserts that contain no life) for biofuel that forces Indigenous and *Quilombola* (Afro-Brazilian former slave) communities from their once-biodiverse, natively managed land. What are these cases if not contemporary corporate colonialism?[33]

As we know from the 2014 IPCC report, 80 percent of fossil fuel reserves must stay in the ground if we are to remain under the critical warming threshold of two degrees Celsius (or more, if we keep it to 1.5 degrees, as recommended at the recent COP21), equivalent, as eco-socialist Chris Williams notes, to writing off some US$20 trillion in assets from the largest corporations on the planet, including ExxonMobil, Chevron, BP, and Shell.[34] Responding to this eventuality, ExxonMobil reassured its shareholders: "The scenario where governments restrict hydrocarbon production in a way to reduce [greenhouse gas] emissions 80 percent during the outlook period [to 2040] is highly unlikely." Instead, as one company executive explained, "All of ExxonMobil's current hydrocarbon reserves will be needed, along

31 See David Harvey, *Spaces of Global Capitalism: Toward a Theory of Uneven Geographical Development* (London: Verso Books, 2006); Neil Smith, *Uneven Development: Nature, Capital, and the Production of Space* (Oxford: Blackwell, 1990); "Oxfam: World's Richest 80 People Own as Much as the Bottom Half," *Democracy Now!*, January 20, 2015, http://www.democracynow.org/2015/1/20/headlines/oxfam_worlds_richest_80_people_own_as_much_as_the_bottom_half; Suzanne Goldenberg, "Just 90 Companies Caused Two-thirds of Man-made Global Warming Emissions," *Guardian*, November 20, 2013, http://www.theguardian.com/environment/2013/nov/20/90-companies-man-made-global-warming-emissions-climate-change; and Michael Klare, *Resource Wars: The New Landscape of Global Conflict* (New York: Holt, 2002).

32 In this regard, Eyal Weizman is right in arguing that climate change is the telos of colonial modernity. See Eyal Weizman and Fazal Sheikh, *The Conflict Shoreline: Colonialism as Climate Change in the Negev Desert* (Göttingen: Steidl, 2015).

33 For more on this argument see Ashley Dawson, "Putting a Human Face on Climate Change," in *Climate Change and Museum Futures*, ed. Fiona Cameron and Brett Neilson (London: Routledge, 2014), 207–18; and Santiago Navarro F. and Renata Bessi, "Green Neocolonialism, Afro-Brazilian Rebellion in Brazil," trans. Miriam Taylor, *Truthout*, December 28, 2014, http://www.truth-out.org/news/item/28232-green-neocolonialism-afro-brazilian-rebellion-in-brazil.

34 Chris Williams, "Why U.N. Climate Talks Continue to Fail," *Indypendent*, September–October 2014, 4. See also Chris Williams, *Ecology and Socialism: Solutions to Capitalist Ecological Crisis* (London: Haymarket Books, 2010).

with substantial future industry investments, to address global energy needs."[35] It's thus not surprising that, as Klein reports, in 2013 in the United States alone the oil and gas industry spent approximately $400,000 *a day* lobbying Congress and government representatives, and expended a record $73 million in federal campaigns and political donations during the 2012 election season, all to support their agenda—economically disastrous for its inequality, environmentally ruinous for its pollution.[36] In this sense, any decolonizing of nature must address our current financial ecologies of democracy, with an eye on challenging the corrupting influx of corporate money in politics today. If reductions are to respect any kind of equity principle between rich and poor nations, then wealthy countries need to cut emissions by something like 8 to 10 percent a year, starting immediately, amounting to what Kevin Anderson and Alice Bows-Larkin call "radical and immediate degrowth strategies in the US, EU and other wealthy nations."[37] Klein writes: "There is still time to avoid catastrophic warming, but not within the rules of capitalism as they are currently constructed. Which is surely the best argument there has been for changing those rules."[38]

Beyond the critical analysis of corporate practice and the international framework of trade policies that privilege economy over environment (including the trade agreements currently operating under the WTO and World Bank), we also need to decolonize our conceptualization of nature in properly political ways. This can be done by moving away from the naturalization of finance (as if it's a universal given); by overturning the philosophy of corporate "personhood" through which economic entities control life; by transforming our laws to introduce a biocentric integration of humans with their environment so that nature's rights to exist will be acknowledged and enforced, as many Indigenous groups demand; and by reinventing economies of selective degrowth and just distribution so that our social systems accord with ecological sustainability and equality. "If a Green Revolution is to happen," explains activist and literature professor Nicholas Powers, "we have to switch from apocalyptic imagery to utopian prophecy, to create a cultural 'wilding' that opens horizontal spaces into which people can enter and join the carnival."[39] I'm convinced that art, given its long histories of experimentation,

35 Cited and discussed in Williams, "Why U.N. Climate Talks Continue to Fail."

36 Klein, *This Changes Everything*, 149. The 2016 presidential race appears no different, excepting the campaign of Bernie Sanders.

37 Ibid., 87–88; Anderson, "Climate Change Going Beyond Dangerous," 18–21; Kevin Anderson and Alice Bows, "A 2°C Target? Get Real, Because 4°C Is On Its Way," *Parliamentary Brief* 13 (2010): 19.

38 Klein, *This Changes Everything*, 88.

39 Nicholas Powers, "Greening Our Desires," *Indypendent*, September–October 2014, 23.

imaginative invention, and radical thinking, can play a central transformative role here. In its most ambitious and far-ranging sense, art holds the promise of initiating exactly these kinds of creative perceptional and philosophical shifts, offering new ways of comprehending ourselves and our relation to the world differently than the destructive traditions of colonizing nature.

Beyond Anthropocentrism

As indicated above, decolonizing nature entails transcending human-centered exceptionalism, no longer placing ourselves at the center of the universe and viewing nature as a source of endless bounty. Fields of inquiry that have recently investigated the terms of such a move include speculative realism, new materialism, ecosophical activism, object-oriented ontology, elementary politics, and post-humanism, each variously proposing innovative methodologies of post-anthropocentric analysis.[40] This diverse and at times conflictual movement represents nothing less than a paradigm shift in the humanities, constitutionally preoccupied in the past with the human, its histories, epistemologies, ethics, and aesthetics.[41] As Levi Bryant, Graham Harman, and Nick Srnicek write, "By contrast with the repetitive continental focus on texts, discourse, social practices, and human finitude, the new breed of thinker is turning once more toward reality itself [...] speculating once more about the nature of reality independently of thought and of humanity more generally."[42] A leading practitioner of this mode of thought and its political ramifications, sociologist Bruno Latour has noted that global environmental governance has largely failed, and he articulates the need for the progressive composition of a common world, where nonhuman entities are integrated into a new commonality and form the basis of a post-anthropocentric social, political, and economic organization.[43] Such a community, grouped around climate as a "non-unified cosmopolitical concern"—a commonality that also maintains difference—would ostensibly recognize the vitality of

40 See, for instance, Jane Bennett, *Vibrant Matter: A Political Ecology of Things* (Durham, NC: Duke University Press, 2010); Levi Bryant, Graham Harman, and Nick Srnicek, eds., *The Speculative Turn: Continental Materialism and Realism* (Melbourne: re.press, 2011); Diana Coole and Samantha Frost, eds., *New Materialisms: Ontology, Agency, and Politics* (Durham, NC: Duke University Press, 2010); Anselm Franke, ed., *Animism* (Berlin: Sternberg Press, 2010); and Bruno Latour, *We Have Never Been Modern*, trans. Catherine Porter (Cambridge, MA: Harvard University Press, 1993).

41 On the humanistic implications of this shift, see Dipesh Chakrabarty, "The Climate of History: Four Theses," *Critical Inquiry* 35, no. 2 (Winter 2009): 197–222.

42 Levi Bryant, Graham Harman, and Nick Srnicek, "Towards a Speculative Philosophy," in Bryant et al., *The Speculative Turn*, 3.

43 Bruno Latour, "The Year in Climate Controversy," *Artforum*, December 2010, 228–29. Also see Bruno Latour, *Politics of Nature: How to Bring the Sciences into Democracy*, trans. Catherine Porter (Cambridge, MA: Harvard University Press, 2004).

materiality and nonhuman agents, and take account of circuits of causality that extend beyond human origins (as in the new materialist philosophy of Jane Bennett). It would also correlate with science-studies approaches to nature as a site of "radical openness, an edgy protean differentiating multiplicity, an agential dis/concontinuity" (as in the theorization of Karen Barad), and invoke the "becoming-with" ontologies that view the human body as a multiplicity of beings (including the bacteriological) all enmeshed within complex multispecies ecologies (as in the work of Donna Haraway).[44] There are indeed many critical resources newly available for political-ecology analysis.

At the forefront of this convergence, art figures as a central platform for the creative practice of speculative realisms, linking with further philosophical inquiry and conceptual experimentation, as well as exploring, for instance, what a "world-without-us" would be like, or what "zoe-egalitarianism" would mean and "becoming-Earth" entail.[45] But there are many potential rifts and discontinuities in this theoretical confluence. Along with Latour, theorists like Morton have gone to great lengths to criticize the traditional Western concept of nature by mobilizing post-anthropocentric terms that are also post-natural. Long positioned as an ahistoric monolith in a separate realm apart from the human, nature's conventional definition appears to critics faulty for its basis in ontological objectification and dualistic thinking, the conceptual platform for extractivist practice. It is also opposed for its ideological manipulations, particularly where it acts as a force of naturalization, fixation, and domination. "Ecology without nature," then, promises to dissolve representational forms that allow for exploitation of a vast realm by agents who exist in the unnatural zone of culture.[46] Yet, in my view, rejecting the term nature is not an option, even while I agree with efforts geared toward its conceptual reorientation in order to undo nature's objectification and ontological isolation. Even more, it's crucial to acknowledge nature's significance as a rallying cry within the contemporary resurgence of Indigenous and

44 Bruno Latour, "Waiting for Gaia: Composing the Common World through Arts and Politics" (lecture, French Institute, London, November 2011), http://www.bruno-latour.fr/node/446; also in *What Is Cosmopolitical Design? Nature, Design and the Built Environment*, ed. Albena Yaneva and Alejandro Zaera-Polo (Farnham: Ashgate, 2016); Karen Barad, "Nature's Queer Performativity (the authorized version)," *Kvinder, Køn og forskning/Women, Gender and Research*, nos. 1–2 (2012), 29; and Donna J. Haraway, *Manifestly Haraway* (Minneapolis: University of Minnesota Press, 2016).

45 On the world-without-us, see Eugene Thacker, *In the Dust of This Planet* (London: Zero Books, 2011); on zoe-egalitarianism and becoming-Earth, see Rosi Braidotti, *The Posthuman* (Cambridge: Polity, 2013), 81.

46 "'Ecology without nature' could mean 'ecology without a *concept* of the natural.' Thinking, when it becomes ideological, tends to fixate on concepts rather than doing what is 'natural' to thought, namely, dissolving whatever has taken form. Ecological thinking that was not fixated, that did not stop at a particular concretization of its object, would thus be 'without nature.'" Morton, *Ecology without Nature*, 24.

environmentalist activism, which also insists that humans are fully integrated in and part of the natural realm. An additional obstacle with some of these approaches is that proposals for new sociopolitical compositions, modeled on a cosmopolitical scenography of global governance, as in Latour's work, often lack a structural critique of neoliberalism (indeed, this absence helps explain Latour's problematic support for techno-fixes and geo-engineering projects, a position directly challenged in Klein's recent work).[47] For there's little in Latour's 2004 book *Politics of Nature*, or in his recent writings about the Anthropocene, that attends to the WTO, free trade arrangements, the World Economic Forum in Davos, or the political economy of petro-capitalism—a complex actor-institutional network that motors the global fossil-fuel ecologies of unsustainability. As a result, we are invited to overlook the manifold violence that is climate change.[48] In this regard, Latour's silence, or lack of direct engagement with corporate globalization, parallels speculative realism's characteristic political diffidence, its general withdrawal from the political sphere of *human* activities, swept aside in its eagerness to theorize object-oriented ontologies.[49]

Given these tendencies, it's necessary to bring these formations into relation with key accounts of political and social ecology; that is, if they are to gain critical use value. For me, these include, but are not limited to, the work of postcolonial and Marxist theorists and activists (for instance, Vandana Shiva, David Harvey, Neil Smith, and Jason Moore), along with the direct political analysis of groups like the International Forum on Globalization, the International Rights of Nature Tribunal, and the Indigenous movement Idle No More, in addition to a more socially engaged eco-criticism (such as that of Rob Nixon, Ashley Dawson, and Ursula Heise), all of which focus on the crises and conflicts of actual environmental

47 Bruno Latour, "Love Your Monsters," in *Love Your Monsters: Postenvironmentalism and the Anthropocene*, ed. Ted Nordhaus and Michael Shellenberger (Oakland, CA: Breakthrough Institute, 2011), 17–25, http://thebreakthrough.org/index.php/journal/past-issues/issue-2/love-your-monsters; and Klein, *This Changes Everything*, 279.

48 Rebecca Solnit writes: "Climate change is global-scale violence against places and species, as well as against human beings. Once we call it by name, we can start having a real conversation about our priorities and values. Because the revolt against brutality begins with a revolt against the language that hides that brutality." Rebecca Solnit, "Climate Change Is Violence," in *The Encyclopedia of Trouble and Spaciousness* (San Antonio, TX: Trinity University Press, 2014), http://truth-out.org/progressivepicks/item/28933-climate-change-is-violence.

49 See Bryant, Harman, and Srnicek, "Towards a Speculative Philosophy," where the authors address Slavoj Žižek's critique of speculative realism as having an inadequate account of political subjectivity, claiming in their defense that "there needs to be an aspect of ontology that is independent of its enmeshment in human concerns. Our *knowledge* may be irreducibly tied to politics, yet to suggest that reality is also thus tied is to project an epistemological problem into the ontological realm" (16).

struggles. As well, environmental concerns in the Global South need to be addressed, and here I've considered what Madhav Gadgil and Ramachandra Guha call the "environmentalism of the poor." Doing so helps to avoid continuing the Global North's legacy of provincialism, prejudice, and privilege regarding ecology, which has led to the multifaceted violence toward the West's colonized peoples, as well as toward its own poor, disenfranchised, and Indigenous populations—part and parcel of what Gadgil and Guha term an "environmentalism of affluence," which also might be said to characterize some of the recent theorizations of the speculative turn.[50]

Decolonizing Methodologies

One step to escape the environmentalism of affluence is to decolonize our research methodologies, in part by acknowledging the conceptual lineages of theories elaborated in the Western academy and tracing their connection to the histories of struggles and perspectives of the colonized, including Indigenous cosmologies, subaltern legal codes, and social movements where appropriate.[51] In doing so, we take seriously the critiques of native thinkers themselves, as when anthropologist Kimberly TallBear takes Jane Bennett to task for her "vital materialism" that invokes a "pluriverse traversed by heterogeneities that are continually doing things," and the "lively matter" of "nonhuman bodies," because she neglects to mention that similar views can be found in the cultural traditions of many Indigenous peoples.[52] Or when anthropologist Zoe Todd criticizes Bruno Latour's discussion of the climate as a "common cosmopolitical concern," pointing out his failure to cite the work of any thinkers from First Nations cultures that have long held such beliefs.[53] One wonders similarly, when

50 Madhav Gadgil and Ramachandra Guha, "Ideologies of Environmentalism," in *Ecology and Equity: The Use and Abuse of Nature in Contemporary India* (London: Routledge, 1995), 98.

51 In some ways, my project parallels related attempts to trace post-anthropocentric theoretical discourse to Indigenous and pre- and postcolonial thinking and practice, as with the "Forensis" project at the Centre for Research Architecture at Goldsmiths, and Anselm Franke's "Animism" research exhibition; see Forensic Architecture, *Forensis*; and Franke, *Animism*. In other ways, it attempts to move beyond these often Latour-inspired conceptualizations that remain—problematically in my view—within Western discourse paradigms, as critically addressed by Jessica L. Horton and Janet Catherine Berlo, "Beyond the Mirror: Indigenous Ecologies and 'New Materialisms' in Contemporary Art," *Third Text*, no. 120 (January 2013): 17–28.

52 See Kim TallBear, "Beyond Life/Not Life: A Feminist-Indigenous Reading of Cryopreservation, Interspecies Thinking and the New Materialisms" (lecture, UCLA, November 5, 2013), https://www.youtube.com/watch?v=TkUeHCUrQ6E; citing Bennett, *Vibrant Matter*, 122.

53 Zoe Todd, "An Indigenous Feminist's Take on the Ontological Turn: 'Ontology' Is Just Another Word for Colonialism," *Urbane Adventurer: Amiskwacî* (blog), October 24, 2014, https://zoeandthecity.wordpress.com/2014/10/24/an-indigenous-feminists-take-on-the-ontological-turn-ontology-is-just-another-word-for-colonialism.

Rosi Braidotti argues for a "postanthropocentric creation of a new pan-humanity,"[54] whether her futurism overlooks present resources located in, for instance, Indigenous heritage and current political engagements that were never anthropocentric in the first place. The point, however, isn't to focus on specific intellectuals who importantly contribute to comprehending political ecology today, but to become sensitive to the general academic tendencies of non-acknowledgment that continue the exclusion of traditions and populations that have historically suffered centuries of colonial violence.

Many Indigenous cosmologies do in fact offer ecological wisdom about localized and sustainable forms of life based on synergies with biodiverse, healthy environments. Pointing this out does not amount to an idealization of Indigeneity, and indeed there are thorough criticisms of this idealization tendency as well as historical examples of the destructive relations of natives to nature in the pre- and post-contact periods.[55] Rather, it remains imperative to register the cultural traditions of peoples living in environmentally sensitive ways, who have rearticulated their forms of life in the context of present geopolitical and ecological conflicts and their ongoing struggles for decolonization and cultural survival—unlike much of Western modernity, which continues to push the world beyond the tipping points of anthropogenic environmental catastrophe. Post-anthropocentric philosophy is not a recent discovery, but rather connects—whether intentionally or not—to long-standing Indigenous views of nature as a pluriverse of agents. These views define a cosmopolitics—a creative social organization merged with world making—existing generally in contradistinction to the nature/human divisions of Western anthropocentric colonial ecologies.[56]

What we need then are new methodologies to acknowledge the voices of historically oppressed peoples, which stand to strengthen the basis of ethico-political solidarity around ecological concerns by joining with current struggles for cultural and environmental survival against corporate

54 Braidotti, *The Posthuman*, 101.

55 On the destruction of North America's megafauna some thirteen thousand years ago, see Alan Weisman, *The World without Us* (London: Virgin, 2008). Also see Shepard Krech III, *The Ecological Indian: Myth and History* (New York: W. W. Norton & Company, 2000); criticisms of Krech in Vine Deloria, Jr., "The Speculations of Krech," review of *The Ecological Indian*, by Shepard Krech, *Worldviews* 4 (2000): 283–93; and criticisms of Deloria in turn in Kimberly TallBear, "Shepard Krech's The Ecological Indian: One Indian's Perspective," IIIRM *Publications*, September 2000, http://www.iiirm.org/publications/Book%20Reviews/Reviews/Krech001.pdf.

56 Isabelle Stengers, "The Cosmopolitical Proposal," in Latour and Weibel, *Making Things Public*, 995. For theoretical innovation that does register Indigenous thinking, see Eduardo Viveiros de Castro, "Perspectivism and Multinaturalism in Indigenous America," in *The Land Within: Indigenous Territory and The Perception of Environment*, ed. Alexandre Surrallés and Pedro García Hierro (Copenhagen: International Work Group for Indigenous Affairs, 2005); and Eduardo Kohn, *How Forests Think: Toward an Anthropology beyond the Human* (Berkeley: University of California Press, 2013).

globalization. With such an effort, non-Indigenous writers and scholars contribute to challenging the situation of academic "research" being associated with colonial domination, and supporting the validity of aboriginal peoples' "right of self-determination, to the survival of our languages and forms of cultural knowledge, to our natural resources and systems for living within our environments," as education scholar Linda Tuhiwai Smith explains.[57] For me this book is only a beginning step in this direction (as a descendent of settler-colonial culture), but this commitment is increasingly imperative. A number of points of connection in these pages consider how current artistic and activist practices have joined the struggles of native and disenfranchised peoples. These include the work of Amar Kanwar and Sanjay Kak relating to the Dongria Kondh and their fight against mining in the Indian state of Odisha; Subhankar Banerjee's photography and writing regarding the Gwich'in people in Alaska and their opposition to Arctic oil drilling; Ursula Biemann and Paulo Tavares's project *Forest Law*, regarding the efforts of the Indigenous people of Sarayaku for self-determination and environmental protection in the Ecuadorian Amazon; and Maria Thereza Alves's work with Indigenous communities in the environmentally degraded Chalco area of Mexico City, work that also connects to the decades-long Zapatista struggle for autonomy and sustainability among the Mayan communities of Chiapas. These projects are exemplary for their refusal to co-opt or idealize Indigenous knowledge systems, and for "standing with" their subjects.[58] As such, they demonstrate a new imperative for artists, as much as writers, to intersect with movements in the global struggle for climate justice, human rights, and ecological sustainability.

One significant example is Biemann and Tavares's *Forest Law* (2014), a multimedia video-based investigation built on research into the formation of the philosophy in Latin America known as *buen vivir* (good living), particularly in relation to Andean-Amazonian cultures. It's a translation of the Quechua term *sumak kawsay*, meaning "living in plenitude, knowing how to live in harmony with the cycles of Mother Earth, of the cosmos, of life and of history,

57 Linda Tuhiwai Smith, *Decolonizing Methodologies: Research and Indigenous Peoples* (London: Zed Books, 2008), 1.

58 On the transformative and politically committed practice of "standing with" one's subject and rejecting false objectivity and liberal academicism in favor of the knowledge production of feminist and Indigenous practices and pedagogy, see Kim TallBear, "Standing With and Speaking as Faith: A Feminist-Indigenous Approach to Inquiry," *Journal of Research Practice* 10, no. 2 (2014), http://jrp.icaap.org/index.php/jrp/article/view/405/371.

59 See Fernando Huanacuni Mamani, *Vivir bien/buen vivir: Filosofía, políticas, estrategias y experiencias regionales* (La Paz: Convenio Andrés Bello y Instituto Internacional Integración, 2010), 32;, cited in Julien Vanhulst and Adrian Beling, "*Buen vivir*: Emergent Discourse within or beyond Sustainable Development?," *Ecological Economics* 101 (May 2014): 56. See also Ricardo Jiménez, "Retrieving and Valuing Other Ethical Pillars: The Concept of Buen Vivir," *Forum for a New World Governance*, July 17, 2011, http://www.world-governance.org/article690.html?lang=en.

and in balance with every form of existence in a state of permanent respect."[59] As the artists make clear, this philosophy has Indigenous origins and joins with academic elaborations and political activism, manifesting, for instance, in recent constitutional amendments and legal codes, including the Law of the Rights of Mother Earth, instituted in Ecuador in 2008. *Buen vivir* politics both challenges the Washington-consensus doctrine of development that has ruled Latin America since the mid-twentieth century (comprised of corporate neoliberalism and antienvironmental neocolonialism enforced by authoritarian military governance) and provides a crucial biocentric model of political economy based on environmental consonance and social equality. "The greatest potential of *Buen vivir*," Julien Vanhulst and Adrian Beling argue, "lies in the opportunities it generates for dialog with other modern discourses and the current forms of development, by enlarging the frame of current debates and allowing for the potential emergence of novel conceptions, institutions and practices through collective learning."[60] In this regard, ecology defines a method of intersectionality, which insists on thinking being and becoming at the cross section of multiple fields of social, political, economic, and material determinations.[61] Such a convergence is forcefully addressed in Biemann and Tavares's work, which maps a network of Global South environmentalism, Indigenous activism, and practices of Earth jurisprudence, all working to extend the rights of nature and contest the corporate and state destruction of Amerindian forest culture. The intersectionalist politics at stake here resonates within and beyond Latin America, touching on the rural US anti-fracking movement and the International Criminal Court's environmental cases in The Hague, sub-Saharan Africa's struggles to protect biodiversity and Indian subsistence farmers' rights to livelihood. This revolutionary Earth-centered legal shift, including its cultural manifestations, represents one forefront of the decolonization of nature.[62]

Climate Justice Now!

This book is organized both thematically and geographically. There are chapters that consider contemporary art and activism in relation to subjects such as climate refugees, the politics of sustainability, the financialization of nature, and contemporary catastrophism. Others focus on the intersection of art and environment in Mexico, India, the Arctic,

60 Vanhulst and Beling, *"Buen vivir,"* 61.

61 Emerging from black feminist legal theory, intersectionality examines overlapping systems of oppression—including those of race, class, gender, and sexuality—in the figuration of social identity. The methodology was first articulated in Kimberlé Crenshaw, "Demarginalizing the Intersection of Race and Sex: A Black Feminist Critique of Antidiscrimination Doctrine, Feminist Theory and Antiracist Politics," *University of Chicago Legal Forum* 140 (January 1, 1989): 139–67.

62 For more on this see my essay "Rights of Nature."

and small island nations like the Maldives and Tuvalu, in addition to the United States and Europe. Chapter 1, "The Art and Politics of Sustainability," traces the conflicted notion of sustainability via scientific, political, and cultural discourses since the 1960s, examining how the term often functions as a privileged instrument of greenwashing and how it might be mobilized otherwise. It examines the restorationist eco-aesthetics of the '60s and '70s that tasked art with the repair of ecosystems (in work by Alan Sonfist, Agnes Denes, Helen Mayer and Newton Harrison, and Robert Smithson); the systems aesthetics of the '70s, where the cybernetic theories of Gregory Bateson and György Kepes offered new ways to consider nature as intertwined with technological systems (addressed in art by Dan Graham, Hans Haacke, and Pulsa); and the formation of political ecology of the '90s and 2000s, whereby artists have investigated nature-culture assemblages, insisting on the political dimensions of ecology and sustainability in relation to social justice and economic equality (in work by Marjetica Potrč, Tue Greenfort, Superflex, and Nils Norman).

Chapter 2, "Climates of Displacement: From the Maldives to the Arctic," considers how distinct (but not unrelated) environmental crises are increasingly bringing about forced displacements of life from the frontline territories of climate change, foremost among them small island states, Far North regions, and low-lying deltas. It examines the contrasting documentary photography of the Argos Collective and of Subhankar Banerjee as models of aesthetic and political engagement, and considers the intricacies of climate-refugee discourse and its assorted problems. These contexts offer ways to approach the intertwinement of political ecology, environmental crisis, forced migration, and artistic-activist aesthetics, a nexus posed to become only more pressing with forecasts of increased climate-driven mass displacement in the near future. In chapter 3, "The Post-natural Condition: Art after Nature?," I investigate political ecology further by focusing on how artists—Lise Autogena and Joshua Portway, Amy Balkin, Nils Norman, and the Laboratory for Insurrectionary Imagination—have challenged what the late geographer Neil Smith termed the "financialization of nature," according to which natural forms, such as atmospheric carbon, are regulated by market dynamics within neoliberal capitalism. This chapter considers how artists have analyzed and challenged this neocolonial logic by visualizing its workings as well as inventing ecologically sustainable alternatives along with permaculture and biodynamic farming (Norman's sculptural and process-based designs synergize experimental architecture, public space, activism, and organic gardening), which also importantly entail experimentation with noncapitalist living, social justice, and environmental activism.

Chapter 4, "*¡Ya basta!* Ecologies of Art and Revolution in Mexico," begins by examining the works of Minerva Cuevas and Marcela Armas that contest the externalities—the environmental and social costs commonly disavowed by corporate industry—of Mexico's post-NAFTA neoliberal economy. Other artists, including Gilberto Esparza, Superflex, and Pedro Reyes, integrate industrial pollution, organic agricultural waste, or social violence in their works, redirecting them toward positive ends. The chapter also considers the revolution in everyday life as practiced by the Zapatistas over the last twenty years, which defines an ecological sustainability merged with revolutionary Indigenous autonomy. Lastly, the chapter looks at the work of Maria Thereza Alves, and particularly her mixed-media research project in Chalco, on the eastern edge of Mexico City, which addresses the colonial history that informs present conflicts over land and water use, turning Mexico's growing capital into an environmental crisis point.

The book transitions to the South Asian subcontinent in chapter 5, "Nature's Sovereignty: Conflicting Environments of Development in India," which investigates the country's worsening environmental predicaments decades into the Green Revolution—the adoption of Western industrial, chemical-based farming to bring greater yields, which has in turn gradually destroyed soil health as much as farmers' livelihoods—paralleling the expansion of neoliberal agricultural governance worldwide. The conflicts accompanying these histories have initiated an urgent debate over the meaning of development and the value of nature, which has occupied many Indian activist-artists as well. The chapter also considers New Delhi's crisis urbanism and the Yamuna River's failed environmental management through the photography of Ravi Agarwal, and explores eastern India's zone of social and military conflict (Chhattisgarh and Odisha in particular), which forms a critical test case for the intersection of ecological commitments and activist-artistic intervention. There, one finds the sustainability of tribal life pitted against multinational corporate interests intent on carrying out resource extraction, throwing land use, Adivasi (Indigenous) rights, and economic development into violent disarray. This geopolitical tension has become the subject of investigation by artists, such as Amar Kanwar, and filmmakers, such as Sanjay Kak, whose recent works offer remarkable and innovative aesthetic approaches to disputes around the biopolitics of sustainability, postcolonial environmental justice, and the financialization of nature.

Chapter 6, "Decolonizing Nature: Making the World Matter," investigates the work of the collective World of Matter. Taking up Michel Serres's proposal for a "natural contract" that would bring human culture into a relation of post-anthropocentric equality with the environment, overcoming humanity's attempted mastery and domination of the earth, the collective critically examines capitalism's subjection of nature to an economic calculus. That situation has led to environmental and social devastation in places as diverse as Brazil, the Netherlands, Ecuador, Bangladesh, India, and Nigeria—the various research areas of World of Matter members, including Mabe Bethônico, Ursula Biemann, Lonnie van Brummelen and Siebren de Haan, Uwe H. Martin, Helge Mooshammer and Peter Mörtenböck, Emily E. Scott, and Paulo Tavares. In their far-ranging work, the group redefines nature as a site of aesthetic-conceptual speculation, taking social struggles against corporate control seriously and considering developments in the rights-of-nature discourse, which resonates with Serres's prescient politico-juridical proposition. The chapter also examines the formation of object-oriented ontologies that decenter human sovereignty, and the group's connection of aesthetics to environmental, social, and political systems. World of Matter's collective artistic and interdisciplinary research is pathbreaking. Through constellations of texts, images, and videos, it advances the imperative to explore how the world matters in material terms and via conflicting forms of valuation, including those beyond the economic.

The final chapter, "Gardening against the Apocalypse: The Case of dOCUMENTA (13)," considers the 2012 mega-exhibition's dedication to environmental concerns and nonhuman agencies. It examines how contributing artists, such as Christian Philipp Müller, Song Dong, and Claire Pentecost, turned to experimental gardening in order to propose sustainable ways of organizing the natural world, in the process opening up new paths of creative expression. The chapter also critically investigates the exhibition's conceptualization, examining conflicts in theories of botanical nature and political ecology by comparing Donna Haraway's post-structuralist approach that celebrates nature-technology hybrids with Vandana Shiva's social-justice activism against corporate biotechnology and its GMO patenting—both were included as guiding lights in the exhibition's programming. As well, the chapter reflects on futurist visions of postapocalyptic landscapes presented at the exhibition in the video works of Moon Kyungwon and Jeon Joonho as well as the Otolith Group. I address the ideological mechanisms of contemporary catastrophism, rife in popular culture, according to which spectacles of disaster repeatedly narrate our potential future. Against this form of destructive nihilism, the chapter poses the urgency of regaining political momentum around ecology in the present, answered in part by the Otolith Group's construction of a politically insistent speculative realism.

With this overview, and during the process of working on the present book, I've immersed myself in material that is as challenging in its complexity as it is expansive in its geographies (certain areas, including East Asia, the Middle East, and sub-Saharan Africa, have received too little analysis owing to limited time and resources, and must await future consideration). My research is a first effort at making sense of the provocative and moving projects of artists, and the multifaceted methodological and theoretical approaches to ecology, that have emerged historically, been mobilized politically, and grown significantly in recent years. I'm convinced that there is nothing more important, timely, and urgent to consider as our present ecological crisis, and in this regard, we can only do so by starting from our bases in our respective fields. Under current forms of governance, our relation to the environment threatens our coming existence, where not only nature is colonized but also our very future, a colonization that we must all struggle to resist. In a way that I find particularly inspirational, Miya Yoshitani, the executive director of the Oakland-based Asian Pacific Environmental Network, has explained:

> *The climate justice fight here in the U.S. and around the world is not just a fight against the [biggest] ecological crisis of all time. It is the fight for a new economy, a new energy system, a new democracy, a new relationship to the planet and to each other, for land, water, and food sovereignty, for Indigenous rights, for human rights and dignity for all. When climate justice wins, we win the world we want. We can't sit this one out, not because we have too much to lose, but because we have too much to gain.*[63]

Indeed, we must all join the struggle for climate justice, doing so from our respective disciplinary, cultural, economic, or otherwise-situated points, and that also means challenging the very divisions of specialization in the first place.

63 Miya Yoshitanti in a speech during People's Climate March, New York, September 2014; cited in Klein, *This Changes Everything*, 155–56.

The Art and Politics of Sustainability

Chapter 1

In their multimedia installation *Greenhouse Britain* (2006–9) Helen Mayer Harrison and Newton Harrison chart the future impact of global warming on Great Britain. Using video animation and multiple projections, a large-scale topographical map of Britain, photographic documentation, analytical texts, and sound elements, their pedagogically oriented presentation portrays a dark future of rising waters, storm surges, and shrinking coastlines. "The news is not good, and it's getting worse. Animals are on the run, plants are migrating. If the temperatures on the average rise over two degrees, one scenario predicts Europe, Asia, America, and the Amazon will lose thirty percent of their forests with concomitant extinctions," notes Newton Harrison in an audio recording that accompanies the presentation. In the United Kingdom, "we're looking at 10,000 square kilometers loss of land with about 2.2 million people displaced."[1] Supplementing this ominous forecast are creative proposals for constructing water barriers and developing environmentally friendly housing for the scores of people who will inevitably be displaced. According to their narrative, the waters will overtake low-lying areas such as the Norfolk Broads and the Thames Estuary, owing to the gradual melting of the Greenland and Antarctic ice sheets over the course of this century and beyond.

Yet while the Harrisons' art has focused on global warming since the early 1970s, when they began their long-standing

1 Helen Mayer Harrison and Newton Harrison, "Greenhouse Britain, 2006–2009," in *The Time of the Force Majeure: After 45 Years Counterforce Is on the Horizon* (New York: Random House, forthcoming).

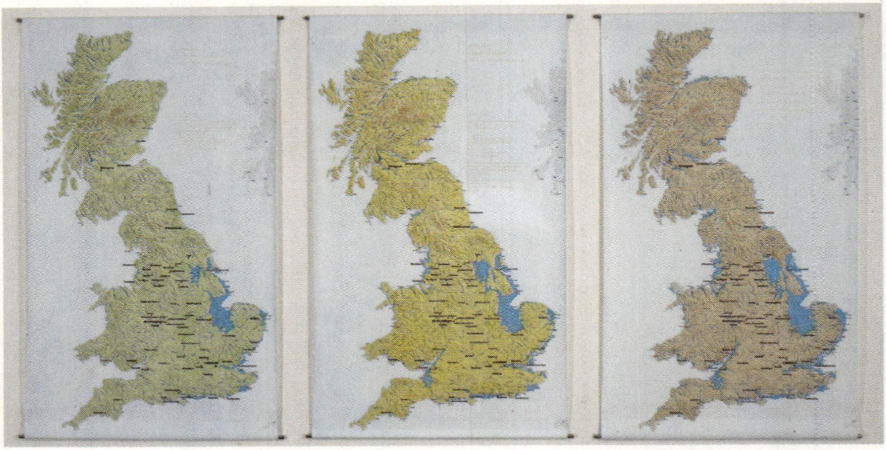

Helen Mayer Harrison and Newton Harrison, *Greenhouse Britain, Green House Britain First Sketch, 2006: Where the loss of land due to ocean rise is first expressed*, 2006

collaboration and climate change was much less discussed, today's context of widespread public information campaigns has subsequently shifted the discourse on the environment—from Al Gore's 2006 educational film *An Inconvenient Truth* or Josh Fox's anti-fracking 2010 documentary *GasLand*, to popular science books like Tim Flannery's *The Weather Makers* and Elizabeth Kolbert's *The Sixth Extinction: An Unnatural History*, and new bestsellers like Naomi Klein's *This Changes Everything* and Gernot Wagner and Martin Weitzman's *Climate Shock: The Economic Consequences of a Hotter Planet*.[2] This recent efflorescence of science writing, environmental reporting, documentary film, and activist movements raises questions about what role art might play now that consciousness-raising is taking place through mainstream mass media, the culture industry, and investigative journalism, even if public knowledge is still plagued by governmental inaction, fossil-fuel lobbying, and climate denialism.[3] As is now widely known—particularly since the consensus established in the 2014 assessment

2 Tim Flannery, *The Weather Makers: How Man Is Changing the Climate and What It Means for Life on Earth* (New York: Atlantic Monthly Press, 2006); Kolbert, *The Sixth Extinction*; Klein, *This Changes Everything*; and Gernot Wagner and Martin L. Weitzman, *Climate Shock: The Economic Consequences of a Hotter Planet* (Princeton, NJ: Princeton University Press, 2015).

3 In fact, things appear to be getting worse: as Naomi Klein reports, "A 2007 Harris poll found that 71 percent of Americans believed that the continued burning of fossil fuels would alter the climate. By 2009 the figure had dropped to 51 percent. In June 2011, the number was down to 44 percent—well under half the population. Similar trends have been tracked in the UK and Australia." Klein, *This Changes Everything*, 35.

report of the Intergovernmental Panel on Climate Change (IPCC)—we live in a changing world of anthropogenic global warming. The IPCC predicts a coming world that will be increasingly uninhabitable and marked by massive species extinction and public health emergencies, riven by rising seas and soaring temperatures, and parched by drought and water scarcity. Such an outlook presents geopolitical challenges of equitable resource distribution, environmental justice between the Global North and South, mitigating and adapting to climate change, and vast migration.[4] This potential future defines new imperatives for an ethics of living and a politics of governing, and in turn provokes new challenges for contemporary art—particularly for those intent on participating in the ethico-political reinvention of life in the face of climate change.

Exhibiting Sustainability?

This state of urgency has led to a slew of art exhibitions and projects over the last decade attuned to ecology. These include: "Beyond Green: Toward a Sustainable Art" (2006) at Chicago's Smart Museum of Art, investigating design-related approaches to environmental sustainability; the 8th Sharjah Biennial (2007), titled "Still Life: Art, Ecology, and the Politics of Change," addressing social, political, and cultural relations to nature, including a symposium that examined ecological practice and everyday life; "Radical Nature: Art and Architecture for a Changing Planet, 1969–2009" (2009), a survey of ecologically engaged art since the late 1960s, at the Barbican Art Gallery in London; "The Oil Show," an examination of our culture's economic, political, and social entanglements with fossil fuel, at the Hartware MedienKunst-Verein in Dortmund; and "Rights of Nature: Art and Ecology in the Americas," considering cultural expressions of post-anthropocentric legality, which I cocurated at Nottingham Contemporary in 2015.[5]

4 On the IPCC and for an account of the recent science and politics of climate change, see IPCC, "Summary for Policymakers," in *Climate Change 2014: Impacts, Adaptation, and Vulnerability. Part A: Global and Sectoral Aspects. Contribution of Working Group II to the Fifth Assessment Report of the Intergovernmental Panel on Climate Change* (Cambridge: Cambridge University Press, 2014), 1–32; https://ipcc-wg2.gov/AR5/images/uploads/WG2AR5_SPM_FINAL.pdf; Suzanne Goldenberg, "IPCC Report: Climate Change Felt 'On All Continents and across the Oceans,'" *Guardian*, March 28, 2014, http://www.theguardian.com/environment/2014/mar/28/ipcc-report-climate-change-report-human-natural-systems; and, for background, Robert Henson, *The Rough Guide to Climate Change* (London: Rough Guides, 2008).

5 This list, of course, is incomplete. Also of note are the following: "Ecotopia: The Second ICP Triennial of Photography and Video," International Center of Photography, New York, 2006; "After Nature," New Museum, New York, 2008; and "Groundworks: Environmental Collaborations in Contemporary Art," Regina Gouger Miller Gallery, Carnegie Mellon, Pittsburgh, 2005. In addition, I cocurated "Rights of Nature: Art and Ecology in the Americas" with Alex Farquharson and Irene Aristizábal at Nottingham Contemporary in 2015.

The growing momentum of such projects is no doubt salutary for focusing public attention on the environment and the threats posed by climate breakdown. However, that achievement should not distract or prevent us from forming a critical assessment of the aims and accomplishments of recent initiatives, as well as evaluating the "promises, perils, and perplexities"—to borrow the subtitle of another exhibition, "Greenwashing"—that may arise with these recent artistic engagements with ecology.[6] One signal peril is the risk of flattening representation's complexity, as if responding to the admittedly real urgency of climate change demands the surrendering of intellectual criticality and aesthetic subtlety.[7] The danger here involves deferring responsibility to scientific expertise and government authority in determining our collective response to environmental change, which makes us vulnerable to solutions forged by exclusive social, scientific, and political interests, and to the forces of commercial exploitation that would use "green" rhetoric for the purposes of economic profit (as much in the art world as elsewhere). And yet, if cultural practitioners refuse to surrender their scrutiny of scientific claims, then what do they do, as Bruno Latour asks, when their commitment to critique, resisting a seemingly self-evident "truth," prevents them from accepting the demonstrable fact of impending ecological crisis, which potentially allies them with climate-change skeptics on the other end of the political spectrum?[8] Facing this dilemma, we must be aware of the fact that what we know about the environment—knowledge that will determine our future actions and chances of survival—is owed to the diverse practices and institutions that represent it. As such, we can only affirm the need for a critical realism that both refuses to relinquish the validity of science and remains dedicated to a guarded analysis of ecological discourse as a representational system forged at the intersection of power and knowledge.

When considering the historical formation of environmental art, it is necessary to scrutinize "sustainability"—its diverse meanings and uses—a term that has been key within governmental and UN discourse on climate change since the 1990s. As polluting corporations increasingly publicize their harmful practices

6 "Greenwashing: Environment, Perils, Promises, and Perplexities," Fondazione Sandretto Re Rebaudengo, Turin, 2008.

7 This tendency is perhaps most clear in the activist art of environmental groups; for instance, those like World Wildlife Fund and Oxfam that stage interventions at UN climate conferences—mounting polar bears made out of slowly melting ice—which target delegates and mass media. For a critique of such presentations, see Gavin Grindon, "Art and Activism," *Art Monthly*, February 2010, 9–12. For creative activist alternatives, see Flood and Grindon, *Disobedient Objects*.

8 On this quagmire, see Bruno Latour, "Why Has Critique Run Out of Steam? From Matters of Fact to Matters of Concern," *Critical Inquiry* 30, no. 2 (Winter 2004): 225–48.

as green and sustainable, we must recognize these buzzwords as deeply political, contentious, and ideological. This chapter therefore critically considers "sustainability" as it examines select historical moments of art's entwinement with ecology—including 1960s practices of environmental restoration, 1970s developments in cybernetic-environmental systems, and contemporary formations of political ecology—which will also provide a framework, however ultimately incomplete, with which to consider contemporary practices in the subsequent chapters.

We need to ask, in this regard, not only what sustainability means when employed, but also whose interests it promotes and whose are excluded. Consider, for instance, the classic articulation of "sustainable development" in the 1987 UN-affiliated report *Our Common Future*: "Development that meets the needs of the present without compromising the ability of future generations to meet their own needs."[9] The UN's embrace of sustainability was a major step forward, and may appear as a decisive world-historical development—although the science of anthropogenic climate change owing to what we now register as heat-trapping gases was first recognized in the 1820s by French physicist Jean-Baptiste Joseph Fourier, and the term "greenhouse effect" was first used in 1917 by the Scottish-born American scientist Alexander Graham Bell.[10] The UN's formulation of sustainability, however, is vague at best, for what are these "needs" exactly? Whose needs count and whose don't? And what is the "development" to be sustained? Whereas the UN placed its agenda under an inclusive commonality (*our* common future), implying a shared responsibility for safeguarding humanity's ecological inheritance, the definition in fact situates the environment as valuable largely from the perspective of *economic* needs. The report grants that "sustainable development does imply limits"—whereby it acknowledges *Limits to Growth*, the influential 1972 report commissioned by the Club of Rome—yet goes on to explain that "technology and social organization can be both managed and improved to make way for a new era of economic

9 World Commission on Environment and Development (WCED), *Our Common Future* (Oxford: Oxford University Press, 1987), 43. The difficult attempt to balance ecological conservation and economic development was already at play in the World Conservation Strategy's 1980 report. See the International Union for Conservation of Nature and Natural Resources (in cooperation with the United Nations Environmental Programme and the World Wildlife Fund), *World Conservation Strategy: Living Resource Conservation for Sustainable Development* (1980), https://portals.iucn.org/library/efiles/documents/WCS-004.pdf.

10 See James R. Fleming, "Joseph Fourier, the 'Greenhouse Effect,' and the Quest for a Universal Theory of Terrestrial Temperatures," *Endeavour* 23, no. 2 (1999): 72–75. On the problems of generalizing responsibility for climate change to the human species, see my forthcoming book *Against the Anthropocene: Visual Culture and Environment Today* (Berlin: Sternberg Press, 2016).

growth," one that will make "development sustainable."[11] This financial priority has guided Western governmental mobilizations of sustainability ever since, where the "needs" and "development" of corporate industry are privileged above all else in what has come to be known as "green capitalism."[12]

Conversely, the terminology of sustainability has been elaborately questioned by critics and theorists, and an analysis in the artistic context should do likewise. Cultural geographer Erik Swyngedouw contends that the term is largely meaningless—for instance, "there is no such thing as an unsustainable city in general, but rather there are a series of urban and environmental processes that negatively affect some social groups while benefiting others."[13] The cipher of sustainability must be qualified within a specific context to capture its slippery meaning; otherwise, it doesn't really mean much. The problem with the generic quality of terminology like "sustainable development" is that it tends to present "a classless vision of ecological justice made in the USA,"[14] as postcolonial theorist Gayatri Spivak puts it, a vision that appears ideologically, and falsely, as uncontestable—who, after all, would oppose sustainability?—even while it furthers corporate interests. As part of the green capitalist agenda, sustainability rhetoric also typically prioritizes the needs of developed nations over others, even though cleaning up European and North American environments under its name has meant transferring their polluting industries and environmental responsibility to the Global South, which, as is widely acknowledged, faces the largest negative impacts of global warming, while having the least economic resources.[15] It

11 WCED, *Our Common Future*, 8. For a critical discussion of the 1972 United Nations Conference on the Human Environment in Stockholm, see Ken Conca and Geoffrey D. Dabelko, eds., *Green Planet Blues: Environmental Politics from Stockholm to Johannesburg* (Oxford: Westview Press, 2004).

12 For a discussion and critique of the economic imperatives of 1990s "green politics," see Timothy Luke, "Environmentality as Green Governmentality," in *Discourses of the Environment*, ed. Éric Darier (Oxford: Blackwell, 1999): 121–51.

13 Erik Swyngedouw, "Circulations and Metabolisms: (Hybrid) Natures and (Cyborg) Cities," *Science as Culture* 15, no. 2 (June 2006): 115. Also see the work of the research collective Critical Sustainabilities, at University of California, Santa Cruz: https://critical-sustainabilities.ucsc.edu/.

14 Gayatri Chakravorty Spivak, "Megacity," *Grey Room*, no. 1 (Fall 2000): 14; cited in Emily Apter, "The Aesthetics of Critical Habitats," *October*, no. 99 (Winter 2002): 21.

15 An infamous example of the logic of inequality is the memo Lawrence Summers wrote when he was Chief Economist at the World Bank in 1991, suggesting that "dirty industries" should migrate to the "least developed countries": because "I think the economic logic behind dumping a load of toxic waste in the lowest wage country is impeccable and we should face up to that. [...] I've always thought that underpopulated countries in Africa are vastly underpolluted; their air quality is vastly inefficiently low compared to Los Angeles or Mexico City." Although Summers apologized for the statement after the memo was leaked, "the trouble with Larry Summers and his memo is not that it was an aberration stemming from a lapse of good judgment. The trouble is that it wasn't [an aberration at all]." Russell Mokhiber and Robert Weissman, "Memo Misfire: World Bank 'Spoof' Memo on Toxic Waste Holds More Irony Than Laughs," *Global Policy Forum*, ac-

is crucial in this regard to challenge environmental proposals under the flag of sustainability that justify the worsening of social inequality, promote authoritarian government, and further concentrate the power of decision-making in the hands of multinationals and their governmental promoters, all in the name of emergency response measures to climate change.

If we still choose to accept the use of the term sustainability—and I believe it remains useful, with qualifications—we must ask, in relation to current artistic practice, how ecological sustainability can meet the demands of environmental justice. "A just urban socio-environmental perspective," Swyngedouw continues, "always needs to consider the question of who gains and who pays and to ask serious questions about the multiple power relations. [...] In other words, environmental transformations are not independent from class, gender, ethnicity, or other power struggles."[16] In this sense, whereas there is a growing need to address the global geopolitics of environmentalism (as in the analysis of art and visual culture), then we should bring greater focus on initiatives based in places like sub-Saharan Africa and Southeast Asia, initiatives that are often absent within Western exhibitions and contemporary art history. Such a focus might include practices like the exposure of the degraded ecologies of Lagos's megaslum by the Nigerian photographic collective Depth of Field, the study of "emerging urbanism" in New Delhi by the Indian research group Sarai, the focus on political ecology in the Global South by the international group World of Matter, and recent exhibition projects like "48°C Public.Art.Ecology" (2008) in Delhi, which investigated the ramifications of climate change on the Indian metropolis.[17] Only then will we avoid the vacuity that terms like sustainability often take on, particularly when set solely in the Euro-American context, which makes them easily appropriable by just about anyone, most often those with corporate interests. Instead, it remains necessary to define such terms in relation to specific practices and their particular geopolitical settings.

Finally, we must also confront the troubling fundamental contradiction of most recent art exhibitions dedicated to sustainability. Even as they seek to raise awareness of climate change and work toward creative

cessed October 15, 2015, https://www.globalpolicy.org/component/content/article/209/43247.html; originally published in *San Francisco Bay Guardian*, May 26, 1999.

16 Swyngedouw, "Circulations and Metabolisms," 115.

17 This handful of references is only a sampling, yet it indicates the commitment of this book: to explore the global geographies where art and environment connect. For further consideration of environmental art, literature, and global justice, see Rob Nixon, *Slow Violence and the Environmentalism of the Poor* (Cambridge, MA: Harvard University Press, 2011); and Yates McKee, "Art and the Ends of Environmentalism: From Biosphere to the Right to Survival," in *Nongovernmental Politics*, ed. Michel Feher, Gäelle Krikorian, and Yates McKee (New York: Zone Books, 2007).

solutions—although certainly not all projects are equally political or pedagogically inclined—they contribute to the very problem of global warming by virtue of their own carbon footprint, the result of transporting artworks, controlling the climate of the galleries, and printing catalogues. Exemplary was dOCUMENTA (13) in 2012: billed as a "sustainable exhibition" in publicity material, its cosmetic green practices largely contradicted its ecological claims.[18] We might conclude that eco-art exhibitions are simply unviable from an environmental perspective—especially one that emphasizes the imperative of material and economic degrowth—even if the urgency of addressing ecological crises only grows by the day. Yet if this response is both inadequate and unrealistic—as much as it would be to insist on immediately discontinuing all unsustainable technologies rather than working gradually and steadfastly toward a state of holistic decarbonized environmentalism—we need at the very least to consider exactly what justifies the continuation of unsustainable art exhibitions committed to the subject of sustainability. With this assortment of deliberations in mind, I will examine three waves of environmental art since 1960.

Fragile Ecologies

The first phase of environmental art in the United States began in the 1960s—including pioneering works such as Hans Haacke's *Grass Grows* (1966), a mound of dirt sprouting grass, installed in Howard Wise Gallery in New York; Newton Harrison's *The Slow Birth and Death of a Lily Cell* (1968), a cell cultivated in lab equipment, also shown at Howard Wise; and Alan Sonfist's *Time Landscape New York City* (proposed 1965, realized 1978), which attempted to return a plot in New York City to its precolonial botanical condition.[19] These pieces were soon followed by the first group shows, including "Earth Art" at Cornell University's art gallery in 1969, which presented diverse models of Land art by Haacke, Robert Morris, Dennis Oppenheim, and Robert Smithson.[20] Surveying these early

18 I investigate dOCUMENTA (13) further in chapter 7.

19 See the very helpful "Short History of Eco-Art Exhibitions" in Sue Spaid, *Ecovention: Current Art to Transform Ecologies* (Corte Madera, CA: Contemporary Arts Center, 2002), 134–36. Additional recent surveys of environmental art include Malcolm Miles, *Eco-Aesthetics: Art, Literature and Architecture in a Period of Climate Change* (London: Bloomsbury, 2014); and Linda Weintraub, *To Life! Eco Art in Pursuit of a Sustainable Planet* (Berkeley: University of California Press, 2012).

20 Subsequent exhibitions, mostly smaller in scale, include: "Earth, Air, Fire, and Water: Elements of Art," Museum of Fine Art in Boston, 1971; "Art in Space," Detroit Institute of Arts, 1973; "A Response to the Environment," Rutgers University Gallery, 1975; and "Earth Net: An Economic System," Baxter Art Museum, California Institute of Technology, 1978. Environmental art exhibitions (with multiple artists) decreased significantly during the 1980s—the era of Reagan-Thatcher conservatism and anti-ecological revanchism—returning with "Fragile Ecologies" in 1992.

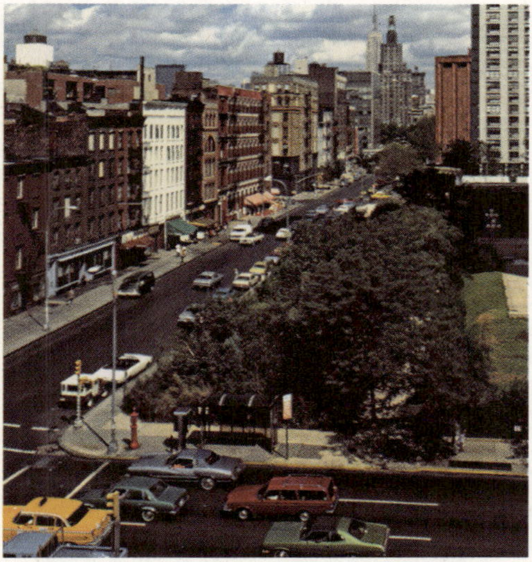

Alan Sonfist, *Time Landscape New York City*, 1965–present

years, the Queens Museum of Art's 1992 exhibition "Fragile Ecologies" was one of the first shows to examine the historical formation of "environmental art." Curator Barbara Matilsky sees it stemming from the "political and social climate during the 1960s," when "an increasing number of people [in the United States] began to question traditional values and governmental policies regarding Vietnam, racial segregation, women's status, and the environment." Spurred on by the publication of signal environmentalist texts—Rachel Carson's *Silent Spring* (1962), Paul Ehrlich's *The Population Bomb* (1968), and the aforementioned *Limits to Growth* (1972)—which helped catalyze the US-based environmental movement, artists "turned to nature and began interpreting its life-generating forces to create radically new kinds of art."[21]

Most of the works in "Fragile Ecologies," as well as the projects referenced in its catalogue, develop a model of what we could term "restorationist eco-aesthetics," referring to art that envisions and enacts the repair of damaged habitats and degraded ecosystems. Sonfist's *Time Landscape*, the Harrisons' *Portable Orchard: Survival Piece #5* (1972–73), Haacke's *Rhine-Water Purification Plant* (1972), Bonnie Ora Sherk's *The Farm* (1974), Agnes Denes's *Wheatfield—A Confrontation* (1982), Joseph Beuys's *7000 Oaks* (1982), and Mel Chin's *Revival Field* (1990–93)—each piece attempts to rescue natural

21 Barbara C. Matilsky, "Environmental Art: New Approaches to Nature," in *Fragile Ecologies: Contemporary Artists' Interpretations and Solutions* (New York: Rizzoli, 1992), 36.

environments from polluted conditions by proposing alternative, nonindustrial uses of land. As such, they fulfilled Matilsky's definition of ecology as "the science of planetary housekeeping" (after Barry Commoner's phrase, derived from the Greek *oikos*, meaning house or habitat) that would sustain "the interrelationship of all forms of life in their diverse environments."[22] Exemplary is Sonfist's stated goal: "To elevate disappearing native landscapes to the status of historical monuments and, by extension, to sensitize people so that they could view nature as an important part of their cultural heritage."[23]

While such aims were once clearly timely and pressing, in retrospect, and with changes to the political and economic systems of environmental management since, these models now present often outmoded approaches to ecological matters. Sonfist's *Time Landscape*, for instance, reconstructed an indigenous biotic realm in New York City's Greenwich Village, a precolonial wilderness of oaks, hickories, junipers, maples, and sassafras that would place urban visitors in touch with the region's preindustrial history, preserving an ecology in the same way one would preserve a historic building, as Sonfist claimed.[24] The landscape would "repair the hole in the psyche which is left when all traces of our biological and ecological roots are obliterated."[25] Sonfist's model of speculative conservationism, however, paradoxically attempted to recover a nonhuman ecology (and quite likely one environmentally managed by Indigenous peoples in the precontact period) via human means. In subsequent decades this conservationism would become a leading strategy of green ecosystem services, where nature's management would be practiced through financial valuations and NGOs in coordination with local communities. In these cases, however, protected "wildernesses"—often acknowledged by critics to be technologically manufactured and shred of all biodiversity, as in monocultural eucalyptus tree farms—proposes something

22 Barbara C. Matilsky, introduction to ibid., 3–4. She references Barry Commoner, *The Closing Circle: Nature, Man, and Technology* (New York: Knopf, 1971), 18. This formation of environmental aesthetics (as practiced by artists such as Haacke, Denes, Sonfist, the Harrisons, and Sherk)—which investigated ecological processes and relations between human culture and natural ecosystems—was generally, if not in every case, distinct from Land art (as practiced by artists like Michael Heizer, Richard Long, Walter De Maria, Dennis Oppenheim, Nancy Holt, and Robert Morris), which examined the aesthetic experience of (often modernist) sculpture situated in, and sometimes merged with, the nonurban landscape, but which did not necessarily engage with its industrial damage or prospective restoration, its biological systems or ecologies. Of course there were also areas of crossover, shared concerns, and critical differences, as with the work of Robert Smithson, which straddled both categories and had a critical relation to both.

23 Cited in Matilsky, "Environmental Art," 40.

24 Eleanor Heartney, "The Garden in the Machine: The Time Landscapes of Alan Sonfist," in *Alan Sonfist: History and the Landscapes* (Iowa City, IA: The Museum, 1997), 15.

25 Sonfist, quoted in ibid.

26 See M. Kat Anderson, *Tending the Wild: Native American Knowledge and the Management of California's Natural Resources* (Los Angeles: University of California Press, 2006).

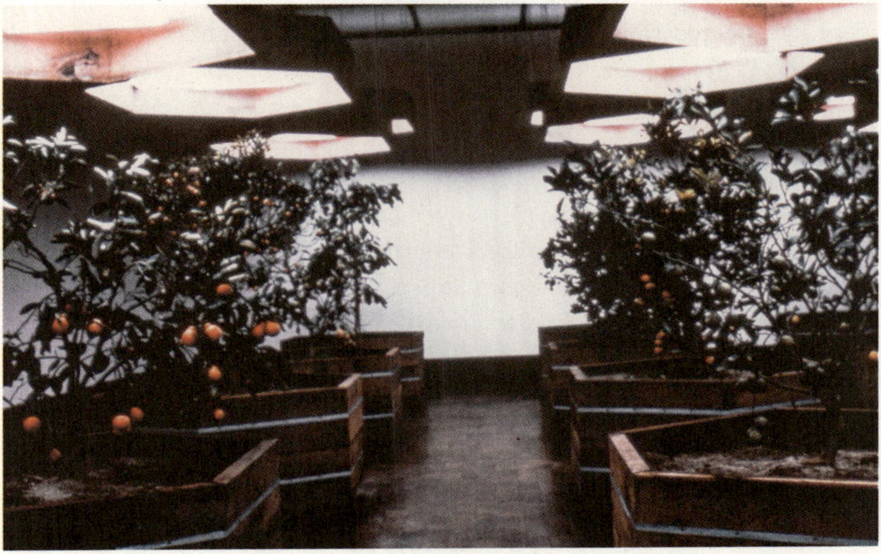

Helen Mayer Harrison and Newton Harrison, *Portable Orchard: Survival Piece #5*, 1972–73

closer to an artificial, human-constructed environment than a restoration of pure nature.[26]

Or consider the Harrisons' *Survival Pieces*, a series of six works that investigate self-sufficient harvesting, for which they brought fish farms and orchards into art galleries, forming experiments in independent pisciculture and agriculture. *Portable Orchard: Survival Piece #5* (1972–73), for instance, installed at the art gallery at California State University, Fullerton, included an assortment of citrus trees growing out of twelve hexagonal redwood boxes. The Harrisons implicitly juxtaposed their plots against "the loss of orchard and farm to ongoing suburban and industrial development," positioning the work as if it were "the last orange orchard in Orange County."[27] The survival works (in particular *Full Farm: Survival Piece #6*, 1974) also parallel Bonnie Ora Sherk's artistic-agricultural experiments, such as *The Farm* (1974), seven acres of communal agricultural land set up under a San Francisco freeway overpass—later turned into a public park. Projects like these adopted organic, self-contained, and independent farming practices, and opposed them to the "silent spring" of industrial farming's carcinogenic pesticides and herbicides, monocrop commercial agriculture, and the division of land into distinct

27 Quoted from the description of the work on the artists' website, *The Harrison Studio*, accessed October 16, 2015, http://theharrisonstudio.net/?page_id=214.

urban and rural zones. These modes of artistic "survival" on the basis of community-based organic farming also tacitly questioned the otherwise nonproductive, sterile context of the art gallery. An element of abstraction is present in these pieces, however, much like the restorationist projects of local environments in subsequent years, insofar as they cultivated pure nature in protected, isolated sites, monumentalized it, or at least neglected to emphasize what the most compelling of later practitioners would foreground: the transformation of ecologies as much as the sociopolitical and economic-legal systems in which agriculture is seen to be increasingly enmeshed.

The dualist thinking implicit in many of these models is apparent, for example, in Agnes Denes's *Wheatfield—A Confrontation: Battery Park Landfill, Downtown Manhattan* (1982), for which the artist planted wheat on two acres of the landfill of earth excavated to build the World Trade Center, cultivating a small farm surrounded by the institutions of global trade. Her project was noteworthy for addressing the ecology of disparate economies: she harvested approximately one thousand pounds of golden wheat a few months later—$158 worth of the cereal grain on land valued at $4.5 billion.[28] In this regard, the said confrontation amounted to a conventional nature-culture opposition, pitting "a leisurely wheatfield," as Denes explained, against "an island of achievement-craze culture and decadence," a "city of competence, sophistication, and crime" against "open fields and the unspoiled farmlands," and "the everlasting" against "the forever changing."[29] Denes's proposal was for a radically different vision of urban land use, one that resisted service to capital via real estate development; like the models by the Harrisons and Sherk, it prefigured the subsequent growth of urban gardening worldwide, particularly in postindustrial American and European cities where local gardens supplement food supply, support economic regeneration, and promote consumption of organic produce.[30] Yet her model of interventionist farming (what curator Sue Spaid calls an "ecovention") had its own limits: unlike subsequent generations of artists who would foreground permaculture's biodiversity in their farming models, as discussed below and in subsequent chapters in this book, Denes planted a monocrop field, a mode of agriculture that inadvertently paralleled the

28 James Clark, "Fields for Thought: The Art of Agnes Denes," *Public Art Review* 8, no. 2 (Spring/Summer 1997): 11.

29 Agnes Denes, quoted in *Agnes Denes*, ed. Jill Hartz (Ithaca, NY: Herbert F. Johnson Museum of Art, Cornell University, 1992), 118.

30 See, for instance, Terri Weisman, "Detroit's Edible Gardens: Art and Agriculture in a Post-Environmental World," *Third Text* 27, no. 1 (January 2013): 1–11; George McKay, *Radical Gardening: Politics, Idealism and Rebellion in the Garden* (London: Frances Lincoln, 2011); and Peter Lamborn Wilson and Bill Weinberg, eds., *Avant Gardening: Ecological Struggle in the City and the World* (Brooklyn: Autonomedia, 1999).

very rationalization and commodification of farming practices by corporate industrial-chemical agribusiness to which her work's anticapitalist spirit was otherwise opposed.

Despite the ecological ethics of the "Fragile Ecologies" exhibition, explicitly posed against industrial capitalism's despoliation of the environment, there are nonetheless several snags within Matilsky's approach—not the least of which is its view of "nature" through a spiritualist lens, which in this case supplants conceptual and self-reflexive rigor as well as political engagement. At the root of the concern is the exhibition's proclivity to separate nature from culture, following from the nature-culture oppositional logic of many of the practices she included. Relegated to a noncultural zone of organic purity, and reminiscent of the mythopoetic realm attributed to the biosphere in chemist James Lovelock and microbiologist Lynn Margulis's Gaia hypothesis from the late '70s—another crucial marker in the development of ecological discourse—nature ends up objectified as an ontology divorced from social, political, and technological processes.[31] Undermining the otherwise laudable environmentalist intentions of the exhibition is the show's depoliticization of its subject, which reproduces the very objectification of nature that got us into trouble in the first place. "Sundered apart, nature and society die in reciprocal conceptual torpor," geographer Neil Smith observed. "The positing of an external nature rationalizes and justifies the unprecedented exploitation of nature (human *cum* nonhuman), the 'massive racket' that capitalism, historically and geographically, represents."[32] Matilsky's definition of nature committed just such a division, if from a perspective critical of capitalism's treatment of the environment.[33]

To Matilsky's genealogy of environmental art, we could add the fact that the period roughly

31 James E. Lovelock and Lynn Margulis, "Atmospheric Homeostasis by and for the Biosphere: The Gaia Hypothesis," *Tellus* 26 (1974): 2–10; and James Lovelock, *Gaia: A New Look at Life on Earth* (Oxford: Oxford University Press, 1979). The hypothesis describes Earth's ecology as a living, self-regulating system, which Lovelock named after the ancient Greek goddess of the earth. For a recent productive redirection of this hypothesis, see Latour, "Waiting for Gaia."

32 Neil Smith, foreword to *In the Nature of Cities: Urban Political Ecology and the Politics of Urban Metabolism*, ed. Nik Heynen, Maria Kaika, and Erik Swyngedouw (London: Routledge, 2006), xiii–xiv.

33 As a counter to this division of nature and culture, see the Haus der Kulturen der Welt's 2013 exhibition, "The Whole Earth: California and the Disappearance of the Outside," curated by Diedrich Diederichsen and Anselm Franke, which presented an analysis of counterculture and environmentalist movements of the 1960s and '70s, mapping connections to cybernetic theory, feedback systems, social networks, experimental music and ecologies, as well as showing how these approaches led to the flexible and libertarian neoliberalism of the subsequent digital revolution. In this regard, the exhibition adopted the narrative of Fred Turner, *From Counterculture to Cyberculture: Stewart Brand, the Whole Earth Network, and the Rise of Digital Utopianism* (Chicago: University of Chicago Press, 2006).

covered in "Fragile Ecologies" marked the emergence of international nongovernmental organizations and intergovernmental protocols, agreements, and cooperative accords for dealing with environmental concerns, framed by the 1972 United Nations Conference on the Human Environment in Stockholm (the first UN conference to focus on international environmental issues) and the 1992 United Nations Conference on Environment and Development in Rio de Janeiro (the "Earth Summit," which led to the Kyoto Protocol, adopted in 1997).[34] The latter event, moreover, gave rise to the growing criticism that UN initiatives failed to address postcolonial concerns and the inequality between so-called postindustrial nations and those in the Global South. Yet "Fragile Ecologies" has nothing to say about this wider context and the political calls for global justice that would challenge a Western-centric environmentalism, favoring instead a new-age eco-aesthetics that overlooks the larger geopolitical stakes. "Environmental artists," Matilsky noted, in what is an extremely limiting view of the complexity of '60s and '70s eco-art, "visualize the forces, processes, and phenomena of nature: organic growth, light, water, crystals and other elements," creating works that "respect nature and establish a reverent relationship between the viewer and the earth."[35]

It is not that the artistic projects represented in "Fragile Ecologies" commit the same abuse of nature as capitalist industry—although they aren't entirely divorced from that framework either, as when they rely on industrial technology or fossil-fuel energy to create their projects. It's rather that the exhibition's conceptualization of nature (as separate, ontologically discrete, and opposed to the human realm) perpetuates a parallel structure of objectification, albeit without the practices of material exploitation relied on by capitalist industry. This very system makes it possible for the exhibition, for instance, to uncritically highlight practices that advance provisional approaches to devastated landscapes, without connecting the repairing of a pond (Haacke), the preserving of a historical landscape (Sonfist), or the growing of a wheat field (Denes) to the technological, social, and economic systems that also construct the environment. In this regard, Matilsky's reference to Robert Smithson's conceptual environmental art is telling, particularly where she notes that Smithson rejected artistic approaches to postindustrial terrains that would merely "cosmetically camouflage the abuse" committed by corporations.[36] Yet by

34 On this history, see Conca and Dabelko, *Green Planet Blues*, esp. the introduction "Three Decades of Global Environmental Politics," 1–24; Donella H. Meadows, Dennis L. Meadows, Jørgen Randers, and William W. Behrens III, "The Limits to Growth," 25–30; and Ken Conca and Geoffrey D. Dabelko, "The 1992 Earth Summit: Reflections on an Ambiguous Event," 68–75.

35 Matilsky, "Environmental Art," 38.

36 Ibid., 44. Matilsky also mentions Robert Morris's criticism of

neglecting to take this skepticism seriously, the exhibition's conceptualization missed an opportunity to nuance its discussion of the included works. What if Smithson's dialectic of "Site and Nonsite"—according to which he theorized the inextricable relationship between the geographical location of a work of art (Site) and its sculptural, photographic, or text-based representations (Nonsite)—had been integrated into the framework of the show?[37] Taking this logic seriously would have precluded the isolation of nature as an autonomous sphere of existence, as a site without a dialectical cultural counterpart. That work would be left to others.

Systems Ecology

An early '90s exhibition that looked back on the formation of eco-centric art since the '60s, "Fragile Ecologies" tended to reduce the complexity of the environment in favor of an ideal essentialist conception of nature. But by the mid-'70s there were already other expanded notions of ecology that encompassed social and technological systems as well as biological ones. These form an alternative and ambitious discourse informed by the midcentury development of cybernetics—the interdisciplinary study of regulatory systems related to systems theory.[38] Advanced in the work of diverse figures such as British anthropologist and social scientist Gregory Bateson, American artist-theorist Jack Burnham, Hungarian-born artist and writer György Kepes, and American architect R. Buckminster Fuller, "systems ecology" provides a key conceptual framework for comprehending the work of artists such as Dan Graham, Robert Barry, Hans Haacke, and Les Levine, who were practicing in the '60s and

eco-art fixes of industrial degradation, which he voiced in his keynote address at the symposium "Earthworks: Land Reclamation as Sculpture" (1979) at the University of Washington, Seattle: "Do those sites scarred by mining or poisoned by chemicals now seem less like the entropic liabilities of ravenous and short-sighted industry and more like long-awaited aesthetic possibilities?"—as if the industrial destruction of environments proposes first and foremost an artistic resource for Land art. Ibid., 47.

37 In his essay "The Spiral Jetty" (1972), Robert Smithson explained, "The range of convergence between Site and Nonsite consists of a course of hazards, a double path made up of signs, photographs, and maps that belong to both sides of the dialectic at once." In *Robert Smithson: The Collected Writings*, ed. Jack Flam (Berkeley: University of California Press, 1996), 153n1. My understanding of Smithson's ambivalent relation to environmentalism benefited from participating in the symposium organized by Ingrid Commandeur, "Rethinking Robert Smithson," at the Royal Academy of Art (KABK), The Hague, March 20, 2012.

38 Systems theory refers generally to self-regulating systems—as found in nature, animal bodies, local and global ecosystems, and climate processes—and was theorized in cybernetic engineering and communications science, which frequently emphasized the self-correcting mechanism of feedback. See Norbert Wiener, *Cybernetics: or, Control and Communication in the Animal and the Machine* (Cambridge, MA: Technology Press, 1948); and Steve Joshua Heims, *Constructing a Social Science for Postwar America: The Cybernetics Group, 1946–53* (Cambridge, MA: MIT Press, 1991).

early '70s.[39] As Jack Burnham presciently wrote in 1968, "Increasingly 'products'—either in art or life—become irrelevant and a different set of needs arise: these revolve around such concerns as maintaining the biological livability of the earth, producing more accurate models of social interaction, understanding the growing symbiosis in man-machine relationships, establishing priorities for the usage and conservation of natural resources, and defining alternative patterns of education, productivity, and leisure."[40] The accuracy of Burnham's insight has been borne out by the subsequent developments of artistic practice until today, even if his eco-systematic "set of needs" has never been quite fulfilled. Even so, the "biological livability of the earth" offers an early account of what later would be termed sustainability.

Bateson, who authored the book *Steps to an Ecology of Mind* in 1972, considered ecology as simultaneously natural, social, and technological, wherein ecological "health" was understood to be dependent on human civilization and the natural-cultural environment, maintaining a sustained and long-term "flexibility [...] to create an ongoing complex system."[41] Defining flexibility as an "uncommitted potentiality for change," Bateson viewed it as a precious resource, for ecological "imbalance" carried unpredictable and potentially catastrophic effects.[42] "Always, in any living (i.e., ecological) system, ever increasing imbalance will generate its own limiting factors as side effects of the increasing imbalance," Bateson warned in the cybernetics and new media journal *Radical Software* in 1972. "In the present instance, we begin to know some of Nature's ways of correcting the imbalance—smog, pollution, DDT poisoning, industrial wastes, famine, atomic fallout, and war. *But the imbalance has gone so far that we cannot trust Nature not to over-correct.*"[43] There are certainly weak points in Bateson's argument from a factual standpoint—no mention of the greenhouse gases already contributing to climate "imbalance," the nostalgic implication that human civilization once lived in an ideal balance with the environment to which modern society could return, and the anthropocentric belief that nature prefers a homeostasis ideally suited to humans. Nonetheless, the culture of systems ecology inspired a range of artistic practices

39 Many of these artists are mentioned in Jack Burnham, "Systems Esthetics," *Artforum*, September 1968, 30–35. Interest in this period of art, ecology, systems aesthetics, and cybernetics has recently resurged in art writing and criticism, including that of David Joselit, William Kaizen, Yates McKee, and Luke Skrebowski.

40 Ibid., 31.

41 Gregory Bateson, "Ecology and Flexibility in Urban Civilization" (1970), in *Steps to an Ecology of Mind: Collected Essays in Anthropology, Psychiatry, Evolution and Epistemology* (Chicago: University of Chicago Press, 2000), 502.

42 Ibid., 505.

43 Gregory Bateson, "Up against the Environment or Ourselves?," *Radical Software* 1, no. 5 (Spring 1972): 33 (emphasis in original).

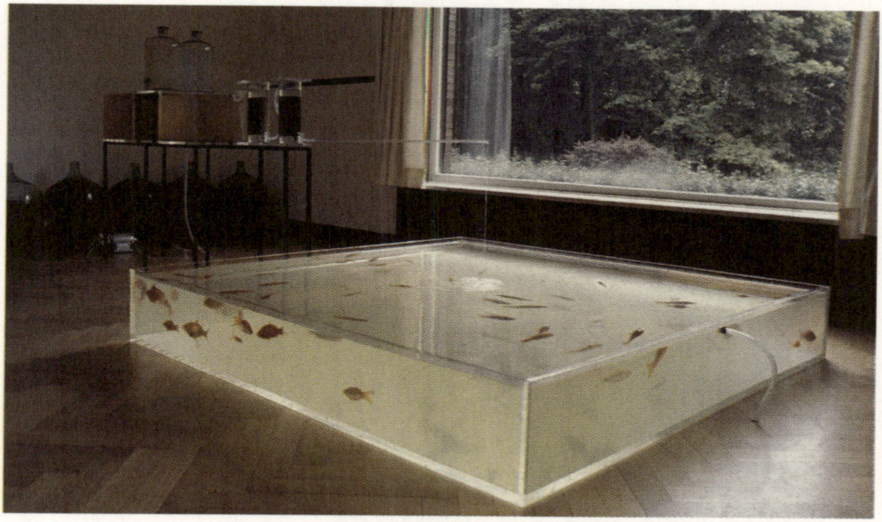

Hans Haacke, *Rhine-Water Purification Plant*, 1972

dedicated to interlinking biological, technological, social, and political ecologies and constructing an environment that can no longer be considered simply natural, and where any output, according to the operations of cybernetic feedback, was simultaneously understood to affect the sustainability of the system as a complex whole.

Consider, for instance, Hans Haacke's modeling of a biotechnological system in *Rhine-Water Purification Plant* (1972), which also advances an artistic and political environmentalism. Invited to produce a two-month-long project for the Museum Haus Lange in Krefeld, former West Germany, the artist set up a chemical-treatment plant with charcoal and sand filtration to process polluted water from the Rhine River. The purified water collected in a large acrylic basin containing goldfish, demonstrating the successful construction of a life-supporting habitat using technology. Yet in referring to the ongoing and systemic problems of industrial and domestic pollution, this project was not limited to the local, cosmetic fix of restorationist eco-aesthetics. And it advanced beyond the smaller-scale physiological systems Haacke created for earlier pieces like *Bowery Seeds* (1970), in which he installed a rooftop mound of dirt in New York's Bowery and allowed it to catch and germinate airborne seeds, and *Grass Grows* (1969), where the foregrounding of the growth of life systems displaced the exclusivity of human artistic agency. In *Krefeld Sewage Triptych* (1972), shown on the same occasion as *Rhine-Water Purification Plant*, Haacke recorded the level of untreated sewage that the city of Krefeld spewed into the Rhine annually (forty-two million cubic meters), included the volume and types of industrial and household sewage, and provided the names of the major polluters. In his description of the piece, Haacke observed that because the Museum Haus Lange is a municipal institution run by civil servants, his project aimed at not merely restoring an ecosystem, but exposing the city's ongoing role in polluting the river (insofar as it allowed such effluence in the first place)—amplified in media coverage of Haacke's work in regional newspapers. The resulting political effects of the techno-biological operation in the art museum would thus be considered part of what Haacke termed a "real-time social system." That system not only intervened in a degraded ecosystem, but also identified the causes of its situation and worked to draw public attention to the broader political and economic culture of environmental abuse.[44]

Nevertheless, Haacke's demonstration of "ecological health," to use Bateson's terminology, might be criticized from the very basis of systems ecology for its failure to involve the audience more directly within its feedback loop; it rather relegated viewers to mere observers of a system that excluded their immediate active participation other than encouraging civic involvement in the ecological governance of their region. Perhaps the pedagogical authority of *Rhine-Water Purification Plant*'s mode of address—one that presented an engineering demonstration coupled with a statement of facts—corresponded to the project's techno-scientific instrumentalism, implying a criticism with which cybernetics has also long contended.[45] It was left to other artists to initiate experiments, including those that were video-based, that developed the socially integrative possibilities of cybernetics systems, particularly as they were conceptualized in *Radical Software*. From 1970 to 1974, the journal—published by the Raindance Corporation, a countercultural media think tank based in New York—served as a platform for articulating the notion of "media ecology," defined by theorist Raymond Arlo in one of the

44 See the description of this project in Brian Wallis, ed., *Hans Haacke: Unfinished Business* (New York: New Museum of Contemporary Art, 1986), 106–7, which also claims that "in response to the exhibition, a regional newspaper reported extensively on the city's part in the pollution of the river." Also see Luke Skrebowski, "After Hans Haacke: Tue Greenfort and Eco-Institutional Critique," *Third Text* 27, no. 1 (January 2013): 115–30.

45 See Bateson, *Steps to an Ecology of Mind*, xii. Haacke did, however, address social ecology in other projects, specifically his statistical polls of museum visitors, even if these also proposed a rudimentary inclusion of the audience-participant. On the relation between Haacke's early ecological works and his later systems aesthetic, see Luke Skrebowski, "All Systems Go: Recovering Hans Haacke's Systems Art," *Grey Room*, no. 30 (Winter 2008): 54–83. For an account of the critical reception of cybernetics in art and architectural discourse, see Felicity D. Scott, "Designing Environment," in *Architecture or Techno-Utopia: Politics after Modernism* (Cambridge, MA: MIT Press, 2007), 89–112.

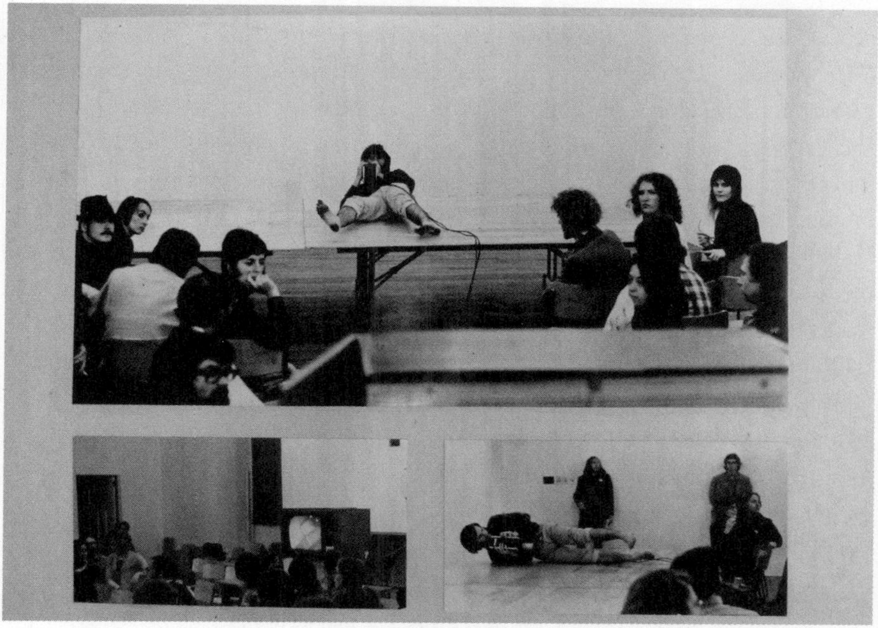

Dan Graham, *TV Camera/Monitor Performance*, 1970

first issues as "the study of a medium of communication and its affect [sic] upon other media/society."[46] Exploiting the possibilities of new low-cost video technology, artists and activist groups affiliated with this formation attempted to construct and mobilize feedback systems for community cable television (connecting to contemporaneous media collectives like Ant Farm, Videofreex, and TVTV) and build closed-circuit video experiments (as in the work of Peter Campus, Dan Graham, Joan Jonas, and Bruce Nauman), to contest the one-way broadcasting control of mainstream media by creating grassroots systems of self-representation in their place.[47] These models insisted that socio-pedagogical elements of media ecology were necessary for sustainability to operate successfully as a system.

With several projects, Graham created what he termed "learning machines."[48] In *TV Camera/Monitor Performance* (1970) he rolled across a stage while pointing a video camera at a monitor located behind the audience that showed the real-time

46 Raymond Arlo, "Media Ecology," *Radical Software* 1, no. 3 (Spring 1971): 19; cited in William Kaizen, "Steps to an Ecology of Communication: *Radical Software*, Dan Graham, and the Legacy of Gregory Bateson," *Art Journal* 67, no. 3 (Fall 2008): 87.

47 See David Joselit, *Feedback: Television against Democracy* (Cambridge, MA: MIT Press, 2007).

48 Cited in Kaizen, "Steps to an Ecology of Communication," 100.

image in a feedback loop, and *Two Consciousness Projection(s)* (1972) involves a closed-circuit video system mediating the spontaneous communication between two participants and an audience. Participants could observe themselves and alter their social system with newly conscious forms of individual and intersubjective behavior immediately perceptible on television monitors. Yet whereas Graham's media ecology interlinked technology, communication, sociability, and affect,[49] nonhuman biological systems (foregrounded, for instance, in Haacke's environmental art) were conspicuously absent (although in his subsequent glass pavilions, particularly when sited in natural environments, Graham developed perceptual feedback loops centering on the figural-environmental assemblage). Arlo had stated, "In a world of biological, chemical and physical pollution, it seems to me that we are overlooking the semantic pollution in our environments, as we attempt to restore our ecological balance."[50] But by addressing semantic pollution, particularly originating in technological media (such as commercial broadcast television), other areas were in turn overlooked. It was precisely the balance between these multiple ecologies that was often difficult to obtain, whether in Graham's socio-technological systems or Haacke's physiological ones, as environmental balance was becoming even more precarious as well.

Another model of cultural ecology is found in the 1972 book *Arts of the Environment*, edited by György Kepes, who founded the Center for Advanced Visual Studies at MIT in 1967. In his introductory essay, Kepes stated: "Environmental homeostasis on a global scale is now necessary to survival. Creative imagination, artistic sensibility, can be seen as one of the basic collective, self-regulating devices that help us all to register and reject what is toxic and find what is useful and meaningful in our lives."[51] Kepes's edited volume includes contributions by the interdisciplinary Pulsa Group, which straddle the division between socio-technological and biopolitical systems. Self-described "researchers in programmed environments," and based for a number of years at the Yale School of Art and Architecture, Pulsa Group created projects in the late '60s and early '70s that interlinked various media and biological systems—*Automation House Installation* (1971) comprised sound and video installations in a domestic space, and Harmony Ranch (1969–73), in Oxford, Connecticut, experimented in communal living, agricultural

49 As Kaizen observes in ibid., 87.

50 Arlo, "Media Ecology," 19.

51 György Kepes, "Art and the Ecological Conscience," in *Arts of the Environment*, ed. György Kepes (New York: Braziller, 1972), 72. Robert Smithson's essay "Spiral Jetty" first appeared in this book.

52 See Yates McKee, "The Public Sensoriums of Pulsa: Cybernetic Abstraction and the Biopolitics of Urban Survival," *Art Journal* 67, no. 3 (Fall 2008): 46–67. McKee deserves credit for retrieving Pulsa Group's activities from (art) historical oblivion.

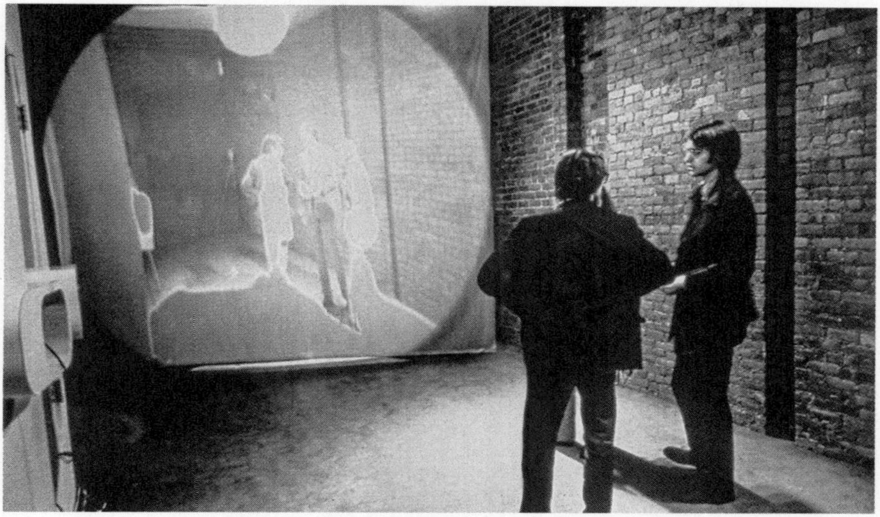

Pulsa Group, *Automation House Installation*, 1971

self-sufficiency, and collaborative art and music projects.[52] In their essay "The City as an Artwork," published in Kepes's volume, Pulsa Group argued that because conventional urban design "is based on an aesthetic of concealment and a concern for picturesque facades," the result, "resembling a pre-technological society," is malfunction, compensating for "a basic human alienation from the systems which make life in a given environment possible."[53] Pulsa Group proposed to repair this systemic breakdown by "creatively expanding the interactive awareness of local populations through media that incorporate principles of feedback: environments, programmed events, cable television, tapes, films."[54] Similarly, at Harmony Ranch, the group experimented with self-organized, collective organic farming to reveal "information about long-term growth rhythms" and "regenerative changes," which were also fed back into the running of the project.[55] Here, agriculture and group-living dynamics became integral to Pulsa Group's experiment in cybernetic systems ecology, whether directed at soil health and vegetable production or cooperative social forms and collaborative music production with acoustic and computerized instruments, with notable visitors from the artistic and musical avant-gardes such as Nam June Paik, Steve Reich, Karlheinz Stockhausen, Richard Teitelbaum, and La Monte Young.

53 Pulsa, "The City as an Artwork," in Kepes, *Arts of the Environment*, 212.

54 Ibid., 217. For a more recent argument on the significance of such media interactivity, see Joselit, *Feedback*.

55 Pulsa, "The City as an Artwork," 217.

Pulsa Group's activities resonated with Kepes's desire to dematerialize and abstract the environment by revealing it as a series of interconnecting flows and dynamics—challenging the sociopolitical, economic, and geographic division between the world of urban crime, warfare, and concentrated poverty, and that of biological engineering, cyborg technology, and communications networks.[56] However, the collective's commitment to moving beyond everyday appearances to diagram environmental workings could be equally taken to task for its very abstraction—as when they created an untitled audiovisual installation at the Boston Public Garden in 1968, positioning fifty-five strobe lights in a four-acre pond with a corresponding number of speakers around the perimeter, creating a sonic-visual ambience that denaturalized the landscape with the help of a signal synthesizer, punched tape reader, digital and analog computers, and magnetic tape. As art historian Yates McKee writes, "The group's understanding of urban crisis as primarily a question of organizational design and ecological maladjustment, to be ameliorated in part by formal experiments in perception, failed to address the structured patterns of inequality of the city that had otherwise become inescapable for urbanism in the aftermath of the ghetto rebellions and claims to rights of the mid- and late 1960s."[57] Pulsa Group did, however, work against idealizing nature, destabilizing its supposed separation from sociopolitical and technological processes and making way for practices to come. The status of nature as an aesthetic object of reverence would nevertheless continue in the work of other artists (such as Andy Goldsworthy, Antony Gormley, and James Turrell), and its basis in sustainability discourse would continue to be subjected to selective abstraction and increasingly to corporate manipulation.

Political Ecology

Because early systems ecology rarely joined with explicit environmental activism—at least in the development of a widely accessible art form—the continued objectification of nature has meant that "the task of new environmental art would be to unsettle the self-evidence of 'environment' itself," as McKee argues, "addressing it as a contingent assemblage of biological, technological, economic, and governmental concerns whose boundaries and agencies are perpetually exposed to conflict."[58] Views of that assemblage have indeed

56 Kepes, "Art and the Ecological Conscience," 9. A discussion of Pulsa was also included in Lucy Lippard, *Six Years: The dematerialization of the art object from 1966 to 1972...* (New York: Praeger, 1973), 83–84.

57 McKee, "The Public Sensoriums of Pulsa," 65.

58 McKee, "Art and the Ends of Environmentalism," 557. Related to this are the conceptualizations of "post-natural" ecology in the writings of Bruno Latour and Timothy Morton.

shifted since 1970, and biopolitical theorists today, such as Timothy Luke, claim that the environment has become the "ultimate domain of being" for the production of knowledge, power, and subjectivity.[59] For Luke, this movement is due to multiple catalysts—including the oil crises of the '70s and the consequent growing awareness of the "limits to growth"; the incipient globalization propelled by the détente between the United States and the Soviet Union and the latter's eventual collapse in the early '90s; corporate biotech investment in, and appropriation of, life systems and their genetic modification; and the expansion of international regulatory bodies, such as the UN World Commission on Environment and Development—all of which would add to the historical momentum driving the increasing inseparability of natural and human worlds.[60]

The result has been the gradual reshaping of governmentality according to the priorities of "enviro-discipline," referring to "the authority of eco-knowledge, geo-powered forces to police the fitness of all biological organisms and the health of their natural environments"—a broad definition of the rise of green capitalism under neoliberalism.[61] One can understand this enviro-discipline as the practice of national, nongovernmental, and international agencies to regulate the "health of our natural environment" so that sustainable development is defined in ways favorable to financial interests, in opposition to comprehending ecology as a field of interlinking systems of biology and technology, social practices and political structures, that might otherwise support natural stability and biodiversity first and foremost. In this sense, enviro-discipline (including during the Obama years) has proved to be concerned more with managing the public's perception of environmental health than with regulating industrial damage to natural systems, or protecting against climate disruption. This conflicted situation gives rise to the following questions: How can artistic practices, operating at the rocky juncture of art institutions, activism, and nongovernmental politics, challenge the emergence of neoliberal eco-governmentality? How can art oppose the commercialization of nature, packaged as an economic resource, or counteract greenwashing to alternatively define the environment with a

59 Luke, "Environmentality as Green Governmentality," 150. While Luke focuses on the Clinton/Gore administration in the '90s and its conjoining of environmental initiatives with strategic economic goals, his reading of "environmental governmentality" (using Foucauldian terms) may yet gain a new relevancy today, even as its opposite "resource colonialism" intervened during the George W. Bush years in the name of national security. For a more recent analysis of such governmentality, regarding the development of biogenetic capitalism, see Cooper, *Life as Surplus*.

60 *Limits to Growth* turned into a bestseller with its arguments that accelerating industrialization, mounting population growth and malnutrition, and the depletion of natural resources defined a natural limit to global growth. See Conca and Dabelko, "The Debate at Stockholm," in *Green Planet Blues*, 17–22.

61 Luke, "Environmentality as Green Governmentality," 146.

focus on global justice and ecological sustainability? How do we define what is to be ecologically sustained, and is it enough to merely sustain current conditions, whatever they be, rather than improving or moving beyond them?[62] How might artists, furthermore, animate an "environmentalism of the poor"—a politics of environmental justice viewed from the perspective of those who have the least access to resources, job protection, political and economic power, and governmental and media representation—to avoid the exclusivity of an "environmentalism born of affluence" in Western capitalist societies?[63] It is also important to avoid a simplistic opposition of global justice in the South and apolitical eco-activism in the North, as each is equally generalizing and reductive. As we'll see throughout this book, the politics of ecological justice transcends all geographical divisions; the spread of economic inequality has already broken down such generically conceived geographies.

In fact, some of the most compelling recent environmental art practices and exhibitions develop a political ecology that not only disrupts the notion of a self-evident environment and questions the assumptions of a self-evident sustainability, but also examines the unequal division of benefits and risks of climate change (how some regions experience positive climate shifts such as greater rainfall, while others face pervasive drought). Consider "Beyond Green: Toward a Sustainable Art," the provocative 2006 exhibition at University of Chicago's Smart Museum of Art, which critically looked at sustainability, the term that has come to replace the emphasis on ecological balance in the '70s and responds to the emergent imperatives regarding global warming. The show included artworks of recycling, housing politics, and community activism (such as the Experimental Station in Chicago, founded by Connie Spreen and Dan Peterman in 2002, and Michael Rakowitz's inflatable homeless shelter, *paraSITE*, 1998); renewable fuels and alternative land use (Nils Norman's *Ideal City, Research/Play Sector, Chicago*, 2005, and *Geocruiser*, 2001–4); resource and infrastructural needs in developing countries and impoverished urban communities (Marjetica Potrč's *A Hippo Roller for Our Rural Times*, 2005, and *Dry Toilet*, 2003); and others that investigate the politics of space in relation to neocolonial militarism—for instance,

62 For instance, philosopher Rosi Braidotti calls attention to the potentially "self-glorifying" and "egotistical" consciousness that drives sustainability as an unimaginative conservationist discourse (which conservation might mean sustaining forms of social and economic inequality), to which she opposes "the multiple dynamic forces of *zoe*"—nonhuman life—"that do not coincide with the human, let alone with consciousness," and calls for a post-anthropocentric redefinition of ecological and sociopolitical well-being (Braidotti, *The Posthuman*, 138).

63 Gadgil and Guha, "Ideologies of Environmentalism," 98–114; and Joan Martinez-Alier, *The Environmentalism of the Poor: A Study of Ecological Conflicts and Valuation* (Cheltenham: Edward Elgar Publishing, 2002).

challenging the US military's former control of Vieques in Puerto Rico and its practice of using the island for bombing practice (Allora & Calzadilla's *Landmark*, 2001–4)—all of which define the terms of a new politico-ecological practice. In general, the show paralleled a growing trend in cultural discourse that relates technologies, economics, and politics to biological systems.[64]

For Stephanie Smith, the show's curator, "sustainability involves meeting the needs of the present without sacrificing the capacity of future generations to meet their own needs."[65] While this statement invokes the 1987 definition in *Our Common Future*, Smith importantly goes on to registers the term's discrepant meanings, which allowed the mythical community signaled by "our common future" to give way to the conflictual geopolitics of sustainability discourse.[66] Following the insights of eco-designer Tony Fry, she distinguishes between "sustainable development" (the greening of existing methods of production without changing consumer habits or altering expectations of capitalist growth and technological progress) and the "development of sustainment," meaning "redirecting development toward a very different basis for the creation of economy, society, and a relation between human beings, the artificial worlds they create, and the biosphere."[67] The distinction is crucial. But against Fry's questionable division of humanity's "artificial worlds" and the "biosphere," Smith calls for an explicit formulation of sustainability that grants "equal attention to social and environmental justice," and turns sustainability effectively into a political ecology.[68] According to Erik Swyngedouw, "The recognition of

64 That trend includes writings such as Latour, *We Have Never Been Modern*; N. Katherine Hayles, *How We Became Posthuman: Virtual Bodies in Cybernetics, Literature, and Informatics* (Chicago: University of Chicago Press, 1999); Francis Fukuyama, *Our Posthuman Future: Consequences of the Biotechnology Revolution* (New York: Picador, 2003); Bill Brown, ed., *Things* (Chicago: University of Chicago Press, 2004); Bennett, *Vibrant Matter*; and Coole and Frost, *New Materialisms*.

65 Stephanie Smith, "Beyond Green," in *Beyond Green: Toward a Sustainable Art*, ed. Stephanie Smith (Chicago: Smart Museum of Art, 2005), 14.

66 Political philosopher Murray Bookchin observed elsewhere that the danger with such a social construction is that a "mythic 'Humanity' is created—irrespective of whether we are talking about oppressed ethnic minorities, women, Third World people, or people in the First World—in which everyone is brought into complicity with powerful corporate elites in producing environmental dislocations." See Murray Bookchin, *Remaking Society: Pathways to a Green Future* (Boston: South End Press, 1990), 9–10; cited in Conca and Dabelko, "Three Decades of Global Environmental Politics," 9.

67 Smith, "Beyond Green," 14. See also Tony Fry, *Design Futuring: Sustainability, Ethics and New Practice* (Oxford: Berg, 2008).

68 Neil Smith writes: "Political ecology provides a powerful means of cracking the abstractions of this discussion about the metabolism or production of nature. Rooted in social and political theory it is also grounded in ecology and has an international scope. When complemented by an environmental justice politics, which is less internationally focused and less theoretical but more politically activist in inspiration, political ecology becomes a potent weapon for comprehending produced natures." Foreword to *In the Nature of Cities*, xiii–xiv.

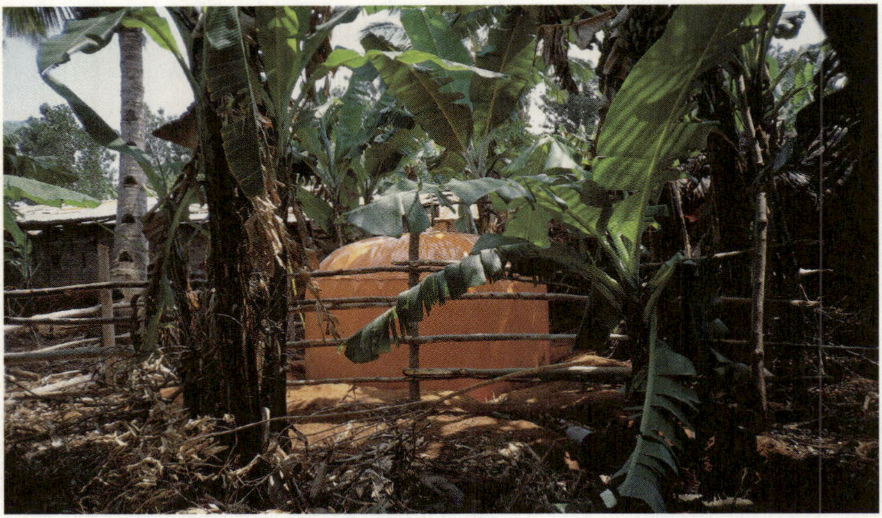

Superflex, *Supergas*, Tanzania, 1997

this political meaning of nature is essential if sustainability is to be combined with a just and empowering urban development; an urban development that returns the city and the city's environment to its citizens."[69] A just theory of sustainable development increasingly calls for a model of "development without growth," which would aim to improve the quality of life of the largest number of people without increasing overall economic production, consumption, or waste.[70] Smith thus corroborates Swyngedouw's political approach to ecology: "Sustainable design posits that a purely green approach, which considers environmental questions in isolation from other factors"—as was the tendency in the "Fragile Ecologies" exhibition—"is incomplete and ineffective."[71]

In terms of situating current environmental art practice, however, "Beyond Green" could go still further. While it reveals an important strain in contemporary art—one that presents "objects, structures, and processes/networks that use aspects of sustainable design to metaphoric, practical, speculative, ironic, and playful ends"—the curator's introduction provides little historical or conceptual explanation

69 Swyngedouw, "Circulations and Metabolisms," 118.
70 For like-minded proposals, see Herman E. Daly and John B. Cobb Jr., *For the Common Good: Redirecting the Economy toward Community, the Environment, and a Sustainable Future* (Boston: Beacon Press, 1989); J. K. Gibson-Graham, *A Postcapitalist Politics* (Minneapolis: University of Minnesota Press, 2006); and Birgit Daiber and François Houtart, eds., *A Postcapitalist Paradigm: The Common Good of Humanity* (Brussels: Rosa-Luxemburg-Foundation, 2012).
71 Smith, "Beyond Green," 14.
72 Ibid., 13.

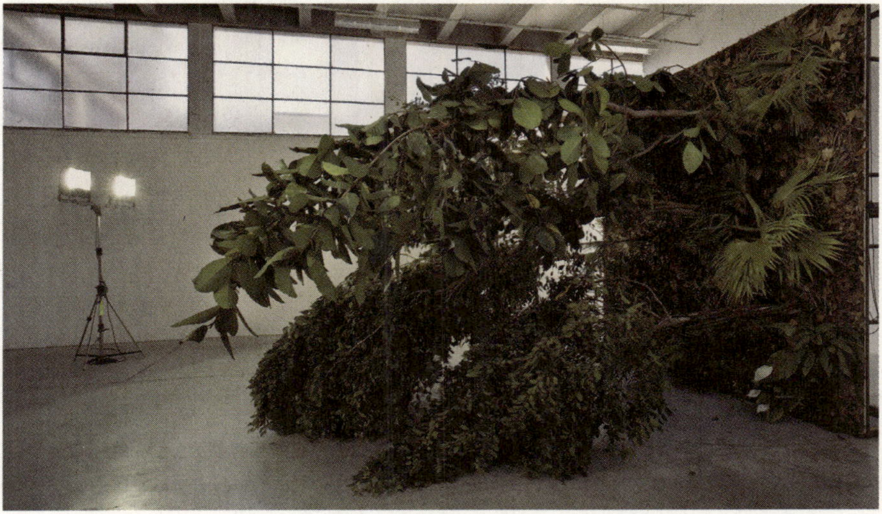

Henrik Håkansson, *Fallen Forest*, 2006

for this development toward play and irony, nor does it differentiate between the practical and the speculative, which nonetheless remain useful terms for comprehending contemporary environmental-artistic and activist practices.[72] Consider a selection of the exhibited works: the *Supergas* "biogas units" by the Danish collective Superflex made for domestic use in villages in Cambodia and Tanzania (and recently in Mexico), which extract methane gas from animal manure; water transportation devices, dry toilets, and wind-energy technology by Marjetica Potrč to provide "urgent architecture" for informal cities; and the inventive usage of recycling technologies by the international collective Learning Group for community-based architecture in Monterrey, Mexico. Each of these projects has an artistic lineage that intersects with 1970s eco-activism and pragmatic models of humanitarian NGO engagement in attempting to improve the everyday conditions of the impoverished or disadvantaged. (Superflex was able to implement its biogas project in Tanzania, where there is a shortage of fuel supplies owing to deforestation and erosion, through the cooperation of the Foundation for Sustainable Rural Development.) Such models demonstrate the resurgent vitality of collectivist practice and artistic collaboration with political and scientific organizations advancing an environmentalism in impoverished areas, which reinvents the place and function of art today.

On the other hand, there is a further formation (related to but going beyond the works in "Beyond Green") that expresses an ironic and subversive neo-conceptualism at the conjunction of contemporary art and ecology, emphasizing the characteristics of autonomy and criticality in art over the exclusivity of pragmatic humanitarian problem-solving. For instance, Henrik Håkansson's *Fallen Forest* (2006) tips a lush section of living woodland vegetation on its side in the middle of an exhibition space equipped with growing lights, recalling the Harrisons' 1972 work of gallery horticulture, *Portable Orchard: Survival Piece #5*. Whereas the Harrisons earnestly worked against environmental degradation, Håkansson exposes the aesthetics of a post-natural condition (one that rejects outmoded notions of pure nature as set apart from culture), in which an organic environment has been immersed in multiple technological, media, and cultural ecologies (including the trend of vertical green walls as part of architectural landscaping). This act of perceptual reorientation, merging organic growth with architectural design, approximates the mesh of nature/culture and opens up new implications for subjective experience, according to which we find ourselves entangled in increasingly multiple worlds—those of biotechnology, media, pharmacology, law, and economics, as well as nonhuman natures.[73] Nature, in this light, proposes a site of unexpected strangeness and becoming, which has always constituted its ever-evolving state.[74]

Consider, as well, Tue Greenfort's *Diffuse Einträge* (2007). For this site-specific work the artist arranged a fertilizer truck, normally carrying liquid manure, to shoot a jet of iron chloride into Lake Aa during Skulptur Projekte Münster. The environmental effects of phosphate pollution from farm runoff, visible in the lake water's persistent algae blooms, were thereby brought into contact with one potential chemical treatment. Yet unlike the hopeful glimmer of, say, Haacke's *Rhine-Water Purification Plant*, which saw the potential success of its ecological intervention actualized in the microcosm of the clean goldfish basin, Greenfort's criticality resides in his ironic exposure of the long-term ineffectiveness of such cosmetic measures to maintain the lake's idyllic appearance. He brings attention to the ridiculousness of restorationist aesthetics when they address the mere local effects of environmental damage but ignore the structural and often global causes.

In these recent projects, irony and playfulness are not meant to simply entertain, but rather indicate a deep skepticism about the motivations, aims, and results of

73 Bennett, *Vibrant Matter*, 115.

74 See, for instance, Karen Barad's reading of nature's "queerness": "a lively mutating organism, a desiring radical openness, an edgy protean differentiating multiplicity, an agential dis/continuity, an enfolded reiteratively materializing promiscuously inventive spatiotemporality" ("Nature's Queer Performativity," 29).

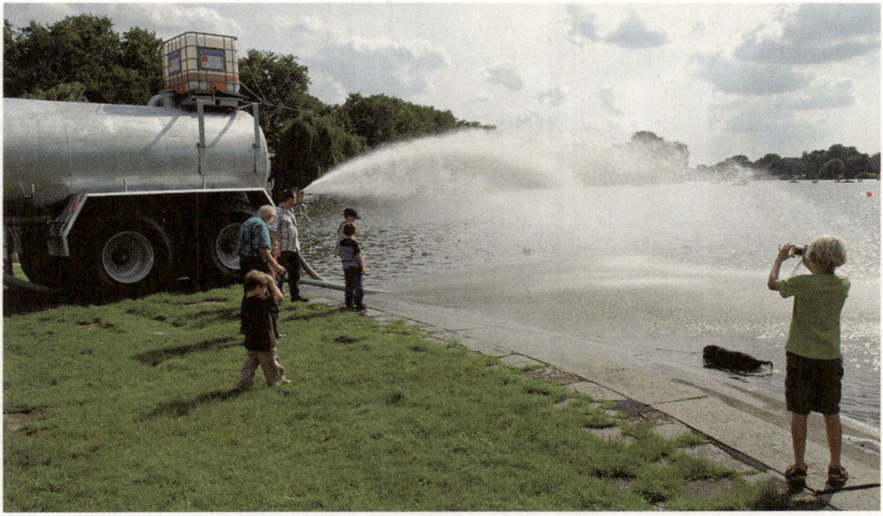

Tue Greenfort, *Diffuse Einträge*, 2007

"pragmatic" environmental art, often aligned with interests uninterested in questioning the structural causes of environmental breakdown. "Artists are now inescapably inscribed within urban regeneration strategies," explains Nils Norman, "and in order to start thinking about this bind critically we need to begin creating more disruptive and experimental methodologies."[75] One such experimental methodology is presented in Norman's mural-sized banner *Ideal City, Research/Play Sector* (2005), typical of the artist's agit-prop signage, which maps out an imaginary playscape and research park composed of a central adventure playground surrounded by several geodesic domes (adventure playgrounds, built by and for children, became prominent at the end of World War II, especially in Britain).[76]

Norman's proposal is certainly playful—it's about play, and takes on ludic dimensions in its cartoon-like diagrams of a nonetheless serious proposal

75 Nils Norman, interviewed in Smith, *Beyond Green*, 91. Consider as well Joshua Decter's prescient reading of Håkansson's practice: "By proposing a new mode of inter-species socialization that is fundamentally constructed, fictive and imperfect, Håkansson defers from offering pragmatic solutions, or the next paradigm model. Instead, his practice asks to be understood as an allegory that illuminates the complex circumstances of species estrangement in general." Joshua Decter, "The Return of Dr. Doolittle: Henrik Håkansson's Inter-species Communications," *Siksi* 7, no. 2 (1997): 73; cited in Spaid, *Ecovention*, 80.

76 See Nils Norman, *An Architecture of Play: A Survey of London's Adventure Playgrounds* (London: Four Corners Books, 2004). For further analysis of Norman's work, see my article, "The Cruel Dialectic: On the Work of Nils Norman," *Grey Room*, no. 13 (Fall 2003): 33–50.

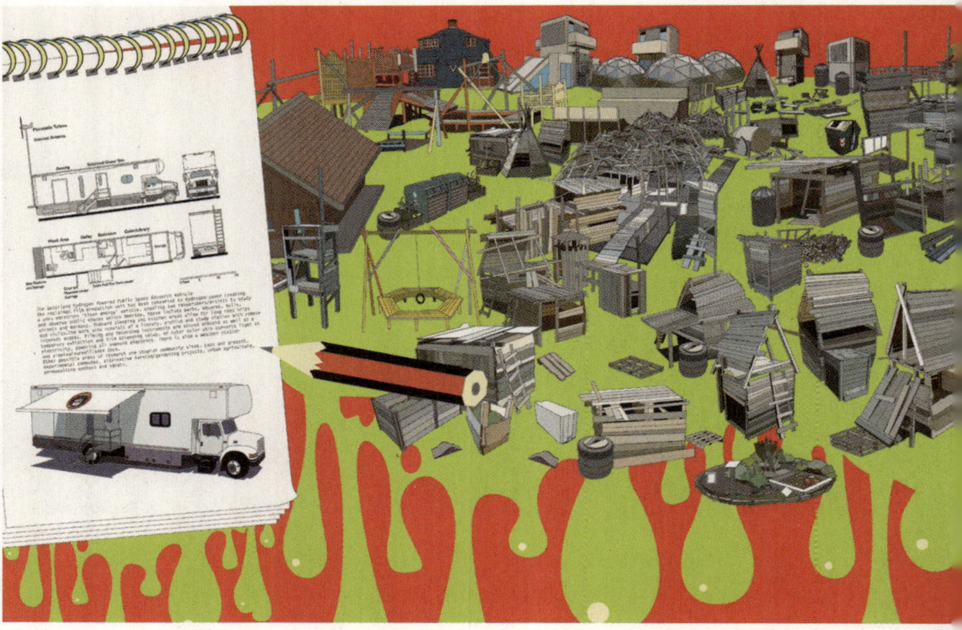

for the reinvention of our educational-environmental-political values, which prioritizes self-sufficient autonomy, deinstrumentalized behaviors, and recycling. *Ideal City* exemplifies how artists are now viewing the environment as formed by a "multitude of ecologies" (in the artist's words), at once biological, technological, political, and social, which can inspire imaginative alternatives to the reality, and representation, of everyday neoliberal urbanism.[77] In this sense, Norman's project points to the continued relevance of Félix Guattari's 1989 book *The Three Ecologies*, which argues for a "transversal" approach that joins the subjective, social, and environmental registers of ecology into an "ethico-aesthetic" practice—one resonating with the subsequent work of theorists such as Swyngedouw, Timothy Luke, Neil Smith, and Ramachandra Guha.[78] Included in Norman's work is a model of a

77 Norman, interviewed in Smith, *Beyond Green*, 91.

78 Félix Guattari, *The Three Ecologies*, trans. Ian Pindar and Paul Sutton (London: Athlone Press, 2000), 69. Also see Eric Swyngedouw, *Liquid Power: Contested Hydro-Modernities in Twentieth-Century Spain* (Cambridge, MA: MIT Press, 2015); Timothy Luke, *Capitalism, Democracy, and Ecology: Departing from Marx* (Chicago: University of Illinois Press, 1999); Neil Smith, "Nature as Accumulation Strategy," *Socialist Register 2007: Coming to Terms with Nature*, ed. Leo Panitch and Colin Leys (London: The Merlin Press, 2006), 16–36; Ramachandra Guha, *Environmentalism: A Global History* (Oxford: Oxford University Press, 2000).

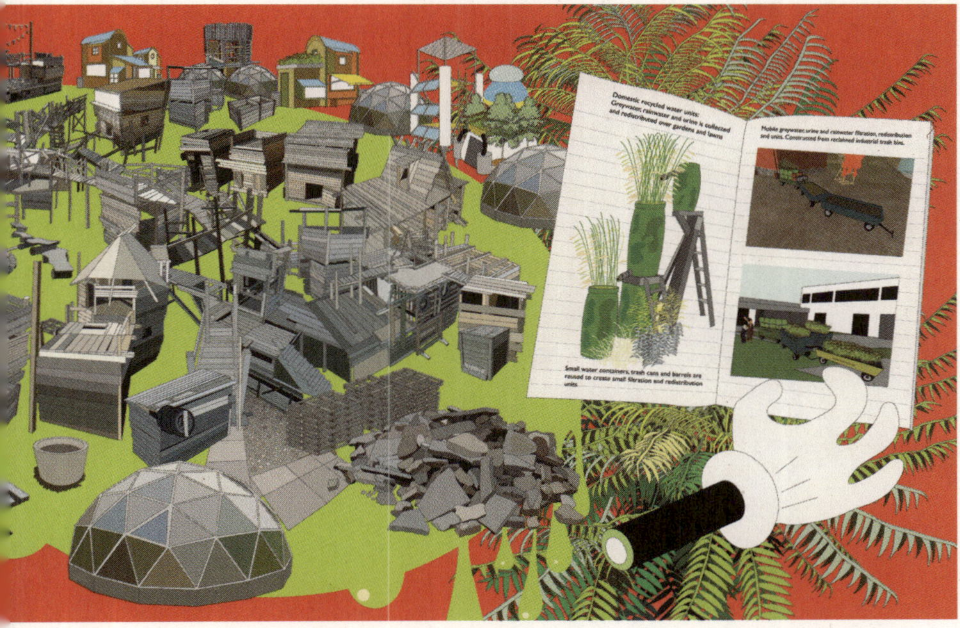

Nils Norman, *Ideal City, Research/Play Sector*, 2005

still-to-be-realized project, "The Solarized Hydrogen Powered Public Space Research Vehicle." The accompanying caption explains: "The reclaimed film production unit has been converted to hydrogen power creating a zero emissions 'clean energy' vehicle, enabling two researchers/artists to study and observe public spaces across America including parks, squares, malls, streets and markets. Onboard sleeping and kitchen areas allow for long road trips and visits. The work area consists of a library, archive and study station with remote internet access. Filming and recording instruments are stored onboard as well as a temporary exhibition and film screening setup. An outer solar skin converts light to electricity, powering all onboard electrics. There is also a weather station and viewing/surveillance deck." While Norman's similarly utopian *Geocruiser* (2001–4)—a refurbished coach running on biodiesel, fitted with solar panels, and containing a community library and a greenhouse—was in fact built, the artist often disassociates his practice from the practical realization of his proposals. "I'm more interested in the ideas and research rather than the vehicle itself," Norman explains. "The vehicle is just a framing device through which to view the content: uses of

79 Norman, interviewed in Smith, *Beyond Green*, 91.

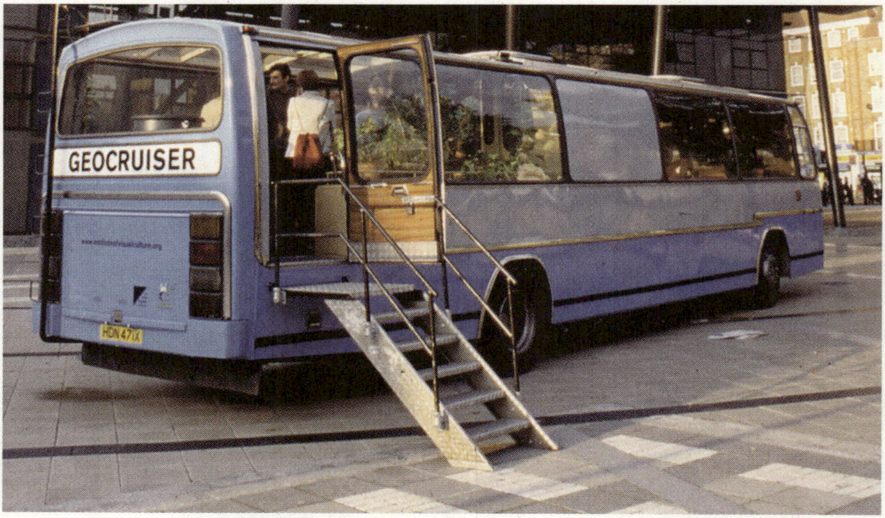

Nils Norman, *Geocruiser*, 2003

public space and the history of U.S. utopian experiments in agriculture, economies, and communal living."[79] (That said, in the last few years Norman has joined a growing international cohort of artists and activists who are now experimenting with what exactly a local sustainable practice might look like, which I consider in the following chapters.)

Both critical-realist and creative-utopian, Norman's work registers the limits of the primarily pragmatic approach of restorationist eco-aesthetics, and insists that we consider ecological crisis in relation to the structural conditions—at once psychological, social, and environmental—of capitalist development. Here, the employment of irony and playfulness becomes politically important for many of today's practitioners: this conceptual, anti-pragmatist emphasis and expansive critique generates an awareness of the challenges of a local sustainable practice within a globally unsustainable system of ecologies. Even while shows dedicated to sustainability may themselves be unsustainable from the perspective of global warming—their very carbon footprint belying the environmentalist desires addressed in these projects—smart and committed exhibitions focusing on art and ecology remain urgent at this time. To contribute to the ongoing public engagement with the politics of sustainability, to advance creative proposals for alternative forms of life based on environmental justice in a global framework, and to do both until art exhibitions can meet the requirements of a just sustainability—these are the imperatives for contemporary environmental art.

Climates of Displacement

Chapter 2

From the Maldives to the Arctic

There is a profusion of scientific accounts today that warn of a near future of forced displacement on a massive scale due to climate change. Inhabitants of small island nations, such as Tuvalu and the Maldives, exposed to the threat of rising ocean levels, commonly figure as imminent "climate refugees." Although these populations are small compared to the millions of impoverished people vulnerable to forced migration in places like the Sahel in Africa, coastal Bangladesh, and Vietnam's deltas, their cases exemplify how climate refugee discourse is currently shaped and visualized, and as such they take on global relevance. According to Koko Warner, an expert on climate change and migration at the United Nations University in Bonn, the displacement of these populations forecasts "a phenomenon of a scope not experienced in human history."[1] Such an eventuality appears credible, especially given the ever-increasing rise in greenhouse gases and quickly approaching tipping points, in addition to the disasters related to extreme weather events in our present—for instance, Hurricane Sandy hitting New York in 2012, and Typhoon Haiyan devastating the Philippines in 2013.

While the scientific basis of that potential future is clear, such narratives do not need to be seen as irrevocable—although it's difficult not to be seduced by frequent spectacular visions of apocalyptic climate disasters and mass migrations (think of the films *The Day after Tomorrow*, 2004, *Flood*, 2007, *The Road*, 2009, and *Oblivion*, 2013). Yet such predictions—whether

1 Cited in Rachel Morris, "What Happens When Your Country Drowns? Meet the People of Tuvalu, The World's First Climate Refugees," *Mother Jones*, November/December 2009, http://www.motherjones.com/environment/2009/11/tuvalu-climate-refugees.

presented in the media, popular visual culture, scientific discourse, or artistic practice—risk being debilitating and fatalist, for they overlook forms of political agency in the present that variously resist the fossil-fuel economy driving climate change. Before we accept the inevitability of climate-refugee narratives, we must ask: How might we invent creative modes of resilience and mitigation in the face of approaching climate chaos, and think aesthetics in relation to the politics of climate justice—as summed up in the slogan "System change, not climate change!"—rather than surrendering to futurist speculation that potentially eclipses real options in the here and now? In what follows, I'll investigate this question in relation to the intersection of visual culture and political discourse that confronts the ecological situations of the Maldives and the Arctic. In particular, I'll examine the work of the Argos Collective and Subhankar Banerjee—examples of photographic and research-based visual culture presented in art exhibitions as well as circulating through NGO publicity, independent media forums, and environmental activism. Addressing geopolitical hotspots from different vantage points, the engagements of these practitioners visualizes the threat of global warming today, where migration is often presented as an unavoidable fate.

The Maldives: A French Requiem?

For the low-lying Maldives, the threat of rising seas is a very present danger, forcing residents to consider migration as a near-future necessity. Moving would mean abandoning their home in the Indian Ocean, which has been inhabited since the third century BCE. Approaching the Maldives' ecologically and socially precarious situation and emphasizing this migration scenario, the Argos Collective created "The Maldives: A Nation at the Water's Edge" (2005–7), a photographic series that documents the islands' inhabitants and their fragile environment. Comprised of eleven writers and photographers from France, the Argos Collective works with environmental and humanitarian NGOs, maintains a website with a full range of visual projects, and publishes books of their documentary journalism, including *Climate Refugees* (2010), which contains photos and essays addressing the situation in the Maldives as well as in parts of Bangladesh, Chad, the United States, Germany, China, and Nepal.[2] "Our job is to tell stories we have heard and to bear witness to what we have seen," writes journalist and member Guy-Pierre Chomette. "The science was already there when we started in 2004, but we wanted to emphasize the human dimension, especially for those most vulnerable."[3] In

2 Argos Collective, *Climate Refugees* (Cambridge, MA: MIT Press, 2010).

3 Cited in "Collectif Argos," *MIT Press*, accessed December 15, 2015, http://mitpress.mit.edu/authors/collectif-argos.

their photo suite, Maldivians are pictured in domestic settings, preparing food, playing on the beach, and swimming, alongside images of their threatened environment beset by coastal deterioration and blanched coral reefs. In relation to one photograph showing a group of youths, the Argos Collective points out that 60 percent of Maldivians are younger than fifteen, and "during their lifetime they will probably see the first exiles leave the island due to sea-level rise and erosion."[4]

Consisting of a double string of twenty-six atolls that join an archipelago of 1,190 islands, two hundred of which are inhabited with a population of almost four hundred thousand, the Maldives form the smallest Asian nation in terms of land and population. Under Portuguese and Dutch reign during the fifteenth and seventeenth centuries and a British protectorate from 1887 to 1965, the country gained its independence only to be subsequently ruled by an authoritarian government for three decades until its first free elections in 2008 brought the progressive Mohamed Nasheed to the presidency. (Nasheed served in office until 2012, when he was forced to resign, later found guilty under the country's Anti-Terrorism Act, and sentenced to thirteen years in prison—all of which has been described by Amnesty International as a politically motivated persecution.) Like other low-lying island states such as Kiribati, Tuvalu, and Nauru, the Maldives are particularly vulnerable to inundation and storm surges.[5] Eighty percent of the country's islands are less than one meter above sea level, and studies predict the Maldives could be completely submerged within one hundred years. The Intergovernmental Panel on Climate Change's (IPCC) fourth climate-change assessment, from 2007, forecast an approximate fifty-centimeter sea-level rise by the end of the twenty-first century, an increase expanded by the IPCC's fifth report, in 2014, to nearly double that amount.[6] The National Oceanic and Atmospheric Administration offers an even direr scenario, predicting as much as a 6.6-foot increase by 2100.[7] While coastal

4 Guillaume Collanges/Argos Collective, "The Maldives: A Nation at the Water's Edge," *Picturetank*, http://picturetank.com/___/series/56f861abb4b0cc98b681c0ebf1d1fdc1/en/a/COG_MALDIVES_1_et_2.html.

5 On the case of Tuvalu, see Alexandra Berzon, "Tuvalu Is Drowning," *Salon*, March 31, 2006, http://www.salon.com/2006/03/31/tuvalu_2/.

6 "A rise in sea level of approximately 50 cm during the 21st century remains the most reliable scenario to employ in future studies of the Maldives." Nobuo Mimura and Leonard Nurse, et al., "Small Islands," in *Climate Change 2007: Impacts, Adaptation and Vulnerability: Contribution of Working Group II to the Fourth Assessment Report of the Intergovernmental Panel on Climate Change*, ed. M. L. Parry et al. (Cambridge: Cambridge University Press, 2007), 694. Also see Pachauri et al., *Climate Change 2014: Synthesis Report*, 13.

7 As reported by Tim Folger, "Rising Seas," *National Geographic*, September 2013, 40–41. There is great uncertainty about the future rate of Greenland and Antarctic glacial melt—if all their ice melted and entered the sea, then waters would rise by 216 feet (as in the Eocene period over 33 million years ago), although such an eventuality, scientists expect, would take thousands of years.

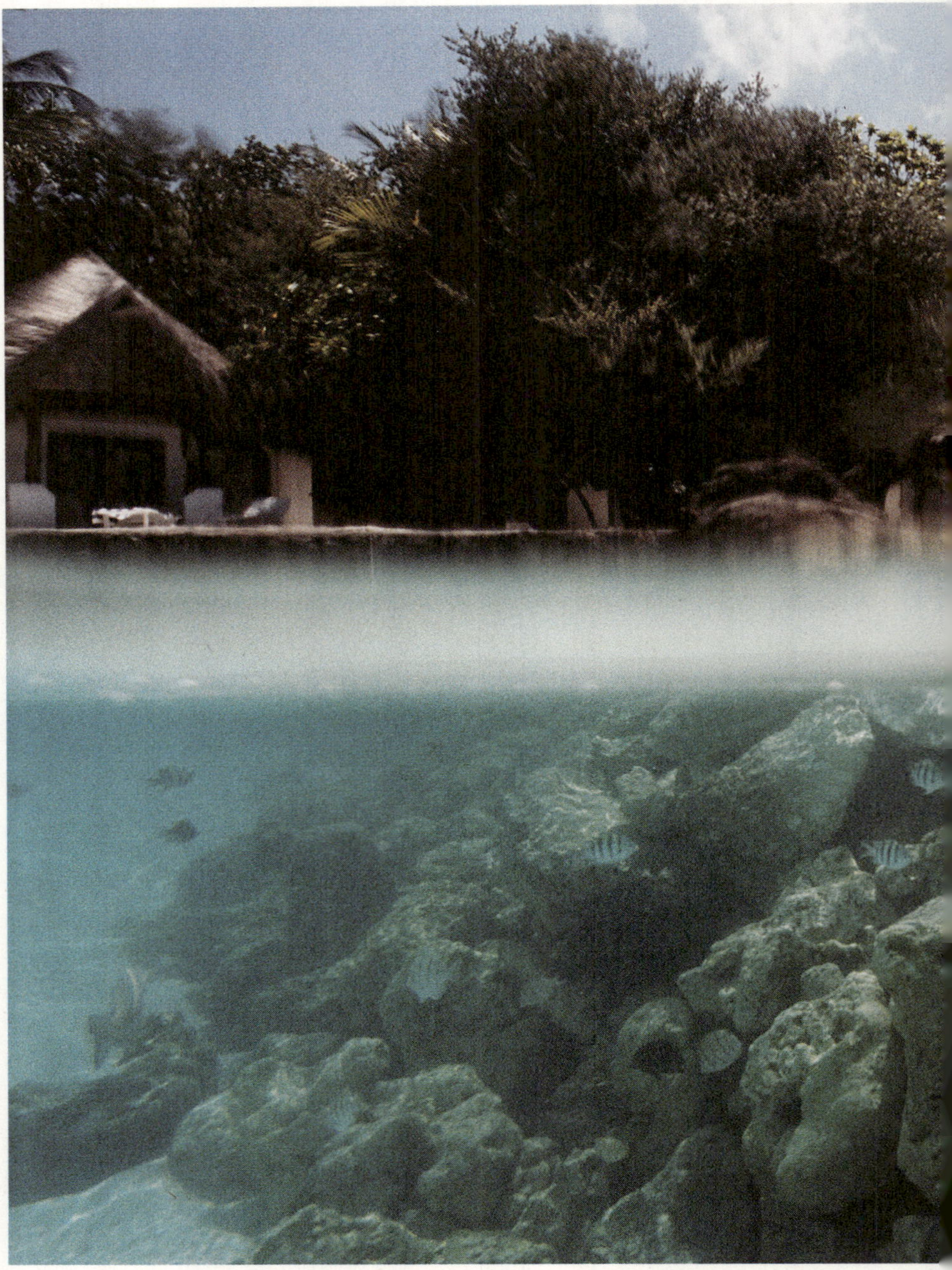

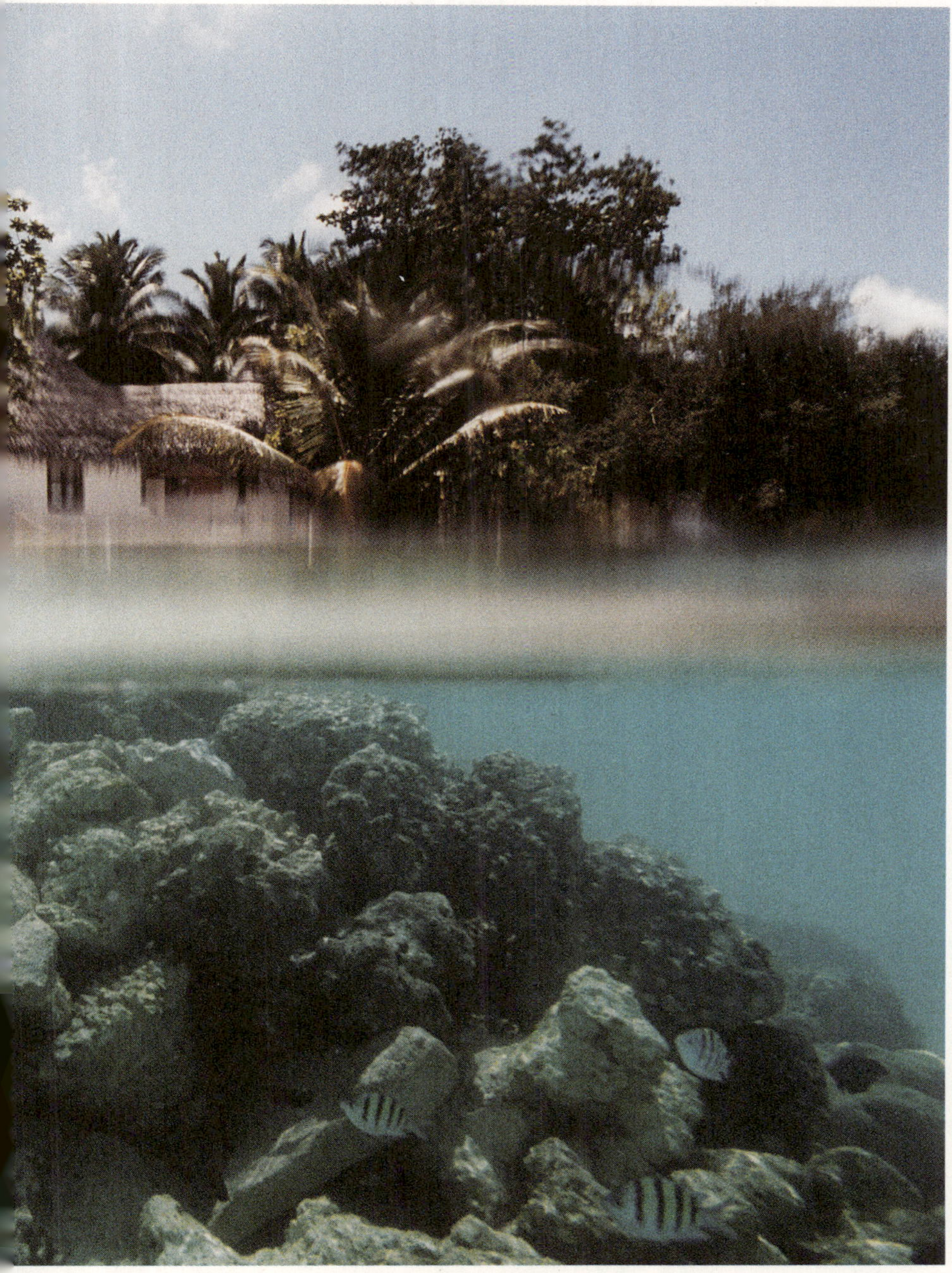

Guillaume Collanges / Argos Collective, Coral reef in the Maldives, 2005

geomorphologists point out that islands are more flexible than often thought, capable of adapting to the vagaries of sea level and currents over time, it remains uncertain how the Maldives will confront a future menaced by water.[8] In addition to inundation and storm surges, the negative effects of sea-level rise include coastal erosion (destroying protective coral reefs), salination of fresh water supplies, and extreme weather events, which in turn threaten infrastructure, human settlements, health, agriculture, and trade. A negative economic hit is particularly harsh for a country that relies on tourism and whose per capita GDP was just US$9,100 in 2013. The Maldives, it is claimed, may be the first nation whose entire population will become climate refugees, foreshadowing "an age of insurgent climate refugees on a far more threatening, chaotic scale."[9] At the same time, nations like the United States and EU members (as we are currently seeing with the response to Syrian refugees, on the move owing to extended Middle Eastern drought, poverty, civil war, and violent militarism), as well as India and Bangladesh, are already preparing for an unprecedented demographic influx by turning their borders into increasingly militarized and high-tech zones to control migration.[10]

The text accompanying the Argos Collective's photographs describes their visits with diverse Maldivian representatives, such as the director of the Maldives Environmental Research Center, the head engineer at a resort on the island Thulhagiri, and the manager of the artificial island Hulhumale. Each contribute to Argos's narrative of the Maldives' vulnerability and likely disastrous future: "A puff of a wind, a wave, and this emerald necklace that appears to be floating precariously on the water might just sink irretrievably into the depths of the Indian Ocean," Chomette explains.[11] While the aim of such depictions may be to raise awareness of the

8 See Paul Kench's research, a coastal geomorphologist at the University of Auckland, as reported in Nicholas Schmidle, "Wanted: A New Home for My Country," *New York Times Magazine*, May 8, 2009, http://www.nytimes.com/2009/05/10/magazine/10MALDIVES-t.html. At Columbia University's Earth Institute, scientists argue that sea rise and surf will reshape islands, not drown them.

9 Nixon, *Slow Violence*, 265.

10 See Steve Wright, "Preparing for Mass Refugee Flows: The Corporate Military Sector," in *Surviving Climate Change: The Struggle to Avert Global Catastrophe*, ed. David Cromwell and Mark Levene (London: Pluto, 2007), 82–101; and Ben Hayes, "The Surveillance-Industrial Complex," in *Routledge Handbook of Surveillance Studies*, ed. Kirstie Ball, Kevin Haggerty, and David Lyon (London: Routledge, 2012). These texts detail the securitization of response to climate change in regard to state, military, and corporate planning for worst-case scenarios. Climate change is viewed as a threat multiplier, where migration, for instance, figures as a criminal menace rather than a mode of behavioral adaptation for human survival. The state/military/corporate response to climate change imagines a nightmare future that demands ever more advanced weaponry and full-spectrum dominance to protect borders, as developed by security-service corporations and defense contractors in a billion-dollar-a-year industry, overriding all concerns for human rights or environmental stability.

11 Guy-Pierre Chomette, "Indian Ocean: Maldives, an Archipelago in Peril," in *Climate Refugees*, 125.

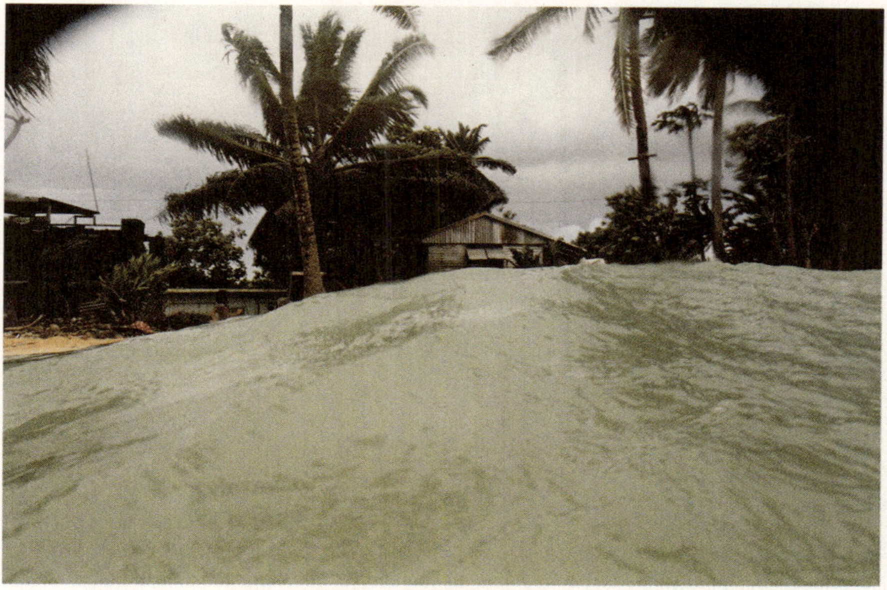

Laurent Weyl / Argos Collective, A Tuvalu island during a tsunami, 2006

current ecological crisis and its effects on frontline communities, the Maldivians themselves are conspicuously allotted little political agency in these images and narratives. By projecting a climate-refugee subjectivity onto the islands' population, the Argos Collective ends up objectifying their subjects, reducing them to anthropological evidence, and casting their situation as urgent according to their own humanitarian criteria, which tends to emphasize victimhood and people deprived of political self-determination. Though the group advocates immediate international cooperation to stop global warming, they expect it will not be enough to halt sea-level rise, and that we must prepare now for the negative consequences. They observe that we can expect two hundred million refugees by the end of the century, claiming it's a question of human rights when a nation's people is "suddenly shorn of their self-determination." To meet this imminent humanitarian disaster, they contend, we must "immediately begin planning for the mass migration of climate refugees that will mark the 21st century."[12]

This story is in fact a familiar one, in mainstream media especially, where it is also often uncritically compared to the very different situation of well-resourced countries similarly at risk from inundation. In a 2013 issue of *National*

12 Argos Collective, "From Global Warming to Climate Refugees," in ibid., 14–16.

Geographic dedicated to the subject of rising seas, for instance, the lead article predicts that developed nations, such as the Netherlands, are already planning to negotiate shifting coastlines and sea levels via experimental architecture, innovative design, and geo-engineering projects—the floating housing project of Ijburg in Amsterdam is exemplary—whereas nations without comparable resources or technical capabilities face the increasingly likely situation of forced migration. Arnoud Molenaar, manager of Rotterdam's Climate Proof program, explains: "To build on water is not new, but to develop floating communities on a large scale and in a harbor with tides—that is new. [...] Instead of fighting against water, we want to live with it." Yet for less prosperous countries the prognosis is very different: "By 2100 rising seas may force Maldivians to abandon their home."[13] The problem with such accounts is that they simply accept the differential effects of climate change, determined by disparate levels of economic and technological capacity, and reproduce environmental injustice, thereby helping to naturalize it. The narratives produced by artists and journalists in the Global North in turn often fail to critically reflect upon the fact that the greenhouse-gas-producing industries of developed countries have historically created the ecological effects that small island states are now confronting. Resigning itself to a doomsday scenario, the title of the Argos Collective's series on Tuvalu is crystal clear: "A Polynesian Requiem." In an act of "wishful sinking," in the terms of environmental anthropologist Carol Farbotko, a critic of just this sort of catastrophe-seeking projection, the island is pictured as if already underwater.[14]

The Maldives have been cast to headline an emergency, an SOS call in geomorphological terms—as visualized in a digitally manipulated photograph produced by Australian artists Josephine Starrs and Leon Cmielewski for the Maldives' newly founded pavilion at the 55th Venice Biennale in 2013 (itself a significant development, curated by the Chamber of Public Secrets to bring international visibility to the plight of the islands

13 Folger, "Rising Seas," 54, 44. "The United Nations Development Programme estimates that $86 billion will need to be spent annually by 2015 to help developing countries adapt to the effects of global warming. The UN has launched a fund for this purpose, but it has only collected $100 million so far. What's more, rich countries commonly use so-called adaptation funds as a bargaining tool to push for lower emissions from the industrializing countries of the developing world." Morris, "What Happens When Your Country Drowns," 2.

14 Carol Farbotko, "Wishful Sinking: Disappearing Islands, Climate Refugees and Cosmopolitan Experimentation," *Asia-Pacific Viewpoint* 51, no. 1 (2010): 47–60. This narrative was also reproduced in Davis Guggenheim's documentary *An Inconvenient Truth* (2006), in which Al Gore observed—falsely—that "the citizens of these Pacific nations have all had to evacuate to New Zealand," a claim accompanied by photographs of a flooded Tuvalu. For a critical review of the Argos Collective's book, see Yates McKee, "On *Climate Refugees*: Biopolitics, Aesthetics, and Critical Climate Change," *Qui Parle* 19, no. 2 (Spring/Summer 2011): 309–25.

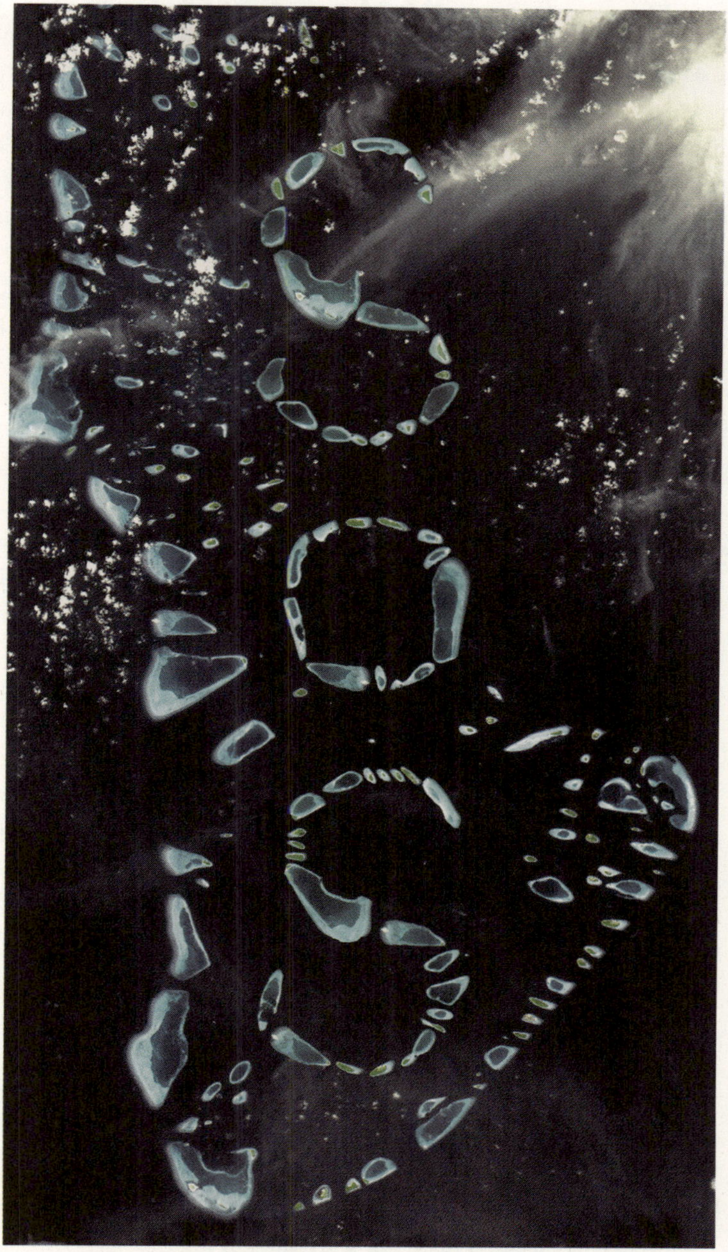

Josephine Starrs and Leon Cmielewski, *SOS*, 2013

in the era of climate breakdown). Yet we do not need to accept such projections, even if we should take the warnings seriously. Consider the alternate approach by artists Christoph Draeger and Heidrun Holzfeind, who recently proposed a very different narrative. In 2011, the Swiss-Austrian duo initiated a research project to investigate countries affected by the 2004 Indian Ocean tsunami, including Thailand, Indonesia, Sri Lanka, the Maldives, and India, resulting in a video also shown at the 2013 Maldives Pavilion.[15] Their video *Tsunami Architecture/The Maldives Chapter Redux* (2011), at just under a half hour, explores the post-disaster architectural achievements and challenges in the Maldives, and offers an early glimpse of future climate-change dangers. Documenting conversations with survivors, aid workers, and rescue personnel, the video looks into how aid money, which flowed into the Maldives following the tsunami, transformed the land and refashioned local economies. Populations were relocated from particularly vulnerable islands so that government services could be more concentrated, and new housing was built on the safer islands, better protected against future tsunamis and sea-level rise. The interviewees—including Abdullah Shahid of the Maldives' Disaster Management Center, Nadine Waheed of the UN Human Settlements Programme for the Maldives, and Wardell Eastwood of the Red Cross, as well as inhabitants of the island of Dhuvaafaru—acknowledge that, while ultimately there is no such thing as a safe island, the new housing is often inadequate, especially for the poor. The video moreover offers critical insights into how the Maldivians possess realistic options in the present, and thereby resists accepting the fatalism of migration as the only response to climate change. "I would say in terms of preparedness, we're quite ready," explains Waheed toward the end of the video. "All of the islands [...] have their own disaster management plans, in case of tsunami or sea-level rise. And we also have early-warning systems established. But obviously if it's a nineteen- or twenty-meter-high wave I don't think we stand much of a chance. It's climate change that's leading to the increase and frequency of disasters and it's something that we'll have to continue to face." As such, Draeger and Holzfeind's video appears in stark contrast to the Argos Collective's photo-text project, in which islanders are reduced to humanitarian victims in need of aid, exposed to an ostensibly implacable future of migration against which they appear powerless, and presented without political agency, scientific knowledge, or legal recourse.

15 Also see Khaled Ramadan's video *Maldives to Be or Not* (2013) shown on the same occasion, which presents an anti-spectacular and sensitive account of the concerns of numerous interviewed Maldivians, questioning the consequences of capitalist modernization and tourism for traditional island life.

Underwater Government

It is telling that the Argos Collective include no mention or image of President Mohamed Nasheed in their photographs or book or on their website. During his first presidential term (2008–12), when the Argos Collective were conducting their research, Nasheed was a particularly visible and vocal proponent for climate justice—a fundamentally different way of framing the environmental crisis and potential responses to it than climate-refugee scenarios or the humanitarian logic of victimhood. For one particular action, in October 2009, he held a cabinet meeting five meters underwater, where, outfitted in scuba gear, he signed into law a commitment to become a carbon-neutral nation within ten years. Nasheed's media appearances have dramatized the urgency of the ecological calamity facing the Maldives for international observers, defining it not as a "natural disaster" in the making, but as a political crisis in the present—created by those governments who live in a psychosis of denial and inaction, operating in league with Big Oil and Gas to prevent global governance systems from addressing the threat of climate change in any substantial way. Nasheed's innovative approach to political theater recalls artistic analogues that perform an aesthetics of politics, creatively reorganizing what can be seen and heard, recorded and distributed—such as the socially engaged projects of filmmaker Abderrahmane Sissako, particularly the fictional court drama and film *Bamako* (2006), where a neighborhood courtyard in Mali's capital is the setting for a trial against the IMF and World Bank for crimes against humanity; and those of Christoph Schlingensief, especially *Foreigners Out! Schlingensief's Container* (2000), a live-theater/reality-TV event and subsequent video, set in Vienna where participating asylum seekers were voted out of the country by viewers in spectacular fashion. The difference is that Nasheed was actually in a position to effect social and political transformation in government.[16]

The underwater session drew large-scale media visibility,[17] amplified by international activist groups like 350.org, which catalyzed the international consideration of climate change ahead of COP15, the 2009 UN climate conference in Copenhagen—even though the Maldivians were subsequently sidelined, along with other "Non-Annex I" developing and small-island nations, by "Annex I" developed nations. Attending

16 I examine Sissako's film in *Return to the Postcolony*, 120–22. Also see James E. Genova, "Re-thinking African Cinema in the Context of Third Cinema: From *Mondabi* to *Bamako* and the Mediascape of Post-colonial Identity," in *Rethinking Third Cinema: The Role of Anti-colonial Media and Aesthetics in Postmodernity*, ed. Frieda Ekotto and Adeline Koh (Berlin: Lit, 2009), 125–46. On President Nasheed and his climate struggle, see Jon Shenk's feature-length documentary, *The Island President* (2011).

17 Nasheed's publicity stunt was covered by the BBC, CNN, *The Hindu*, *Le Monde*, and *Mother Jones*.

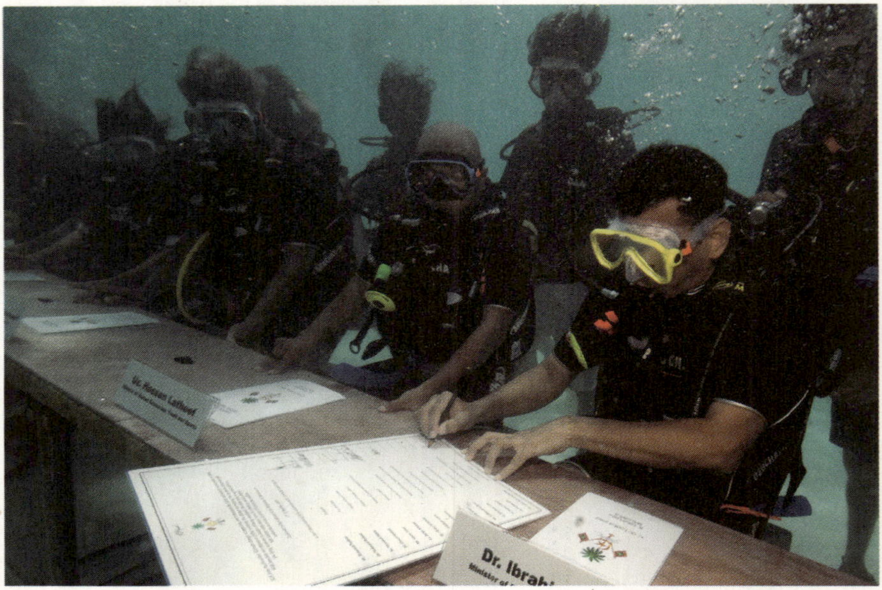

Underwater cabinet meeting, Maldives, October 17, 2009

the meeting, Nasheed explained to an audience of world leaders: "Developed countries created the climate crisis. Developing countries must not turn into a calamity. Therefore, I invite the leaders of big developing countries to recognize their responsibilities."[18] Yet the final Copenhagen deal, concluded in a private meeting between the United States, Brazil, China, India, and South Africa—and controversially accepted by the Maldives, owing to the promise of US financial assistance—contained no binding agreements on greenhouse-gas reductions and was widely criticized as undemocratic and ineffective—an outcome repeated at annual UN climate meetings since. At COP16, the 2010 UN climate talks in Cancun, forty-three island nations (constituting the Alliance of Small Nation Island States, the Maldives included) announced that they face the "end of history" if rich countries (the UN's "Conference of Polluters") fail to act now against

18 Quoted in "Voices from Small Island States: Maldives President Mohamed Nasheed, a Tuvaluan Delegate and a Youth Activist from the Solomon Islands," *Democracy Now!*, December 17, 2009, http://www.democracynow.org/2009/12/17/voices_from_the_island_states_maldives.

19 Nixon, *Slow Violence*, 265. See also Banerjee, "A Climate for Change," 1761–86. "Despite more than fifteen years of high level efforts led by the United Nations to broker a binding agreement on emissions reduction, negotiations at every annual meeting have failed to establish a global agreement, mainly due to significant disagreements between industrialized and developing countries over differentiated responsibilities in reducing emissions" (ibid., 1761).

climate change.[19] The situation has remained unchanged for the last few years, and analysts frequently talk of how we are basically "burning the planet, one climate COP at a time."[20]

Counter to the facile assumption that the islands will inevitably be abandoned, Nasheed has argued for investment in a post-hydrocarbon future, on a global scale, in order to avoid future catastrophe. Governments must halt carbon emissions, he urges, and keep future warming within the two degrees Celsius recommended by scientific consensus as a safe level, meaning an 80 percent reduction of emissions from 1990 levels by 2050 (the 2014 IPCC report revealed that global temperatures are likely to rise by as much as 4.8 degrees Celsius by the end of the century should governments maintain the status quo).[21] Nasheed's position is largely continuous with the goals of the climate-justice movement, which demands the inclusive participation of marginalized communities in the global climate negotiation process, and highlights the fact that climate change negatively impacts human rights and worsens economic inequality worldwide. As activist groups like Climate Justice Now! and the Global Justice Ecology Project argue, environmental justice is inextricable from the struggle for economic equality, democratic politics, and the rights of Indigenous and marginalized communities.[22] Environmental justice for the Maldives would require that developed countries acknowledge their role in causing global warming and assume their responsibilities regarding climate debt and in overcoming the crisis in the present, not simply accepting the narratives of future anthropogenic catastrophe.[23]

Nonetheless, after winning the country's first truly democratic elections in October 2008, Nasheed announced plans to create a sovereign wealth fund financed from tourism, the Maldives' main industry, that could be used to buy a new homeland in India, Sri Lanka, or even Australia, should migration—whether together as a nation or as post-national refugees—eventually become inevitable. Other island states in the Pacific, such as Kiribati and Tuvalu, facing a similar threat of submergence, have followed the same course, and have already asked Australia and New Zealand to accept its citizens as permanent

20 Mary Louise Malig, "Burning the Planet, One Climate COP at a Time," *people forests rights* (Global Forest Coalition blog), December 13, 2014, https://peopleforestsrights.wordpress.com/2014/12/13/burning-the-planet-one-climate-cop-at-a-time; and Brian Tokar, "Is the Paris Climate Conference Designed to Fail?," *Common Dreams*, November 11, 2015, http://www.commondreams.org/views/2015/11/11/paris-climate-conference-designed-fail.

21 Mimura et al., "Small Islands"; Mark Hertsgaard, *HOT: Living through the Next Fifty Years on Earth* (New York: Mariner, 2012); and Pachauri et al., *Climate Change 2014: Synthesis Report*.

22 See http://globaljusticeecology.org; and Frances Williams, "Climate Is Rights Issue, Says Maldives Minister," *Financial Times*, March 4, 2009, http://on.ft.com/1MBKAZI.

23 See Ross, "Climate Debt Denial."

refugees—as yet to no avail.[24] Importantly, such a plan is not Nasheed's only solution, and it was no doubt a further act of media publicity to gain more visibility for the country's dire situation in advance of COP15. Still, such a proposal, along with the visual politics that endorse it, prompts further consideration of "climate refugees" as a prospective legal and conceptual category.

Climate Refugees?

Some legal theorists argue that offering environmental refugees recognition under the Geneva Conventions will grant them internationally assured protection, independent of the laws of their own governments.[25] Yet this suggestion raises complex legal questions, beginning with the fact that Article 1A of the 1951 Geneva Convention only grants refugee status for those fleeing persecution for reasons of race, religion, nationality, social association, or political opinion. The term "environmental refugees" was defined subsequently in a 1985 United Nations Environment Programme policy paper as "those people who have been forced to leave their traditional habitat, temporarily or permanently, because of a marked environmental disruption," which means "any physical, chemical, and/or biological changes in the ecosystem (or resource base) that render it temporarily or permanently unsuitable to support human life."[26] But this definition has yet to be recognized in international law.

Recognition could occur, analysts point out, by expanding the Geneva Conventions, developing existing international law (the UN Framework Convention on Climate Change, for instance), or extending the mandate of the UNHCR (United Nations High Commissioner for Refugees), as the Argos Collective proposes.[27] There are nonetheless several reasons to question this route as a proposed response to the displacement brought on by climate

24 To date, New Zealand has rejected requests to classify Tuvaluans as climate refugees, and instead calls them "labor migrants," agreeing to admit seventy-five per year under its Pacific Access Category. See Berzon, "Tuvalu Is Drowning"; and Angela Oels, "Asylum Rights for Climate Refugees? From Agamben's Bare Life to the Autonomy of Migration" (lecture, "Bridging Multiple Divides," 49th Annual Convention of the International Studies Association, San Francisco, March 26, 2008), http://citation.allacademic.com/meta/p_mla_apa_research_citation/2/5/1/0/8/pages251088/p251088-1.php.

25 See Molly Conisbee and Andrew Simms, *Environmental Refugees: The Case for Recognition* (London: New Economics Foundation, 2003), 39.

26 Essam El-Hinnawi, *Environmental Refugees* (Nairobi: United Nations Environment Programme, 1985), 4; cited in Oels, "Asylum Rights for Climate Refugees," 10. For more on climate refugees, see Jane McAdam, *Climate Change, Forced Migration, and International Law* (Oxford: Oxford University Press, 2012); Laura Westra, *Environmental Justice and the Rights of Ecological Refugees* (London: Routledge, 2009); and Gregory White, *Climate Change and Migration: Security and Borders in a Warming World* (Oxford: Oxford University Press, 2011).

27 See Oels, "Asylum Rights for Climate Refugees," 10; and Argos Collective, *Climate Refugees*, 15.

change. First, it is difficult to define strictly environmental causes and separate them from poverty, war, or any of the multifarious factors that are co-extensive with the effects of climate change. The climate refugee thus, by definition, represents an intangible figure, owing to the difficulty in disaggregating the causality of its circumstances. Climate change exacerbates an already complex set of challenges for vulnerable populations, including uneven access to diverse resources, such as water, land, infrastructure, institutions, capital, and the rule of law.[28] Indeed, political theorists, such as Angela Oels, remain skeptical of establishing such confusing and complex distinctions in classifying refugees, as "it will leave plenty of room for thresholds of indistinction that leave the final decision on the status of life up to sovereign power," which can then abuse any ambiguity in oppressive ways.[29] As well, placing climate refugees under the UNHCR's jurisdiction will not simply grant rights to refugees; it will also potentially transform them into objects (or victims) of humanitarianism, which can withdraw aid at any time.[30] Consider, for example, the displaced of Hurricane Katrina and their effective relegation to the status of bare life—a form of life stripped of political agency, reduced to mere biological existence—in their sports-stadium-turned-camp environment. That dystopian real-life scenario foreshadows the potential future treatment of climate migrants in the United States, European Union, and elsewhere (as those migrants, deemed "illegal," are in fact already treated).[31]

We should be skeptical of proposals to institutionalize the climate-refugee category; they imply a proliferation of distinctions between "good" and "bad" migrants and an intensification of biopolitical regimes of control, including measures such as automated and weaponized surveillance systems, the militarization of borders, expanded refugee

28 See Carol Farbotko and Heather Lazrus, "The First Climate Refugees? Contesting Global Narratives of Climate Change in Tuvalu," *Global Environmental Change* 22, no. 2 (2012): 382–90. Also see Neil Smith, "There's No Such Thing as a Natural Disaster," *Understanding Katrina: Perspectives from the Social Sciences*, June 11, 2006, http://understandingkatrina.ssrc.org/Smith.

29 Oels, "Asylum Rights for Climate Refugees," 11. Here Oels references the political theory of Giorgio Agamben and his discussion of the power of sovereignty to designate a state of exception, or internal exclusion from the law, and deny rights on that basis, particularly as outlined in Agamben's *Homo Sacer: Sovereign Power and Bare Life*, trans. Daniel Heller-Roazen (Stanford, CA: Stanford University Press, 1998).

30 "Assistance to refugees is conceived of in terms of charity rather than as a means of enabling refugees to enjoy their rights. There are insufficient resources to meet needs, with the power to decide their allocation placed in the hands of humanitarian workers who are said to be responsible to the donors but not to the recipients." Barbara Harrell-Bond, "Can Humanitarian Work with Refugees Be Humane?," *Human Rights Quarterly* 24, no. 1 (February 2002): 53; cited in Oels, "Asylum Rights for Climate Refugees," 8.

31 "The social practice of the politics of migration in Europe shows that such 'exceptions' are becoming more and more the rule" (Oels, "Asylum Rights for Climate Refugees," 8). On contemporary art and migration, see my book *The Migrant Image*.

camps, biometrics, and the commodification of migration via the increasingly Kafkaesque bureaucracy of visas and work permits.[32] Not surprisingly, many islanders reject the refugee role allotted to them by humanitarian groups and NGOs who wish to enlist them as poster children in their political campaigns.[33] "In the eyes of Tuvaluans," write Carol Farbotko and Heather Lazrus, "permission to cross a western border as a refugee falls far short of the climate change remedies required: extensive, immediate reductions in global greenhouse gas emissions, and significant legal and financial action to redress lost livelihoods and self-determination if emissions reduction is not achieved."[34] One final problem regarding the climate-refugee category is that migration narratives—and even those that stress the "autonomy of migration" perspective, arguing for open borders and protesting the growing criminalization of migration[35]—tend to minimize the resilience of both political agency and climate justice in the present. Many experts argue that adaptation strategies are currently most important.[36] Still, even if joined to human rights claims, this solution tends to shift the conversation to geotechnical fixes (such as buttressing seawalls) instead of cutting emissions.[37] In this regard, advocates for adapting to the effects of climate change come all too close to those who deny the anthropogenic causes of climate change in the first place: in both cases, the danger remains that people will stop trying to act to counter the causes of global warming.[38]

32 Wright, "Preparing for Mass Refugee Flows," 85; and Christian Parenti, *Tropic of Chaos: Climate Change and the New Geography of Violence* (New York: Nation Books, 2012).

33 One conflict involved the campaign by Friends of the Earth to aid Tuvaluan "climate refugees" at the 2008 Climate Camp in Newcastle, Australia, only to be told by islanders that they rather wished to receive training to become skilled migrants should they have to leave their land. Farbotko and Lazrus, "The First Climate Refugees," 383.

34 Ibid., 388.

35 The autonomy of migration perspective supports "the call for legislation of *all* migrants, without distinction," and "the recognition of fundamental human rights like the right to reside, to work and to non-discrimination. Migration activists believe that only open borders will eventually trigger policymaking to address the perpetuation of global injustice." Oels, "Asylum Rights for Climate Refugees," 18.

36 See "UN Expert Urges Maldives to Tackle Displacement Caused by Climate Change," *UN News*, July 21, 2011, http://www.un.org/apps/news/story.asp?NewsID=39111; and World Bank, *Maldives – Climate Change Adaptation Project: Environment and Social Assessment and Management Framework*, 2014, http://documents.worldbank.org/curated/en/2014/11/23008510/maldives-climate-change-adaptation-project-environment-social-assessment-management-framework.

37 Adaptation discourse also allows governments to abdicate responsibility for climate change in the first place. For instance, the US Chamber of Commerce, in a bid from 2009 to prevent the EPA from regulating carbon emissions, argues that in the event of global warming, "populations can acclimatize to warmer climates via a range of behavioral, physiological, and technological adaptations." Cited in Klein, *This Changes Everything*, 48.

38 See Eddie Yuen, "The Politics of Failure Have Failed: The Environmental Movement and Catastrophism," in *Catastrophism: The Apocalyptic Politics of Collapse and Rebirth*, ed. Sasha Lilley, David McNally, Eddie Yuen, and James Davis (Oakland, CA: PM Press, 2012), 15–43.

Climate Justice Now!

Representatives of small island nations, figuring as some of the most vulnerable populations, are thus on the forefront of demanding climate justice in the present rather than accepting a future of forced migration. Consider the case of Tuvalu, the Pacific island nation halfway between Hawaii and Australia, which international media and NGOs, the Argos Collective included, predict will succumb to future submergence. The IPCC warns, however, that such narratives silence alternative voices of resilience (even if that means accepting the unavoidability of global warming)—for them, it is "adaptation, perhaps even more than relocation or mitigation initiatives, which is of immediate importance in island places [... especially] in the face of changes brought about by 'global warming.'"[39] The danger of future environmental chaos "is as much associated with the narrowing of adaptation options [...] as it is with uncertain potential climate-driven physical impacts."[40] Yet instead of reproducing a form of environmentalist determinism—which portrays global warming as one-directional and irreversible—it's crucial to consider climate change as part of a "web of vectors," where gradually unfolding outcomes depend on multiple factors, including the circumstances of people (including social and class-based distinctions), geopolitical conditions, and sociopolitical structures.[41]

Against the "narrowing of adaptation options," the Maldives' (formerly named) Ministry of Home Affairs, Housing and Environment, for instance, outlined the following goals: coastal protection, reduction in the number of inhabited islands, the development of hydroponic agricultural systems, solar energy and rainwater harvesting, public awareness and education campaigns, and increasing coastal elevation through engineering.[42] An additional measure is for these small states to become "renewable energy islands" and model a path away from fossil fuel dependency, as Fiji, Samsoe, Pellworm, and La Réunion have done, all of which presently generate more than 50 percent of their electricity from renewable

39 Farbotko, "Wishful Sinking."

40 Jon Barnett and W. Neil Adger, "Climate Dangers and Atoll Countries," *Climatic Change* 61, no. 3 (December 2003): 321–37; cited in Mimura et al., "Small Islands," 707. "The enhancement of resilience at various levels of society, through capacity building, efficient resource allocation and the mainstreaming of climate risk management into development policies at the national and local scale, could constitute a key element of the adaptation strategy" (ibid., 711).

41 Farbotko and Lazrus, "The First Climate Refugees," 384.

42 Adaptation strategies can also include internal migration: consider the examples of Niue and Tokelau, two islands in the Realm of New Zealand, whose populations have almost entirely emigrated to New Zealand. See the work of anthropologist Michael Goldsmith, as discussed in Berzon, "Tuvalu Is Drowning"; also Mimura et al., "Small Islands," 705.

43 Ibid., 702. The 1989 Male Declaration on Global Warming and Sea Level Rise, initiated under then Maldivian President Maumoon Abdul Gayoom, had already called on the UN and developed nations to adopt alternative energy sources to reduce pollution. See Argos Collective, *Climate Refugees*, 133.

energy sources.[43] Reference to these various approaches is completely absent in the Argos Collective's overview. The group might also have considered the legal recourse taken up by island nations as an emerging mode of exerting political power in relation to global warming, as the governments of the Maldives and Tuvalu have done by demanding that polluting countries pay for damage caused by climate change. The argument is framed as a matter of climate justice, rather than one of humanitarian charity, aid, or loans for adaptation.[44] "Rather than relying on aid money, we believe that the major greenhouse polluters should pay for the impacts they are causing," claimed Tavau Teii, the deputy prime minister of Tuvalu, expressing support for the principle of climate debt.[45] In 2002, Tuvalu even considered initiating a lawsuit in the International Court of Justice in The Hague to sue major greenhouse gas emitters like the United States and Australia, though they decided ultimately against the idea, given the difficulties in winning such a case.[46] Nevertheless, the example points to a potentially litigious future in addressing the effects of and responsibilities for climate change, as well as corporate environmental malfeasance, a future where one could imagine the situation where a small island nation like Tuvalu could sue the oil giant ExxonMobil.[47] Proponents of this legal strategy have been steadily developing an emerging model of "Earth jurisprudence," attempting to reconcile human governance structures with a paradigm-shifting biocentric—rather than market-centered—global legal system, which forms one source of hope for climate justice in the near future.[48]

44 Tuvalu has lobbied for effective policy making on climate change, and the rejection of refugee status for its population, with Tuvalu UN Ambassador Enele Sopoaga arguing against the rhetoric of relocation: "To relocate is a short-sighted solution, an irresponsible solution. We're not dealing here with Tuvalu only. All of the low-lying island coastal areas are going to be affected. You tell me whether the world is ready to evacuate everybody." Cited in Berzon, "Tuvalu Is Drowning"; see also Oels, "Asylum Rights for Climate Refugees," 15.

45 Teii estimated that helping countries to adapt to the negative impacts of climate change, such as installing seawalls, or raising land levels by dredging sand, would amount to around US$80 billion per year. He proposed the creation of a global insurance institution financed by the polluters that would compensate vulnerable countries for the damages they have suffered from climate change. See the press release by the Permanent Mission of Tuvalu to the United Nations, "Tuvalu Calls for Climate Change Polluters to Pay," September 29, 2007; cited in Oels, "Asylum Rights for Climate Refugees," 16.

46 "Until the United States takes significant action, it is vulnerable to this type of lawsuit." Jennifer Morgan, cited in Reuters, "Tiny Tuvalu Sues United States over Rising Sea Level," August 29, 2002, http://www.tuvaluislands.com/news/archived/2002/2002-08-29.htm; see Oels, "Asylum Rights for Climate Refugees," 16.

47 See Rachel Morris, "Tuvalu v. ExxonMobil?," *Mother Jones*, May/June 2010, http://www.motherjones.com/environment/2010/04/climate-desk-climate-change-legislation.

48 Earth jurisprudence, or "wild law," encompassing the juridico-political project organized around enshrining the rights of nature, has seen substantial development in recent years. See Cullinan, *Wild Law*; and Burdon, *Exploring Wild Law*.

The Argos Collective has little to say in regard to these juridico-political developments, choosing only to acknowledge the Maldivians' migrant fate. They write: "Where will the Maldives get the billions of euros necessary to construct more artificial islands? Where will they find the funds to build tetrapod seawalls around the 200 inhabited islands?"[49] Declining to think of solutions, they embrace a migration framework devoid of climate-justice claims. The inadequacy of their analysis and prognosis, however, is evident in a short informational video accompanying their Maldives project, which presents a montage of still photos with voice-over testimonies in English and Dhivehi, both ultimately drowned out by the Argos Collective's fatalistic commentary. It begins by quoting the UN's predictions that 150 million people will have to migrate by the end of the century due to global warming (which is translated into grammatically awkward English in the subtitles). The voices of everyday Maldivians are then heard reflecting on their uncertain future: "What will we do if the sea level rises? Climb the coconut trees or live on boats!"[50] With this, viewers are presented with a narrative of isolated localism (where the effects of climate change are foregrounded with no reflection on the global causes), constructing the Maldivians as victims. Ultimately this story serves the interests of those sectors of the humanitarian industry that accept climate change as a fait accompli; meanwhile, the Argos Collective position themselves to document the expected consequences.[51]

The Arctic Oil Rush

An atmospheric carbon dioxide concentration today of roughly 400 parts per million, up from 275 in the eighteenth century, due to the burning of fossil fuels and deforestation, is unprecedented since the Pleistocene eight hundred thousand years ago, when extreme volcanic outgassing trapped heat in the atmosphere. This shift has introduced significant environmental transformations in the Far North (comprising the Arctic and Subarctic regions), including warmer temperatures leading to the loss of permafrost, freezing rain instead of snow, and ever-accelerating ice melting in the polar region (which leads to sea-level rise in coastal zones—especially low-lying deltas like

49 Argos Collective, *Climate Refugees*, 134.

50 Argos Collective, *The Maldives: A Nation at the Water's Edge*, accessed October 22, 2015, http://www.collectifargos.com/en/interactive-documentary-blogs/multimedia-reports/the-maldives-a-nation-at-the-water-s-edge/multimedia#.VXhbcRPtlBc.

51 On the humanitarian industry, see Linda Polman, *The Crisis Caravan: What's Wrong with Humanitarian Aid?*, trans. Liz Waters (New York: Metropolitan, 2010); Alex De Waal, *Famine Crimes: Politics and the Disaster Relief Industry in Africa* (London: African Rights & the International African Institute, 1997); and T. J. Demos, "The Haunting: Renzo Martens's *Enjoy Poverty*," in *Return to the Postcolony*, 97–123.

those in India, Bangladesh, and island nations like the Maldives).[52] The consequences for Arctic life are severe—invasive species increasingly move north and disrupt fragile ecosystems and food chains established over millennia, migratory animals lose their habitat, and villages of Arctic Indigenous peoples are pressured to relocate (such as those in Shishmaref and Kivalina, Alaskan villages located on the Chukchi Sea, just north of the Bering Strait—Arctic corollaries to the Maldives).[53]

One-fifth of the planet's undiscovered oil and natural gas is thought to be buried in the Arctic floor, according to the US Geological Survey in 2013, making the region, in the agency's words, "the largest unexplored prospective area for petroleum remaining on earth."[54] As a result, oil prospecting has led to a new geopolitical contest over rights to ocean territory, fought between countries such as Russia, the United States, Denmark, Canada, and Norway. In 2007, Russian scientists boarded the submersibles *Mir-1* and *Mir-2* to descend through a hole in North Pole ice to assert a claim on the region by planting a flag on the ocean floor—"The Arctic is Russian," declared the expedition leader.[55] This mediagenic gesture—reproduced by artist Caleb Larsen in a diptych that elicits the humor resulting from the discrepancy between the geopolitical maneuver and its modest symbolic marker—a new submarine landgrab, a race to the bottom of the sea, and forms a poignant counterimage to the Maldivian president's underwater cabinet meeting. The comparison suggests an irony of energy politics in the age of climate change: fossil-fuel-induced global warming is melting ice caps in the Arctic only to reveal more sources of fossil fuel that were previously unreachable. The result is that inhabitants of the Far North—people and wildlife alike—have become "both the leading suppliers and the leading subjects of humanity's current experiment in warming the planet."[56] Far from a remote wilderness of natural splendor, the Arctic, according to arts writer Nicola Triscott, is a place where competing worlds jostle: landgrabs supported by high-tech electronic fortresses and military encampments share space with migrating animals, oil extraction plants, mines, launch sites, and nuclear reactors, while submarines glide beneath the

52 See Alex Shoumatoff, "The Arctic Oil Rush," *Vanity Fair*, May 2008, 237–39; Suzanne Goldenberg, "Arctic Sea Ice Shrinks to Sixth-Lowest Extent on Record," *Guardian*, September 18, 2013, http://www.theguardian.com/environment/2013/sep/18/arctic-sea-ice-shrinks-record-low; and Frank Sejersen, *Rethinking Greenland and the Arctic in the Era of Climate Change: New Northern Horizons* (London: Routledge, 2015).

53 Christine Shearer, Kivalina: A Climate Change Story (London: Haymarket, 2011).

54 Cited in Jad Mouawad, "Energy Hunt Is Focusing on the Arctic," *New York Times*, July 24, 2008. See also Basia Rosenbaum, "The Battle for Arctic Oil," *Harvard International Review*, March 9, 2015, http://hir.harvard.edu/the-battle-for-arctic-oil/.

55 Cited in Nixon, *Slow Violence*, 267.

56 Karl Jacoby, "The Near North," in *Subhankar Banerjee* (Hanover, NH: Dartmouth College, 2009), 10.

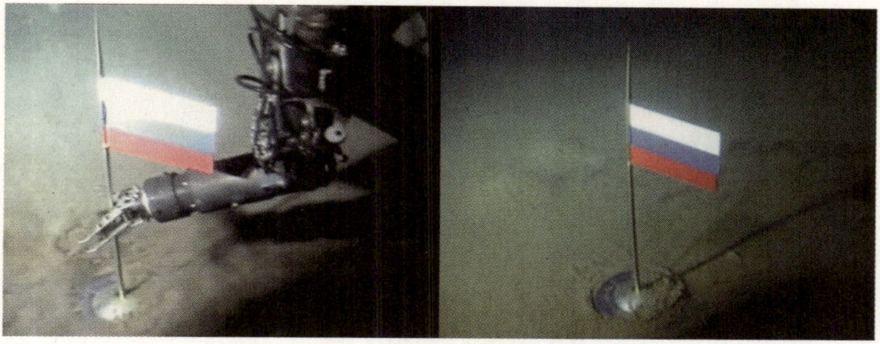

Caleb Larsen, *Land Grab*, 2008

ice—the vast plains interspersed with scientific research stations and remote Indigenous settlements.[57]

It is this conflicted geography that the photographer and writer Subhankar Banerjee has approached in a further model of visual culture that addresses a region threatened by the effects of global warming, the energy industry, and narratives of migration. Banerjee's work operates at the intersection of aesthetics and politics, more in the tradition of eco-activism than ethnography, photojournalism, or fine art photography, even if it also broaches each of these areas. An Indian-born American photographer, writer, and environmental activist, Banerjee has worked for the protection of ecologically significant areas since 2000, particularly in the Arctic, and for Far North Indigenous human rights in the era of climate change; in 2010 he founded ClimateStoryTellers.org, a website that gathers his writings on these subjects.[58] In the introduction to his edited anthology on the subject, *Arctic Voices: Resistance at the Tipping Point*, Banerjee explains: "The Arctic has become our planet's tipping point—climate change is wreaking havoc up there. Resource wars continue to spread. Industrial toxins continue to accumulate widely. But also, the voices of resistance are gathering, are getting louder and louder—and that is the story this volume presents. It is the noise and the music of all our voices bundled together."[59] Those voices

57 See Nicola Triscott, "Critical Art and Intervention in the Technologies of the Arctic," in *Arctic Geopolitics and Autonomy*, ed. Michael Bravo and Nicola Triscott, *Arctic Perspective Cahier*, no. 2 (Ostfildern: Hatje Cantz, 2001), 21.

58 Banerjee's articles on ClimateStoryTellers.org include: "Destabilization of Arctic Sea Ice Would Be Game Over for Climate," September 27, 2013; "Colorado's Thousand-Year Flood: Repeated Assaults Culminate with Epic Floods in Colorado," September 16, 2013; and "Walking the Waters: How to Bring the Major Oil Companies Ashore and Halt the Destruction of Our Oceans," August 2, 2012.

59 Subhankar Banerjee, "From Kolkata to Kaktovik: En Route to Arctic Voices," in *Arctic Voices: Resistance at the Tipping Point*, ed. Subhankar Banerjee (New York: Seven Stories Press, June 2012), 20.

include Inupiat cultural activists and tribal leaders, a Gwich'in elder and activist, NGO conservationists, environmental writers, wildlife and conservation biologists, and environmental activists, joined together in this interdisciplinary study of the Arctic, a micro-version of a larger social movement, supplemented with Banerjee's writing and images.

Banerjee's photographs are wide-ranging, from aerial landscape shots to close-ups of animal life in the Arctic National Wildlife Refuge (ANWR), spanning over nineteen million acres in northeastern Alaska. One stunning panorama, *Snow Geese I*, shows the autumnal coastal plain of the ANWR, the ocher of the land and blue of the water speckled with the white of migrating birds in flight. Another aerial shot, *Caribou Migration II*, depicts a bluish ice landscape punctuated with ant-like progression of the circumpolar species (both are from the 2002 series "Oil and the Caribou"). There are also shots of Indigenous communities that Banerjee has spent time with while researching the environment, including landscape images of Evens in northeastern Siberia herding reindeer in a snowy mountain range (from the series "Even and the Climate," 2007); close-ups of Yukaghirs in eastern Siberia ice fishing (from "Yukaghir and the Climate," 2007); and intimate portrayals of Gwich'ins hunting caribou, dressing the bloody carcasses besides their snowmobiles (from "Gwich'in and the Caribou," 2007). While these images startle with visual power, owing to the awesome environments and saturated colors, they are also accompanied by extended captions that disclose the regions' ecological transformations, placing images in relation to traditional knowledge of First Nations peoples and the scientific insights of recent geology and climatology. We learn that shifting environmental conditions that lead to wetter snow and freezing rain make foraging difficult and cause a decline in reindeer and caribou populations, which threatens Indigenous food supplies in turn; that fish species, such as the Arctic char, are particularly vulnerable to displacement owing to warming waters, and migrating fish threaten to introduce new parasites and diseases to northern regions, carrying health risks for the Yukaghir population; and that oil development in the ANWR endangers the calving area of the Porcupine River caribou herd, which adversely affects the Gwich'ins since they rely on the animals for sustenance.[60] The captivating aesthetics of these images, in other words, is backed up by substantial research, with Banerjee's project intertwining conceptual substance and visual seduction.

Banerjee's images and texts reveal how climate change impacts the mobility of Indigenous Arctic peoples, as well as animals, in

60 See the exhibition catalogue *Subhankar Banerjee: Resource Wars* (New York: Sundaram Tagore Gallery, 2008), 22. Banerjee's expansive captions are available on his website; owing to their length they unfortunately could not be reproduced here. See http://www.subhankarbanerjee.org.

a number of ways (these communities, although traditionally nomadic and settling only in the last century owing to colonialist government policies and economic reasons, are now subjected to climate-change induced mobility). Transformations in habitat and weather alter foraging and hunting practices, changing the usual range of herd animals, and fragment landscapes, where thinning ice makes rivers and lakes harder or impossible to cross.[61] In this regard, Banerjee's work resonates with Indigenous documentary practices, such as Isuma Productions, based in Igloolik, Nunavut, which has focused on the changing environment from a native perspective since the mid-1990s.[62] The company focuses on the independent production and distribution of community-produced films, TV programming, and Internet content to preserve and widen the culture and languages of the Inuit, mainly located in First Nations' territory in the Canadian Arctic, and presents storytelling traditions for Indigenous and non-native audiences. For instance, the TV series *Nunavut: Our Land*, directed by Zacharias Kunuk in 1995, comprises thirteen half-hour programs that reconstruct traditional Inuit life, and was presented at documenta 11 in 2002, which was especially attuned to documentary media and postcolonial approaches to cultural politics (Kunuk also made the first Aboriginal-language feature in 2001, *Atanarjuat: The Fast Runner*, which received international acclaim). In 2010, Kunuk and Ian Mauro directed the hour-long documentary *Inuit Knowledge and Climate Change*, in which elders discuss how environmental transformation has altered traditional modes of living, hunting, and harvesting, and modified weather and atmospheric conditions. Video is a memory medium here, recording culture and tradition and transmitting eyewitness testimony to the environmental changes caused by a warming climate over the last eighty years. The medium helps Isuma Productions fulfill its aim: to use modes

61 "About five years ago the sea ice used to take longer to melt. It lasted about 10 months but now it's only 8 months. This harms our way of life, our way of hunting, our way of fishing, and our way of traveling from one place to another." Charlie Nakqashuk, of Pangnirtung, Nunavut, cited in Alex Randall, "Moving Stories: The Arctic, Migration and Displacement Linked to Climate Change," *UK Climate Change & Migration Coalition* (blog), March 18, 2013, http://www.climatemigration.org.uk/moving-stories-the-arctic-migration-and-displacement-linked-to-climate-change.

62 Also see the work of Arctic Perspective Initiative, a transnational artistic and scientific collaboration with offices in Canada and Slovenia, founded by Marko Peljhan and Matthew Biederman in 2006, which seeks to challenge dominant visual representations of Artic geopolitics through its media interventions and collaborations with the Igloolik community. They have also covered Isuma Productions. On Indigenous uses of new media, see Katarina Soukup, "Traveling through Layers: Inuit Artists Appropriate New Technologies," in Bravo and Triscott, *Arctic Geopolitics and Autonomy*, 57–69; Triscott, "Critical Art and Intervention"; and Emily Eliza Scott, "Artists' Platforms for New Ecologies," online supplement to *Third Text* 27, no. 1 (January 2013), http://www.thirdtext.org/domains/thirdtext.com/local/media/images/medium/scott_ee_artists__platforms_cc.pdf.

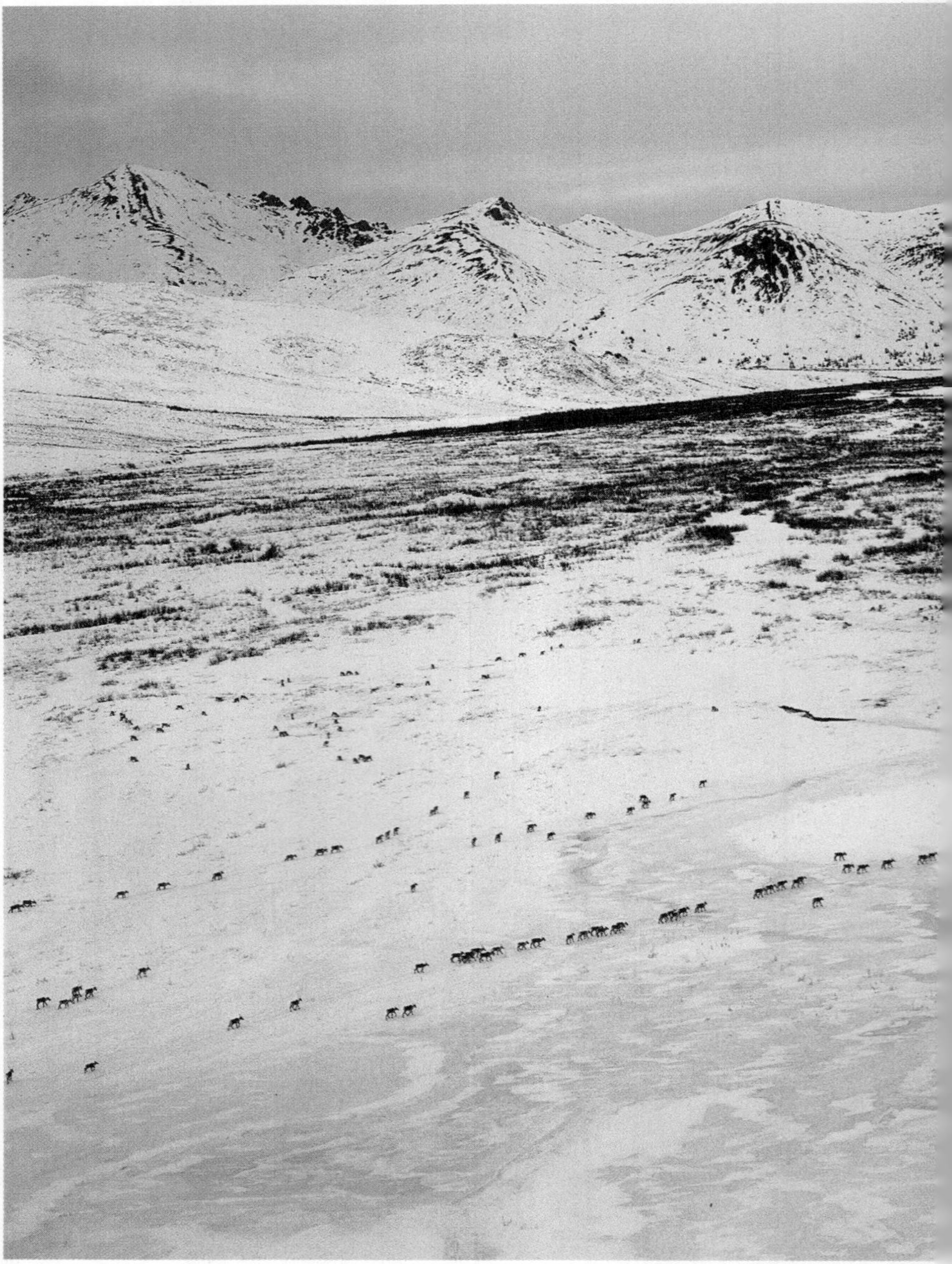

Subhankar Banerjee, *Caribou Migration II*, 2002; from the series "Oil and the Caribou"

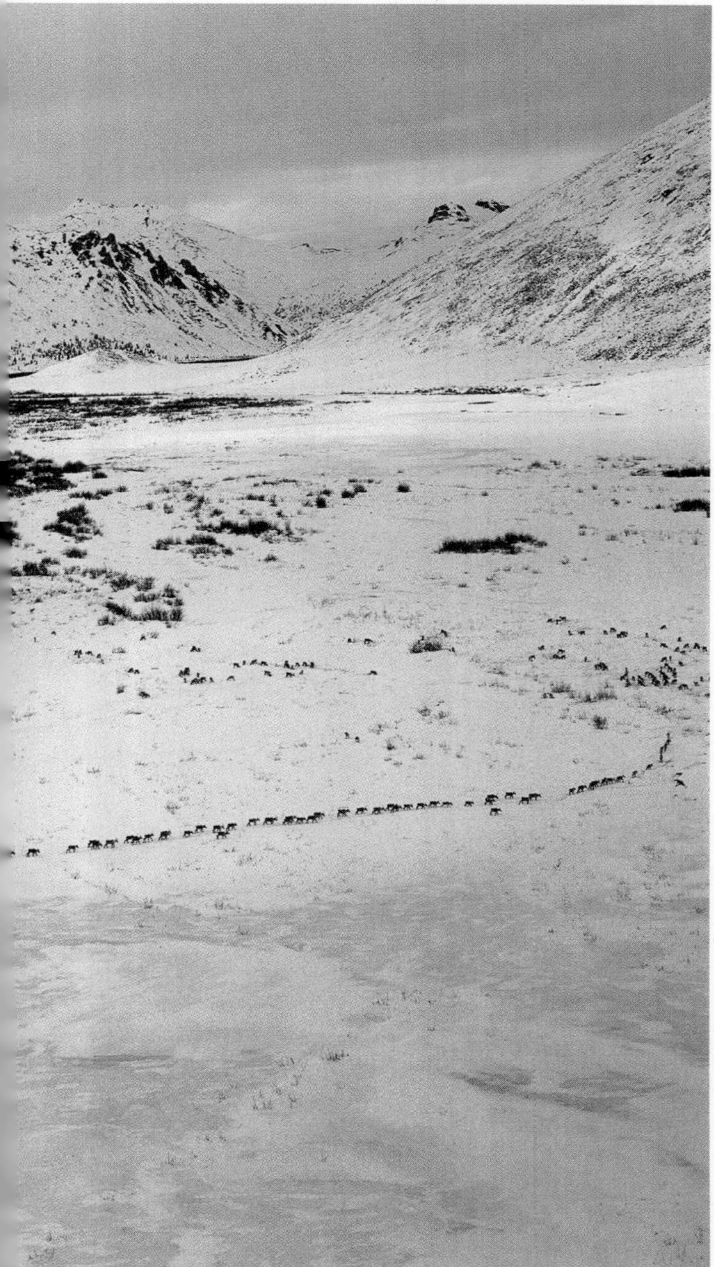

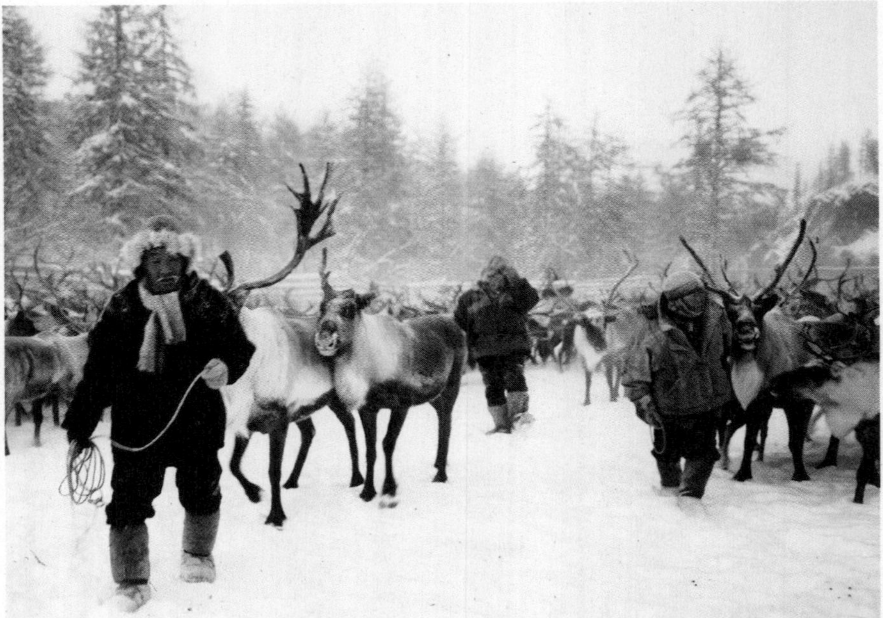

Subhankar Banerjee, *At the Corral III—Ilya Golikov, Nikolayev Matvey and Osenina Dariya Mikhailevna*, 2007; from the series "Even and the Climate"

of community-based cultural representation to respond to the transformation of traditional forms of life and begin to decolonize four thousand years of oral-history suppression by the Canadian state, demonstrating that the Indigenous people of Igloolik can control their self-representation in word and image.[63]

Banerjee's work forms a parallel aesthetics of survival, focusing on signs of ecological breakdown rather than depicting an idealized purity of the nature preserve, to contribute to a politics of resistance.[64] This aspect of destruction resonates with the theories of the

63 See Zacharias Kunuk, "The Art of Inuit Story-Telling," *Isuma Productions*, accessed October 27, 2015, http://www.isuma.tv/isuma-productions/art-inuit-story-telling. On the political history of Far North Indigenous peoples, see Lassi Heininen, "Post–Cold War Arctic Geopolitics: Where Are the Peoples and the Environment?," in Bravo and Triscott, *Arctic Geopolitics and Autonomy*, 89–103.

64 "Rarely, despite the increasing interest in the Arctic, does the political complexity of the region find visual representation as a contested arena of aspirations—a fragile set of ecosystems that are simultaneously a storehouse of resources, both renewable and nonrenewable, a transport zone and a theater for military operations, as well as homelands to dozens of different indigenous groups" (Triscott, "Critical Art and Intervention," 23). Yet Triscott neglects to mention the biodiverse flora and fauna of the region, which Banerjee investigates in relation to fossil fuel extraction and industrialization of the landscape via mining infrastructure.

photographic medium and its ontology of death, materialized in Banerjee's melancholy visual imaginary of threatened forms of life stranded in time and space.[65] More literally, Banerjee's photography exposes how climate chaos brings about destructive alterations to the food chain, and compounds environmental pollution that afflicts the Arctic's cold zone, where toxic substances such as PCBs, DDT, and mercury have settled, wreaking havoc on animal, plant, and human life.[66] In a particularly grisly image, *One Polar Bear Eating Another* (2000), Banerjee's perspective juxtaposes two animals, one desperate and alive, the other eviscerated, caught in a cannibalistic act that is the direct outcome of climate change's reduction of traditional food sources.[67] In a shot from 2006, a caribou skeleton lies on the shore in the ANWR, marking a quest for food far from the animal's traditional migration area around Teshekpuk Lake, a couple hundred miles to the west.[68] Banerjee's images form an iconography of the Arctic ecology's ruins, and, as critic Yates McKee observes, extend environmental relevance to "[theorist Eduardo] Cadava's axiom that 'there can be no [photographic] image that is not about destruction and survival, and this is especially the case in the image of ruin.'"[69]

The titles of Banerjee's series situate his images within the larger conflicts between nature and human industry that determine such cycles of destruction and survival today—"Coal and the Caribou," "Oil and the Caribou," "Oil and the Geese," "Even and the Climate." Integral to the meanings of the photographs, they express divergent values regarding nature, signifying both a "natural resource" in the capitalist petro-economy and a biodiverse ecology, and resonating with Indigenous approaches to the environment (evident in the photographer's writings, and exhibitions like "Resource Wars" from 2008). The photograph *Caribou Tracks on Coal Seams II* (2006) brings the two together visually: the tracks of centuries of migrating herds are etched on the surface of coal beds, testimony to the close physical connection in this habitat between human energy supplies and animal environments. It is exactly this coexistence that is often covered up by those

65 See, for instance, the classic text by Roland Barthes, *Camera Lucida: Reflections on Photography*, trans. Richard Howard (London: Vintage, 1993); and for contemporary political implications, Ariella Azoulay, *Death's Showcase: The Power of Image in Contemporary Democracy* (Cambridge, MA: MIT Press, 2003).

66 Jacoby, "The Near North," 10–16. Also see Marla Cone, *Silent Snow: The Slow Poisoning of the Arctic* (New York: Grove Press, 2005).

67 See Subhankar Banerjee, "Thankful for Polar Bear Habitat But Shell Must Not Go There," *ClimateStoryTellers.org*, November 26, 2010, http://www.climatestorytellers.org/stories/subhankar-banerjee-polar-bear-habitat/.

68 See http://www.subhankarbanerjee.org/photohtml/oilncaribou10.html.

69 Yates McKee, "Of Survival: Climate Change and Uncanny Landscape in the Photography of Subhankar Banerjee," in *Impasses of the Post-Global: Theory in the Era of Climate Change*, vol. 2, ed. Harry Sussman (Ann Arbor, MI: Open Humanities Press, 2012), 76.

Subhankar Banerjee, *Caribou Tracks on Coal Seams II*, 2006; from the series "Coal and the Caribou"

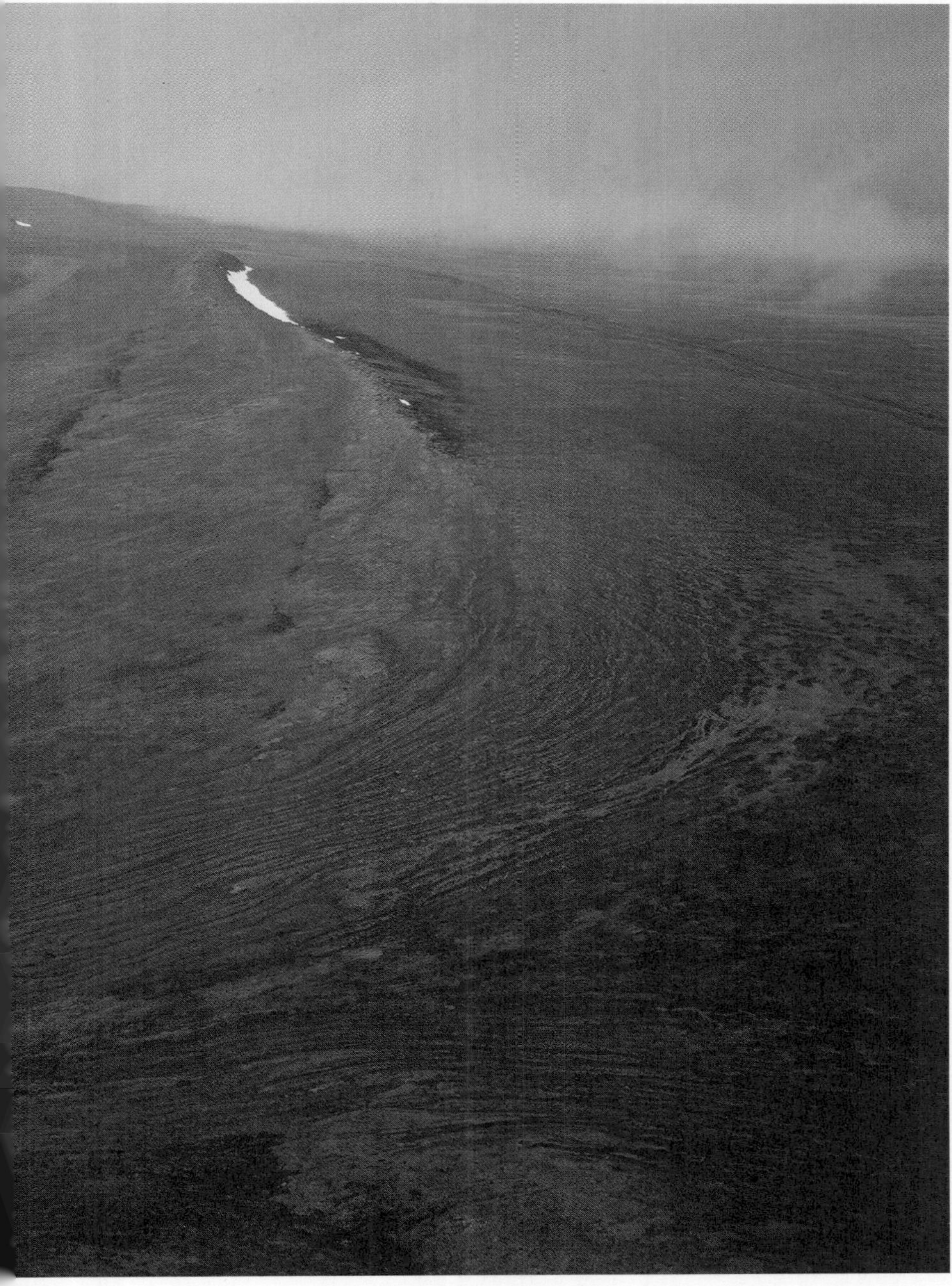

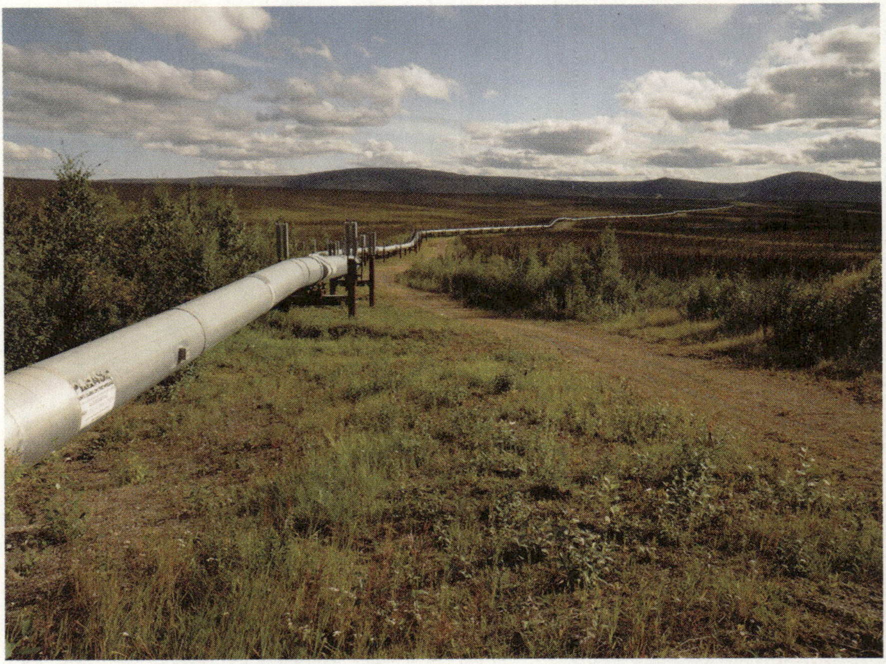

Center for Land Use Interpretation, from *The Trans-Alaska Pipeline*, 2008

supporting fossil-fuel development in the Arctic, as if the extraction industry's object of interest can be clearly disassociated from the region's fragile ecologies. Investigating this nature-culture conflict, other artists and collectives tend to focus on technological interventions in the Arctic landscape—such as the Center for Land Use Interpretation's *The Trans-Alaska Pipeline* (2008), a forty-minute slideshow of photographs of the oil conduit as it traverses eight hundred miles across the state; or Bureau d'Études's *Conquête du Grand Nord* (2009), a map detailing military and industrial activity in the Far North, showing military bases, nuclear reactors, radar stations, sites of nuclear tests, mines, oil extraction plants, and polluted areas. In contrast, Banerjee foregrounds the ecosystems, both fragile and sublime, of the open Arctic expanses and animal migrations, showing its precarious existence, ever threatened by industry, which has already led to present scenes of ecological breakdown.

The Arctic Image Complex

More than practicing photography as an artistic activity—one that focuses attention exclusively on the aestheticized picture—Banerjee has deployed his images within the fields of politicized visual culture and mainstream media to raise consciousness about climate-justice grievances. In 2003, Banerjee's ANWR photographs, just before they were to be exhibited at the Smithsonian Institution's National Museum of Natural History, made a fascinating detour into the very environmental deliberations of US government policy. Republican politicians under President George W. Bush's administration were arguing that the Arctic is empty of wildlife and therefore opening up the area to oil drilling should pose little environmental risk. Secretary of the Interior Gale Norton described the region as a "flat, white nothingness," and Alaska Senator Frank Murkowski held up a blank white poster and claimed it showed an accurate picture of the Far North.[70] Such hyperbole is only the latest example of a self-serving politics of erasure, going back to the colonial days of forced displacements and violent resettlements of native peoples, as well as nineteenth- and twentieth-century conservation practices that attempted to define and protect unsettled lands as pure wildernesses, depopulated of Indigenous inhabitants, a practice now extended to Arctic life.[71] It's just this view—politically instrumental to the energy industry—that Banerjee's images have opposed by highlighting the biodiversity of the region, and by locating First Nations peoples and nonhuman nature alike within distinct political, ecological, and aesthetic constellations.

Intervening in that same congressional debate, Democratic California Senator Barbara Boxer displayed a reproduction of Banerjee's 2001 photograph depicting a polar bear walking amid pools of melting ice on the coast of the Beaufort Sea, having been given an advance copy of Banerjee's book *Seasons of Life and Land: Arctic National Wildlife Refuge* by the Alaska Wilderness League, with whom the photographer had been collaborating.[72] She used the image, entitled *Polar Bear on Bernard Harbor, Barter*

70 See Finis Dunaway, "Reframing the Last Frontier: Subhankar Banerjee and the Visual Politics of the Arctic National Wildlife Refuge," in Braddock and Irmsher, *A Keener Perception*, 259. Murkowski's stunt figured in the 2004 documentary *Oil on Ice*, directed by Bo Boudart and Dale Djerassi.

71 See Ramachandra Guha, "Radical American Environmentalism and Wilderness Preservation: A Third World Critique," in *Philosophical Dialogues: Arne Næss and the Progress of Ecophilosophy*, ed. A. Brennan and N. Witoszek (Lanham: Rowman & Littlefield, 1999), 313–24; and Rebecca Solnit, *Savage Dreams: A Journey into the Landscape Wars of the American West* (Berkeley: University of California Press, 1999), 215–385.

72 Banerjee explained: "My first book, *Seasons of Life and Land: Arctic National Wildlife Refuge* was published in 2003. The official publication date was in April, but my publisher The Mountaineers Books received a few early copies from the printer in March and immediately sent it to the Alaska

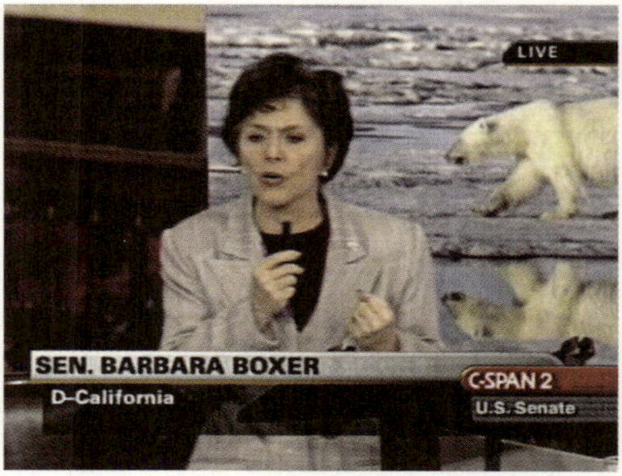

Senator Barbara Boxer, with Subhankar Banerjee's 2001 photograph *Polar Bear on Bernard Harbor, Barter Island*, on C-SPAN, March 19, 2003

Island, to mobilize Banerjee's visual evidence in support of the continued protection of the region, showing the Northern environment to be a life-filled habitat, counter to the claims of the likes of Norton and Murkowski. The March 19 debate was shown on the TV network C-SPAN, and Banerjee's work featured prominently in the movement that successfully stopped the drilling proposal on the floor of Congress. As a result of this politicized framework, Banerjee's extensive captions were subsequently abridged for the Smithsonian exhibition, an act of censorship that occasioned a further exhibition that same year—with restored captions—at the California Academy of Sciences in San Francisco.[73] Through these intersecting fields of exposure, in the media, exhibition spaces, and governmental politics, Banerjee reinforced the work of various activist groups, including the Alaska Wilderness League and Greenpeace, who in recent years have focused their energies on protecting the Arctic from oil drilling and stopping Canadian tar sands exploitation. A further example of this collaboration is Banerjee's *Caribou Migration I* (2002), which shows a herd traveling over the frozen Coleen River in the ANWR, its

Wilderness League office in Washington, DC, a national conservation organization fully dedicated to conservation of Alaska's wild places. I was already working with AWL since 2001, and was contributing my images for the campaign and also visited DC several times to lobby Congress. The debate was coming up on March 19. Alaska Wilderness League gave a copy of the book to Senator Boxer who was to lead the opponent voice on the Senate floor against drilling in the Arctic Refuge." E-mail to the author, June 23, 2015.

73 Banerjee wrote this caption to accompany a photograph of a buff-breasted sandpiper before the Senate debate: "This species, a long-distance traveler that migrates each year from Argentina to the Arctic Refuge coastal plain to nest and rear their young, is one of the top five bird species at greatest risk if their habitat is disturbed." After the Senate vote, the Smithsonian edited the caption to read: "Buff-Breasted Sandpiper/Coastal Plain of the Jago River." See Tricia Louvar, "Pressing Forward: Arctic Refuge Photography by Subhankar Banerjee," *Orion*, January/February 2004, https://orionmagazine.org/article/pressing-forward/. For the larger context of the controversial political reception and censorship of Banerjee's work when it was displayed at the Smithsonian, see Dunaway, "Reframing the Last Frontier."

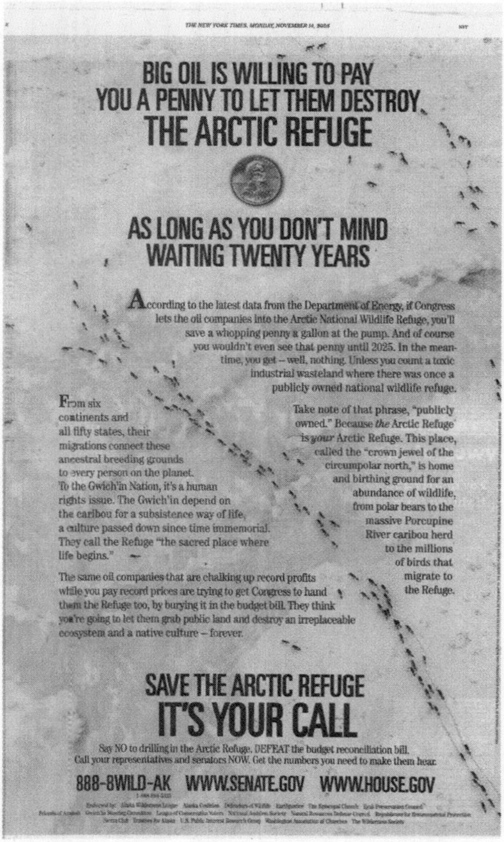

Political advertisement with Subhankar Banerjee's 2002 photograph *Caribou Migration I*, in the *New York Times*, November 2005

aerial viewpoint emphasizing the connectedness of animal life and land as an integrated ecosystem. Banerjee put this image to task as part of a carefully considered political campaign mounted in the pages of the *New York Times* in November 2005, in collaboration with US environmental NGOs, including Alaska Wilderness League, Natural Resources Defense Council, and Earthjustice, and endorsed by the Gwich'in Steering Committee. The ad asked readers to take responsibility for the "public" land of ANWR, in part by contacting Senate and House representatives to voice opposition to its proposed sell-off to the energy industry.

Banerjee's work forms part of a movement that links climate-change threats in the Far North to the oil and gas industry in the United States: connecting his photography to environmental movements produces a network of visuality that exerts pressure on governmental politics. This results in an "image complex," which, as described by Meg McLagan and Yates McKee, identifies "the channels of circulation along which cultural forms travel, the nature of the campaigns that frame them, and the discursive platforms that display and encode them in specific truth modes."[74] Banerjee's work opens up channels connecting environmentalist photojournalism, grassroots activism, and media imagery; discourses of art, science, politics, and Indigenous community groups—corresponding to ecology's very definition as the science of connection. It thus adds further momentum to the collective will to act, both against the oil and natural gas rush in the Arctic and for native rights. And it is the visual legibility of his images that renders them capable of addressing multiple audiences and constituencies.

On May 14, 2015, Banerjee's iconic polar bear image made another appearance, this time on *Democracy Now!*, accompanying a video interview with the artist-activist regarding the Obama administration's recent decision, opposed by many environmentalists, to approve Shell's request to conduct offshore drilling in the Chuckchi Sea, which scientists estimate contains approximately fifteen billion barrels of oil.[75] In his interview with Amy Goodman, Banerjee explained his support of protestors fighting to stop Shell's drilling plans, including the "kayaktivists" blocking Shell's oil rig off Seattle's coast before it headed to the Arctic. The flotilla constituted a protest action by the "Shell No" coalition, comprising environmentalist and activist groups like 350Seattle, the Mosquito Fleet, Rising Tide, Bayan USA, and the Backbone Campaign. Given the likelihood of industrial accidents in waters where there's inadequate infrastructure for cleanup operations, the presidential decision supporting oil drilling can only be "irresponsible and reckless," according to Banerjee, placing "a national and an international ecological treasure" at unnecessary risk—and in fact the governmental approval was rescinded months later owing to environmental concerns.[76] Throughout the struggle, Banerjee's polar bear has come to figure metonymically as an image of precarious survival, and equally one of popular resistance, visualizing the terms of the wider debate around the manifold impacts of climate change, as it documents a threatened life-form endemic to the biodiverse Arctic.

74 McLagan and McKee, introduction to *Sensible Politics*, 12.

75 See Nadia Purpis, "Chorus of Outrage as Obama Administration Approves Arctic Drilling for Shell Oil," *Common Dreams*, April 1, 2015, http://www.commondreams.org/news/2015/04/01/chorus-outrage-obama-administration-approves-arctic-drilling-shell-oil.

76 "'Irresponsible & Reckless': Environmentalists Decry Obama's Approval for Shell Drilling in Arctic," *Democracy Now!*, May 14, 2015, http://www.democracynow.org/2015/5/14/irresponsible_reckless_environmentalists_decry_obamas_approval.

The Politics of Legibility

By employing visual forms that emphasize legibility over experimental imagery or conceptualist opacity, the photography of both the Argos Collective and Banerjee takes on a populist dimension. Both models distinguish themselves from the Western avant-garde's politics of representation—its attempts to revolutionize modes of perception through unconventional, experimental aesthetics—which, however, tend to cater to exclusive audiences versed in the highly specialized discourses of contemporary art. In contrast, this embrace of legibility, privileging the representation of politics rather than the politics of representation, recognizes the imperative to directly visualize the growing crisis of habitat loss, species extinction, environmental calamity, and mass displacement. As such, it invests in the potential of that imagery to reach wide audiences via accessible media, inclusive education, and informative framing devices, which can better contribute to social transformation in the present, unlike those forms of artistic specialization presented in galleries. This openness extends as well to sites of exhibition: Banerjee's photography, for instance, has been shown by such diverse hosts as the California Academy of Sciences, the Smithsonian Institution, and contemporary art institutions (such as in Nottingham Contemporary's 2015 exhibition "Rights of Nature: Art and Ecology in the Americas"). It has, in addition, been featured in nature magazines such as *Orion*, *Audubon*, and *Sierra*, and independent media websites like *TomDispatch*, *Truthout*, *Common Dreams*, and *Democracy Now!*, where its aesthetic versatility—and its image complex—allows it to fit into this expanded field of reception. At the same time, his work has a representational and political complexity not shared by the visuality and discourse of the Argos Collective or conventional conservationism, as found in the photographic illustrations of media platforms like *National Geographic*, to which it might also occasionally bear superficial similarity in terms of composition, image style, and referential lucidity.

In contrast to photography and its histories that emphasize landscape as an anthropocentric enterprise, Banerjee's work creatively approximates what Bruno Latour calls "hybrid" formations, by bridging cultures and natures, the pictorial and the geophysical, the image and the trace, the photograph and the text.[77] The result restructures perception so that it no longer reaffirms human sovereignty over nature, which has defined photography's long-standing focus on human subjects (from Nadar to the Argos Collective), or its production of aestheticized landscapes

77 See Latour, *We Have Never Been Modern*, 42. He argues that in addition to the "purifying" practices that characterize modernity, there are other "hybrid" models that mix politics, science, technology, and nature, which open our culture anew to others past and present.

as human-constructed zones of experience (from Ansel Adams to Andreas Gursky).[78] Conversely, Banerjee's photography and texts, whether focusing on caribou and coal or Yukaghirs ice fishing in Siberia, reveal a world of ecologies that are interrelated as much as conflictual. On the one hand, his work provides a post-anthropocentric account of biodiversity, part of which is to depict a more egalitarian composition of a common world (again in Latour's terms);[79] on the other, it forms a critical view of the increasingly destructive effects of corporate and industrial activity on nonhuman life-forms and their environs.

Banerjee's writing contributes further to this speculative discourse, expressed visually as an inclusive space for nonhuman life and natural environments. Consider his 2012 essay, "Ought We Not Establish 'Access to Food' as a Species Right?," which grants a legal-status claim to his photography's animal subjects. There, Banerjee defends his rights-expanding proposal by referencing the precedents of the World People's Conference on Climate Change in Bolivia in 2010, attended by some thirty thousand people from over one hundred countries, and the UN resolution of the same year that declared, for the first time, access to clean water and sanitation as "a fundamental human right," with 122 nations voting in favor, none against, and forty-one abstaining (the United States and Canada among the latter).[80] Banerjee contends that access to food as an animal-rights claim is not only necessary for the survival of other-than-human life, but is also at the root of the struggle of First Nations peoples against habitat loss caused by the industrial exploitation of their lands: "By making this claim they are fighting to protect access to food for human and non-human communities—caribou for the Gwich'in, and cotton grass for the caribou, during calving time."[81] In 2009, Indigenous representatives from the Arctic, North America, Asia, Pacific, Latin America, Africa, Caribbean, and Russia met in Alaska to demand the "inherent

78 Banerjee made this observation on photography and human subjects in his presentation at a conference I organized on the release of the issue of *Third Text*, "Contemporary Art and the Politics of Ecology," at University College London, March 2, 2013. On the typical dominance of human-portrait photography in current major Western exhibitions, see Subhankar Banerjee, "Ought We Not Establish 'Access to Food' as a Species Right?," *Third Text*, no. 120 (January 2013): 34; and Liz Wells, *Land Matters: Landscape Photography, Culture and Identity* (London: I.B. Tauris, 2011), 2. The traditional anthropocentric bias of photography theory is also expressed in Deborah Bright, "Of Mother Nature and Marlboro Men: An Inquiry into the Cultural Meanings of Landscape Photography," in *The Contest of Meaning*, ed. Richard Bolton (Cambridge, MA: MIT Press, 1989): "Whatever the aesthetic merits, every representation of landscape is also a record of human values and actions imposed on the land over time" (126).

79 See Latour, *Politics of Nature*, 8.

80 See "In Historic Vote, UN Declares Water a Fundamental Human Right," *Democracy Now!*, July 29, 2010, http://www.democracynow.org/2010/7/29/in_historic_vote_un_declares_access.

rights of Indigenous Peoples," including the "rights to our lands, territories, environment and natural resources," and to declare their traditional lands as Food Sovereignty Areas, "free from extractive industries, deforestation and chemical-based industrial food production systems."[82] By extension, Banerjee's photographs of caribou and snow geese can be considered as speculative "portraits" of rights-bearing subjects, rather than as natural objects whose value is defined by human criteria of usefulness, pragmatic or aesthetic. In this regard, his work visualizes one modeling of an interspecies democratization of politics, working toward the composition of a common world—the result of an image complex formed out of photography, political theory and practice, legal testimony, activism, and exhibitions between the fields of science, visual culture, and environmental humanities. Banerjee's politicization of visual culture exists at a far remove from the fatalism of climate-refugee narratives, and shows that resigned adaptation to the dislocations of climate change is hardly our only option.

81 Banerjee, "'Access to Food' as a Species Right," 38. For further consideration of contemporary art's relation to this judicial discourse, see my essay for the exhibition "Rights of Nature" at Nottingham Contemporary, "Rights of Nature: The Art and Politics of Earth Jurisprudence."

82 Indigenous Peoples' Global Summit on Climate Change, *The Anchorage Declaration*, April 24, 2009, http://library.arcticportal.org/635.

The Post-natural Condition

Chapter 3

Art after Nature?

The night sky never looked as different as it does in *Black Shoals Stock Market Planetarium* (2001/4). For the mixed-media installation, London-based artists Lise Autogena and Joshua Portway projected an array of constellations onto the inner surface of a large dome hanging above beanbags where viewers could sit and gaze upward; however, the heavenly bodies correspond not to real suns or planets, but rather to publicly traded companies, as a computer program translates the real-time financial activity of the world's stock exchanges into glimmering stars. Included in the 2001 group exhibition "Art and Money Online" at Tate Britain, the piece connected to a Reuters market-data feed; in 2004, at the Nikolaj Kunsthal, Copenhagen Contemporary Art Centre, it was wired to the local stock market. The points of light flash brightly whenever their stocks are traded, gathering into constellations or dispersing according to market momentum, only to be preyed on by digital creatures. Designed by the artificial-life researcher Cefn Hoile, evolutionary algorithms—computations that allow the entities to selectively reproduce, mutate, and recombine over time—program these critters to feed on the energy of the artificial astral bodies. Nourished, they grow into complex beings, composite structures of luminescence, and regenerate in order to adapt and survive. The famine of a market downturn leads them to die out, overcome by the darkness.

But this extraordinary ecosystem is also, pointedly, devoid of natural life. The title of Autogena and Portway's project puns on the Black-Scholes option-pricing formula, developed in 1973 by University of Chicago professors Fischer Black and Myron

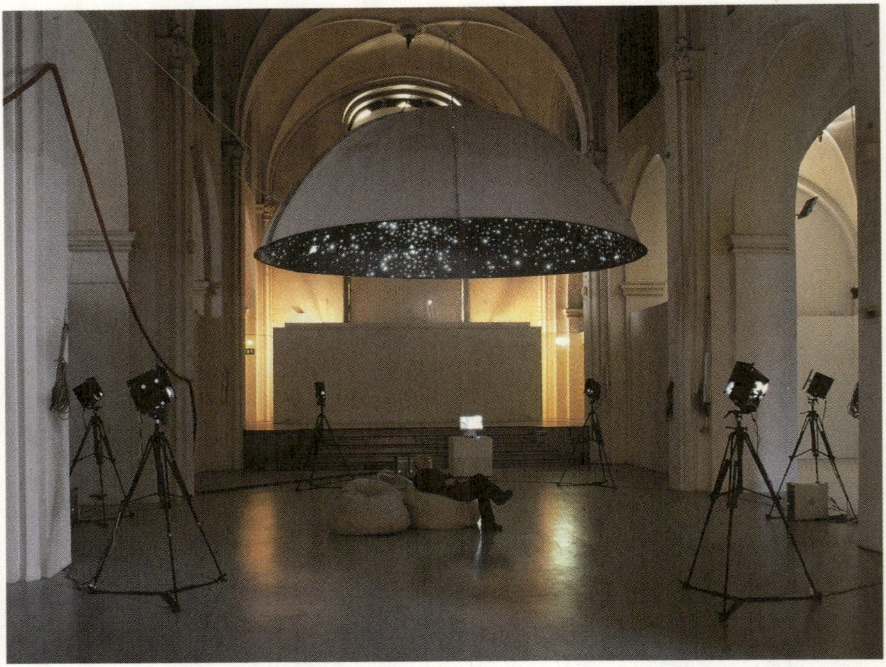

Lise Autogena and Joshua Portway, *Black Shoals Stock Market Planetarium*, 2004

Scholes, which set the course for an unprecedented trading of financial derivatives. These market-based contracts contributed to an increasing abstraction in the world of finance, and the Black-Scholes formula lent scientific credibility and economic legitimacy (both later revealed to be erroneous) to the activities of the Chicago Board Options Exchange, also founded in 1973 as the first marketplace for trading listed options. In the mid-'90s, this exchange would also expand the trading of derivatives from stocks to natural events, such as futures that bet on the outcome of regional temperature fluctuations, rainfall intensity, drought conditions, and hurricanes. These mechanisms amounted to financial strategies for corporations to minimize risk to their operations and maximize economic returns, even though this trading is mostly done by speculators without concern for economic or ecological sustainability.[1] The title of the artwork thus casts a negative pall over such financial logic, evoking the automated groupthink of schools of fish as well as the unanticipated and ominous sandbars that sink ships.

1 See Donald MacKenzie, *An Engine, Not a Camera: How Financial Models Shape Markets* (Cambridge, MA: MIT Press, 2006).

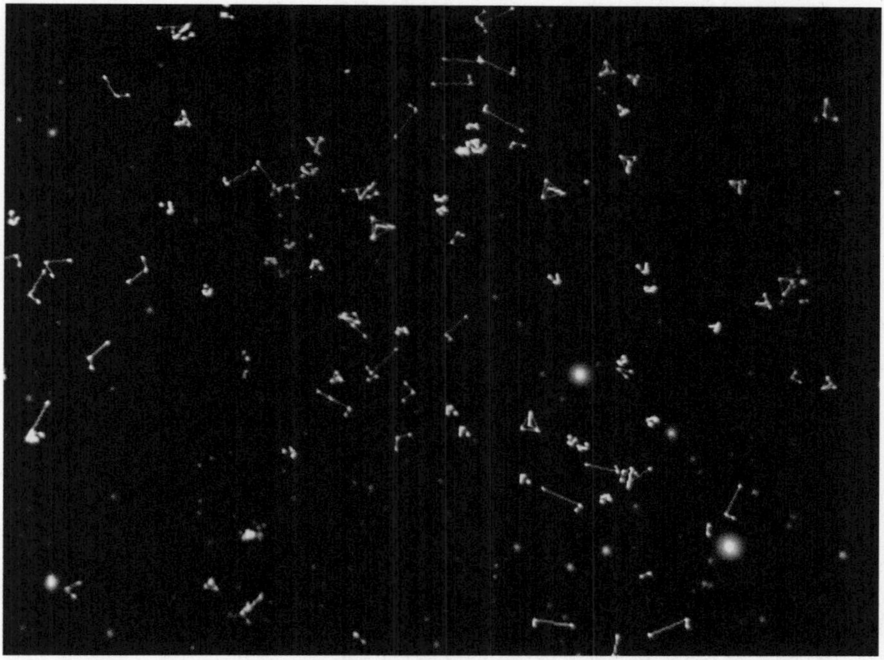

Lise Autogena and Joshua Portway, *Black Shoals Stock Market Planetarium*, 2001; detail

Indeed, *Black Shoals Stock Market Planetarium* reduces such complex mathematical-financial calculations to the level of the seductive visuals of a video game, whereby the ravenous animal programs simulate the speculative passions that have led to real-life fortunes and much suffering. It equally intimates the pseudoscience of astrology, which nonetheless might be closer to the heavens and earthly ecosystems than derivatives-based finance. Either way, the piece comments directly on our grim socioeconomic condition. Building on an idea of Portway's, Hoile stated, "The creatures' relationship with their artificial world of stars is a mirror of our relationship with the financial markets—they strive to survive, competing with each other in a world whose complexity they are too simple to fathom."[2] In other words, when viewers watch this cannibalistic drama unfold, they are peering at their own contemporary world: these creatures are nothing but a distilled expression of self-entrepreneurship—approximating what Michel Foucault, in his

2 Cefn Hoile, "Black Shoals: Evolving Organisms in a World of Financial Data," *Black Shoals Stock Market Planetarium*, accessed October 29, 2015, http://www.blackshoals.net/ALife.html.

later writings on biopolitics, called "homo economicus," the subject of neoliberalism, the dominant economic condition of our times.[3] The piece is not just a means of visualizing data, it's also an existential model that shows predatory life under advanced capitalism, within a zone where nothing else matters—not bodies, nature, social life, religion, or aesthetics. As Naomi Klein writes, "This, without a doubt, is neoliberalism's single most damaging legacy: the realization of its bleak vision has isolated us enough from one another that it became possible to convince us that we are not just incapable of self-preservation but fundamentally *not worth saving*"—owing to the conviction that, at its basis, human nature is nothing but competitive greed, murderous envy, and survivalist selfishness.[4] The fact that the creatures have repeatedly died out during successive exhibitions leads to the extreme proposal that the *Black Shoals* project be taken as a dark allegorical warning about our precarious existence as a species whose activities are putting its very viability at risk.[5]

Picturing a lifeworld merged with capital, Autogena and Portway's starry sky presents the activity of the stock market via a technology that naturalizes perception, translating the processing of economic data into the visualization of the universe. Insofar as the piece is upfront about its technological apparatus, it also reveals the artificiality of that financial-perceptual system, exposing in turn the vulnerability of life exposed to a purely economic, and falsely naturalized, rationality. The work thus invokes and troubles the idea that "the market is in human nature," a neoliberal proposition that Fredric Jameson has said "cannot be allowed to stand unchallenged," arguing that to contest the ideology of the market as a biological fact is "the most crucial terrain of ideological struggle in our time."[6] Writing in

3 The term was first used in the 1880s by John Stuart Mill in relation to the self-interested subject. See also Michel Foucault, *The Birth of Biopolitics: Lectures at the Collège de France, 1978–1979*, trans. Graham Burchell (New York: Palgrave Macmillan, 2008), 226; David Harvey, *A Brief History of Neoliberalism* (Oxford: Oxford University Press, 2005); and Jason Read, "A Genealogy of Homo-Economicus: Neoliberalism and the Production of Subjectivity," *Foucault Studies*, no. 6 (February 2009): 25–36. For further analysis of the political economy of Autogena and Portway's piece, see Brian Holmes, "Is It Written in the Stars? Global Finance, Precarious Destinies," *Continental Drift: The Other Side of Neoliberal Globalization* (blog), November 6, 2009, https://brianholmes.wordpress.com/2009/11/06/is-it-written-in-the-stars/.

4 Klein, *This Changes Everything*, 62. For a counterargument about the generosity of human nature, as seen in the selfless care for others in times of environmental crisis, see Rebecca Solnit, *A Paradise Built in Hell: The Extraordinary Communities That Arise in Disaster* (New York: Penguin, 2010).

5 It is hard not to relate this conclusion to the argument of conservation scientists that we are in the midst of a global "mass extinction event" as a result of human activity. See Kolbert, *The Sixth Extinction*.

6 Fredric Jameson, "Postmodernism and the Market" (1990), in *Postmodernism: or, The Cultural Logic of Late Capitalism* (Durham, NC: Duke University Press, 1991), 263.

1990, Jameson was mostly concerned about the naturalization of finance, but around the same time, the first glimmerings of the inverse of this neoliberal doctrine emerged: the financialization of nature, which threatens to have even greater consequences.

The process began when the Reagan administration, reeling from the recession of the '70s, developed a science policy that put the biotech revolution in motion.[7] As a consequence, over the following decades the "limits to growth" environmentalism of the '70s became gradually marginalized and a new paradigm was inaugurated, in which life itself was mobilized to save free-market capitalism from the threat of regulatory system change, in the name of ecological sustainability. No longer seen as finite, nature was conceptualized as technologically reproducible, which led to the biogenetic capitalism of the '80s and '90s, when individual genes, cells, proteins, and bodies were first commodified for pharmaceutical, medical, military, and agricultural applications, from gene therapy to biological weapons. As part of this development, nature became prey to the financial markets: transformed into an object of venture capital speculation ("nature as an accumulation strategy," as geographer Neil Smith called it), its value came to be defined economically based on the promise of profits as determined by derivatives in the stock market. Natural disasters, including the predicted effects of anthropogenic climate change, have also been commodified according to this logic, whereby *environmental* crisis becomes first and foremost an *economic* crisis, to be addressed via economic means (in other words, to battle deforestation, we must financialize trees; to save rhinos, we must create a market for their horns). Capitalist catastrophism, as sociologist Melinda Cooper explains, tends to view crisis as an integral part of an endless Schumpeterian process of breakdown, reproduction, and innovation. According to this logic, the life of species and habitats, defined by a continuous cycle of death and rebirth, extinction and regeneration, becomes a model for the new bio-economy, thereby providing the conceptual means to overcome the finite resources of the fossil-fuel system of the earlier Fordist model of capitalism.[8] Such thinking underlies the 1997 Kyoto Protocol and related efforts to stem climate change via market mechanisms—including emissions trading, pollution permit systems, and carbon taxation. Driven by the interests of developed countries, these strategies turn catastrophe itself into a profitable opportunity, while each passing year sets a new record for CO_2 emissions and a still warmer world.

With environmental calamity forecast for our near future, it has become all the more urgent to

7 Such policy "respond[ed] point by point to the ecological and biospheric limits painstakingly detailed by the Club of Rome" in *Limits to Growth*. Melinda Cooper, "Life beyond the Limits," in *Life as Surplus*, 18.

8 Ibid., 15–50.

dismantle the logic that sees and treats nature as a financial object, viewing its breakdown as an economic opportunity—the most recent step in a long history of colonizing people and the environment.[9] Artists and activists have not only addressed this task, dramatizing its cruel effects—including mass species extinction—in experimental media projects like Autogena and Portway's, they have also attempted to imagine and realize the definancialization of nature, whether through innovative legal constructions of the commons on a global as well as local scale, or through inventing and implementing collective experiments in sustainable living according to a postcapitalist ethos. As we move from the sky and heavens to the workings of the soil and earth—as in projects by Nils Norman and the Laboratory of Insurrectionary Imagination—we witness a new movement toward the materialization of utopias once thought to be ungraspable and beyond reach, or politically misguided and dangerously authoritarian. Now these proposals for creative—and importantly, self-critical—alternatives are more necessary than ever.

The Atmosphere as World Heritage Site

With *Public Smog* (2004–ongoing), Amy Balkin furthers the artistic exploration of the complex systems that link nature and finance. The project details the Sisyphean attempts of the San Francisco–based artist to set up a clean-air "park" in the atmosphere, one whose location, dimensions, and duration are contingent on the contracts of the emission credits purchased by the artist.[10] Balkin mimics the market-based approach to controlling carbon pollution (favored by the Kyoto Protocol), which provides economic incentives for reducing greenhouse gas emissions. According to this logic, a central authority (such as a state) sets a cap on the amount of pollution and sells emissions permits on the stock market that can be traded among companies, while intending to lower allowances over time. The real-world results, however, have been far from ideal. While the 2010 UN Convention on Biological Diversity supported "innovative financial mechanisms" to mitigate biodiversity loss, NGOs like Carbon Trade Watch—linked on Balkin's website—point out how such economic instruments fail to address the drivers of environmental and social damage, and instead merely create markets for wealth accumulation without mitigating overall emissions.

9 On the long history of the expropriation and colonization of nature and the commons, see Peter Linebaugh, *Stop Thief! The Commons, Enclosures, and Resistance* (Oakland: PM Press, 2014).

10 *Public Smog* was shown at dOCUMENTA (13) in 2012 and more recently at Nottingham Contemporary in the 2015 exhibition "Rights of Nature." For more on dOCUMENTA (13), see chapter 7.

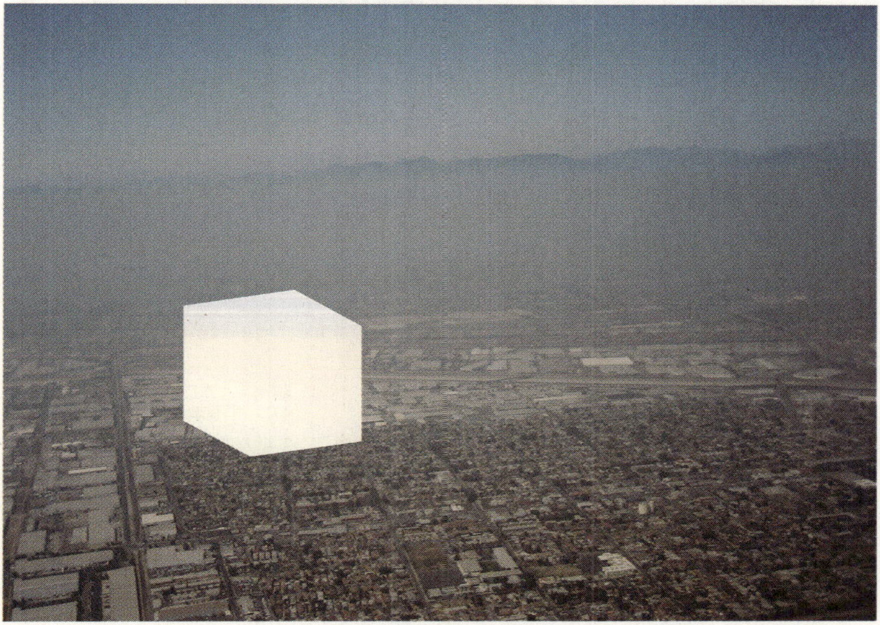

Amy Balkin, *Public Smog over Los Angeles*, 2004

Balkin not only acquired carbon offsets for *Public Smog*, she also subverted, if on a small scale, the cap-and-trade system, by withholding and retiring those emissions credits from industrial use. The strategy helped her to create "clean-air parks" in the atmosphere. A twenty-one-minute slide show on the *Public Smog* website shows the financial and legal documents that created these parks, and excerpts from letters Balkin wrote to traders to acquire offsets and their sale contracts. Balkin opened the "Lower Park" in California's South Coast Air Quality Management District for the month of June in 2004; the "Upper Park," over the European Union, existed for a year beginning in the fall of 2006, then again over the United States from April to August 2010. Expanding the geographical possibilities of her project during a residency at the Centre Culturel Français Blaise-Cendrars in Douala, Balkin installed a series of thirty billboards across Cameroon's capital to announce the inauguration of a clear-air park over Africa, which never came to pass, as the artist's disillusionment with her strategy grew, owing to its proximity to the very logic she meant to contest.[11] Nonetheless, as a critique of the

11 "I was feeling uncertain about continuing with market-based activities as an approach to open the park, and at the time didn't find a pursuable strategy." Amy Balkin, e-mail to the author, August 5, 2015.

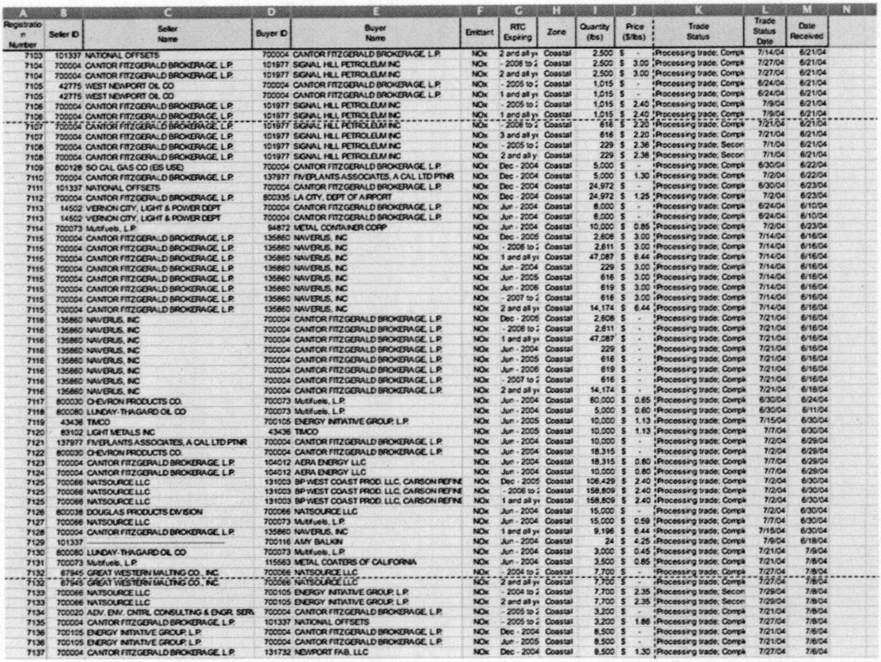

Registration Number	Seller ID	Seller Name	Buyer ID	Buyer Name	Emittant	RTC Expiring	Zone	Quantity (lbs)	Price ($/lbs)	Trade Status	Trade Status Date	Date Received
7103	101337	NATIONAL OFFSETS	700004	CANTOR FITZGERALD BROKERAGE, L.P.	NOx	2 and all y	Coastal	2,500	$ -	Processing trade; Compl	7/14/04	6/21/04
7104	700004	CANTOR FITZGERALD BROKERAGE, L.P.	101977	SIGNAL HILL PETROLEUM INC	NOx	- 2006 to 2	Coastal	2,500	$ 3.00	Processing trade; Compl	7/27/04	6/21/04
7104	700004	CANTOR FITZGERALD BROKERAGE, L.P.	101977	SIGNAL HILL PETROLEUM INC	NOx	2 and all y	Coastal	2,500	$ 3.00	Processing trade; Compl	7/27/04	6/21/04
7105	42775	WEST NEWPORT OIL CO	700004	CANTOR FITZGERALD BROKERAGE, L.P.	NOx	- 2005 to 2	Coastal	1,015	$ -	Processing trade; Compl	6/24/04	6/21/04
7105	42775	WEST NEWPORT OIL CO	700004	CANTOR FITZGERALD BROKERAGE, L.P.	NOx	1 and all y	Coastal	1,015	$ -	Processing trade; Compl	6/24/04	6/21/04
7106	700004	CANTOR FITZGERALD BROKERAGE, L.P.	101977	SIGNAL HILL PETROLEUM INC	NOx	- 2005 to 2	Coastal	1,015	$ 2.40	Processing trade; Compl	7/9/04	6/21/04
7106	700004	CANTOR FITZGERALD BROKERAGE, L.P.	101977	SIGNAL HILL PETROLEUM INC	NOx	1 and all y	Coastal	1,015	$ 2.40	Processing trade; Compl	7/9/04	6/21/04
7107	700004	CANTOR FITZGERALD BROKERAGE, L.P.	101977	SIGNAL HILL PETROLEUM INC	NOx	- 2006 to 2	Coastal	616	$ 2.20	Processing trade; Compl	7/21/04	6/21/04
7107	700004	CANTOR FITZGERALD BROKERAGE, L.P.	101977	SIGNAL HILL PETROLEUM INC	NOx	3 and all y	Coastal	616	$ 2.20	Processing trade; Compl	7/21/04	6/21/04
7108	700004	CANTOR FITZGERALD BROKERAGE, L.P.	101977	SIGNAL HILL PETROLEUM INC	NOx	- 2005 to 2	Coastal	229	$ 2.36	Processing trade; Secon	7/1/04	6/21/04
7108	700004	CANTOR FITZGERALD BROKERAGE, L.P.	101977	SIGNAL HILL PETROLEUM INC	NOx	2 and all y	Coastal	229	$ 2.36	Processing trade; Secon	7/1/04	6/21/04
7109	800128	SO CAL GAS CO (EIS USE)	700004	CANTOR FITZGERALD BROKERAGE, L.P.	NOx	Dec - 2004	Coastal	5,000	$ -	Processing trade; Compl	6/30/04	6/22/04
7110	700004	CANTOR FITZGERALD BROKERAGE, L.P.	137977	FIVEPLANTS ASSOCIATES, A CAL LTD PTNR	NOx	Dec - 2004	Coastal	5,000	$ 1.30	Processing trade; Compl	7/2/04	6/22/04
7111	101337	NATIONAL OFFSETS	700004	CANTOR FITZGERALD BROKERAGE, L.P.	NOx	Dec - 2004	Coastal	24,972	$ -	Processing trade; Compl	6/30/04	6/23/04
7112	700004	CANTOR FITZGERALD BROKERAGE, L.P.	800335	LA CITY, DEPT OF AIRPORT	NOx	Dec - 2004	Coastal	24,972	$ 1.25	Processing trade; Compl	7/2/04	6/23/04
7113	14502	VERNON CITY, LIGHT & POWER DEPT	700004	CANTOR FITZGERALD BROKERAGE, L.P.	NOx	Jun - 2004	Coastal	8,000	$ -	Processing trade; Compl	6/24/04	6/10/04
7113	14502	VERNON CITY, LIGHT & POWER DEPT	700004	CANTOR FITZGERALD BROKERAGE, L.P.	NOx	Jun - 2004	Coastal	8,000	$ -	Processing trade; Compl	6/24/04	6/10/04
7114	700073	Multifuels, L.P.	94872	METAL CONTAINER CORP	NOx	Jun - 2004	Coastal	10,000	$ 0.85	Processing trade; Compl	7/2/04	6/23/04
7115	700004	CANTOR FITZGERALD BROKERAGE, L.P.	135860	NAVERUS, INC	NOx	Dec - 2005	Coastal	2,608	$ 3.00	Processing trade; Compl	7/14/04	6/16/04
7115	700004	CANTOR FITZGERALD BROKERAGE, L.P.	135860	NAVERUS, INC	NOx	- 2006 to 2	Coastal	2,611	$ 3.00	Processing trade; Compl	7/14/04	6/16/04
7115	700004	CANTOR FITZGERALD BROKERAGE, L.P.	135860	NAVERUS, INC	NOx	1 and all y	Coastal	47,087	$ 6.44	Processing trade; Compl	7/14/04	6/16/04
7115	700004	CANTOR FITZGERALD BROKERAGE, L.P.	135860	NAVERUS, INC	NOx	Jun - 2004	Coastal	229	$ 3.00	Processing trade; Compl	7/14/04	6/16/04
7115	700004	CANTOR FITZGERALD BROKERAGE, L.P.	135860	NAVERUS, INC	NOx	Jun - 2005	Coastal	616	$ 3.00	Processing trade; Compl	7/14/04	6/16/04
7115	700004	CANTOR FITZGERALD BROKERAGE, L.P.	135860	NAVERUS, INC	NOx	Jun - 2006	Coastal	619	$ 3.00	Processing trade; Compl	7/14/04	6/16/04
7115	700004	CANTOR FITZGERALD BROKERAGE, L.P.	135860	NAVERUS, INC	NOx	- 2007 to 2	Coastal	616	$ 3.00	Processing trade; Compl	7/14/04	6/16/04
7115	700004	CANTOR FITZGERALD BROKERAGE, L.P.	135860	NAVERUS, INC	NOx	2 and all y	Coastal	14,174	$ 6.44	Processing trade; Compl	7/14/04	6/16/04
7116	135860	NAVERUS, INC	700004	CANTOR FITZGERALD BROKERAGE, L.P.	NOx	Dec - 2005	Coastal	2,608	$ -	Processing trade; Compl	7/21/04	6/16/04
7116	135860	NAVERUS, INC	700004	CANTOR FITZGERALD BROKERAGE, L.P.	NOx	- 2006 to 2	Coastal	2,611	$ -	Processing trade; Compl	7/21/04	6/16/04
7116	135860	NAVERUS, INC	700004	CANTOR FITZGERALD BROKERAGE, L.P.	NOx	1 and all y	Coastal	47,087	$ -	Processing trade; Compl	7/21/04	6/16/04
7116	135860	NAVERUS, INC	700004	CANTOR FITZGERALD BROKERAGE, L.P.	NOx	Jun - 2004	Coastal	229	$ -	Processing trade; Compl	7/21/04	6/16/04
7116	135860	NAVERUS, INC	700004	CANTOR FITZGERALD BROKERAGE, L.P.	NOx	Jun - 2005	Coastal	616	$ -	Processing trade; Compl	7/21/04	6/16/04
7116	135860	NAVERUS, INC	700004	CANTOR FITZGERALD BROKERAGE, L.P.	NOx	Jun - 2006	Coastal	619	$ -	Processing trade; Compl	7/21/04	6/16/04
7116	135860	NAVERUS, INC	700004	CANTOR FITZGERALD BROKERAGE, L.P.	NOx	- 2007 to 2	Coastal	616	$ -	Processing trade; Compl	7/21/04	6/16/04
7116	135860	NAVERUS, INC	700004	CANTOR FITZGERALD BROKERAGE, L.P.	NOx	2 and all y	Coastal	14,174	$ -	Processing trade; Compl	7/21/04	6/16/04
7117	800030	CHEVRON PRODUCTS CO.	700073	Multifuels, L.P.	NOx	Jun - 2004	Coastal	60,000	$ 0.65	Processing trade; Compl	6/30/04	6/24/04
7118	800080	LUNDAY-THAGARD OIL CO	700073	Multifuels, L.P.	NOx	Jun - 2004	Coastal	5,000	$ 0.60	Processing trade; Compl	6/30/04	6/11/04
7119	43436	TIMCO	700105	ENERGY INITIATIVE GROUP, L.P.	NOx	Jun - 2005	Coastal	10,000	$ 1.13	Processing trade; Compl	7/15/04	6/30/04
7120	83102	LIGHT METALS INC	43436	TIMCO	NOx	Jun - 2005	Coastal	10,000	$ 1.13	Processing trade; Compl	7/7/04	6/30/04
7121	137977	FIVEPLANTS ASSOCIATES, A CAL LTD PTNR	700004	CANTOR FITZGERALD BROKERAGE, L.P.	NOx	Jun - 2004	Coastal	10,000	$ -	Processing trade; Compl	7/2/04	6/29/04
7122	800030	CHEVRON PRODUCTS CO.	700004	CANTOR FITZGERALD BROKERAGE, L.P.	NOx	Jun - 2004	Coastal	18,315	$ -	Processing trade; Compl	7/2/04	6/29/04
7123	700004	CANTOR FITZGERALD BROKERAGE, L.P.	104012	AERA ENERGY LLC	NOx	Jun - 2004	Coastal	18,315	$ 0.80	Processing trade; Compl	7/7/04	6/29/04
7124	700004	CANTOR FITZGERALD BROKERAGE, L.P.	104012	AERA ENERGY LLC	NOx	Jun - 2004	Coastal	10,000	$ 0.80	Processing trade; Compl	7/7/04	6/29/04
7125	700066	NATSOURCE LLC	131003	BP WEST COAST PROD. LLC, CARSON REFINE	NOx	Dec - 2005	Coastal	106,429	$ 2.40	Processing trade; Compl	7/2/04	6/30/04
7125	700066	NATSOURCE LLC	131003	BP WEST COAST PROD. LLC, CARSON REFINE	NOx	- 2006 to 2	Coastal	158,809	$ 2.40	Processing trade; Compl	7/2/04	6/30/04
7125	700066	NATSOURCE LLC	131003	BP WEST COAST PROD. LLC, CARSON REFINE	NOx	1 and all y	Coastal	158,809	$ 2.40	Processing trade; Compl	7/2/04	6/30/04
7126	800038	DOUGLAS PRODUCTS DIVISION	700066	NATSOURCE LLC	NOx	Jun - 2004	Coastal	15,000	$ -	Processing trade; Compl	7/2/04	6/30/04
7127	700066	NATSOURCE LLC	700073	Multifuels, L.P.	NOx	Jun - 2004	Coastal	15,000	$ 0.59	Processing trade; Compl	7/7/04	6/30/04
7128	700004	CANTOR FITZGERALD BROKERAGE, L.P.	135860	NAVERUS, INC	NOx	1 and all y	Coastal	9,196	$ 6.44	Processing trade; Compl	7/15/04	6/30/04
7129	101337	———	700116	AMY BALKIN	NOx	Jun - 2004	Coastal	24	$ 4.25	Processing trade; Compl	7/9/04	6/18/04
7130	800080	LUNDAY-THAGARD OIL CO	700073	Multifuels, L.P.	NOx	Jun - 2004	Coastal	3,000	$ 0.45	Processing trade; Compl	7/21/04	7/9/04
7131	700073	Multifuels, L.P.	115563	METAL COATERS OF CALIFORNIA	NOx	Jun - 2004	Coastal	3,500	$ 0.85	Processing trade; Compl	7/21/04	7/8/04
7132	67945	GREAT WESTERN MALTING CO., INC.	700066	NATSOURCE LLC	NOx	- 2004 to 2	Coastal	7,700	$ -	Processing trade; Compl	7/27/04	7/8/04
7132	67945	GREAT WESTERN MALTING CO., INC.	700066	NATSOURCE LLC	NOx	2 and all y	Coastal	7,700	$ -	Processing trade; Compl	7/27/04	7/8/04
7133	700066	NATSOURCE LLC	700105	ENERGY INITIATIVE GROUP, L.P.	NOx	- 2004 to 2	Coastal	7,700	$ 2.35	Processing trade; Secon	7/29/04	7/8/04
7133	700066	NATSOURCE LLC	700105	ENERGY INITIATIVE GROUP, L.P.	NOx	2 and all y	Coastal	7,700	$ 2.35	Processing trade; Secon	7/29/04	7/8/04
7134	700020	ADV. ENV. CNTRL CONSULTING & ENGR. SERV	700004	CANTOR FITZGERALD BROKERAGE, L.P.	NOx	- 2005 to 2	Coastal	3,200	$ -	Processing trade; Compl	7/21/04	7/8/04
7135	700004	CANTOR FITZGERALD BROKERAGE, L.P.	101337	NATIONAL OFFSETS	NOx	- 2005 to 2	Coastal	3,200	$ 1.86	Processing trade; Compl	7/27/04	7/8/04
7136	700105	ENERGY INITIATIVE GROUP, L.P.	700004	CANTOR FITZGERALD BROKERAGE, L.P.	NOx	Dec - 2004	Coastal	8,500	$ -	Processing trade; Compl	7/21/04	7/6/04
7136	700105	ENERGY INITIATIVE GROUP, L.P.	700004	CANTOR FITZGERALD BROKERAGE, L.P.	NOx	Jun - 2005	Coastal	8,500	$ -	Processing trade; Compl	7/21/04	7/6/04
7137	700004	CANTOR FITZGERALD BROKERAGE, L.P.	131732	NEWPORT FAB, LLC	NOx	Dec - 2004	Coastal	8,500	$ 1.30	Processing trade; Compl	7/27/04	7/6/04

Amy Balkin, *Public Smog*, 2004; detail

financial instrumentalization of the environment and climate change, Balkin's project mirrors the approach of eco-activists such as Tim DeChristopher. At a Bureau of Land Management auction in 2008 to parcel out land to oil and gas companies next to national parks in southern Utah, the US activist, inspired by the disruptive tactics of the Yes Men, successfully bid $1.8 million for 22,500 acres without the means or intention to pay for his purchase.[12] Managing to jam the auction's workings, he was fined and jailed for nearly two years for the disruption—even after the US Department of the Interior subsequently voided many of the sales, including most of those that involved DeChristopher, acknowledging that they lacked sufficient prior environmental and scientific review. Using the same logic of turning the system against itself, Balkin's work is no doubt less risky than DeChristopher's direct action as well as more conceptually mediated in casting a self-reflexive, critical regard toward its

12 See Bryan Farrell, "The Monkey-Wrench Prank: An Interview With Tim DeChristopher," *Mother Jones*, November 13, 2009, http://www.motherjones.com/environment/2009/11/monkeywrench-prank-interview-tim-dechristopher; and *Bidder 70*, the 2013 documentary on DeChristopher by Beth Gage and George Gage.

own processes and imagined effectiveness. Still, both share a certain humor expressive of the pleasure of anarchistic intervention, an artistic-activist monkey wrenching that also inspires further momentum in the rejection of nature's financialization.

Also included in *Public Smog* are transcribed snippets of conversations Balkin had with various NGO and governmental bureaucrats regarding the attempt to register the earth's atmosphere as a UNESCO World Heritage Site to protect it against further pollution. This aspect of the work allowed Balkin to raise questions about who is entitled to nominate and enforce such protections, and in turn about the (in)justice of the current system. Some of the responses—"Mmhm, right. Right, right."—indicate the wall of unsympathetic bureaucracy Balkin ran into along the way. One responder, UNESCO legal consultant Francesco Francioni, explained that "the nomination could be possible only if all parties agreed [...] that the atmosphere is a part of the general environment of 'outstanding universal value' and that its conservation is essential to the conservation of the 'territorial' environment of every state"—as if those conclusions were debatable![13]

Since only UNESCO States Parties—countries that have adhered to the World Heritage Convention—can nominate a world heritage site, Balkin invited them, as part of her project for dOCUMENTA (13), to lead a coalition process. She received thirteen responses out of the 186 letters sent, all declining the invitation. One expression of interest came from 'Ana Taufe'ulungaki, Minister of Education, Women's Affairs, and Culture of Tonga, an island nation in the Pacific Ocean, who had given a talk in 2011 titled "Safeguarding of Intangible Cultural Heritage,"[14] even as she acknowledged that her small country, at risk from global warming's rising seas, was insufficiently equipped to begin or lead a coalition effort. To gather public support, Balkin invited visitors to urge their respective countries "to initiate an extraordinary nomination process to inscribe Earth's atmosphere on the UNESCO World Heritage List on an emergency basis," as her freely available postcards explained, to which visitors could add their names and then send on to government representatives of their "Nation." Using language reminiscent of UN bureaucracy and officialdom, these postcards explain the petition:

13 A precedent to Balkin's project, the March 1969 issue of the *Whole Earth Catalog*, edited by Stewart Brand, called for subscribers to write to President Nixon urging the establishment of the entire earth as a national park.

14 Dr. 'Ana Taufe'ulungaki, "Safeguarding of Intangible Cultural Heritage" (keynote address, workshop on safeguarding cultural heritage, Tonga National Cultural Center, Tofoa, March 29, 2011), http://www.mic.gov.to/ministrydepartment/14-govt-ministries/moet/2318-dr-hon-ana-taufeulungaki-safeguarding-of-intangible-cultural-heritage. Thanks to Balkin for pointing this out.

> *Recognizing the outstanding universal value of Earth's Atmosphere, and responding to the formidable threats and risks to its integrity from greenhouse gases, including a forecast global temperature rise of 3 to 6 degrees Celsius by 2100,*
> *Finding it in the common interest to protect the Atmosphere for present and future generations, and acknowledging that its preservation is the duty of the international community,*
> *Further recognizing the impacts of climate change on sites of tangible and intangible natural and cultural heritage currently inscribed on the World Heritage List,*
> *The Nation should undertake and faithfully carry out a coalition-led effort for inscription of Earth's Atmosphere on the World Heritage List, consistent with the aims and goals of the World Heritage Convention.*

In the case of Germany, fifty thousand signed postcards were collected and sent to the country's environmental minister in August 2012, with a further forty thousand going out in September (the month documenta ended); in November, Germany declined the request (as did all the other nations). Other hindrances to this goal of atmospheric protection, which might help explain the general lack of political will, are revealed by *Public Smog* and Balkin's ongoing work.[15] One concerns the virtuality of the project—a park in the air can neither be seen nor exist in any stable state—which mirrors the invisibility and instability of atmospheric carbon dioxide and, indeed, climate change itself; fencing off one small section of the atmosphere for protection is clearly an impossible proposition. "Given the privileging of the landscape as a powerful symbolic image of nature since the Enlightenment," media researcher Julie Doyle observes, "global warming and climate change have limited symbolic resonance, signifiable only when their impact has been seen on the landscape, thus effectively too late."[16] This very invisibility eases the denial of global warming, informing the lack of concern for the state of the earth's atmosphere, and facilitates its similarly abstract economic manipulation, opening onto its potential colonization by private interests.[17] Those outcomes

15 For a 2015 "climate festival" in Melbourne, positioned against Australia's poor record of greenhouse gas reductions and protection of the Great Barrier Reef (nearly listed "in danger" recently by UNESCO), Balkin approached Australians to sponsor her initiative, once again to little effect. E-mail correspondence with author, August 5, 2015.

16 Julie Doyle, "Seeing the Climate? The Problematic Status of Visual Evidence in Climate Change Campaigning," in *Ecosee: Image, Rhetoric, Nature*, ed. Sidney I. Dobrin and Sean Morey (Albany: SUNY Press, 2009), 286.

17 Balkin points out: "The atmosphere is a complex dynamic system, it's true, but there can be positive remediation. Two very different examples are the 1979 Convention on Long-range Transboundary Air Pollution, and the successful activism in 1999 by a coalition of residents and farm workers from Westley, California, who fought to have an enormous toxic smoke plume from a tire fire extinguished rather than

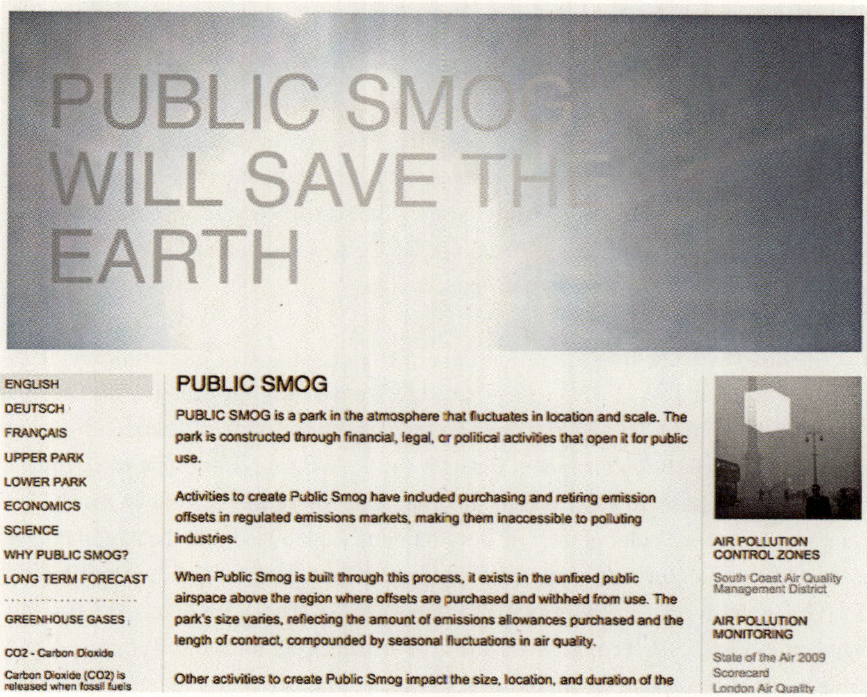

Amy Balkin, screenshot of *Public Smog* website, 2015

are indicated in the piece's emphasis on the various bureaucratic challenges of protecting the atmosphere, and directly addressed in the research Balkin presents as part of the project's website, including its various links to critical literature on the offsets market. The website states: "Ultimately, as the logic of privatization points to the commodification of all common pool resources, a reduction model based on trade is contradictory to a socially just solution to global air pollution. We need another model. In the meantime we have *Public Smog*, a way for the global public to buy back the sky on the open market."[18] Balkin's work thus reproduces the financial practice of offsetting as a

allowed to burn out. And while fraught both in origins and at present, the World Heritage model strongly supports local and regional approaches for protection of varied types of 'cultural landscapes' of 'outstanding universal value' including 'ongoing ecological and biological processes.'" Quoted in T. J. Demos, "The Law of the Land: An Interview with Amy Balkin," *International New Media Gallery*, November 2013, http://www.inmg.org/archive/balkin/catalogue/demos/#.VR1BWjuUcww.

18 See publicsmog.org, which also references Tamra Gilbertson and Oscar Reyes, *Carbon Trading: How It Works and Why It Fails* (Uppsala: Dag Hammarskjold Centre, 2009), http://www.carbontradewatch.org/publications/carbon-trading-how-it-works-and-why-it-fails.html.

response to climate change only to reveal its specious logic, an ironic gesture to expose the inherent failure of attempts to marketize pollution to ameliorate global warming (rather than reduce greenhouse gas emissions, cap and trade only makes banks and traders wealthier). Yet in declaring, on the website, "*Public Smog* is no substitute for direct action," the artist also acknowledges that merely drawing attention to the problem is not enough; what is needed is further collective mobilization to pressure government institutions, and intergovernmental organizations like UNESCO, in order to bring about real solutions to the mounting threats of climate change.

Exceeding Two Degrees

Part of the growing tide of exhibitions dedicated to these issues, the 8th Sharjah Biennial (2007), titled "Still Life: Art, Ecology and the Politics of Change," filtered its consideration of art and the environment through the United Arab Emirate's stark contradiction of attempting to address ecological sustainability while relying on a fossil fuel economy and spectacular real estate development. Acknowledging the biennial's significant carbon footprint alongside its broader concerns for ecology, the Danish artist Tue Greenfort produced *Exceeding 2 Degrees* (2007). The work involved a thermo-hygrograph (a chart recorder measuring temperature and humidity) placed on a table made of Malaysian wood that was fabricated in Japan and sold in Dubai. In this regard, Greenfort's piece recalls Hans Haacke's *Recording of Climate in Art Exhibition* (1969–70), which also used chart recorders and graphs to record the atmospheric conditions inside an art gallery. Art historian Luke Skrebowski writes that Haacke's piece exemplified the artist's "proto-institutional critique"—that is, "a condensed and elegant invocation of the museum's function as the preserver of artworks' capital value (both financial and symbolic)," done most directly by maintaining the works' material existence.[19] But Greenfort also goes beyond Haacke's site-specificity by dramatizing the dispersed conditions of globalized commodity production, which formed one part of the work's eco-institutional critique.[20] Another consisted of raising the temperature in the entire museum by two degrees Celsius—the interval then set as a plausible goal (seemingly unreachable now, even while not being ambitious enough) in the fight against global warming in the authoritative 2006 report *The Stern Review*, excerpts of which were also on view as part of the piece. Greenfort then used the

19 Skrebowski, "After Hans Haacke," 121; also see Skrebowski, "All Systems Go," 54–83.

20 For more on Greenfort's relation to ecology, see T. J. Demos, "Gas, Glass, and Polar Bears: Tue Greenfort and GASAG," in *Tue Greenfort: GASAG Art Prize 2012*, ed. Berlinische Galerie (Bielefeld: Kerber Verlag, 2012), 20–27.

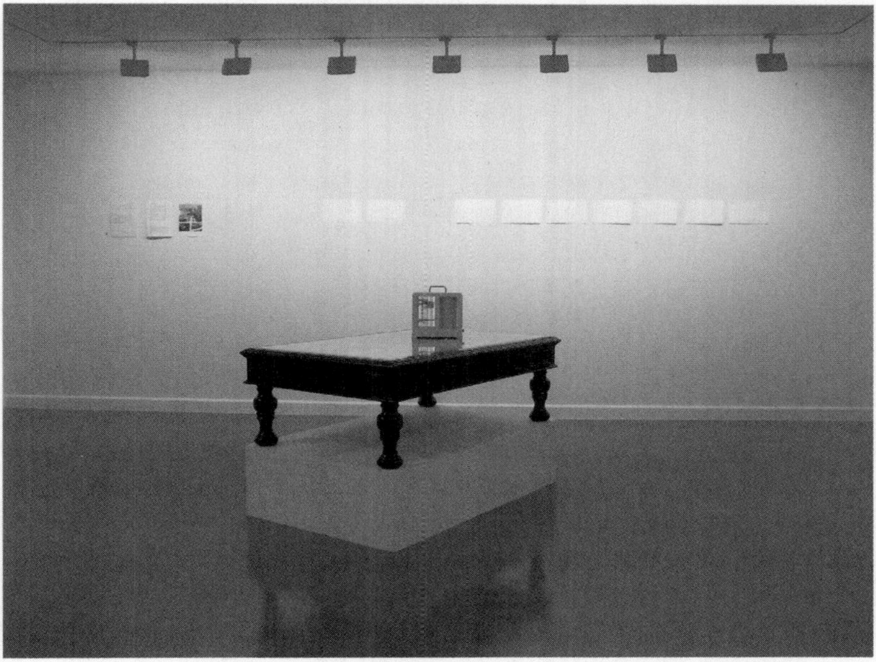

Tue Greenfort, *Exceeding 2 Degrees*, 2007

money saved on air-conditioning to preserve an area of Ecuadorian rain forest through a Danish environmental organization. This alternative version of offsetting, however, was hardly presented as a solution; rather, in an act of critical negation, the piece revealed the daunting complexity of the problem it addressed by entangling itself in its paradoxes. Although it rescued only a tiny piece of rain forest—around two square miles were purchased for around four hundred dollars, making this intervention at best a token gesture—Greenfort's work demonstrated how the global economy joins regional ecologies via institutional connections. In addition, his project points to the inherent flaw in the logic of offsetting, which involves trading environmental damage in prosperous developed areas (in this case, Sharjah) for nature conservation in politically and economically disenfranchised areas (such as the Ecuadorian Amazon). Such thinking fails to take into account the impossibility of exchanging natural elements between discrete systems of biodiversity.

Like Balkin's project on emission-credits trading, the piece taps into a now common (although still dubious) model to address climate change, a policy with roots in the Kyoto Protocol, by mitigating atmospheric carbon.[21] Titled "Reducing Emissions from Deforestation and Forest Degradation," or UN-REDD, the scheme has been deployed worldwide in subnational, national, and international policies. The UN has explained that the goal is "to make forests more valuable standing than they would be cut down, by creating a financial value for the carbon stored in trees"—a formula for eco-economics, where nature is marketized and companies integrate the environmental impacts of production into their spreadsheets.[22] The proposal of REDD is that developed countries (or corporations in those countries) pay developing ones carbon offsets for not cutting down their standing forests; in exchange, these agents can then continue their polluting activities elsewhere.

REDD (and its variations) has been met with major resistance from the very beginning, from environmental justice activists, Indigenous peoples' organizations, and social movements in the Global South (including the Global Forest Coalition, Grassroots Global Justice Alliance, Indigenous Environmental Network, and La Via Campesina). They have all pointed out the program's manifold problems: it allows biodiverse forests to be clear-cut and replaced by tree monocultures and genetically engineered varieties; it's based on a false equivalence between volatile forest carbon (emitted via deforestation) and the carbon stored underground for tens of thousands of years; it treats forests as carbon sinks rather than integrated and biodiverse ecosystems; and it opens the door to carbon trading and speculation, which is at odds with forest conservation, local communities (who are forced into a market logic), and ecological sustainability. Moreover, REDD programs allow rich countries and companies to continue to pollute while presenting themselves as green. The provision to secure land in Africa and South America often ends up encouraging forest enclosures, privatization, and militarization, inviting fraud, corruption, and the forced displacement of Indigenous peoples.[23] For these

21 See Vivienne Holloway and Esteban Giandomenico, *The History of REDD Policy* (Adelaide: Carbon Planet, 2009), http://www.forestcarbonportal.com/resource/history-redd-policy.

22 On eco-economics, see the Natural Capital Project (a ten-year partnership founded in 2006 between the Nature Conservancy, WWF, University of Minnesota Institute on the Environment, and Stanford University), http://www.naturalcapitalproject.org; Lester R. Brown, *Eco-Economy: Building an Economy for the Earth* (New York: W. W. Norton, 2001); Jonathon Porritt, *Capitalism as if the World Matters* (London: Earthscan, 2005); and Nicholas Stern, *The Economics of Climate Change: The Stern Review* (Cambridge: Cambridge University Press, 2007).

23 For further critical appraisals of REDD and carbon offsetting, see "No REDD! A Reader," *No REDD: Papers, Volume 1*, accessed July 25, 2015, http://noredd.makenoise.org; "Why REDD Is Wrong," *Global Justice Ecology Project*, November 25, 2010, http://globaljusticeecology.org/why-redd-is-wrong-2/; "Reaping Profits from Evictions, Land Grabs, Deforestation and Destruction of Biodiversity," *Indigenous Environmental Network*, accessed July 25, 2015,

various reasons, Carbon Trade Watch contends that the scheme "could be the biggest land grab of all time with no enforceable safeguards at the national or subnational level that would guarantee protection of the rights of Indigenous Peoples and forest-dependent communities."[24]

The model of offsetting utilized in Greenfort's *Exceeding 2 Degrees* offers the opportunity to consider these assorted problems. Its underlying theory of environment/monetary equivalence transforms nature into a commodity, introducing a generalization that abstractly exchanges a South American rain-forest allotment for the Sharjah atmosphere. Making this logic appear ridiculous by virtue of its miniscule proposal for the massive problem it evokes, Greenfort's work echoes as well the thought of eco-critics such as Timothy Morton, who insists that we think of "ecology without nature," arguing that the very idea of nature has become too ideologically compromised to warrant continued conceptual and aesthetic usage—as when anthropogenic warming is naturalized, as if it were not a man-made process intertwined with the fossil fuel economy. The post-natural condition doesn't mean, of course, that there isn't an ecosystem filled with diverse life-forms; rather, it warns against objectifying "nature" as separate and external, because living and nonliving things are all embedded within a "mesh" of social, political, and economic relations.[25] *Exceeding 2 Degrees*, like *Public Smog*, visualizes all three aspects of this network. By literalizing them within an all-too-pat scenario, risible in its simplicity (as if environments can be precisely measured and thereby financially valued), Greenfort reveals the logic of offsetting to be dependent upon exactly that conceptualization of nature as homogenous, commodifiable, and exchangeable.

http://www.ienearth.org/REDD/index.html; and "REDD: An Introduction," *REDD Monitor*, last modified February 2011, http://www.redd-monitor.org/redd-an-introduction.

24 "REDD+," *Carbon Trade Watch*, accessed July 25, 2015, http://www.carbontradewatch.org/issues/redd.html. Also see the statement of opposition contained in the Kari-Oca II Declaration of 2012, authored by over five hundred representatives of Indigenous peoples from around the world: "We demand that the United Nations, governments and corporations abandon false solutions to climate change, like large hydroelectric dams, genetically modified organisms including GMO trees, plantations, agro-fuels, 'clean' coal, nuclear power, natural gas, hydraulic fracturing, nanotechnology, synthetic biology, bio-energy, biomass, biochar, geo-engineering, carbon markets, Clean Development Mechanism and REDD+ that endanger the future and life as we know it. Instead of helping to reduce global warming, they poison and destroy the environment and let the climate crisis spiral exponentially, which may render the planet almost uninhabitable. We cannot allow false solutions to destroy the Earth's balance, assassinate the seasons, unleash severe weather havoc, privatize life and threaten the very survival of humanity. The Green Economy is a crime against humanity and the Earth."

25 See Morton, *Ecology without Nature*; and Timothy Morton, *The Ecological Thought* (Cambridge, MA: Harvard University Press, 2010).

Definancializing Nature

The projects by Balkin and Greenfort contrast with the essentialist idea of nature, both presented and complicated by pioneers of eco-art in the '70s, as a separate realm of purity in need of protection from industrial degradation, pollution, and economic exploitation. This earlier defense, however, frequently risked reifying nature—ironically paralleling the very objectifications of industry. But artists such as Joseph Beuys, Agnes Denes, Peter Fend, Hans Haacke, Helen Mayer Harrison and Newton Harrison, and Alan Sonfist nonetheless helped to focus on the representation of often ignored natural sites and industrially degrading practices and, like Balkin and Greenfort, addressed ecological issues by visualizing processes that are normally hidden. Sonfist's *Time Landscape New York City* (1965–ongoing) is a telling example: the artist returned a half block of Greenwich Village to its native precolonial condition, protected from surrounding invasive species, urbanization, and development—although since its founding, the land has been continually challenged by the encroachment of Manhattan's urban life.

Building on these pioneering experiments with art and nature, the models of Balkin and Greenfort nonetheless engage with a different breadth and conception of ecology. Rather than consisting of generally private or individual artistic gestures, they advance new modes of the commons, working with social movements and NGOs alike. Rather than being directed toward a specific place (like an open mine or enclosed lot), they concern the spaces of global geography, whose borders are crossed in networked systems of exchange, forming relational and post-natural areas (the earth's atmosphere, a "protected" section of the Ecuadorian rain forest, assemblages of inextricable nature-culture elements). Finally, instead of solely intervening in the ecological condition and context of a particular region, they address the terrain of the institutions of international law and finance that govern land and environment, further enmeshing nature within human systems. Balkin and Greenfort thereby reinvent earlier practices of eco-aesthetics—established in the work of Haacke, Smithson, Denes, Sonfist, and others—within the specifics of contemporary climate change and the legal and economic structures that address and regulate it, and forge connections with the international climate justice movement and environmental law on that basis.

In this manner, contemporary artists are increasingly responding to the recent calculations of green capitalism. Separating "nature" from human activities is no longer possible, since the environment, as we've seen, has become ever intertwined with economic speculation and legal regulations—which becomes all the more clear as the industrial domination and biotechnological reinvention of nature grow and lead to environmental disasters caused by climate change, even as corporate and state powers attempt to keep the invisible drivers hidden.[26] These ecological breakdowns are in turn further exploited by industry and finance, as the market-state nexus prefers big-technology fixes like carbon sequestration and geo-engineering (large-scale projects that address the symptoms rather than the causes of climate change) in addition to carbon credit trading to reduce emissions, and international banks continue to provide the financial infrastructure, as indicated in the activist discourse forming around recent UN climate meetings.[27] Within this system, carbon trading serves to impose a system of property rights that, in an act of atmospheric and resource colonialism, "licenses enclosures of land, air, water and labor in the global South to serve the 'carbon needs' of the North," as scholar and activist Larry Lohmann observes.[28] It helps to create a form of neoliberal climate change governmentality that, as corporate-policy critic Subhabrata Bobby Banerjee writes, "isolates the economic in such a way that institutions and policies focus more on the anti-competitive effects of climate change regulation rather than on the negative environmental and social effects of unbridled economic growth."[29] Indeed, free trade is valued so highly as a global right these days that corporations (such as those in the mining and fossil fuel energy industries) now commonly bring lawsuits against governments for introducing "unfair subsidies" to green industries like solar or wind power, or for creating environmental regulations that reduce their corporate profits (which is bound to get even worse as international policies like TTIP, the Transatlantic Trade and Investment Partnership, are enacted).[30]

Historian Dipesh Chakrabarty has argued that the present Anthropocene era challenges us to write the "species history of humans" directly alongside the

26 For additional studies of this post-natural condition, see Scott and Swenson, *Critical Landscapes*.

27 See Banerjee, "A Climate for Change," 1763.

28 Larry Lohmann, "The Endless Algebra of Climate Markets," *Capitalism Nature Socialism* 22, no. 4 (December 2011): 101.

29 Banerjee, "A Climate for Change," 1765.

30 See ibid., 1774–75; and Lori M. Wallach, "The Corporation Invasion," *Le Monde diplomatique*, December 2013, http://mondediplo.com/2013/12/02tafta. For instance, the Air Transport Association (the industry advocacy group for the major US airlines) took the European Union to court in 2009 for new regulations capping jetliner emissions and requiring airlines to pay for exceeding emission limits (in this case, the EU court ruled in favor of EU regulations). Under NAFTA, Canada and Mexico have each lost or settled five investor-state suits, with multimillion-dollar settlements going to foreign companies. In one example from 2012, the International Center for Settlement of Investment Disputes, a World Bank–affiliated institution in Washington that conducts arbitration, ordered Ecuador to pay $1.77 billion to Occidental Petroleum for nullifying its contract with the corporation. See Manuel Pérez-Rocha, "When Corporations Sue Governments," *New York Times*, December 3, 2014, http://www.nytimes.com/2014/12/04/opinion/when-corporations-sue-governments.html.

"global histories of capital." We might add to this the challenge of disentangling the Anthropocene's generic positing of human activities as the driver of geological change from what activist Vandana Shiva has termed "the corporate control of life" by biotechnology and intellectual property law. This historical condition of politico-ecological conflict represents a new stage in the "death of nature" (Shiva citing ecofeminist Carolyn Merchant), whereby genetically modified living organisms have come to be seen as "man-made" phenomena, stripped of their autonomous, self-organizing capacity, in an effort to guarantee the claims—and, of course, profitability—of corporate invention.[31]

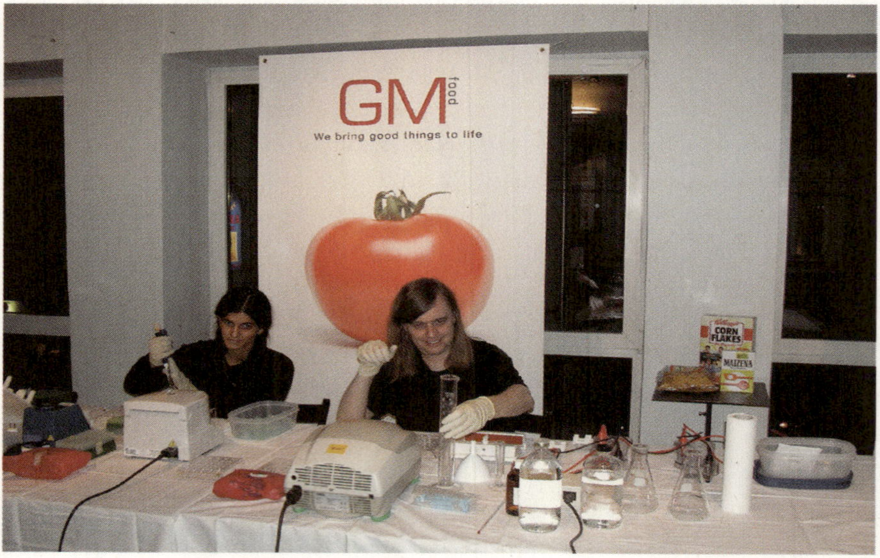

Critical Art Ensemble, *Free Range Grain*, 2003–4

Critical Art Ensemble (CAE) has staged interventions in this realm with, for example, *Free Range Grain* (2003–4, in collaboration with Beatriz da Costa and Shyh-shiun Shyu). This mobile laboratory/performance piece traveled to various European art venues, where visitors were invited to bring in store-bought groceries for CAE members to test for genetically modified ingredients. The project exposes the tenuous anti-GM regulations in the European Union, which leave openings in the trade market for the import of processed foods, especially from the United States,

31 Chakrabarty, "The Climate of History," 212; and Shiva, *The Corporate Control of Life*.

where corporations have spent millions blocking popular legislation that would enforce the labeling of GM products. While the piece represented "a means to visualize the material reality of theories of global trade," as the artists explained, it also demonstrated how scientific detection techniques can be utilized by nonspecialists in radical ways that work against corporate obfuscation—dramatized by the casually dressed artists operating lab equipment to identify hidden ingredients in consumer products.[32] Yet such cases also reveal complications of the post-natural condition: the activists who resist GMOs and commonly support small-scale organic agriculture maintain a steadfast belief in the natural and defend it as an area in need of protection against the onslaughts of the biotech industry. Just as some writers (like Morton) wish to put the term "nature" to rest theoretically, activists such as Shiva—and a whole host of environmental movements and Indigenous groups, as well as some governments, like Ecuador's and Bolivia's—take recourse to the "rights of nature," which, invoking a politico-juridical strategy parallel to Balkin's UNESCO initiative, they have defended in court, using "universal jurisdiction" to protect against the encroachments of corporate globalization.[33]

If artists rarely approach such legal activism (Balkin aside), they do excel at unraveling some of the utopian and critical myths of separate holistic nature—as well as reasons why we might want to retain some element of the natural in the struggle against a biotech post-natural condition.[34] The works by CAE, Greenfort, Balkin, and Autogena and Portway visualize environmental, technological, and economic processes as a means to comprehend and critique: the artists each give shape or visibility, to varying degree and with varying emphasis, to the abstractions or unseen flows, networks, and conflicts on which both finance and global ecology depend. Yet these manifestations—an index of environments, institutions, economics, and subjectivities—are not simply mimetic, but point to transformations and deformations of the systems they engage. In this sense, the entire endeavor of ecologically minded art presses the age-old

32 See Beatriz da Costa and Shyh-shiun Shyu, "Free Range Grain," *Critical Art Ensemble*, http://www.critical-art.net/FRG.html; and Steve Kurtz, Lucia Sommer, and Brian Holmes, eds., *Critical Art Ensemble: Disturbances* (London: Four Corners Books, 2012).

33 Among the pertinent examples here are the Bolivian 2011 Law of the Rights of Mother Earth and the 2010 Ecuadorian lawsuit against BP following the Deepwater Horizon disaster. I address the rights-of-nature discourse at greater length in chapter 6. See also the 2015 exhibition I cocurated, "Rights of Nature: Art and Ecology in the Americas," Nottingham Contemporary, http://www.nottinghamcontemporary.org/art/rights-nature.

34 One additional leading example of artistic practice that does compellingly address rights-of-nature legality is Ursula Biemann and Paulo Tavares's *Forest Law* (2014), which I address in "Rights of Nature: The Art and Politics of Earth Jurisprudence."

modernist question of art and life—the union of which long glimmered in the dreams of the avant-garde—into literally new terrain that is not only social, but more specifically biopolitical and eco-financial. As is the case with our so-called post-natural condition, where nature can no longer be seen as discrete from human activity, art's autonomy is all the more untenable when faced with ecological catastrophe. Some artists are now demonstrating as such, by going far beyond institutional (and eco-institutional) critique and opting for an explicitly activist, interventionist practice, acknowledging that there is no Edenic existence to return to, yet also unwilling to surrender control of nature to corporate neoliberalism.

These artist-activists—perhaps there is no better term—often avoid the enclosure of art institutions, and certainly reject biogenetic capitalism's control of life, privileging instead local projects and communities as well as traditional and organic horticulture. In some cases of contemporary practice, the distinctions between art and activism are blurred in favor of self-sufficiency and an ethical eco-aesthetics. Bobby Banerjee writes: "In a critical political economy of climate change the 'exercise of power in the form of economy' is not the sole provenance of governments but emanates from a loosely woven web of interconnected actors and institutions whose interests sustain existing material inequalities and forms of political power. Thus, the key question for a more progressive and equitable climate regime is how can groups that are excluded from participation at the global level resist policies that undermine their sustainability?"[35] A number of figures dedicate themselves to inventing precisely this kind of resistance—practitioners such as Nils Norman, the Laboratory of Insurrectionary Imagination (Labofii), Bureau d'Études, Marjetica Potrč, Art Not Oil, Allora & Calzadilla, and the Yes Men, who have each focused on artistic-activist interventions that promote models of community-driven ecological sustainability. Pursuing these examples of the definancialization of nature, I'll consider projects by Norman and Labofii in the remaining pages of this chapter.

Models of Utopia

As we've seen in chapter 1, the artistic practice of Nils Norman contests prevailing economic conditions and redirects urbanism to ecological sustainability and activist creativity. *Geocruiser*, in operation from 2001 to 2004, was a refurbished bus that used biodiesel and solar power and contained a

35 Banerjee, "A Climate for Change," 1782; citing Michel Foucault, "Governmentality" (1978), trans. Rosi Braidotti and Colin Gordon, in *The Foucault Effect: Studies in Governmentality*, ed. Graham Burchell, Colin Gordon, and Peter Miller (Chicago: University of Chicago Press, 1991), 92.

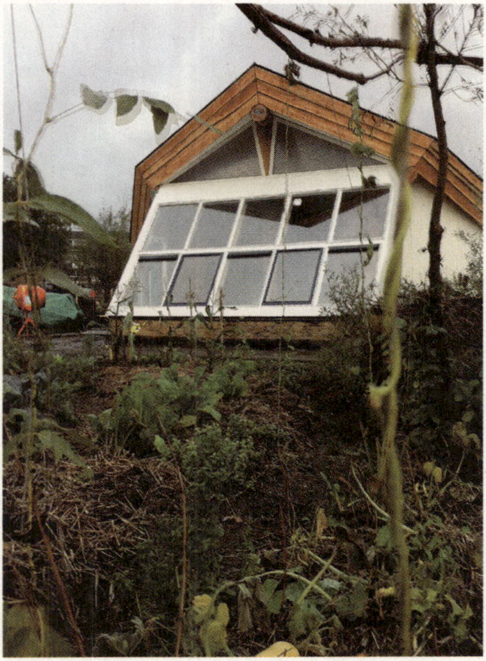

Nils Norman, *Edible Park*, 2010

community library and greenhouse; and *Ideal City, Research/Play Sector* (2005) was one of a series of utopian architectural proposals for urban public spaces, integrating child-directed playscapes, permaculture gardening, and anti-neoliberal activist training grounds.[36] Following suit, *Edible Park*, initiated in 2010 in The Hague, is a longer-term and more ambitious laboratory for community-based city planning, where sustainability equals an ecological and socioeconomic durability opposed to its conventional green-capitalist definition. The project was conceived, in part, as a response to a 2006 proposal by the Office for Metropolitan Architecture for a new creative hub in a former industrial area near the city center, including an amusement park and leisure district, beach, glass-and-steel skyscrapers, contemporary art museum, and Formula 1 racetrack—in other words, a high-impact, energy-intensive "spontaneous city" that has become a model of ready-made urbanism in global-city architecture. Plans were shelved,

36 For analyses of other design projects by Norman, see T. J. Demos, "Designs for a New Economy: Nils Norman's *Public Workplace Playground Sculpture for Graz, 2009*," in *Utopia and Monument: On the Validity of Art between Privatisation and the Public Sphere*, ed. Sabine Breitwieser (Graz: Steirischer Herbst, 2011); and Norman's website, accessed May 31, 2016, http://www.dismalgarden.com/projects.

however, following the financial meltdown of 2008 (in retrospect, the proposal appears as exactly the kind of design that should be abandoned to the past). In striking contrast to OMA's visions of grandeur—reflective of neoliberalism's unsustainable version of utopia—Norman's low-tech "anti-master plan" joined organic agriculture and self-sustaining practices (rainwater harvesting, forest gardening, composting) to craft a model of eco-communalism and bioregionalism, and was realized in collaboration with a local group of permaculture activists. Permaculture, for Norman, supports regional self-sufficiency and "would hopefully be developed in tandem with a self-critical discussion around the nature of public and community-type art projects in a time of forced austerity and economic crisis."[37] Commissioned by the art and architecture foundation Stroom Den Haag, Norman's project was granted eight hundred square meters of land in the city's Zuiderpark for three years, as well as a nearby meadow (a term that was extended indefinitely owing to the project's popularity).

Norman worked with Dutch architect Michel Post to build a central timber-frame pavilion with a sedum-covered roof, large "passive solar" windows, reused materials, cob, straw bales, and store-bought lumber. This low-impact, inclusive architecture of recycled elements (rarely deployed in the Netherlands, owing to architectural codes) suited the project's investment in agroecology education for the general public, where high-school groups and permaculture students could learn about bringing ecological principles of sustainability and nonchemical farming into agro-ecosystems.[38] The structure's shape recalls the modernism of German architect Bruno Taut, who worked closely in the 1920s with landscape architect Leberecht Migge to design social housing based on models of communal socialism—references that helped Norman distinguish the pavilion from "the cliché of hobbit-like eco-architecture," relating it more to the underrepresented history of green socialist modernism.[39] Instead of merely being an instance of trendy urban gardening—and Norman acknowledges that "systems like permaculture, forest gardening, deep ecology, Transitional Towns, bioregionalism, eco-communalism and urban agriculture [...] are becoming increasingly popular"[40]—*Edible Park* experiments with socioeconomic construction through agriculture design: How to think differently about the link between ecology and economy (in particular local economics committed to degrowth and

37 Nils Norman, "Edible Park with Permacultuur Centrum Den Haag, 2010," http://www.dismalgarden.com/collaboration/edible-park-permacultuur-centrum-den-haag.

38 See the book that accompanies the project, which offers a range of essays, a guided tour of the garden's plants, and a DIY permaculture kit: Nils Norman et al., *Eetbaar Park/Edible Park* (Amsterdam: Valiz, 2012).

39 Nils Norman, "Utopia: It's Here, If Not Now," in ibid., 23.

40 Ibid., 21.

sustainability), with art functioning as a space for theory and praxis? Indeed, Norman chose permaculture as a trial system because it unfolds onto inclusive social processes of collaboration, localization, and group learning, taking account of regional weather, soil conditions, geography, and collective subsistence farming. Norman explains: "[Permaculture] is primarily a form of agro-forestry: using the forest as a paradigm for growing food. It is a design strategy where energy production, water conservation, social organisation and food production are considered. You could call it a design methodology that uses nature as its teacher."[41] The project's garden was designed by students from the local permaculture course, its form based on a series of plant circles radiating out from fruit and nut trees in order to maximize contact between different species of flora, in contrast to the rigid grid of mono-crops.[42]

Indebted to historical utopian and socialist models of social and economic life—especially the 1960s San Francisco anarchist collective the Diggers, who aimed to create a "free city" through free food, provisions, and theater, and who took their name from a group of English Protestants in the 1600s, forerunners of agrarian socialism, who mobilized against land enclosures—Norman's plan is no doubt more modest, if also more pragmatic. It is based on the idea that changing the organization of energy, food, and land will in turn effect change on the level of social and economic organization and distribution, based on degrowth, de-globalization, and postcapitalist principles.[43] Although Norman's work was initiated through an art context—as part of Stroom's programming—it is in effect an outdoor, public, and volunteer-led project that also represents a withdrawal from commercial art-institutional practice. (Nonetheless, its categorization as art was strategic: it allowed the project to be realized in an area whose strict zoning and planning codes would otherwise have not allowed such unconventional architecture.) In his proposal for the project, Norman asks: "Can a grassroots, biodynamic system that comes out of a utopian tradition operate

41 Nils Norman, quoted in Nina Folkersma, "A Conversation with Nils Norman and Peter de Rooden," in ibid., 67. For a broader definition of sustainability, see "Ten Principles for Sustainable Societies," in Cavanagh and Mander, *Alternatives to Economic Globalization*, 77–104.

42 On permaculture, see the movement's founding text: Bill Mollison and David Holmgren, *Permaculture One: A Perennial Agricultural System for Human Settlements* (Melbourne: Corgi Publishing, 1978).

43 In fact, recent theories of postcapitalist "degrowth economics" have been promulgated as necessary means to forestall catastrophic climate change. See Gibson-Graham, *A Postcapitalist Politics*; Daiber and Houtart, *A Postcapitalist Paradigm*; François Schneider, Giorgos Kallis, and Joan Martinez-Alier, "Crisis or Opportunity? Economic Degrowth for Social Equity and Ecological Sustainability: Introduction to this Special Issue," *Journal of Cleaner Production* 18, no. 6 (April 2010): 511–18; Serge Latouche, *Farewell to Growth* (Cambridge: Polity, 2009); and the work of the Community Economies Research Network (CERN) and the Community Economies Collective (CEC).

city-wide, become integrated in the city's existing planning processes and possibly eventually replace them? Is this in itself a naive and misplaced utopian idea?"[44] In fact, the naive and misplaced (bad) utopian idea would be *not* to try to think differently—believing, all evidence to the contrary, that we can simply continue down our current self-destructive path. Norman's practice is part of a widespread move, growing internationally and exponentially, to invigorate community-based urban gardening with art and political activism.[45]

Resist, Organize, Nourish, Create, Exist!

Another artist-activist manifestation of utopian anticapitalist politics and community gardening, the Laboratory of Insurrectionary Imagination has turned these shared commitments into a long-term ambition—particularly with its experimental living and work space la r.O.n.c.e. Founded in 2004 in London by John Jordan and Isa Frémeaux, Labofii combines art and activism, and, while drawing on similar lineages as Norman, directs its work more toward a mix of radical theater, performance, and civil disobedience. For *Put the Fun between Your Legs: Become the Bike Bloc* (2009), they remade cycles from hundreds of discarded bikes in Copenhagen to contribute swarms of self-powered vehicles to the protests against the continued nonaction and ineffectiveness of the UN Climate Change Conference. For the Clandestine Insurgent Rebel Clown Army, in 2005, they dressed in clown costumes to neutralize police aggression while demonstrating against the neoliberal policies of the G8 summit in Gleneagles, Scotland.[46] These activities emerged from the collective Reclaim the Streets (also cofounded by Jordan), which pioneered theatrical protest tactics in London to take back public space from its motorization in the mid-to-late '90s.[47] The group successfully blocked automobile traffic in

44 Norman, "Utopia: It's Here, If Not Now," 26.

45 Exemplary is artist-run 16 Beaver Group's approach to New York City's regional community gardens in relation to their support for the newly formed Garden Solidarity Network, a movement "at the juncture of food sovereignty, housing activism, opposition to ecocidal infrastructure, opposition to gentrification and development according to the interests of capital, and practices of reclaiming urban spaces. The capacity to grow food locally is essential to reducing our dependence on fossil fuels and to counterbalancing the effects of fossil fuel consumption." See "Saturday – 10.04.14 – First Meeting of the Garden Solidarity Network, El Jardin del Paraiso," *16 Beaver*, October 2, 2014, http://16beavergroup.org/mondays/2014/10/02/777/. For a wider study of artistic gardening and farming in the West since the 1960s, see Sue Spaid, *Green Acres: Artists Farming Fields, Greenhouses and Abandoned Lots* (Cincinnati: Cincinnati Contemporary Arts Center, 2012).

46 For more on these artist-activist models, see Gavin Grindon, "Art, Activism and Climate Change," *Art Monthly*, February 2010, 9–12; and the exhibition catalogue, Flood and Grindon, *Disobedient Objects*.

47 Jordan also codirected the London-based artist-activist group Platform from 1987 to 1995, and worked as a cinema-

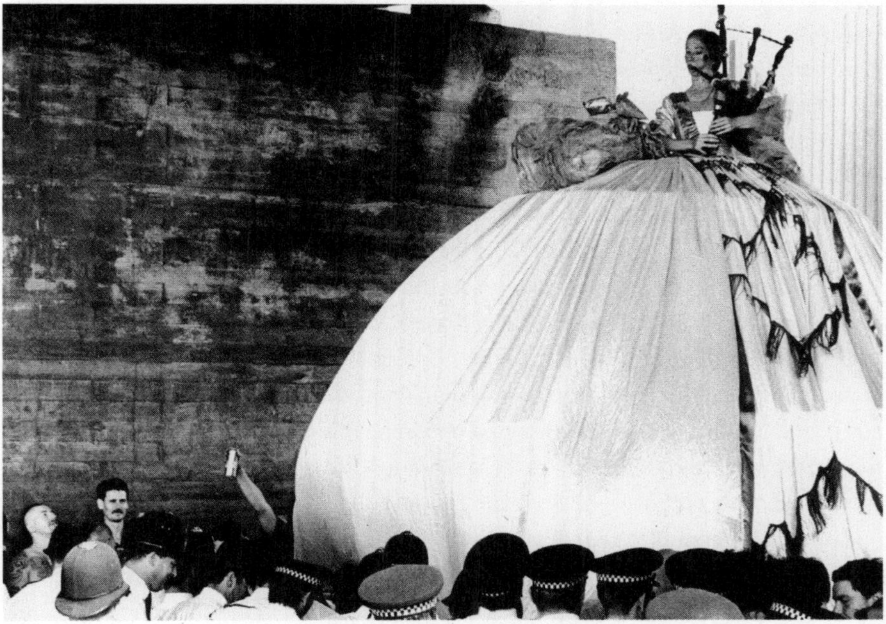

Reclaim the Streets, M41 Party, July 13, 1996

London, to protest the polluting instruments of capital with play and guerilla gardening—throwing spontaneous raves on city streets, digging up the asphalt to plant flowers, and setting up sandboxes and bouncy castles in the middle of the capital's busy intersections, with thousands of protestors joining the party. These injected a joyful, carnivalesque celebration into the demonstrations, overcoming the serious, dour, and angry tone often associated with protests.[48] Jordan and Frémeaux subsequently coauthored the 2007–8 book and film project *Paths through Utopias*, which took them on a road trip to visit different utopian communities across Europe—from the "socialist" town Marinaleda in Andalusia to the "articulteur"

tographer for Naomi Klein and Avi Lewis's film *The Take* (2004), which investigated the financial crisis in Argentina and the formation of workers' cooperatives.

48 See John Jordan, "Reclaim the Streets," in *The International Encyclopedia of Revolution and Protest: 1500 to the Present*, ed. Immanuel Ness (Oxford: Wiley-Blackwell, 2009), 2807; Chris Mosey, *Car Wars: Battles on the Road to Nowhere* (London: Vision, 2000); and Derek Wall, *Earth First! and the Anti-Roads Movement: Radical Environmentalism and Comparative Social Movements* (London: Routledge, 1999). See also Marcelo Expósito's film *Radical Imagination (Carnivals of Resistance)* (2004), which documents some of the activities of Reclaim the Streets; and Julia Ramírez Blanco, "Reclaim the Streets! From Local to Global Party Protest," in "Global Occupations of Art," ed. Jonathan Harris, special issue, *Third Text* 27, no. 4 (July 2013): n.p.

(artist-farmer) hamlet La Vieille Valette near Avignon; from autonomous Freetown Christiania in Copenhagen to the eco-community ZEGG (Center for Experimental Culture Design) outside of Berlin.[49] The trip taught them that "alternatives are not only possible but already exist in their thousands and that Utopias are transgressive in that they allow the 'creation of a space where previously there was none, in which new and different ways of relating to the world can be practiced'"[50]—clearly an important point of departure for the formation of la r.O.n.c.e.

Developed in 2012 by participants in the alter-globalization and climate camp movements in the United Kingdom and France, la r.O.n.c.e.—"resist, organize, nourish, create, exist," the acronym meaning "bramble" in French—provides a space for experiments in postcapitalist collective living and creative interventions supporting social and ecological justice.[51] Situated on a rehabilitated farm in France's Brittany region, the project's name refers to the beginnings of a forest ecology, as young growth is shielded by thorny, fast-growing, and fruit-producing shrubs. Like these protective and pioneering brambles, the collective's goal is to bring artistic creativity, activist commitment, and permaculture-based self-sufficiency together as utopian possibilities in our otherwise untenable present. Unsatisfied with simply criticizing fossil fuel capitalism and its destructive ecology, let alone the financialization of nature, or merely imagining future solutions, la r.O.n.c.e. implements sustainable living, environmental justice, and a pedagogical activist-artistic practice in the here and now.

Following Frémeaux's resignation from higher education in 2011 "to escape wage labor and academia" (she was a lecturer in media and cultural studies at Birkbeck, University of London), the pair joined like-minded folks in Brittany, where they acquired a disused farm and founded their new home, a mix of Bauhaus and the Highlander Folk School; in other words, joining the avant-garde community-based crafts and experimental living of the former with the pedagogy of the oppressed and civil rights and labor activism of the latter.[52] As such, la r.O.n.c.e. intervenes both critically and creatively in the world: if the critique of the current

49 See the book, Isabelle Frémeaux and John Jordan, *Les sentiers de l'utopie* (Paris: La Découverte, 2012); the blog, https://lessentiersdelutopie.wordpress.com; and the film, https://vimeo.com/21919175. For a study of the city of Marinaleda, see Dan Hancox, *The Village against the World* (London: Verso Books, 2014).

50 The Laboratory of Insurrectionary Imagination, "Geographies of Hope," in *A Guidebook of Alternative Nows*, ed. Amber Hickey (Los Angeles: Journal of Aesthetics and Protest Press, 2012), 245; they cite Lucy Sargisson, *Utopian Bodies and the Politics of Transgression* (London: Routledge, 2000).

51 For an overview of alter-globalization, see Cavanagh and Mander, *Alternatives to Economic Globalization*.

52 As Jordan explained to me during my visit to la r.O.n.c.e in August 2014. Also see Notes from Nowhere, eds., *We Are Everywhere: The Irresistible Rise of Global Anticapitalism* (London: Verso Books, 2003).

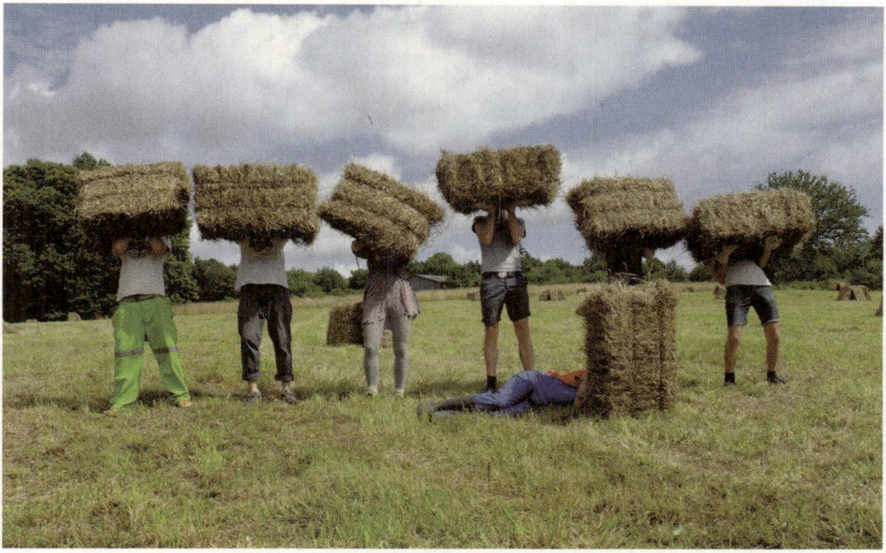

Playing after a harvest at la r.O.n.c.e., ca. 2012

order "is not grounded in a certain optimism, a shred of belief that the imagined *better* world can exist in some form in *this* world now," Jordan and Frémeaux write, "it risks turning into another theoretical model, abstract and cynical or another excuse to wait for the perfect moment—the revolution, the collapse, the last judgement—a sure recipe for hopelessness."[53] As an experiment in autonomous living, la r.O.n.c.e.'s combination of activist politics and sustainable ecology is based in the principle that aesthetics equals ethics.[54] Their seven-hectare farm, located in an area of France long known for its regional autonomy, includes a nineteenth-century longhouse, working barn, and large organic vegetable farm with several poly-tunnels (providing climate control and shelter for plants); here, permaculture's agroecological ethics feeds into the ambience of a non-mechanized, chemical-free, collectively managed site. The group numbers around eight individuals—political activists, botanists,

53 Labofii, "Geographies of Hope," 242.

54 Labofii locate la r.O.n.c.e. in the "autonomous geographies" defined as "personal freedom, a mistrust of power and rejection of hierarchy, and the advocacy of self-management, decentralised and voluntary organisation, direct action and radical change." The Laboratory of Insurrectionary Imagination, "An Open Letter in the Dark," *The Laboratory of Insurrectionary Imagination* (blog), October 26, 2014, https://labofii.wordpress.com/2014/10/28/an-open-letter-in-the-dark. Also see Paul Chatterton and Jenny Pickerill, "Notes towards Autonomous Geographies: Creation, Resistance, and Self-Management as Survival Tactics," *Progress in Human Geography* 30, no. 6 (December 2006): 730–46.

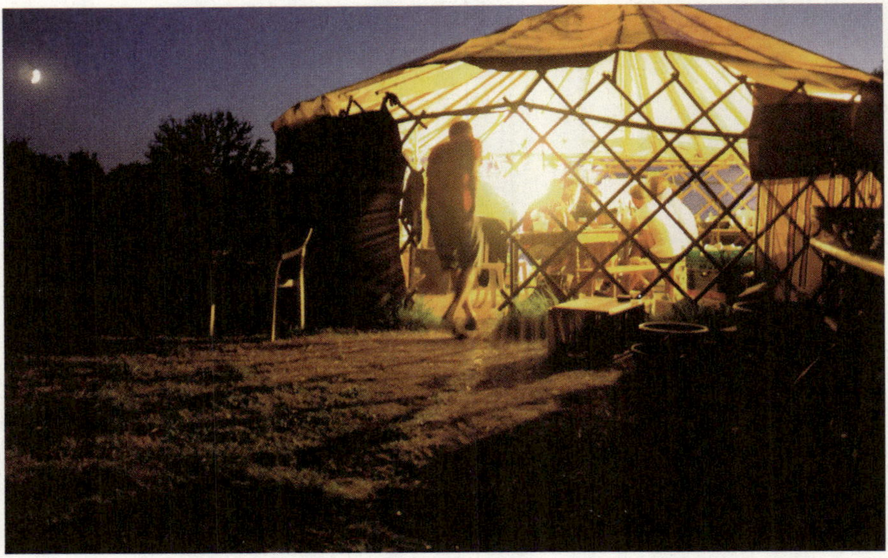

Summer night in one of the yurts at la r.O.n.c.e., ca. 2012

farmers, and artists—who shared the initial investment in the disused property. Their project has little interest in what they term "picture politics"—that is, the political aesthetics claimed for art in galleries or institutions—which for these practitioners is akin to taking a "holiday in representation." Distinguishing themselves from the gallery-bound elements of other utopian projects or eco-critiques, la r.O.n.c.e. members insist on getting their hands dirty.[55]

As such, la r.O.n.c.e. encompasses multiple elements: an organic vegetable farm, since "growing organic, healthy, wholesome, high-quality food is a fundamental step in regaining autonomy and control over our health, global sustainability, energy security and income";[56] Radikales Cocottes (Radical Pots), a mobile kitchen that serves vegan food at demonstrations for more just and fair immigration and environmental laws; L'Atelier, a workshop based in the barn for bike and car repair (which feeds their long-term goal to move off the electrical grid, relying on solar and wind power for their energy needs); and a base for Labofii's workshops on creative activism, experimental living, and

55 Labofii, "An Open Letter in the Dark." I support Labofii's ambition to "do" politics instead of "represent" it, but I wouldn't dismiss the contemporary politics of aesthetics, which can also transform subjective positions and educate through critique, even if situated in an institutional context. For support of this position, see my recent books *Return to the Postcolony* and *The Migrant Image*.

56 Labofii, "Geographies of Hope," 250.

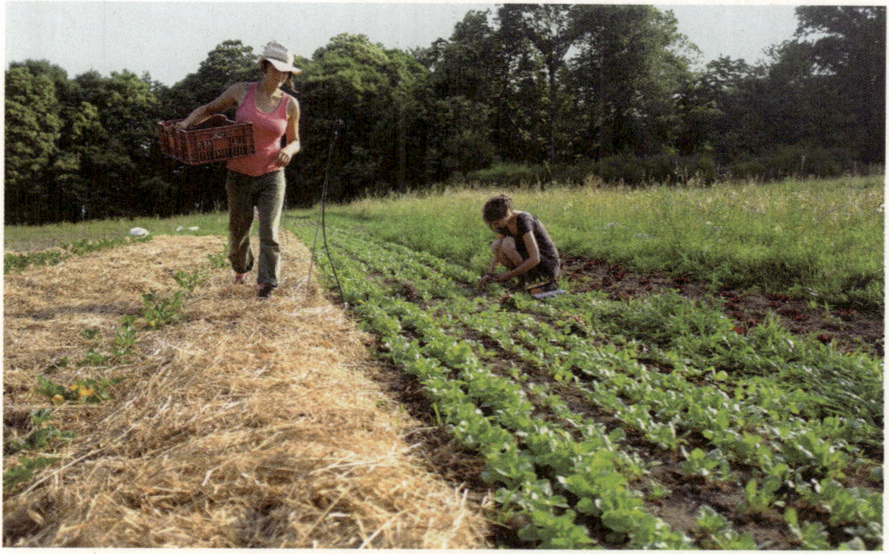

Working with an ex-landless farmer to produce local food at la r.O.n.c.e., ca. 2012

permaculture (in addition to the market farm, tuition for these workshops provides a subsistence income).[57] These aims follow from Labofii's commitment to overcome the calcified hierarchies, authoritarianism, and asceticism of the traditional Left. "Capitalism works because it is constantly manipulating our desires. We think it is important to reclaim such desires, therefore, our work involves pleasure, play and adventure, but not within the frame of art," Jordan explains.[58] In this regard, la r.O.n.c.e. intends to transform the pleasures associated with capitalism—arrayed around its unsustainable throwaway material culture, fossil-fueled transportation, and alienating, often sexist and classist, commercial spectacle—with those of postcapitalist ecological sustainability, localized egalitarian community, political engagement, and self-sufficiency. For them, like Norman, permaculture, which emphasizes the points of connection between organic forms so as

57 Labofii's first workshop at la r.O.n.c.e., "Living Like a Forest: Art, Activism, and Permaculture," in September 2011, merged the ecology and design of permaculture with forms of creative resistance, and aimed to expand a network of artists and activists from western and eastern Europe. The California-based activist pedagogy of Starhawk, Erik Ohlsen, and Penny Livingston-Stark has been formative for la r.O.n.c.e.; see the Earth Activist Training website, www.earthactivisttraining.org.

58 Quoted in an interview by Lars Kwakkenbos, "Art, Activism, and Permaculture," *Foreign Policy in Focus*, January 20, 2011, http://fpif.org/art_activism_and_permaculture/.

to maximize biodiversity, provides a compelling model for sociopolitical life: "Utopia is a beautiful edge (by beautiful we mean something that excites all of our senses), an edge between fiction and reality, between the conceptual and the concrete, between an imagined reality and the construction of it. We learn to value edges from the observation of the natural world."[59]

Reinventing Nature

While in some ways representative of a contemporary return to nature, la r.O.n.c.e. and Norman's *Edible Park* avoid any relapse to regressive idealism, as certain eco-art communal experiments of the 1960s may have done.[60] As well, these contemporary models are distant from the drug-induced escapism of the "tune in, turn on, drop out" ethos characterizing some countercultural moments of decades past, just as they reject the flexible neoliberal subjectivities of subsequent years, when the antiauthoritarianism of the '60s transmogrified into the '90s economy of corporate techno-utopianism.[61] These current artist-activist practices distinguish themselves from past forms by creating and expanding connections to regional and global circuits of antiglobalization politics—such as Labofii's interventions at COP21 in Paris in late 2015,[62] or Norman's work with inner-city organic agriculture, collaborative pedagogy, and experimental designs for transforming social life and the capitalist economy that mediates it. By connecting self-sufficient farming to eco-activism, they challenge the mythopoetic models of the past that tended to essentialize nature. In addition, current practitioners of this variety reject the social hierarchies of preceding communal organizations—including the patriarchy and personality cults that past charismatic leaders sometimes obtained, as well as the virtual (non)communities of the friending-frenzies of Facebook and other social networks—in favor of an engaged and meaningful

59 Labofii, "Geographies of Hope," 244. Labofii defines permaculture as "a strong ethical framework that consists of three core values: *earth care* (i.e. the acknowledgement that we must work *with* our ecosystems not against them, and oppose the destruction of our soils, wild habitats, water systems and atmosphere), *people care* (i.e. the need to look after ourselves and our community, and strive for justice for all), and *fair share* (i.e. the acknowledgement that we live on a finite planet, with finite resources which we must share and distribute equally amongst all people and species)" (ibid., 249).

60 For an excellent analysis of the diversity of 1960s experiments in collective living, see Iain Boal, Janferie Stone, Michael Watts, and Cal Winslow, *West of Eden: Communes and Utopia in Northern California* (Oakland: PM Press, 2012).

61 See Turner, *From Counterculture to Cyberculture*.

62 For an overview of Labofii's Climate Games, their artistic activism around COP21, see T. J. Demos, "Playful Protesters Use Art to Draw Attention to Inadequacy of Paris Climate Talks," *Truthout*, December 13, 2015, http://www.truth-out.org/news/item/34006-playful-protesters-use-art-to-draw-attention-to-inadequacy-of-paris-climate-talks.

proximity with others, expressed through consensus-based decision-making and embedded in the long-term temporality and multifaceted materiality of collective living.[63] The withdrawal from capitalism exemplified in la r.O.n.c.e. is a creative act of affirmation and experimental form of life, building social connections and forming real alternatives to contemporary European austerity-based neoliberalism.[64]

Recalling Norman's queries around *Edible Park*, we might nonetheless ask: Are local projects that bridge art and sustainable gardening applicable in a larger context? Are they scalable upward? And do they provide models for expanding that won't follow the protocol of Big Organic—industrial farming greenwashed?[65] In fact, according to recent research by the UN, the world's agricultural needs can be met with small-scale, localized organic farms, which are versatile enough to ensure future food security in a destabilized era of climate change—against agribusiness's claims that chemical-based GM farming is the only way forward.[66] Countering the criticism that the organic food craze in the West forms part of an ecology of affluence for only the well-heeled, food and environmental author Michael Pollan writes that this false notion is premised on the misunderstanding of the "value" of nonorganic foods, one that doesn't take into account their dependence on hidden state subsidies that support fossil-fuel-dependent agribusiness (especially for corn and soy) that destroys the soil and environment but avoids paying for these externalized costs.[67] Rejecting this corporate path, the smaller-scale artistic experiments looked at in this chapter also mirror the

63 On utopian social experiments such as Drop City (one of many, including Libre, Olympali, Hog Farm, Red Rockers, New Buffalo, Lama), see Scott, *Architecture or Techno-Utopia*. For the critique of new media's virtual communities, see Franco "Bifo" Berardi, "The Paradox of Media Activism: The Net Is Not a Tool, It's an Environment," in *Uncommon Grounds: New Media and Critical Practices in North Africa and the Middle East*, ed. Anthony Downey (London: I. B. Taurus, 2014), 39–46.

64 This approximates Paolo Virno's thoughts on exodus in relation to the Italian autonomism movement: "Exodus—exodus from wage labor and toward activity, for example—is not a negative gesture, exempt from action and responsibility. On the contrary, because defection modifies the conditions within which conflict takes place, rather than submit to them, it demands a particularly high level of initiative—it demands an affirmative 'doing.'" Paolo Virno, "The Ambivalence of Disenchantment," in *Radical Thought in Italy: A Potential Politics*, ed. Paolo Virno and Michael Hardt (Minneapolis: University of Minnesota Press, 1996), 33.

65 Permaculture is increasingly "going global," with the twelfth, and biggest yet, International Permaculture Convergence in London in summer 2015.

66 Maryam Henein, "United Nations Calls for an End to Industrialized Farming," *Truthout*, November 26, 2014, http://www.truth-out.org/opinion/item/27636-united-nations-calls-for-an-end-to-industrialized-farming.

67 Pollan explains that with industrial foods, "society is not bearing the [true] cost of water pollution, of antibiotic resistance, of food-borne illnesses, of crop subsidies, of subsidized oil and water—of all the hidden costs to the environment and the taxpayer that make cheap [conventional] food seem cheap." Michael Pollan, *The Omnivore's Dilemma: A Natural History of Four Meals* (New York: Penguin, 2006), 243.

organic farming movements in India, Asia, Africa, and Latin America.[68] If, as Naomi Klein argues, we need to rebuild the public sphere, reverse privatizations, relocalize large parts of our economies, scale back overconsumption, initiate forms of selective degrowth, and heavily regulate and tax corporations—that is, if we are to avoid societal breakdown in a near future dominated by climate chaos—then these artist-activist practices are opening up crucial potential trajectories of current collective action.[69] As laboratories of the possible, they represent experimental prototypes that prefigure a world of localized and sustainable food production. In this sense, these artist-activist practices connect current imperatives to Félix Guattari's plea in *The Three Ecologies*, first published in 1989, that we develop new "stock exchanges" of value that exit from the domination of "general equivalence," according to which everything, including nature, becomes a form of currency, without value outside the capitalist economy.[70] In other words, the solutions to the environmental crisis must precede and predetermine economic decisions—not vice versa. Fredric Jameson, in 1990, had focused on the naturalization of finance, "the most crucial terrain of ideological struggle in our time," while the contemporary artists who have put issues of the (de)financialization of nature at the core of their practice are occupying today's most crucial terrain of struggle.

68 On organic farming in Latin America, see Movimento dos Trabalhadores Sem Terra (Landless Workers' Movement) and La Via Campesina (International Peasant's Movement), the latter which, representing some two hundred million farmers worldwide, describes itself on its website as "an international movement which coordinates peasant organizations of small and middle-scale producers, agricultural workers, rural women, and indigenous communities from Asia, Africa, America, and Europe," and which advocates sustainable farms.

69 See Klein, *This Changes Everything*, esp. 89–93.

70 See Guattari, *The Three Ecologies*, 65.

¡Ya basta!

Chapter 4

Ecologies of Art and Revolution in Mexico

For *Seascape* (2012), the Mexican artist Minerva Cuevas dipped an ocean landscape painting in a tarry black substance, mimicking the scene of an offshore oil spill. The medium-sized canvas was painted by an anonymous amateur artist, the kind found a dime a dozen in thrift stores, and depicts a romanticized view of waves crashing on a rocky shore. Now a shiny goo covers the seashore along the bottom of the canvas and hangs off in solidified drips. The painting, it appears, was carefully immersed so that only the sandy-beach portion bears the traces of gunk. The piece is part of a larger series by Cuevas of hydrocarbon-soaked objects that mimic the remnants of an oil spill, a frequent occurrence in the Gulf of Mexico.[1] The state-owned Mexican petroleum company Pemex has had a series of offshore industrial accidents that altogether rival the destructiveness of the 2010 BP *Deepwater Horizon* disaster off the coast of Louisiana, in terms of barrels of oil lost and habitats destroyed. Uncontainable, the oil-like substance of *Seascape* not only overwhelms the pictorial illusion, it also seeps into actual space, forming an apt metaphor for the tendency of fossil fuel—from extraction to consumption—to not stay where it's supposed to, and with calamitous results.

The piece provides a dramatic entrance into the uneven ecologies of Central America as addressed by contemporary Mexican artists. Together with national and international colleagues such as Marcela Armas, Gilberto Esparza, Superflex, Pedro Reyes, and Maria Thereza Alves, Cuevas is part of a wave of activist-artists working in Mexico's capital who are critically

1 Cuevas worked with chapopote, a black asphalt used in Indigenous ceramics for waterproofing since Olmec times, ca. 1500–400 BCE.

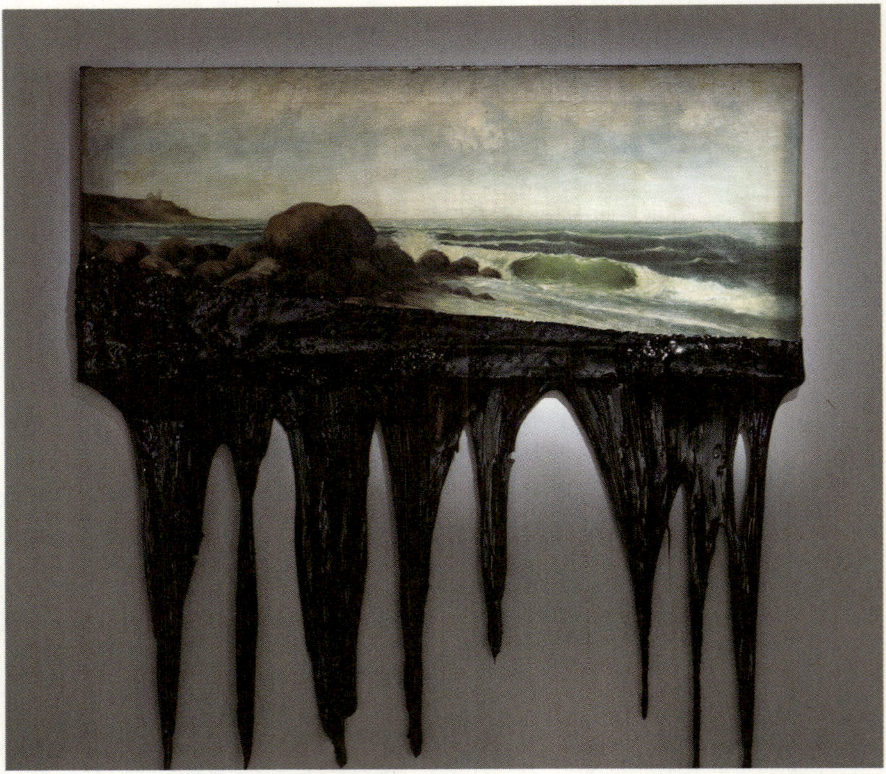

Minerva Cuevas, *Seascape*, 2012

examining environmental issues, including the pollution and toxicity of industrial modernity and the many deleterious socio-ecological effects of NAFTA, the North American Free Trade Agreement implemented in 1994, especially for small-scale farmers and their land. That same year, the Zapatistas proclaimed their revolutionary intentions, consisting of a creative and globally resonant resistance to corporate neoliberalism, to which they responded *¡Ya basta!* (Enough already!). Indeed, their ongoing rebellion—subsequently nonviolent following a series of conflicts with the Mexican army at the beginning of their struggle—remains pledged to regional autonomy and Indigenous rights, and is also a leading example of sustainable organic ecology in Latin America. Their revolution is the most ambitious version of political ecology; its lessons for the decolonization of nature are addressed later in this chapter. First, I will further consider the diverse range of environment-related positions of the artist-activists mentioned above.

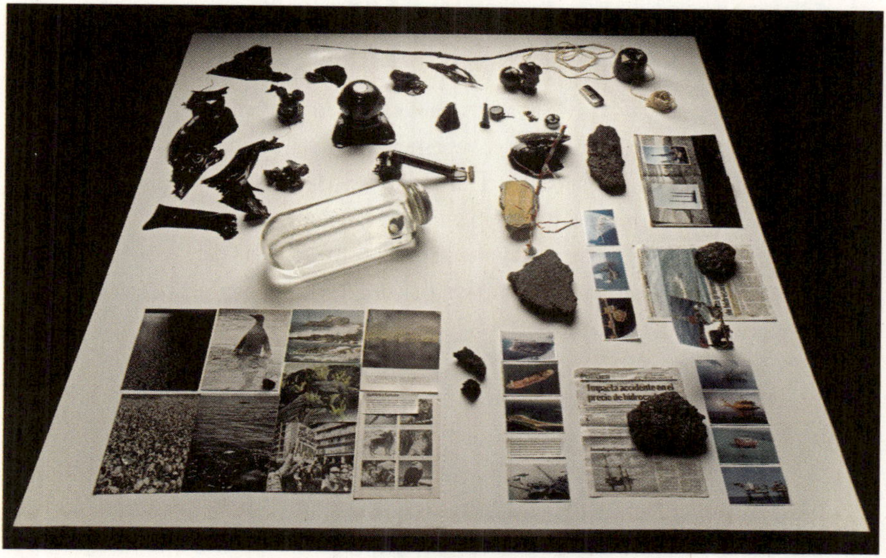

Minerva Cuevas, *Serie hidrocarburos*, 2007

Pure Del Montte

Cuevas's oil-befouled seascape counters idealized nature with abject materialism—a sculptural maneuver that parallels the artist's works of tactical media to take down corporate spectacle. These pieces are enacted in painted murals (as in the mixed-media installation *Nation State*, 2003) that put the lie to the claims of biotech multinationals, which have infused the Mexican landscape with genetically modified products in recent years, destroying Indigenous farming techniques, traditions, and communities. In *Del Montte* (2003), an aesthetics of appropriation shows how commercial product design blankets the neocolonial violence of corporate globalization. The latter includes what appear to be canned tomatoes mass-produced by Del Monte Quality, but the labels proclaim the product's name as "Pure Murder" by the brand "Del Montte Criminal"—a strong condemnation of the US food corporation for its deadly legacy in Guatemala. Following its purchase of United Fruit Company's holdings in Guatemala in 1972, and to increase profits, minimize labor-union power, bypass environmental regulations, and maintain a pro-corporate political climate, Del Monte colluded with the country's extremely repressive military dictator, José Efraín Ríos Montt, and his CIA-supported regime, which ruled the country from 1982 to '83. Ríos Montt was responsible for the killings and land dispossession of thousands of Indigenous people who were suspected of supporting the opposing side in the country's civil war.[2] *Del Montte* lays out its case explicitly on the cans' back label by listing the "ingredients" that have gone into the region's geopolitics (which also applies, more broadly, to corporate and US collaboration with paramilitary governments across Latin America): "The best land in Guatemala is administered by Del Monte Fresh Produce, Dole and Chiquita. These are criminal companies, having benefitted from the CIA wars that left the people of North and Central America bloodied and impoverished. Their cooperation with U.S. military, police and various groups of paramilitaries has never ceased and their ties have strengthened since the U.S.A. launched the War against Terrorism."

Direct and confrontational, Cuevas's projects call attention to the devastation of multinational corporate exploits that aim to secure new markets and accumulate wealth at all costs: the sludge of oil extraction that creates major environmental damage, whether spilled or consumed as intended; and the social costs of corporate activities on disadvantaged or unstable foreign soil, including labor exploitation, forcible dispossessions, pauperization, even disappearances and death via police-state violence. Cuevas returns to our field of vision these negative "externalities"—a term from economics designating the disowned environmental and social offshoots of corporate production[3]—thereby constructing, in condensed visual form, a more accurate and critical history of geopolitics and capitalist industry in Latin America than what official versions typically provide. As such, Cuevas's work signals some of the central ecological and political concerns of contemporary art in Mexico (and in Central America more broadly) that contests neoliberal corporate practice, which, forging ahead on its path of economic growth while disregarding all else, leaves a trail of social, political, and environmental destruction in its wake.

Cuevas connects the Cold War-era ravages of CIA-supported Latin American dictatorships, and governments working with US corporate partners, to the wreckage caused by contemporary

2 The US-supported coup in Guatemala in 1954 set the stage for "a bloody, 36-year civil war in which more than 200,000 people were killed—the vast majority at the hands of the military." See Ana Perez, "U.S. Needs to Atone for CIA Coup in Guatemala," *Progressive* (blog), May 26, 2011, http://progressive.org/mpperez052611.html; Noam Chomsky, "The US Remains Guilty in Guatemala," *Truthout*, June 6, 2013, http://truth-out.org/opinion/item/16801-the-us-remains-guilty-in-guatemala; and Stephen G. Rabe, *The Killing Zone: The United States Wages Cold War in Latin America* (Oxford: Oxford University Press, 2015). In May 2013, a court in Guatemala convicted Ríos Montt with genocide and crimes against humanity for his massacre of the country's Ixil population in the 1980s (the conviction was overturned ten days later, likely the result of political compromise).

3 According to economist Joseph E. Stiglitz, externalities occur "when the actions of an individual have impacts on others for which they do not pay or for which they are not compensated." Quoted in Daniel Altman, "Joseph Stiglitz Q&A," *Economist's View* (blog), October 11, 2006, http://economistsview.typepad.com/economistsview/2006/10/joseph_stiglitz.html.

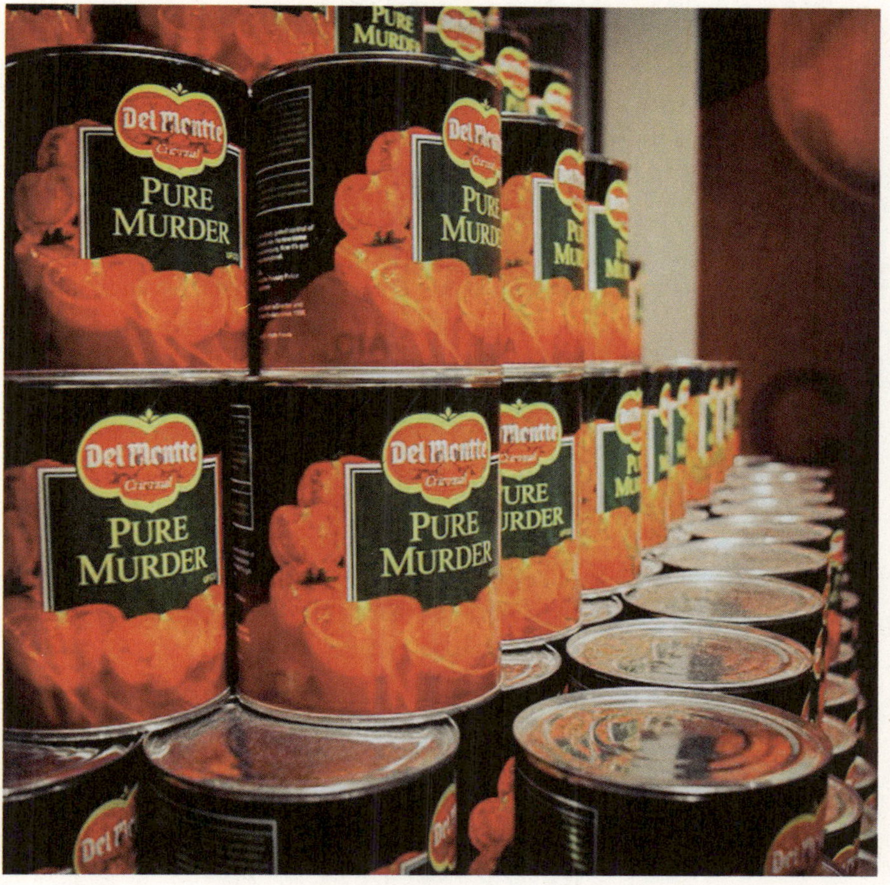

Minerva Cuevas, *Del Montte*, 2003

bioprospecting and agribusiness. The labels in *Del Montte*, for instance, describe how Del Monte has exposed millions of farm workers to chemical pesticides over the years, leading to "respiratory diseases, asthma, babies born with defects, spontaneous abortion and male sterility." Biotech multinationals such as Monsanto have continued this reckless endangerment, forcibly introducing GM seeds (under the antidemocratic terms of international "free trade" deals) that compete with the Indigenous heritage and regional biodiversity in Latin America—the prickly pear cactus, maize, wheat, cocoa, and plantains, as alluded to in the illustrated plants native to Mexico in *Nation State*—and contaminating traditional farming ecologies, genetically and chemically.

The labels in *Del Montte* explicate further: "The extensive arrival of U.S. economic interests in Latin America can be considered the origin of the armed conflicts that Indigenous populations have fought against their governments and paramilitary forces for some decades."[4]

Art and cultural historian Jean Fisher calls Cuevas's approach of attacking corporate advertising imagery a "para-sitic intervention," whereby the artist leeches onto her semiocapitalist hosts in order to create "a space of critical agency in the field of social activism."[5] Similarly, curator and art historian Cuauhtémoc Medina contends that "the effectiveness of these interventions lies precisely in their adherence to detour and narrative-sabotage techniques that ensnare corporate advertising icons in a tear-down of the mercantile illusions that feed them."[6] While these are accurate descriptions, Cuevas's work can also be seen to perform a fundamental ecological operation: to elicit—viscerally or conceptually, materially or textually—the repressed elements of the capitalist economy, disavowed by corporations but nonetheless essential to its continued functioning. Insofar as Cuevas deconstructs corporate illusions and the price of their profits, her work also points to the ultimate financial impossibility of this system once externalities are factored in—from greenhouse gas emissions to water and land use, from the destruction of cultural heritage to social and antidemocratic violence.[7]

Eco-homeopathy

Like Cuevas, Marcela Armas insists on an ethical and ecological aesthetics that confronts the waste products of the capitalist economy rather than disavowing or disappearing them. Both feature the viscous presence of fossil fuel: Cuevas dips quotidian and fine-art objects into the black matter in her *Serie hidrocarburos*, and Armas constructs motorized sculptures lubricated with oil. Formed into geographical shapes, such as the inverted outline of Mexico in *I-Machinarius* (2008), these metal contraptions have been shown in galleries, dripping crude oil down the white walls.

4 This struggle could also be seen as beginning with sixteenth-century colonialism. See Eduardo Galeano, *Open Veins of Latin America: Five Centuries of the Pillage of a Continent*, trans. Cedric Belfrage (London: Serpent's Tail, 2009); and Anibal Quijano, "Coloniality of Power: Eurocentrism and Latin America," *Nepantla: Views from South* 1, no. 3 (2000): 533–80.

5 Jean Fisher, "Minerva Cuevas and the Art of Para-sitic Intervention," *Afterall*, no. 27 (Summer 2011): 57.

6 Cuauhtémoc Medina, "Interiorized Exterior," in *Limitless: Contemporary Art in Mexico City, 2000–2010*, ed. Edgar Alejandro Hernández and Inbal Miller (Mexico City: Editorial RM, 2013), 28.

7 The "unpriced natural capital costs" are from greenhouse gas emissions (38%), water use (25%), land use (24%), air pollution (7%), land and water pollution (5%), and waste (1%). Trucost, *Natural Capital at Risk: The Top 100 Externalities of Business*, April 2013, http://www.naturalcapitalcoalition.org/js/plugins/filemanager/files/TEEB_Final_Report_v5.pdf, 7.

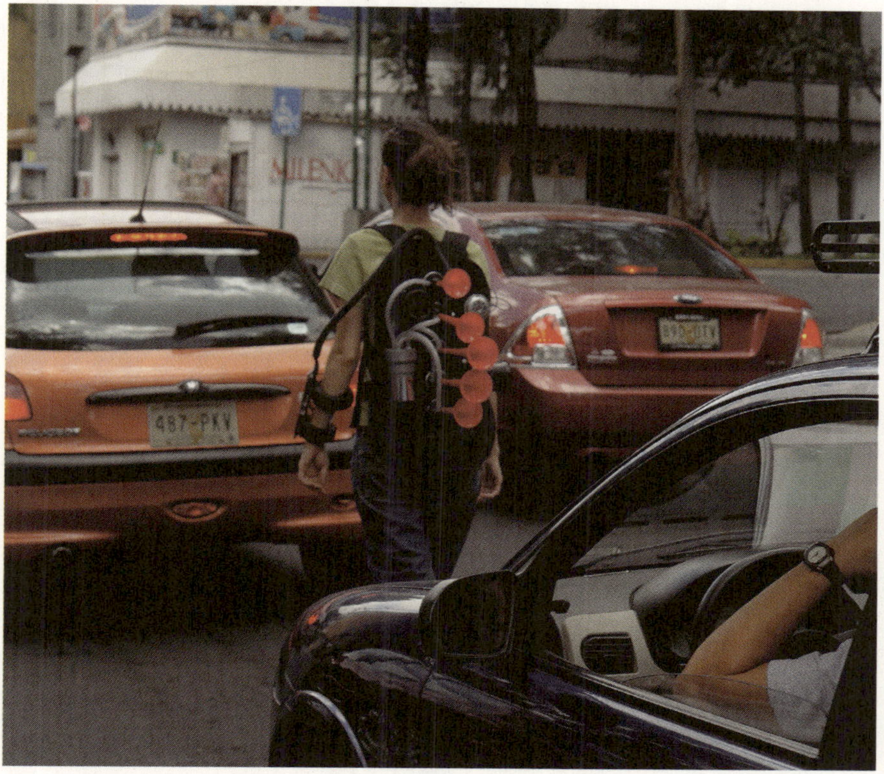

Marcela Armas, *Occupation: Sound Action for Car Space with Seven Car Horns*, 2007

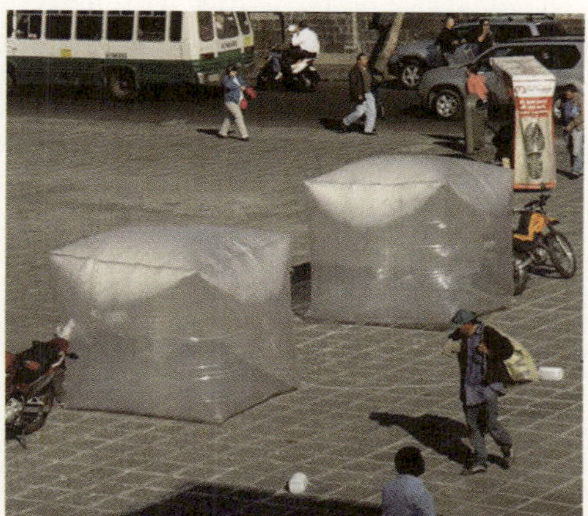

Marcela Armas, *Obstruction with Two-Stroke Engine: Two Motorcycles, Gasoline, Plastic Container, Gas Combustion*, 2009

Armas has also performed eco-activism in public space. For *Occupation* (2007) she walked the traffic-filled streets in Mexico City wearing a specially made backpack equipped with seven air horns, her physical and sonic presence competing with cars; by continuously sounding her sirens, she transformed herself into a human noise generator.[8] Further interventions on the capital's streets briefly rendered visible pollution from internal combustion engines. For *Obstruction with Two-Stroke Engine*, the exhaust pipes of two motorcycles were connected to separate plastic inflatables, and as their engines ran, the giant transparent containers filled to capacity with hazy fumes and condensation (the piece was installed twice in Mexico City: in Colonia Roma in 2009, and Santo Domingo Square in 2011). And with *Exhaust* (2009), Armas set up a twelve-meter-high plastic inflatable, mimicking the shape of a concrete supporting pillar, under a highway overpass in Iztapalapa, one of Mexico City's most populous and poorest boroughs. The piece was fully inflated by the exhaust of six stationary cars as their engines ran continuously for one day.

Armas's sculptural staging of urban pollution recalls earlier art projects that occupied public space to address environmental issues, such as Mexican artist Helen Escobedo's *Negro basura, negro mañana* (Black garbage, black future, 1991). For this weekend-long installation, Escobedo created a pathway in the capital's Chapultepec Park with ten tons of trash spray-painted black—assembling a mere seventh of the weekly refuse generated by visitors—which catalyzed a large public response. Armas's work also invokes German artist Gustav Metzger's "auto-destructive art," particularly *Project Stockholm, June (Phase 1)*, an ambitious installation-event scheduled to coincide with the UN Conference on the Human Environment in Stockholm in 1972 (but never fully realized).[9] Metzger's intention was for 120 stationary vehicles, lined up side-by-side, to run their engines for two weeks, their exhaust pipes affixed to a large hanger-like plastic container. The installation's duration would correlate with the UN event, expressing the urgency of addressing industrial air pollution that threatens environmental biodiversity by visualizing its everyday consumer production process. "Phase 2" would involve moving the cars into the tent, engines still running, until they spontaneously combusted; if they failed to ignite, Metzger planned to throw several small explosive devices into the tent to catalyze the blast. Providing a small dose of the "disease" of global pollution in order to raise defenses, the auto-destructive strategy, in the artist's terms, was meant to be

8 See video documentation of Amras's work on the artist's website, www.marcelaarmas.net. On art in public space in Mexico, see Hernández and Gurfinkel, *Limitless*.

9 A partial realization of the piece took place at the 8th Sharjah Biennial in 2007.

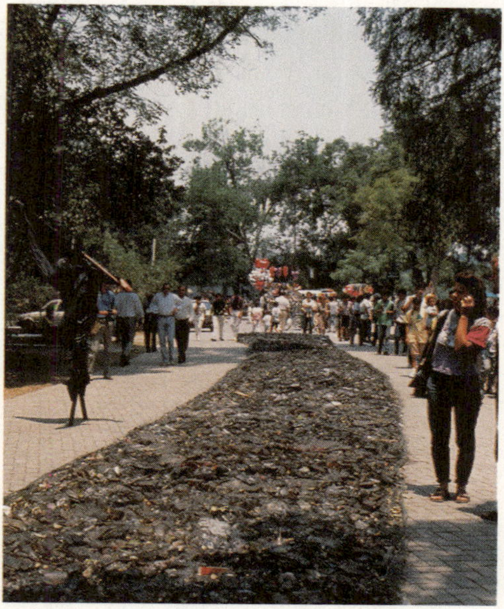

Helen Escobedo, *Negro basura, negro mañana*, 1991

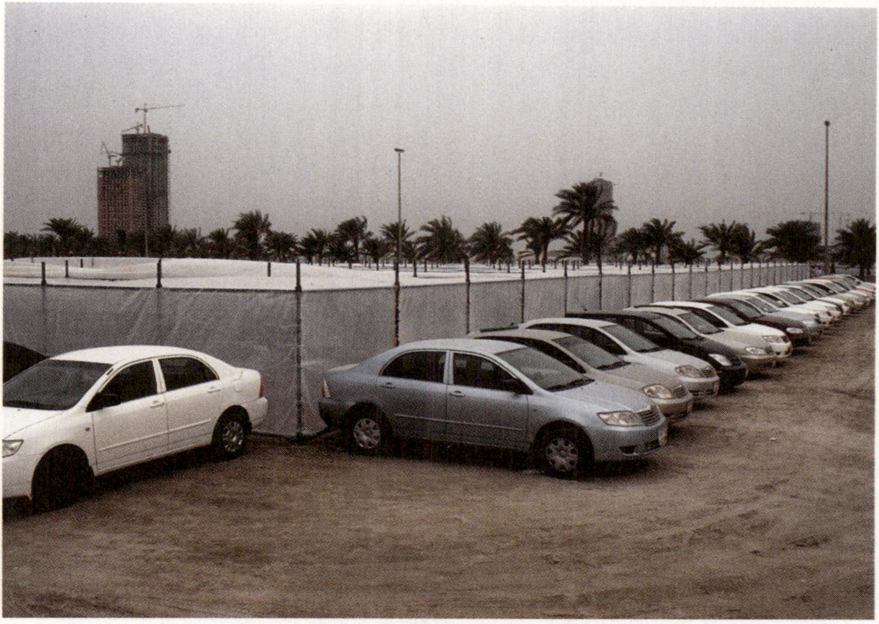

Gustav Metzger, *Project Stockholm, June (Phase 1)*, 1972/2007

"homeopathic": "By forcing people to look at the pollution created by one hundred and twenty cars over a period of two weeks [...] you are forcing them to confront what happens daily on the roads of all major countries," Metzger explained. "That was one of the ideas behind this concept, forcing people to see 'this is what it looks like', when it's deliberately concentrated."[10]

Aware of these precedents, Armas similarly argues that it's imperative for people in Mexico City to see what normally invisible air pollution looks like (not as smog on the horizon, but the result of vehicles up close, on the street), which overtakes any art-historical risk in repeating earlier work or strategies.[11] The goal is to address the governing politico-economic system as simply unsustainable ecologically. More specifically, Armas's work shows that automobile pollution in Mexico City is a major concern—and insufficiently addressed by decades of neoliberal governance—driven by the state's recent defunding of public transportation according to policies that favor privatization, especially at the level of individual mobility. Indeed, in recent years, we have witnessed what Mike Davis calls the "motorization of the Third World"—a logic cloaked in the language of development but based on individual consumption at the cost of environmentally sensitive public transportation.[12] In Mexico City, one response to the increase in air pollution has been to remove older and less efficient cars from the road, especially to reduce the growth of *contingencias ambientales*, air-quality crisis days when workers are given the day off and children stay home from school. With her public performances and sculptural installations, Armas not only momentarily disrupts everyday life by highlighting normally overlooked sound and air pollution, in acts of Metzger-like critical mimicry, she also generates discussions through these works, inviting passersby to consider and debate the destructive environmental conditions of Mexico City's motorized urbanism. As a form of practice-led ecological pedagogy, she uses videos of her actions and works in schools, universities, and community centers to expand conversation about the dangerous environment in the city, and inspire the search for creative alternatives.

10 Gustav Metzger, in conversation with T. J. Demos, "On *Project Stockholm, June (Phase 1)*," in *Catastrophe*, ed. Michael Corris et al., Transmission Annual no. 3 (London: Artwords Press, 2012), 90–98.

11 Marcela Armas, interview with the author, Mexico City, November 2013.

12 "International development agencies encourage destructive transport policies by their preference for financing roads rather than rails, as well as by encouraging the privatization of local transportation." Mike Davis, "Slum Ecology," in *Planet of Slums* (London: Verso Books, 2006), 131–33. Also see Paulina Oliva, "Environmental Regulations and Corruption: Automobile Emissions in Mexico City," *Journal of Political Economy* 123, no. 3 (2015): 686–724; and Lilian Calderón-Garcidueñas et al., "Megacities Air Pollution Problems: Mexico City Metropolitan Area Critical Issues on the Central Nervous System Pediatric Impact," *Environmental Research* 137 (February 2015): 157–69.

NAFTA Ecology

Environmental pollution, antidemocratic politics, human-rights abuses, violations of Indigenous sovereignty—corporate externalities in Mexico have been multiplying as neoliberal policies privilege a bottom line of profits and steadily increase the number of values deemed inessential or irrelevant. Biodiversity and seed heritage, labor value and social welfare, public health and social equality, thought to be "market distortions," have all been tossed to the side by the state, their worth and viability downgraded owing to a lack of clear economic value. This situation began in the 1980s: in 1982, amid falling oil prices, currency devaluations, inflation, and capital flight, Mexico experienced a massive debt crisis, leading to an emergency bailout by the IMF and the Federal Reserve under Reagan. The terms forced Mexico—like other countries across the developing world during that decade, such as Chile, Argentina, and Brazil—to accept austerity plans comprising sharp cuts to real wages and public spending and the elimination of subsidies for basic goods to prioritize paying back debts (which increased by billions of US dollars during this time).[13]

The implementation of NAFTA in 1994 introduced economic conditions that brought disaster to Mexican peasant farmers, as the country's market was pried open for the import of cheap industrialized agriculture from the United States. The drastic reduction of Mexican farming subsidies drove down the wages and living standards of those working for small-scale operations unable to compete with the subsidized, industrial, chemically fertilized, and genetically modified imports from the north.[14] The result brought a new dependence on imported corn and beans, which for millennia had been staples of homegrown Mexican cuisine.[15] "SAPs [structural adjustment

13 See Susan George, *A Fate Worse Than Debt: The World Financial Crisis and the Poor* (New York: Grove Press, 1988); Naomi Klein, *The Shock Doctrine: The Rise of Disaster Capitalism* (London: Penguin, 2007); and Harvey, *A Brief History of Neoliberalism*, 159–64. Harvey defines neoliberalism as a system of "accumulation by dispossession," with four main components: the privatization and commodification of public goods; financialization, in which objects are transformed into an instruments of economic speculation; the management and manipulation of crises through free trade; and state redistribution, in which the state defunds welfare, education, and health-care services, and supports upwardly mobile wealth.

14 For critical assessments of NAFTA, see, for instance, "NAFTA at 20: Lori Wallach on U.S. Job Losses, Record Income Inequality, Mass Displacement in Mexico," *Democracy Now!*, January 3, 2014, http://www.democracynow.org/2014/1/3/nafta_at_20_lori_wallach_on; and Public Citizen's Global Trade Watch, *NAFTA's 20-Year Legacy and the Fate of the Trans-Pacific Partnership*, February 2014, http://www.citizen.org/documents/NAFTA-at-20.pdf.

15 "Mexico, for example, has become dependent on imported food (including maize and beans that are the basis of the Mexican diet) which had represented 10 per cent of the total before the signing of the North American Free Trade Agreement (NAFTA) and which rose to a little over 40 per cent at the end of the first decade of the 21st century." Gian Carlo Delgado

programs] devastated rural smallholders by eliminating subsidies and pushing them sink or swim into global commodity markets dominated by heavily subsidized First World agribusiness," notes Mike Davis.[16]

In fact, NAFTA magnified the effects of earlier waves of structural adjustment in the 1980s. Social welfare programs, state-supported health care, and public-works projects were gradually defunded and privatized, as Mexico's budgets for social services were slashed (except the military's), fulfilling loan contingencies, which introduced a cascading of negative effects—economic, social, and environmental—written off as irrelevant to the purely financial priorities of the neoliberal market. One consequence was general impoverishment following the shift of formal employment toward precarious labor, including the move of former agricultural laborers to exploitative *maquiladora* sweatshop work, trailed, not surprisingly, by the growth of organized crime.[17] With the dismantling of rural farming, people swelled the capital and headed north to the United States. As northward-bound migration and Mexican urbanization intensified, so did protests, including the many "IMF riots" in debtor countries that had already begun in the late '80s.[18]

Mexico City, with more than twenty million inhabitants, is now one of the world's largest metropolises (along with Delhi, Shanghai, Lagos, and Jakarta) and promises to expand in the next few decades by incorporating neighboring cities, with a projected population of thirty-five million in 2050.[19] World population is predicted to peak at ten billion in 2050, with the majority of the growth occurring in cities of developing countries, upping

Ramos, "Common Goods, Socio-ecological Metabolism and the Common Future of Humanity: A North/South Analysis," in Daiber and Houtart, *A Postcapitalist Paradigm*, 75.

16 Davis, "SAPing the Third World," in *Planet of Slums*, 153. Ironically, many environmental groups—such as the National Wildlife Federation, Environmental Defense Fund, Conservation International, National Audubon Society, Natural Resources Defense Council, and World Wildlife Fund—supported NAFTA, owing to "reflexive political centrism" and "the growing influence of corporate 'partners' and donors" (Klein, *This Changes Everything*, 83–84).

17 See Agustín Escobar Latapí and Mercedes González de la Rocha, "Crisis, Restructuring and Urban Poverty in Mexico," *Environment and Urbanization* 7, no. 1 (April 1995): 63–64; and Anabel Hernández, *Narcoland: The Mexican Drug Lords and Their Godfathers* (London: Verso Books, 2013). Criminal cartels not only traffic drugs and weapons, but also sex workers, undocumented migrants, toxic waste, oil and gas, high-tech industry, black-market products, and automobiles.

18 See Davis, "SAPing the Third World"; David Bacon, "How US Policies Fueled Mexico's Great Migration," *Nation*, January 4, 2012, http://www.thenation.com/article/165438/how-us-policies-fueled-mexicos-great-migration; and John Walton and David Seddon, *Free Markets and Food Riots: The Politics of Structural Adjustment* (New York: John Wiley & Sons, 2011).

19 See Keith Pezzoli, "Mexico's Urban Housing Environments: Economic and Ecological Challenges of the 1990s," in *Human Settlements and Planning for Ecological Sustainability: The Case of Mexico City* (Cambridge, MA: MIT Press, 2000); and María Cristina Bayón and Gonzalo A. Saraví, "The Cultural Dimensions of Urban Fragmentation: Segregation, Sociability, and Inequality in Mexico City," *Latin American Perspectives* 40, no. 2 (March 2013): 35–52.

the pressure on already stressed infrastructure, governance, and resources.[20] In Mexico City, where a large section of the population lives in informal or slum conditions, the reality is the spread of precarious housing without basic services like running water, sewage, or electricity, and declining access to well-functioning schools and decent hospitals. NAFTA has also increased governmental neglect of environmental protections, transferring disaster risk to the poor. As we know, poverty magnifies geologic and climatic hazards, creating urban environments that are vulnerable to fires, landslides, floods, and earthquakes (in 1985, when the last major trembler struck Mexico City, its effects were felt mostly in poor areas).[21] Slums ramify urban blight and are subjected to concentrations of toxic industrial waste that middle-class zones would never tolerate (in 1984, a Pemex natural gas plant in the poor district of San Juanico exploded, killing two thousand residents).[22] Meanwhile, peripheral greenbelts have been transformed into wastelands, and up to 90 percent of sewage in Latin America is released untreated into streams and rivers.[23]

The "SAPing" of Mexico has nonetheless been countered by the positive growth of environmentalism, with groups like the Movimiento Ecologista Mexicano, Pacto de Ecologistas, and Alianza Nacional de Ecología focusing on conditions in the capital, where worsening air, land, and water pollution has dramatized the ecological costs of NAFTA-era externalities and environmental transformations.[24] Part of this mobilization has been an emerging eco-critique of the Washington-imposed development model, a critique informed by Indigenous cultural traditions and ecological knowledge, infused as well with the armed insurgency of the Zapatistas in Chiapas, whose very rebellion corresponded with the day NAFTA was implemented—January 1, 1994. Bottom-up rural organizations, such as Centro de Ecodesarrollo and Centro de Estudios Sociales y Ecológicos, supporting Indigenous ecology (based on local, organic farming),

20 Cited in Davis, *Planet of Slums*, 2. See also Eduardo López Moreno, *Slums of the World: The Face of Urban Poverty in the New Millennium?* (Nairobi: United Nations Human Settlements Program, 2003). The situation is exemplary of global trends: "In 1950 there were 86 cities in the world with a population of more than one million; today there are 400, and by 2015 there will be at least 550" (Davis, *Planet of Slums*, 1–2).

21 See Kenneth Hewitt, *Regions of Risk: A Geographical Introduction to Disasters* (Harlow: Longman, 1997), 217–18; and Davis, "Slum Ecology," 126.

22 See Joel Simon, *Endangered Mexico: An Environment on the Edge* (San Francisco: Sierra Club Books, 1997), 157; and Pezzoli, *Human Settlements*.

23 Davis, "Slum Ecology," 137; Ivo Imparato and Jeff Ruster, *Slum Upgrading and Participation* (Washington, DC: World Bank, 2003), 61; and Pezzoli, *Human Settlements*, 20.

24 Víctor M. Toledo, David Garrido, and Narciso Barrera-Bassols, "The Struggle for Life: Socio-environmental Conflicts in Mexico," *Latin American Perspectives* 42, no. 5 (September 2015): 133–47; and Nemer E. Narchi, "Environmental Violence in Mexico: A Conceptual Introduction," *Latin American Perspectives* 42, no. 5 (September 2015): 5–18.

have since joined with the formation of the agroecology movement to oppose Mexico's "Green Revolution" of GM biotechnology and chemical fertilizers, monoculture cash crops, and high energy costs.[25] Against neoliberalism's economics of externalities, they insist on recognizing human, social, and cultural factors as intrinsically valuable; for instance, the socioeconomic welfare of subsistence farmers, local cultural heritage, and environmental health.

Such is the long-standing project of eco-economics: to integrate externalities within the economic rationale of production and consumption and achieve a socio-ecological and political sustainability by weaving the defense of biodiversity with that of cultural diversity, food sovereignty with democratic regional governance.[26] "True-cost pricing," where, for instance, the environmental costs of a car's lifetime of use will be taken into account in determining its sales price, provides new criteria for revolutionizing industry and agriculture.[27] It thus avoids "externalizing the social burden," which, for Indian environmentalist Vandana Shiva, "is the very basis of profits and capital accumulation."[28] It's not that the current market is flawed and stands to be repaired; rather, neoliberal economics, in categorizing environmental destruction as an externality to render the market more efficient, is entirely backward. "At present, ecology movements are the primary voice stressing the full economic value of these natural processes," Shiva writes, insisting that natural goods, far from being dismissible as externalities, are ultimately more important than the market economy itself.[29] Without them, the economy could not even function.

25 Occurring between 1950 and 1970, Mexico's Green Revolution, like those in developing countries elsewhere, was a move toward chemical-intensive and corporate-supported farming technologies and practices, including the use of high-yielding types of cereal grains and hybridized seeds, irrigation infrastructure, modernized management techniques, and synthetic fertilizers and pesticides. For an introduction to its opposite, agroecology, see Stephen R. Gliessman and Eric W. Engles, *Agroecology: The Ecology of Sustainable Food Systems* (Boca Raton, FL: CRC Press, 2014). On the politics of GM agriculture in Mexico, see Silvia Ribeiro, "Monsanto Protection Act," trans. Joana Chelo, *ETC Group*, June 6, 2013, http://www.etcgroup.org/content/monsanto-protection-act; Kathleen McAfee, "Beyond Techno-science: Transgenic Maize in Fight over Mexico's Future," *Geoforum* 39, no. 1 (January 2008): 148–60; and Mark Schapiro, "Sowing Disaster?," *Nation*, October 10, 2002, http://www.thenation.com/article/sowing-disaster.

26 See Robert Hunziker, "Eco Economics Takes on Neoliberalism," *CounterPunch*, April 20, 2015, http://www.counterpunch.org/2015/04/20/eco-economics-takes-on-neoliberalism; and Peter G. Brown and Peter Timmerman, eds., *Ecological Economics for the Anthropocene: An Emerging Paradigm* (New York: Columbia University Press, 2015).

27 See Kevin P. Gallagher, *Free Trade and the Environment: Mexico, NAFTA, and Beyond* (Stanford, CA: Stanford University Press, 2004). Gallagher calls for "nation-states in the developing world and international institutions to address market failures related to environmental externalities" (80).

28 Vandana Shiva, *Earth Democracy: Justice, Sustainability, and Peace* (Cambridge, MA: South End Press, 2005), 17.

29 Ibid., 16.

Plants, Biogas, Guns, Shovels

A number of socially engaged art practices in Mexico have taken on this integrative ecological initiative, offering creative ways to repair damaged ecosystems. They move beyond merely rendering visible the negative externalities of material, industrial, and social waste, and attempt to redirect the repressed, unaccounted, and disavowed toward positive ends. Consider Gilberto Esparza's *Plantas Nómadas* (Nomadic plants, 2008–13), a mobile biorobotic hybrid capable of cleaning polluted rivers by collecting organic residues, metals, and petroleum-based effluents, and using them as energy sources. Developed through a collaboration with Dr. Carlos Godínez, an expert in power systems and microbial fuel cells, and Dr. Alejandro Rodríguez Ángeles, a specialist in mechanical electronics, the ten-legged cyborg is the size of a small dog and capable of independent movement, and grows its own plants that assist with bioremediation. Energized by solar cells, biosensors direct its motion as it seeks out industrial waste to process as food, its metabolism working inside a microbial fuel cell. The cell generates oxidation, stimulating the growth of microbes that begin, with the help of its mechanical system, to internalize, process, and clean the river, in the process generating energy to keep the cyborg operating. Esparza tested the prototype in the Río Lerma, Mexico's second largest river, commonly known as the most polluted waterway in Mexico, finding that it successfully contributed to the river's remediation, if on a minimal scale.

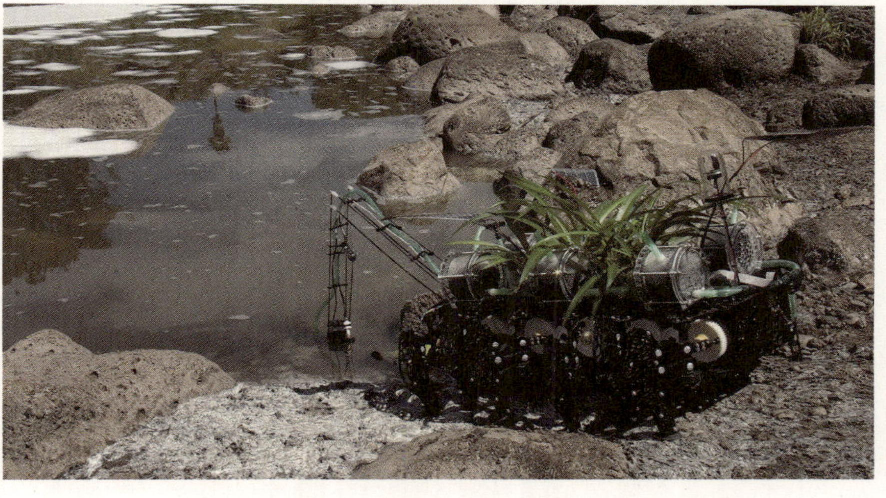

Gilberto Esparza, *Plantas Nómadas*, 2008–13

In a like-minded effort to recuperate waste in Mexico, Superflex, working between artistic practice and small-scale geo-engineering, developed a model of *Supergas*. The Danish collective, in collaboration with biogas engineer Jan Mallan, had previously deployed the system in the late 1990s in underdeveloped regions, such as Tanzania, Cambodia, Thailand, and Zanzibar. The ten-foot-tall ovoid unit is set in the ground and converts organic matter into combustible fuel (methane and carbon dioxide) and ammonia-based fertilizer, producing from the dung of two or three cattle approximately three to four cubic meters of gas per day—enough for the cooking needs of a large family. From 2010 to 2012, Superflex collaborated with Taller de Operaciones Ambientales (Studio of Environmental Operations), a Mexican engineering and product design firm, on a *Supergas* prototype for mass production. The aim is to provide an alternative source of energy, especially for people too poor or isolated to access electricity or fuel.[30] Designed to be sold at affordable rates to individual families, particularly in agricultural areas in the equatorial belt, *Supergas* is a model for a self-sufficient recycling technology enabling communities to access low-cost fuel not otherwise provided by state infrastructure (owing partly, in Mexico, to NAFTA-related cutbacks).

One might ask: Do the eco-designs of Esparza and Superflex merely reproduce green-capitalist ventures, as prototypes for mass-produced commodities? Or are they an urgently needed conceptual model of energy sovereignty? Esparza explains: "The energy issue is fundamental. The maintenance of a system based practically on a single energy source—oil—subordinates the weaker economies to a small core of power, with devastating consequences for the planet in social and environmental terms."[31] By transforming waste into energy, merging technology and organic refuse in ecological symbiosis, these models assist communities in being more independent and self-sufficient. That said, they are far from perfect solutions. When I asked Esparza what critical traction his prototypes possess in the very techno-scientific capitalist economy on which they depend for food, he acknowledged their "monstrous" character, immersed in "paradox"[32]—much like his *Parásitos Urbanos* (2010). Built from discarded technology, these bizarre mechanico-insectoid miscreants scavenge energy from city infrastructure by crawling along electric wires and tapping into their power flows (occasionally

30 See the *Supergas* website, http://www.supergas.dk/; and Superflex's essay contribution to *SITAC IX: Theory and Practice of Catastrophe*, ed. Eduardo Abaroa (Mexico City: Patronato de Arte Contemporáneo, 2013).

31 Gilberto Esparza, "Introducción," *Plantas Nómadas* (blog), January 2010, http://plantasnomadas.blogspot.de/2010/01/plantas-nomadas.html (my translation).

32 Gilberto Esparza, conversation with the author, Mexico City, November 2013.

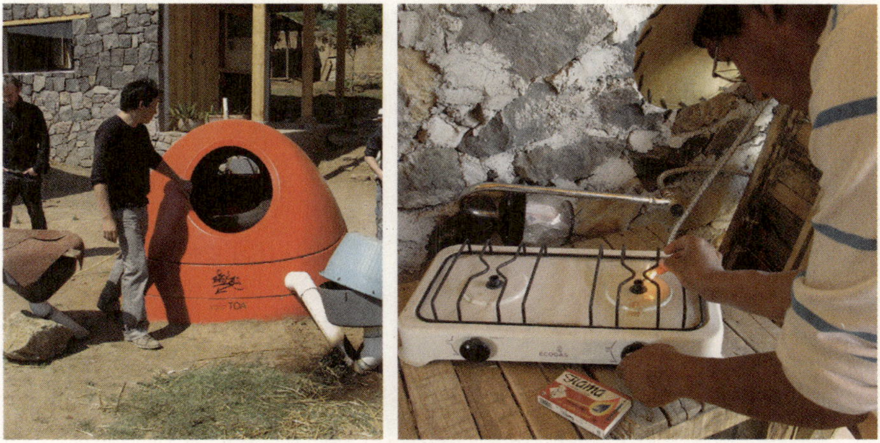

Superflex, *Supergas*, Mexico, 2014

spotted by bewildered passersby).[33] These models, given their small scale and isolated occurrences, acknowledge the limited effectiveness of their techno-fixes, yet still try to operate within the world and ameliorate its dysfunctional conditions.

Further repurposing objects of capitalist destruction, akin to an eco-Situationist *détournement*, Pedro Reyes's *Palas por Pistolas* (Guns for Shovels, 2008) transforms the dehumanizing violence of narco-trafficking, itself a symptom of the NAFTA-era economy, into an ecologically recuperated form.[34] Offering a model of social and biological remediation that is also a machine for integrating externalities, his project was commissioned by the botanical garden in Culiacán, a city in western Mexico plagued with mafia-related gun violence. Reyes ran ads on local television stations that invited citizens to donate weapons in exchange for coupons for domestic appliances and electronics. Residents traded in a total of 1,527 guns, nearly half of which were clandestinely circulated military-grade arms. The guns were taken to a military zone and crushed by a bulldozer, the metal rubble then melted down in a foundry and brought to a hardware factory to make 1,527 gardening shovels (their handles inscribed with legends describing the story behind their fabrication). These shovels, a contemporary version of the biblical "swords-into-plowshares" story, were then sent to schools and art institutions (in

33 See Gilberto Esparza, *Parásitos Urbanos* (blog), http://urbanparasites.blogspot.com.

34 On the integral connections between the US-sponsored drug war, Mexico's narco-violence, and NAFTA-related neoliberalism, see Peter Watt, *Drug War Mexico: Politics, Neoliberalism and Violence in the New Narcoeconomy* (London: Zed Books, 2012).

addition to participating international art institutions), where they were used to plant 1,527 trees, primarily in the Cualiacán region, forming what the artist calls a "ritual [that] has a pedagogical purpose of showing how an agent of death can become an agent of life."[35]

Clearly it would be simplistic to suggest that Mexico's gang violence could be repaired through gardening, or similarly, to propose that environmental concern for trees can solve mass drug-related murder. Yet Reyes's project has no such pretense; rather, it unleashes symbolic power as well as an exemplary, if microcosmic, pragmatism, by transforming human systems of destruction into ecological repair. It thereby approaches an ambitious project of political ecology by exposing the deathly social costs of current economic priorities and glimpsing an alternative system that, if implemented at a larger scale, would place the welfare and value of life, community, and environment above market efficiency and corporate profits. Still, like Esparza's *Plantas Nómadas* and Superflex's *Supergas*, Reyes's project addresses social, economic, and environmental effects without locating their systemic causes directly in neoliberal capitalism, whose focus on corporate wealth accumulation makes it appear, as Noam Chomsky contends, that "the survival of the [human] species is an externality."[36] Esparza and Superflex (through environmental techno-science) and Reyes (intervening into gun regulation) variously recuperate the damaging by-products of our irrational economy. Yet in doing so, these artistic models point to a further quandary: Should we support green entrepreneurs who favor measures such as environmental taxes and full costing to integrate corporate externalities, which keeps us within the same system that produced the problems in the first place? Or should we be skeptical of such commodification and call for new forms of government to address the environmental crisis by venturing outside of capitalist priorities, and placing ecological and sociopolitical concerns above economic growth imperatives? If life as we know it is at stake, as Chomsky implies, then

35 Cited from the artist's website, accessed August 10, 2015, http://pedroreyes.net/palasporpistolas.php. Continuing this series, Reyes used revolvers, shotguns, and machine guns collected by the government in Ciudad Juárez to create musical instruments for *Imagine* (2012), and weapons collected by the Mexican army to make mechanical instruments for *Disarm* (2013). In 2013, Mexico City's government introduced a buyback program offering citizens cash, bikes, and computers for their firearms.

36 Cited in "Chomsky on Governance, Science and Art," *Para_Doxa* (blog), April 17, 2010, https://neodoxa.wordpress.com/2010/04/17/chomsky-on-governance-science-and-art/; first published in *Z Magazine*, May 2010. In addition, the piece appears as mere token gesture when one realizes that "about 2,000 guns per day enter illegally into Mexico across the border with the United States." Santiago Navarro F., "Michoacan and the Economics of Crime," *Truthout*, January 28, 2014, http://www.truth-out.org/news/item/21431-michoacan-and-the-economics-of-crime.

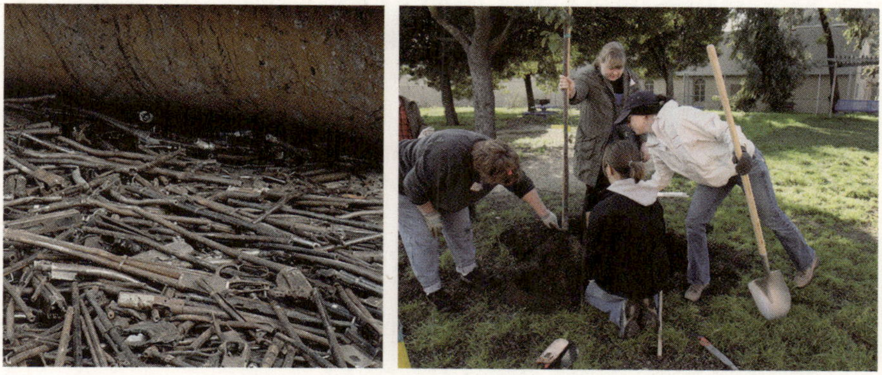

Pedro Reyes, *Palas por Pistolas*, 2008

perhaps the best approach is to ecologize the economy instead of economizing the environment.[37]

Zapatista Ecology

Closest to this last approach in the Mexican context is the Zapatista Army of National Liberation (Ejército Zapatista de Liberación Nacional, EZLN), a revolutionary formation in the southeastern state of Chiapas not explicitly aligned with socialism, environmentalism, or artistic experimentation, although creatively incorporating elements from each.[38] The insurgency merges both Indigenous-agricultural and radical-democratic practices with the imperatives of the worldwide alter-globalization movement for social justice, which took off in the late 1990s with anti-IMF protests (inspired partly by the EZLN). With former leading spokesperson Subcomandante Marcos proclaiming that "NAFTA is the death certificate for the Indigenous people of Mexico,"[39]

37 Eco-socialist Richard Smith summarizes: "All such market-based efforts are doomed to fail, and a sustainable economy is inconceivable without sweeping systemic economic change. The project of sustainable capitalism based on carbon taxes, green marketing, 'dematerialization' and so forth was misconceived and doomed from the start because maximizing profit and saving the planet are inherently in conflict." Arguing that capitalism is incapable of turning away from profit maximization to save the planet from ecological disaster, Smith supports a democratically planned eco-socialist economy. Richard Smith, "Green Capitalism: The God That Failed," *Truthout*, January 9, 2014, http://www.truth-out.org/news/item/21060-green-capitalism-the-god-that-failed.

38 "Despite its religious and ethnic overlays, the Zapatista revolt was essentially an ecological struggle, one that focused on two central questions: Who controls the land, and what do they use it for?" James D. Nations, "The Ecology of the Zapatista Revolt," *Cultural Survival Quarterly* 18, no. 1 (Spring 1994), http://www.culturalsurvival.org/publications/cultural-survival-quarterly/mexico/ecology-zapatista-revolt.

39 Marcos, cited in ibid.

the movement of native peasant farmers, largely Tzotzil Maya, countered NAFTA's inauguration with a proclamation of their own agenda, which linked their rebellion to five hundred years of struggle against Spanish colonialism, subsequent and ongoing North American imperialism, and the continuous oppression of Mexican governments in the twentieth and twenty-first centuries. Allying themselves with the fight for *tierra y libertad* (land and liberty) by early twentieth-century Mexican revolutionaries Pancho Villa and Emiliano Zapata, the Zapatistas initiated "a plan that struggles for work, land, housing, food, health care, education, independence, freedom, democracy, justice and peace," and the protection of natural resources for the benefit of the people of Chiapas.[40] The Zapatistas employ a radical combination of aesthetics, high-tech acumen, and grassroots organizing. Ecology, for them, was never a superficial, inessential element of the struggle; from the beginning it has been integral to the Zapatistas' political goals and revolutionary way of life, and has come to serve as a key model of politico-ecological commitments for the wider environmentalist movement in the Americas, from the US-based Indigenous Environmental Network to the climate justice struggles in Bolivia, Chile, Ecuador, and beyond.

Due to its natural wealth, Chiapas has been site of intensive resource extraction since Spanish colonial times, with water, oil, gas, and pine and oak trees expropriated for the rest of the country, leaving the region's inhabitants resource-poor. More recently, highland forests have been converted to cash crops, the Ocosingo Valley cleared for sugarcane and coffee plantations, and the Lacandon jungle partly transformed into pastureland and cattle ranches and explored for fossil fuel deposits, all with destructive results for the local ecosystem and population.[41] Zapatista ecology has conversely emphasized, and aimed at implementing, sustainable technologies, including

40 General Command of the EZLN, "First Declaration from the Lacandon Jungle," December 31, 1993, reprinted in *¡Ya basta! Ten Years of the Zapatistas' Uprising*, ed. Ziga Vodovnik (Oakland, CA: AK Press, 2004), 645. Among the extensive literature on the Zapatistas, see John Holloway, "Change the World without Taking Power," in *Alternative Economics, Alternative Societies*, ed. Oliver Ressler (Gdansk: Wyspa Institute of Art, 2007), 172–75; John Holloway and Eloína Peláez, eds, *Zapatista! Reinventing Revolution in Mexico* (London: Pluto Press, 1998); Jan Rus, Rosalva Aída Hernández Castillo, and Shannan L. Mattiace, eds., *Mayan Lives, Mayan Utopias: The Indigenous Peoples of Chiapas and the Zapatista Rebellion* (Lanham, MD: Rowman & Littlefield, 2003); and Gloria Muñoz Ramírez, *The Fire and the Word: A History of the Zapatista Movement* (San Francisco: City Lights Publishers, 2008).

41 NAFTA-era reforms also included the elimination of Article 27 of the Mexican Constitution, which had guaranteed small plots of land (*ejidos*) to millions of Mexicans living in rural areas, allowing them instead to be bought by foreign firms and large plantations, a dispossession that became a major catalyst for the Zapatista uprising. See David Carruthers, "Indigenous Ecology and the Politics of Linkage in Mexican Social Movements," *Third World Quarterly* 17, no. 5 (December 1996): 1007–28.

locally produced electricity via wind, solar power, and biogas, and collective public transportation powered by recycled oil. They practice organic subsistence farming, fair trade, zero waste, and low-cost water treatment. Their protection of the region's rich seed heritage opposes GM biotechnology, corporate monocultures, and the use of petrochemical fertilizers and pesticides.[42] And their valuing of nature as a noneconomic resource rejects the financial imperatives of green capitalism, such as offsetting programs like REDD that entail corporations paying Indigenous communities to maintain forests in the south so that industry can continue polluting elsewhere.[43] In contrast, the EZLN place collective ecological considerations above individualist consumption (hardly an option for impoverished farmers), and view the inclusive, participatory sharing of resources as the only answer to safeguarding the future of the earth's ecology. This commitment is reflected in their popular slogan, derived from Subcomandante Marcos: *Para todos todo, para nosotros nada*, "Everything for everyone, nothing for us."[44] As reaffirmed in their long-standing motto, *¡Ya basta!*, their form of life represents a direct retort to neoliberal market-based solutions that cause wanton destruction of the environment as well as economic and political inequality, produce expendable people, and eradicate Indigenous culture. Environmental journalist Jeff Conant has observed, "In the 1990s, the Zapatistas told the world 'Enough already!' That message resonates in today's climate crisis."[45]

The Zapatistas provide a crucial antidote to the sociopolitical, agrarian-economic system designed to maximize corporate profits, while consigning all else—the lives of farmers, environmental biodiversity, a healthy ecosystem—to externalities. But as they struggle to maintain and develop their autonomy in remote Chiapas, what does their model of existence mean for those in the technologically developed and urban world? For environmental economist Gian Carlo Delgado Ramos, the Zapatista model proposes nothing less than a revolutionary turn toward biophysical, or sustainable, *degrowth*: "an equitable down-scaling of production and

42 Jeff Conant, "What the Zapatistas Can Teach Us about the Climate Crisis," *Foreign Policy in Focus*, August 3, 2010, http://fpif.org/what_the_zapatistas_can_teach_us_about_the_climate_crisis. Also see Jeff Conant, *A Poetics of Resistance: The Revolutionary Public Relations of the Zapatista Insurgency* (Oakland: AK Press, 2010).

43 Tom Goldtooth, director of the US-based Indigenous Environmental Network, calls REDD a "corruption of the sacred"; in Chris Lang, "'The REDD train is going pretty fast and it's left us at the station': Interview with Tom B. K. Goldtooth," *REDD Monitor*, January 14, 2009, http://www.redd-monitor.org/2009/01/14/interview-with-tom-bk-goldtooth/; and *The Stern Review*, released in 2006, called climate change "the biggest market failure in history." Meanwhile, most developed nations continue to push for REDD and other offset mechanisms.

44 Subcomandante Marcos, "Votán—Zapata or Five Hundred Years of History, April 10, 1994," in *Our Word Is Our Weapon: Selected Writings*, ed. Juana Ponce De Leon (New York: Seven Stories Press, 2004), 20.

45 Conant, "What the Zapatistas Can Teach Us."

consumption that increases human well-being and enhances ecological conditions at the local and global level, in the short term and long term."[46] The objective is a "genuine socio-environmental sustainability" and a "harmonious socio-ecological metabolism," which offers one potential future world approximated in the present by the Zapatistas.[47]

While the Zapatistas have declared their autonomy and refused to work within state structures, the insurgency has also taken important steps toward collaborating with international activists and Indigenous movements, and reaching out to alter-globalization politics beyond their region.[48] Three examples should suffice. In 2005, the Zapatistas undertook a six-month "Other Campaign" in opposition to the concurrent Mexican presidential campaign, which led them across Mexico's thirty-one states to discuss shared political goals with national leftist organizations, Indigenous groups, and NGOs. In 2007, they initiated Intercontinental Indigenous Encounters, a series inviting native peoples from around the world to gather in Guaymas in northwestern Mexico, to mark "515 years since the invasion of ancient Indigenous territories and the onslaught of the war of conquest, spoils and capitalist exploitation."[49] And in the summer of 2013, the Zapatistas organized Escuelita de la Libertad, inviting international activists to the "little school of freedom" in Chiapas to learn from ten years of Zapatista autonomy and mobilize support for grassroots resistance movements worldwide.[50] With these campaigns their struggle has reached out to an international Indigenous and activist network organized around political ecology, including the Workers' Landless Movement in Brazil, which took an active role in 2010 at the World People's Conference on Climate Change and the Rights of Mother Earth in Cochabamba, Bolivia, the alternative to the UN climate change negotiations in Cancun.[51]

46 Ramos, "Common Goods, Socio-ecological Metabolism," 73. Ramos also refers here to Schneider et al., "Crisis or Opportunity," 512.

47 Ramos, "Common Goods, Socio-ecological Metabolism," 74.

48 See John Holloway, *Change the World without Taking Power: The Meaning of Revolution Today* (London: Pluto Press, 2002); and Peter Rosset, María Elena Martínez-Torres, and Luis Hernández-Navarro, "Zapatismo in the Movement of Movements," *Development* 48, no. 2 (June 2005): 35–41. This latter article argues that the Zapatistas' approaches to diversity, autonomy, power, and resistance to neoliberalism have been valuable in elaborating proposals to confront the challenge of European societies. Also see Kara Zugman Dellacioppa, "The Bridge Called Zapatismo: Transcultural and Transnational Activist Networks in Los Angeles and Beyond," *Latin American Perspectives* 38, no. 1 (January 2011): 120–37.

49 Comandante David said in an interview, "The object of this meeting is to meet one another and to come to know one another's pains and sufferings. It is to share our experiences, because each tribe is different." Brenda Norrell, "Zapatistas Select Yaqui to Host Intercontinental Summit in Mexico," *Narco News Bulletin*, April 23, 2007, http://www.narconews.com/Issue45/article2637.html.

50 See Leonidas Oikonomakis, "Zapatistas Celebrate 10 Years of Autonomy with 'Escuelita,'" *ROAR Magazine*, August 6, 2013, http://roarmag.org/2013/08/escuelita-zapatista-10-year-autonomy. See also Natalia Arcos, "Relato de la Escuelita Zapatista," *El Ciudadano*, August 27, 2013, http://www.elciudadano.cl/2013/08/27/79979/relato-de-la-escuelita-zapatista.

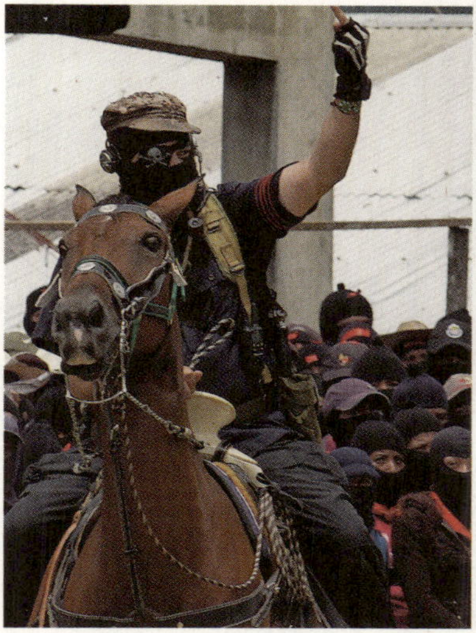

Grupo de Investigación en Arte y Política (GIAP), *The Farewell of Subcomandante Marcos*, 2014

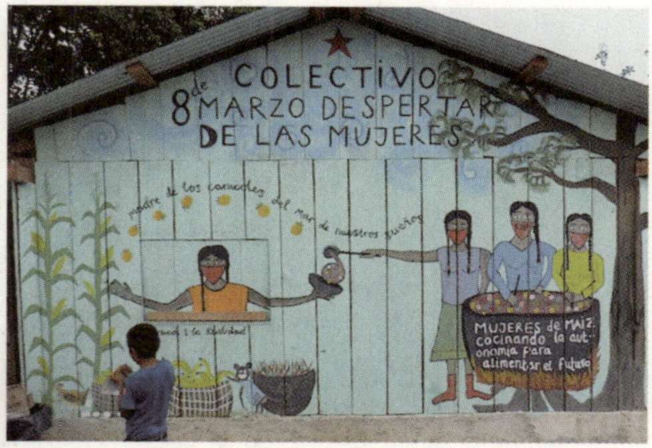

Grupo de Investigación en Arte y Política (GIAP), *Mural in La Realidad*, 2014

Integral to the Zapatistas' politics of aesthetics has been impassioned displays of revolutionary collectivism involving music and speeches, as well as carnivalesque parades and protests, and Indigenous craft traditions and mural painting. Going beyond their Chiapas-based manifestations, they have also developed online media platforms and networks to disseminate political messages and news, and to link with activists, NGOs, and political organizations worldwide. (They have drawn extensively on the potency of Marcos's appearance, which resonates with a powerful revolutionary iconography in Latin America of charismatic rebels such as Zapata and Che Guevara.)[52] Extending their international reach further, the Zapatistas' multifaceted political appearance is frequently

51 In Cochabamba, participants declared that the dignity of climate justice demands "that equity between North and South can only be reached when the Northern notion of environmental sustainability (preservation of resources for planetary needs and future generations) is matched with the Southern demand for social sustainability (equity, and full social, environmental, political and cultural rights)." "Peoples Agreement," *World People's Conference on Climate Change and the Rights of Mother Earth*, April 22, 2010, https://pwccc.wordpress.com/support. See also Conant, "What the Zapatistas Can Teach Us."

52 On Marcos's image economy, see Antigoni Memou, "The Zapatistas and the Media Spectacle," and "Zapatistas, Photography and the Internet or Winning the Game of Visibility," in *Photography and Social Movements: From the Globalisation of the Movement (1968) to the Movement against Globalization (2001)* (Manchester: Manchester University Press, 2013), 32–50, 86–100. On Zapatista aesthetics more broadly, see the analysis by Grupo de Investigación en Arte y Politica, in particular "Dialogo No. 1," *GIAP* (blog), accessed May 17, 2016, https://elblogdegiap.wordpress.com/dialogo-no1.

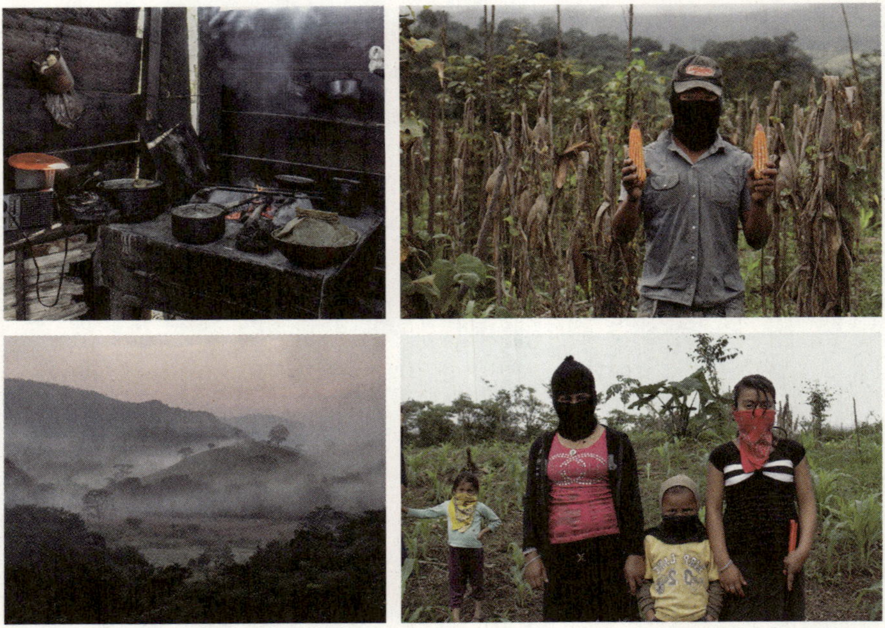

Grupo de Investigación en Arte y Política (GIAP), Zapatista farmers practicing agroecology, 2014–15

referenced and idealized in international art and cultural discourse, especially in relation to socially engaged art, where the Mexican rebels function as an exemplar for artist-activists in other contexts. For instance, curator Nato Thompson writes: "There is no way to conceive of the protest in Seattle in 1999 as anything but inspired by the Zapatistas' use of the carnivalesque, poetics, the Internet, and social networking culture. This is to say that over the last twenty years, we have seen the integration of cultural manipulation into its most poignant social movements and accompanying forms of activism. Certainly the antics of the Yes Men—who poke fun at corporate power through their numerous appearances on television and in print media, positing as executives—is another example of resistance manifesting itself in the media-sphere via the manipulation of cultural symbols."[53] Yet

53 Nato Thompson, "Living as Form," in *Living as Form: Socially Engaged Art from 1991–2011*, ed. Nato Thompson (Cambridge, MA: MIT Press, 2012), 30. For additional recent reference to the Zapatistas in the international artistic-cultural context, see Flood and Grindon, *Disobedient Objects*, 57. Also consider the Electronic Disturbance Theater, which has generated agit-prop actions since 1998—such as jamming the Mexican government's website to hinder its repressive policies—"to mobilize micro-networks to act in solidarity with the Zapatistas in Chiapas." Ricardo Dominguez, "Electronic Disturbance Theater," in *Corpus Delecti: Performance Art of the Americas*, ed. Coco Fusco (London: Routledge, 1999), 284.

while the EZLN clearly remain a powerful ideal for those outside of Chiapas who wish to reject the terms of neoliberal capitalism, such a comparison also potentially fails to take seriously the expansive scale and radical ambition of the Zapatista rebellion on its own terms. There, art becomes nothing less than a politico-aesthetic means of building an alternate revolutionary world whose anticapitalist, sociopolitical, and ecological elements define a holistic and sustainable form of life.

Return of a Lake

The Zapatista rebellion is clearly singular in its eco-politics, distinct from the models of Mexican contemporary art considered above although integral to their discursive context. In addition, it is relatively isolated geographically, based in the mountainous highlands and rainforests of Chiapas, not the urban environment of Mexico City. In light of the preceding discussion, we might ask again what alternatives are available in Mexico's metropolitan regions for a sustainable ecology, where revolutionary withdrawal from the state isn't an option at present. In this chapter, we've examined practices that make visible the deleterious waste of corporate capitalism, and others that invent experimental technologies and social systems to exploit the potential of these normally discarded products. Let's now look at an artistic practice that both amplifies a local urban struggle through a critical reckoning with colonial history and empowers demands for democratic regional governance and ecological sustainability.

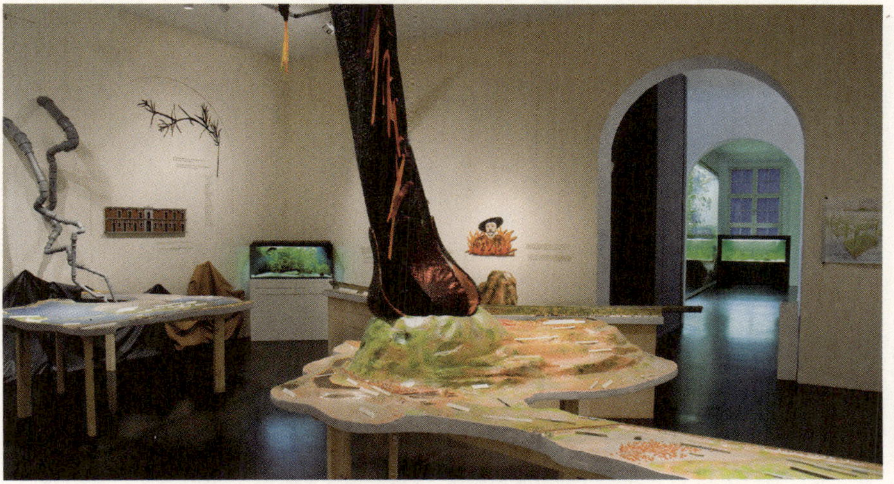

Maria Thereza Alves, *Return of a Lake*, 2012

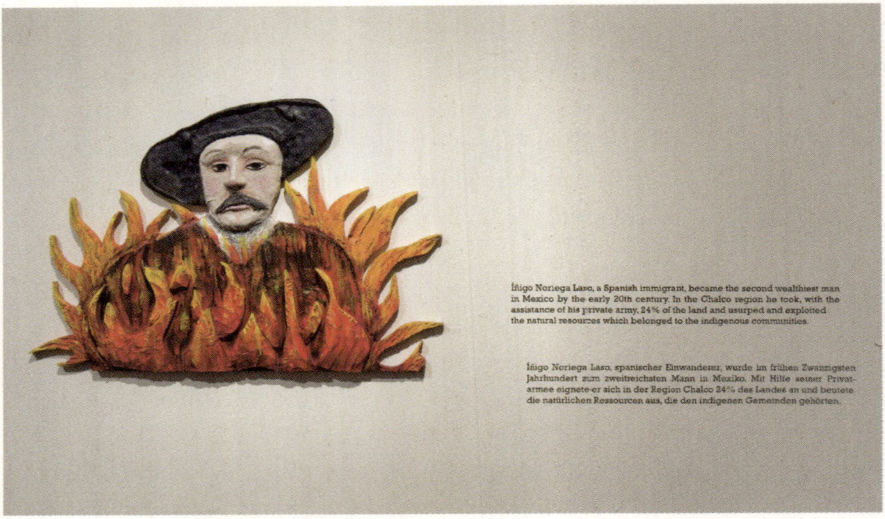

Maria Thereza Alves, *Return of a Lake*, 2012

For her mixed-media installation *Return of a Lake* (2012), Brazilian artist Maria Thereza Alves investigated the area of Chalco on the eastern edge of Mexico City, presenting her project at dOCUMENTA (13). The local lake, as if possessing a will of its own, reappeared more than a century after it was drained to make way for farmland, rebelling against the degradation of colonial and economic exploitation. Alves's work shows how the lake's return has inspired the imagination of a different world, one that is politically just, equitably resourced, and ecologically viable. In 1985, water began emerging from the ground after the construction of several wells to tap the aquifer and deliver water to the capital. As the water was withdrawn from subterranean cavities, the ground began to sink; by 2013 it was twelve meters lower than its level almost thirty years ago, and it filled with water. In an area previously dedicated to agriculture, Lake Tláhuac-Xico—named after the borough and another nearby town—has now become a substantial body of water, and a new source of conflict for regional disputes, real estate interests, and competing water management systems.

Alves maps this conflict in her installation, which comprises three dioramas that represent Chalco: a scaled model of the region, showing the lake and bordering land developments; another of the nearby volcanic mountain now ringed by housing projects, an extension of the informal urbanism of Mexico City; and a reproduction of a section of an open-air canal that, used for waste disposal and notoriously plagued with inefficiency, regularly overflows during rainy seasons, pouring untreated sewage into local homes. (When its walls broke in 2010, eighteen thousand people were forced to flee, as one of the many descriptive cards on the sculpture explains). Giant ramshackle pipes extend from the lake scene, indicating the interventionist technology of water extraction for use in the capital, and the volcano appears in blazing eruption, as if responding angrily to humanity's treatment of the land. (The eruption also refers to local tradition: belief has it that the Mesoamerican deity Quetzalcoatl fled to safety from the Spanish conquistadors by diving into the Xico volcano, where he now slumbers.) Cast in a folk aesthetic, Alves's models employ a vernacular handmade style reminiscent of displays in community museums, such as the Museo Comunitario del Valle de Xico, with whom the artist collaborated in her research.

The visual argot, more broadly, speaks to the artist's politics of localism, here posed against the environmental devastation wrought by real estate development, the swelling capital's water needs, and informal dumping and industrial waste. These elements are revealed in a selection of Mexican newspaper clippings in one corner of her installation that report of ongoing governmental, industrial, and political threats to the region's ecology as well as the community museum's existence. The piece, in this regard, develops the artist's long-standing commitments to environmental justice and political activism—in 1979, she created the Brazilian Information Center, which lobbied for the human rights of Indigenous peoples; in 1981, she cofounded the Green Party in São Paulo; and from 1987 to 1994 she lived in Cuernavaca, Mexico, with her partner, artist Jimmie Durham, where she extended her politico-ecological agenda via art exhibitions, collective practice with Espacio Verde and La Estación, and helping to found the Green Party in Mexico. These interlinked concerns have broadly defined her artistic commitments, as with projects such as *Seeds of Change* (1999–ongoing), for which Alves creates gardens from seeds found in ships' ballast during the maritime trade of colonial and industrial modernity.[54] What's more, *Return of a Lake* continues Alves's longstanding interest in collaborative practice: circulated internationally, the local environmental self-determination in the work amounts to an aesthetics of resistance for postcolonial justice, Indigenous rights, and ecological sustainability.

54 Alves describes the project, which began in Marseille: "*Seeds of Change* is an investigation based on original research (no previous scientific studies exist on ballast flora in Marseille) to unearth historical ballast sites and ballast flora while studying the emergent flora at the sites in the Port of Marseille. This project raises questions on the parallels between the discourses of defining what epoch in the geographical history of place classifies its 'naturalness'? At what moment do seeds become native? What are the socio-political histories of place that classify the framework of belonging?" In *Maria Theresa Alves*, ed. Mai Tran (Nantes: École des beaux-arts, 2013), 14.

The resurgence of waters in Chalco is the most recent in a series of geographical changes since precolonial days when the actors in the basin were Indigenous populations and biodiverse flora and fauna. In the history that Alves presents, as represented in both her installation and its detailed catalogue, one figure stands out who substantially altered the region's habitat in a manner verging on ecocide: Íñigo Noriega Laso (1853–1923), a Spanish landowner and businessman whose modernizing projects brought about the brutal dispossession of Indigenous lands. Having immigrated to Mexico in 1867, Noriega, a close friend of President Porfirio Díaz, mobilized his political connections and gained the right to drain what was formerly called Lake Chalco—an ecosystem that had supported native life for thousands of years—carrying out a massive geo-engineering project between 1885 and 1903 that created agricultural lands to surround his opulent hacienda. Noriega soon became one of the country's richest men through his agricultural industries, though he was forced to flee Mexico when the revolution broke out in 1910, as we learn from the research by Alves and the Museo Comunitario.[55] In Spain, Noriega is still considered a heroic *indiano* (a primitivizing term describing Spanish colonials), celebrated in the Museo de la Emigración in Colombres, for his colonial entrepreneurialism. The museum is located in a mansion Noriega built in 1906, and Alves's installation represents its facade in a relief sculpture.[56]

The research by Alves and the Museo Comunitario refutes this triumphalist history, detailing how Noriega amassed his immense wealth by exploiting Indigenous campesinos and destroying their habitat. His many crimes are detailed in the catalogue, in chapters such as "Íñigo Noriega Laso: The Destroyer of My Pueblo" by Raymundo Martínez (a Chalca whose grandparents were expelled from San Martín, a village in Xico, by Noriega) and Alves's "Why the Indigenous People Did Not Like Íñigo and Held Prejudices against the Spanish." He was responsible for forcibly resettling native communities on inferior land and thereby eliminating the Indigenous community's subsistence-based livelihood, eradicating the lake's biodiversity as well, including numerous species of birds and fish (in the installation, Alves

55 This is corroborated through independent research: Noriega's interests included his agricultural enterprises, factories producing turpentine and resin, textiles, tobacco, mining, and railroads. See the bibliographic entry "Íñigo Noriega Laso Papers, 1586–1928," *Texas Archival Resources Online*, http://www.lib.utexas.edu/taro/utlac/00277/lac-00277.html.

56 "It is thought by the Museo de la Emigración [founded in 1987] in Íñigo's hometown of Colombres, Asturias, in Spain, and by his descendents in Mexico, that Íñigo was 'a great man' who was outstanding in his business due to his grand vision as an impresario." Maria Thereza Alves, "Some Points of View of Íñigo Noriega," in *The Return of a Lake* (Cologne: Verlag der Buchhandlung Walther König, 2012), 149.

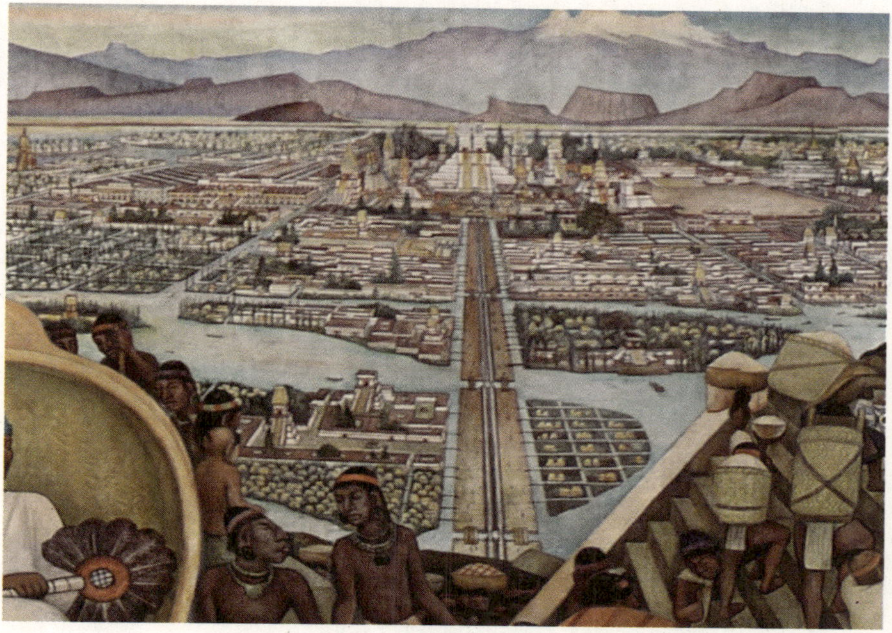

Diego Rivera, *The Great City of Tenochtitlán*, 1945; detail

includes a fish tank with axolotl salamanders, borrowed from an owner in Kassel, to reference the species once endemic to Lake Chalco). Noriega assigned those who resisted to military service or had them killed and their houses burned—acts carried out in collusion with the Mexican military under the repressive Díaz regime.

In *Return of a Lake*, a wall sculpture depicts Noriega engulfed by flames, as though condemned to hell—a form of environmental and political justice, rendered in the iconographic language of Noriega's Catholicism.[57] Yet Noriega's actions formed only one episode, however significant and brutal, in a longer history of colonialism in the region. Another was Hernán Cortés's sixteenth-century conquest and demolition of Tenochtitlán, the Aztec island city-state in Lake Texcoco, connected at the time to Lake Chalco, and which formed the historical site that would become Mexico City. Established over hundreds of years as a sustainable agroecology, Aztec farming involved an ingenious system of *chinampas*, floating gardens that integrated organic materials and waste recycling for heightened fertility, depicted in

57 "In my research, I encountered a statement by an academic who hoped that Íñigo Noriega and his brother would burn forever in the fires of hell for the destruction that they had caused in Chalco". (Alves, "Some Points of View of Íñigo Noriega," 149).

watercolor diagrams in Alves's installation. (In his mural *The Great City of Tenochtitlán*, 1945, Diego Rivera provides an inspired, if idealized portrayal of the precolonial capital, including its extensive aquaculture system.) After Cortés subdued the Aztecs by murdering their leaders, he destroyed their temple complex (whose ruins now lie in the center of Mexico City), filled in the canals, demolished the chinampas, and began the process of Hispanicizing the geography and people—prefiguring Noriega's later expropriations in the same region.

While assigning Noriega the blame for Chalco's ecological devastation over the last century, Alves's project also addresses contemporary political conflicts that have exacerbated conditions originating with that history. With competing demands for water resources by both the Mexican state and the local municipality, Chalco's social demographic has been profoundly altered by NAFTA policies, which, as we've seen, had a devastating impact on Mexico's small-scale commercial and subsistence farming, skyrocketing rates of urbanization and internal immigration (visible in Chalco's informal housing and overcrowding). In addition, commercial real estate interests supported by shady government deals (echoing the corrupt relations between Noriega and Díaz a century earlier) threaten to develop Chalco, which is already stressed by poorly constructed housing and inadequate sewage and water facilities. All in all, local commitments to bringing land management in line with ecological criteria and social well-being remain ever challenged.

Alves's project approaches this region's history and contemporary politics through an understanding of the land that approximates the geologic "now," defined by media theorist Elizabeth Ellsworth and artist Jamie Kruse as "a teeming assemblage of exchange and interaction among the bio, geo, cosmo, socio, political, legal, economic, strategic, and imaginary."[58] Indeed, there are numerous heterogeneous actants in Alves's project—the lake waters, animal life, Indigenous populations, real estate arrangements, colonial legacies, and governmental forces—that form the interconnecting structures driving this narrative of conflict. Alves suggests that the lake has "returned" by a complex set of causes beyond the solely human.[59] New sociology's actor-network theory comes close to theorizing

58 Elizabeth Ellsworth and Jamie Kruse, "Making the Geologic Now: Intentions, Motivations, Provocations," in *Making the Geologic Now: Responses to Material Conditions of Contemporary Life*, ed. Elizabeth Ellsworth and Jamie Kruse (Brooklyn, NY: Punctum, 2012), 23. See also Klaus K. Loenhart, "Vibrant Matter, Zero Landscape: An Interview with Jane Bennett," *GAM*, no. 7 (October 2011), http://www.eurozine.com/articles/2011-10-19-loenhart-en.html.

59 The object-oriented philosophy of speculative realism focuses as well on the nonhuman realm beyond what Quentin Meillassoux calls the "correlationism" that asserts an unsurpassable connection between human thinking and being. Yet Alves retains an emphasis on historical political systems, namely colo-

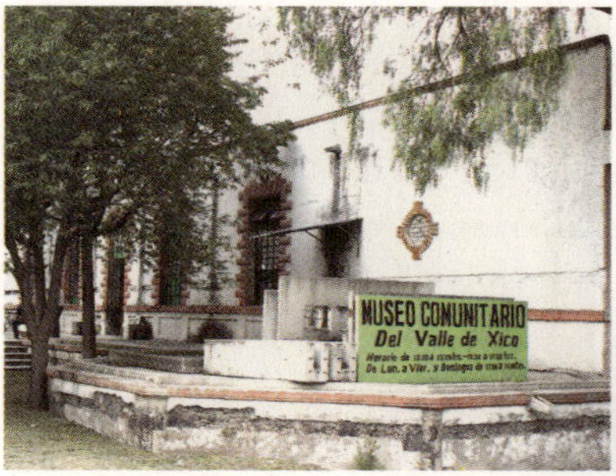

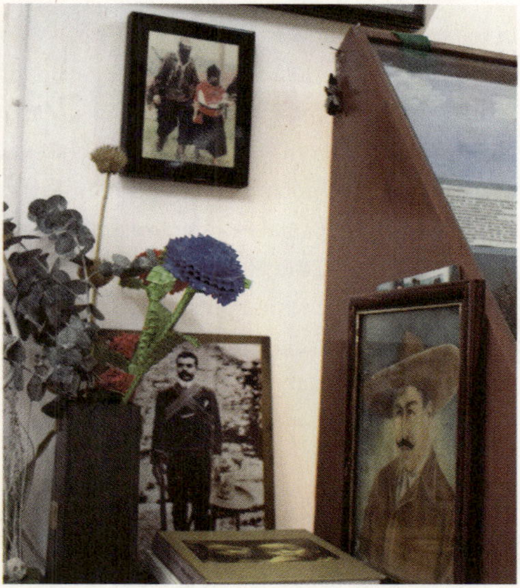

Museo Comunitario del Valle de Xico, Mexico, 2013

this condition; however, when pushed to extremes, it risks dissolving human responsibility for environmental change amid the diffused causality of non-anthropocentric networks of agents. Yet this risk is circumvented by Alves, who, along with Genaro Amaro Altamirano (director of the Museo Comunitario), takes to task human agents like Noriega and contemporary formations like neoliberal capitalism as those primarily responsible for the history she tells. At the same time, her project celebrates the contributions of the numerous "heroes of the lake," whose photographic portraits hang on the walls of the installation. These local community members, like Altamirano and Martínez, are presented as initiators of progressive transformation.

The possibilities of political ecology are also expanded by the project, from historical research to contemporary socioeconomic and environmental struggles. It recovers local cultural heritage and Indigenous knowledge (for instance, the kind that developed the chinampas system) via substantial collaboration, by which it translates, develops, and amplifies the research of the Museo Comunitario for wider audiences and awareness.[60] In the process, Alves's investigation uncovered a fascinating archaeology: Noriega's hacienda was built

nialism, which sets her project apart from this philosophical movement's political detachment. See Bryant, Harman, and Srnicek, "Towards a Speculative Philosophy," 1–18.

60 The museum presents local archaeological objects that narrate a pre-Columbian history of the region (used extensively in community educational initiatives), and through its installations, programming, and events also supports social and environmental well-being.

in the same area as Cortés's country estate—a palimpsest bringing the initial conquest of the Americas into contact with industrial modernity's neocolonial incursions into Indigenous land and labor. Additionally, Zapata had worked in mines run by Noriega's company, and his experience of labor exploitation and economic inequality lead to the 1913 revolutionary uprising, when Noriega's Chalco mansion was occupied and turned into the regional headquarters of Zapata's movement.[61]

When I visited the Museo Comunitario in October 2013, next to a recent painting of Daniel Rivera (the first president of the local *comisariado ejidal*, or cooperative farm commission) was a display of framed photographs—one of Zapata, from the early twentieth century, and a recent one of two masked Zapatistas, Subcomandante Marcos and Comandante Ramona. This display highlights the local recognition of the radical political lineage extending from Zapata's revolution to today's Zapatistas and their demands for Indigenous rights, autonomy, and cultural dignity in Chiapas (in fact, the museum frequently offers its space to Zapatistas for meetings when they are traveling through the area).[62] The museum's struggle for local self-determination, greater autonomy, community solidarity, and ecological sustainability resonates with the Zapatistas' program.

In addition to illustrating an ideological solidarity with past and present revolutionary struggles, Alves's project magnifies the politico-ecological mission of the Museo Comunitario by reproducing community proposals in the exhibition and catalogue to realize local demands for self-determination, the recovery of the natural surroundings of the valley of Chalco, and sovereignty over local resources—against what museum director Altamirano defines as "a capitalist dynamics" that "in its attempts to obtain the highest economic benefit possible does not refrain from putting into practice policies that result in the rape of the social resources of the nation and privatizing them for the benefit of a capitalist class." For instance, Alves's catalogue reprints and translates the museum's 2006 booklet, *Cultural and Ecological Patrimony of Xico*, which includes proposals for "the sustainable use of natural resources," and "a program for the orientation and management of the micro-basins in the Chalco-Amecameca area with the purpose of assuring the social use and usufruct of the resources for the original communities of the region."[63] This agenda, as set out in the booklet, welcomes the

61 "The Zapatistas took possession of the mine operated by [Noriega's] Compañía Minera Tlalchichilpa where Emiliano Zapata had once worked, as well as Xico, Río Frío, and the Hacienda de Zoquiapam, exploiting the properties and appropriating the revenues and assets for themselves" (see "Íñigo Noriega Laso Papers, 1586–1928").

62 On the relation between past and present revolutionary struggles, see James D. Cockcroft, *Mexico's Revolution Then and Now* (New York: Monthly Review Press, 2010).

63 Genaro Amaro Altamirano, "Recuperacion del Entorno Natural del Municipio de Valle de Chalco Solidaridad (Propuesta

participation of the residents of the region's thirteen municipalities as "autonomous and self-managed" agents to create communal land committees to reforest the hill area and prevent further urban sprawl; provide education for local farmers in sloped crop cultivation; establish community-based water management to counter real estate privatization; restore the Xico lagoons; and promote recycling, rainwater collection, and environmental education.

In sum, Alves's piece performs a museological and historiographic intervention in the name of ecological and social justice, in more than merely representational terms (as when Noriega is shown suffering in a fiery inferno). Toward this end, her project facilitated Altamirano's trip in 2012 to Colombres (funded by Mexico's National Council for Culture and the Arts), to deliver a written report on Noriega's leading role in Chalco's ecological destruction, and to donate a copy of the catalogue to the director of the Archivo de Indianos and Museo de la Emigración, where Noriega is still lionized. The reemergence of the lake water is thus translated into a political act of the return of the repressed, a historical reckoning that, as Alves observed, presented "an excellent moment for Europe to face its colonial history."[64] The project was also exhibited at the Museo Universitario de Arte Contemporáneo in Mexico City during the summer of 2014, provoking the capital as well to reconsider the destructive terms of its environmental and political present, and find future ways to support movements like the one in Chalco that offer a sustainable and socially just way forward.

de Acción)," in *Cultural and Ecological Patrimony of Xico* (Chalco: Museo Comunitario del Valle de Xico, 2011), 25; translated and cited in Alves, *Return of a Lake*, 143.

64 Cited in Teobaldo Lagos, "The Lake That Disappears, the Lake That Emerges: *The Return of the Lake* by Maria Thereza Alves," *A*DESK*, September 18, 2013, http://www.a-desk.org/highlights/The-lake-that-disappears-the-lake.html. I examine a younger generation of European artists who have recently investigated similar colonial histories in *Return to the Postcolony*.

Nature's Sovereignty

Chapter 5

Conflicting Environments of Development in India

Sanjay Kak's *Red Ant Dream* (2013) addresses the fundamental question of how we define the value of nature and thereby choose to live in the world today. The feature-length documentary film portrays the violent conflict unfolding in the hills of Niyamgiri, a remote forested area of Odisha in eastern India. The Dongria Kondh tribe has lived there for countless generations, and recently has become embroiled in a contest over the meaning of the land beneath their feet—whether it represents a sacred place that is integral to tribal sustainable ecology, or whether it will provide a source of tremendous profit for multinational corporations, such as Vedanta Resources, who are invested in mining the land. In India's conservative mainstream media and political discourse, the story is frequently described as one of bringing "development" to a "backward" world mired in outmoded tradition. Kak's film serves as a corrective. It tracks that discourse and its opposing voices, depicting the efforts of the Maoist insurgent group People's Liberation Guerrilla Army (PLGA) for control of the eastern part of the country, known for its militant leftists, or "Naxalites," as they are commonly called. The armed conflict, in Kak's film, represents a microcosm of a larger debate about India's future—whether the country will continue to embrace a Western-style modernization that forcibly assimilates Indigenous and rural villagers into its great neoliberal project of industrial development, or whether it will cultivate democratic participation in determining land use and an economic and environmental approach to life designed to support long-term human and ecological well-being.[1]

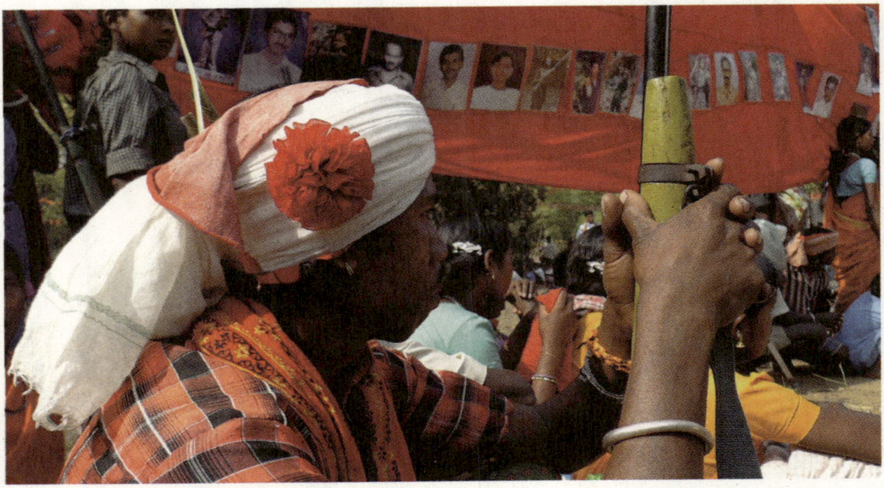

Sanjay Kak, still from *Red Ant Dream*, 2013

Over the course of the documentary, *Red Ant Dream* depicts diverse participants in this conflict, including PLGA cadres training in the Chhattisgarh forests bordering Odisha to the west; tribal members of the Save Niyamgiri movement, who speak out against their prospective displacement to make way for mining operations; and members of the Counter Terrorism & Jungle Warfare College in Chhattisgarh, where military troops prepare to execute their "political, military, social, economic, psychological counter-Naxal campaign," as their brigadier explains. In addition to this remarkable footage—a testimony to Kak's extensive investigative research—the film also includes various audio recordings of rebels past and present, such as 1930s Indian revolutionary Bhagat Singh, 1970s Naxalite poet-activist Avtar Singh Pash, and Azad, late spokesperson for the Communist Party India (Maoist). Alongside these are several tribal members who state, "Niyamgiri is under attack," and speak about their backgrounds, motivations, and political views. Kak's voice-over narration draws the film's diverse strands together and helps explain the complex history and politics, at the same time presenting his own position, which remains particularly attentive to the plight of the tribals and the

1 For a critical overview of development discourse, see William M. Adams, *Green Development: Environment and Sustainability in a Developing World* (London: Routledge, 2009); and Vandana Shiva, *Staying Alive: Women, Ecology and Survival in India* (London: Zed Press, 1988). On the Dongria and their environmental practice, see Felix Padel and Samarendra Das, *Out of This Earth: East India Adivasis and the Aluminium Cartel* (New Delhi: Orient Blackswan, 2010).

struggle of the PLGA. "These are fragile communities fighting to save themselves from annihilation," he intones. A filmic corollary to "Walking with the Comrades"—a rousing 2010 article by political essayist Arundhati Roy that sparked national controversy for its similarly positive portrayal of the Maoist rebellion[2]—Kak's documentary, by depicting the life-and-death stakes of the struggle, reveals its sympathy for the fierce resistance to India's corporate-military complex. If *Red Ant Dream* opens onto an impassioned and sometimes deadly conflict in present-day India over just what "development" means, then it sides with those who strive for an as-yet-unrealized form of life that prioritizes environmental sustainability along with socio-political equality. It also opens onto a growing counternarrative, advanced as well in other contemporary cultural practice in India, which views the cultural and religious elements of traditional life as valuable for modeling a politically and ecologically just future.

In this chapter I offer a historical contextualization of India's current environmental conflicts, and a discussion of the creative eco-aesthetics found in artistic and filmmaking practices leaning toward an activist basis. Following a detailed analysis of *Red Ant Dream*, I consider the work of two additional contemporary practitioners, Ravi Agarwal and Amar Kanwar, who have contributed far-reaching projects at the conjunction of political ecology and visual culture that propose further vantage points on the clash over development in India.

From the Green Revolution to Revolutionary Red

Current socio-environmental conflicts caused by industrialization and modernization come on the heels of India's long history of becoming an independent state; I'll quickly survey the definitive moments for understanding the meanings of development today. In the 1960s and '70s India underwent its "Green Revolution." Like other developing nations, the subcontinent—under Prime Minster Lal Bahadur Shastri and Director General of the Indian Council of Agricultural Research, M. S. Swaminathan, known as the father of the Green Revolution in India—eagerly adopted Western methods of industrial agriculture to increase production as part of a national project to feed its growing populations and alleviate poverty. Development, in this sense, implied the turn toward modern infrastructure, advanced technology, applied science, and biogenetic and chemically intensive agriculture,

2 Arundhati Roy, "Walking with the Comrades," *Outlook*, March 29, 2010, http://www.outlookindia.com/article/walking-with-the-comrades/264738.

applying neo-Keynesian tactics to planning and Marxist theories of progress (dominated by state control of markets and protectionist trade policies that mirrored the "five-year plans" of the Soviet Union, reflecting positive postwar Indo-Soviet relations). These policies eventually gave way to the doctrine of economic liberalization in the '80s emphasizing free markets, denationalization of industries (steel, mining, telecommunications, electrical, etc.), and minimization of state welfare.[3] "Liberalization, privatization, globalization"—or LPG, a common acronym in India today—dominated the following decade, especially in the mining, communications, biotech, and dam-building industries, accompanying an intensified development rhetoric that increasingly sacrificed environmental costs to economic growth (a situation that has intensified under the conservative Bharatiya Janata Party Prime Minister Narendra Modi, elected in 2014).[4]

Mounting evidence of the industrial damage (including the "externalities" of land degradation, deforestation, and anthropogenic climate change), along with its social impacts (forced displacement, pollution-related health problems, economic inequality, and loss of subsistence-based livelihood), has led in recent years to a widespread rejection of Green Revolution ideology, particularly by activists and increasingly by small-scale farmers. Starting in the '80s, environmentalists and writers such as Madhav Gadgil, Ramachandra Guha, Medha Patkar, and Vandana Shiva began chronicling debates around political ecology, emphasizing the imperatives of social justice when addressing environmental problems.[5] Shiva, in particular, has critiqued India's postindependence discourse of development as a neocolonial mechanism that subjugates nature, women, and Indigenous cultures alike: "The Green Revolution has been a failure. It has led to reduced genetic diversity, increased vulnerability to pests, soil erosion, water shortages, reduced soil fertility, micronutrient deficiencies, soil contamination, reduced availability of nutritious food crops for the local population, the

3 Adams, *Green Development*, 8–10.

4 See Armin Rosencranz, "Modi and the Environment," *Truthout*, October 2, 2014, http://www.truth-out.org/opinion/item/26547-modi-and-the-environment. "In under a year, [Modi] has begun to undo policies of fair land acquisition, undermine environmental protection and reverse the fight for tribal rights." Rohini Mohan, "Narendra Modi's War on the Environment," *Al Jazeera America*, April 10, 2015, http://america.aljazeera.com/multimedia/2015/4/narendra-modis-war-on-the-indian-environment.html.

5 See, for instance, Vandana Shiva, *Ecology and the Politics of Survival: Conflicts over Natural Resources in India* (Thousand Oaks, CA: Sage Publications, 1991); Vandana Shiva, *Biopiracy: The Plunder of Nature and Knowledge* (Boston: South End Press, 1997); Madhav Gadgil and Ramachandra Guha, *This Fissured Land: An Ecological History of India* (New Delhi: Oxford University Press, 1992); Madhav Gadgil and Ramachandra Guha, *Ecology and Equity: Use and Abuse of Nature in Contemporary India* (London: Routledge, 1995); and Guha, *Environmentalism*.

displacement of vast numbers of small farmers from their land, rural impoverishment and increased tensions and conflicts. The beneficiaries have been the agrochemical industry, large petrochemical companies, manufacturers of agricultural machinery, dam builders and large landowners."[6] Shiva emphasizes the long-term environmental risks of Green Revolution development, whose violence is never more apparent than following industrial accidents. In December 1984, for instance, a leak sprung in Union Carbide's Bhopal pesticide plant, releasing toxic methyl isocyanate gas that immediately killed thousands of people and in subsequent years led to more than twenty thousand dead and one hundred fifty thousand severely disabled. The International Campaign for Justice in Bhopal, a coalition of disaster survivors and environmental, social justice, and human rights groups, continues to struggle to hold the Indian government and the chemical corporation accountable. The disaster exemplifies the attritional temporality of effects, and often difficult-to-represent lived conditions, of what literature and environmental scholar Rob Nixon terms the "slow violence" that plagues the environments of the poor—those consigned to the sacrifice zones of industrial development, as in Bhopal.[7]

The longer history of modern environmentalism in India, however, begins in the 1920s, when Gandhi's decolonization struggle mounted a resistance politics of localist self-sufficiency, encapsulated in his concept of *swaraj*, or self-governance, scaled up to the national level as the embrace of independence from foreign rule.[8] The *khadi* (homespun cloth) movement, set in a traditional India of village communities, distant from the megacities of the current nation, defined the context of his nonviolent boycott of foreign-made goods, especially British ones; and *satyagraha* (insistence on truth), a civil disobedience protest against taxes and the British colonial salt monopoly, begun in 1930, formed a key element of the Indian decolonization movement. Establishing an environmentalism of low-impact subsistence living, traditional knowledge, and nonviolent politics, Gandhi was crucial

6 Vandana Shiva, "The Green Revolution in the Punjab," *Ecologist* 21, no. 2 (March–April 1991): 57. Also see Vandana Shiva, *The Violence of the Green Revolution: Ecological Degradation and Political Conflict in Punjab* (Dehra Dun: Natraj Publishers, 1989); and Shiva, "Development, Ecology and Women," chap. 1 in *Staying Alive*, 1–13.

7 Nixon discusses Bhopal in *Slow Violence*, 43, 48. Also see Bridget Hanna, Ward Morehouse, and Satinath Sarangi, eds., *The Bhopal Reader: Remembering Twenty Years of the World's Worst Industrial Disaster* (Sydney: Apex Press, 2005). The Yes Men's intervention on BBC regarding Bhopal on its twenty-year anniversary in 2004 is discussed in "The Yes Men in Bhopal: Interview with Andy Bichlbaum, Mike Bonanno, and Satinath Sarangi," in Feher, Krikorian, and McKee, *Nongovernmental Politics*, 524–29.

8 On Gandhi and environmentalism, as well as the history of the Indian environment under colonialism, see Guha, *Environmentalism*.

for subsequent eco-activist formations, such as the Chipko movement in the 1970s against deforestation and the Save Narmada movement in the 1990s against damming the Narmada River. Both practiced nonviolent resistance and demonstrated a socio-ecological awareness of the links between the exploitation of nature and disenfranchised humans; Chipko activists hugged trees to protect them, and their ecosystems, from the logging industry in the Garhwal Himalayas (the name of the movement comes from the Hindi word for "embrace"). Their anti-deforestation politics spread throughout India, leading to policies sensitive to the needs of local communities,[9] which was foundational for the movement against the World Bank–financed construction of a series of major dams along the course of the Narmada River. Bypassing community consultation, the antidemocratic project would displace whole villages and hundreds of thousands of people from land they had occupied for generations. The activist Medha Patkar established the Save Narmada movement in 1989, joining with allied groups and forming a national coalition of environmental and human rights activists, scientists, academics, and local populations affected by the project, protesting with marches, sit-ins, and fasting. The struggle has been portrayed in documentaries that have situated the dam projects amid India's rise in social, political, and economic inequality: Anand Patwardhan and Simantini Dhuru's *A Narmada Diary* (1995) optimistically depicts the social movement, foreshadowing prospective political-judicial success; in contrast, Sanjay Kak's *Words on Water* (2002) remains pessimistic after the Supreme Court, appearing to bow to industry demands, decided to support the dam project's completion.

From Gandhi to Save Narmada, these various precedents inform current ecological conflicts, including the contemporary struggles against mining, tribal displacement, industrial pollution, and GM agriculture. "India today is a veritable cauldron of social conflicts, many of which pertain directly to the control and use of natural resources," write Madhav Gadgil and Ramachandra Guha, who have stressed an approach to "social ecology" that highlights a postcolonial awareness of social and environmental inequity in green politics between North and South, and criticizes the uneven development in India since LPG began in the early 1990s after decades of central planning, state

9 See Jayanta Bandyopadhyay and Vandana Shiva, *Chipko: India's Civilisational Response to the Forest Crisis* (New Delhi: INTACH, 1986); and Guha, "A Chipko/Chico Comparison: The Parallels between Two Famous Forest Movements," and "Redefining Development: Bringing Back Nature and the People," in *Environmentalism*, 98–137.

10 See Gadgil and Guha, *Ecology and Equity*, 2–3; and Ramachandra Guha, ed., *Social Ecology* (Delhi: Oxford University Press, 1994).

11 Shiva, *Staying Alive*, 5–6 (emphasis added).

socialism, and Nehru's modernization efforts.[10] Rather than characterize such large-scale social transformations as "development," Shiva writes that we should be speaking of an "anti-life model of *maldevelopment*," meaning "the violation of the integrity of the organic, interconnected and interdependent systems, that sets in motion a process of exploitation, inequality, injustice and violence."[11]

These debates over development have also been taken up by cultural practitioners (Kak, for instance), and perhaps nowhere more so than in New Delhi, a city of diverse and energetic artistic practice, particularly owing to the surging art market, but also a megalopolis suffering under the strains of overpopulation and pollution, and existing in a state of infrastructural and environmental crisis. One key site of discourse and practice has been the Sarai program at the Centre for the Study of Developing Societies (CSDS), founded in 2000 by Ravi Sundaram, Ravi Vasudevan, and Raqs Media Collective members Jeebesh Bagchi, Monica Narula, and Shuddhabrata Sengupta. A platform for interdisciplinary research on urbanism, media, information technology, and politics, the program also publishes the Sarai Reader book series and, more recently, the film-studies journal *BioScope*. Another leading institution is Khoj International Artists' Association, the artist-led residency and exhibition space, founded in 1997, which held the two-week-long project "48°C Public. Art.Ecology" in 2008 (its title a reference to record-high temperatures in the city) that involved twenty-five artworks throughout Delhi's public spaces—including Ravi Agarwal's photographs investigating the extinction of India's vultures; Amar Kanwar's early iteration of *The Sovereign Forest*, considering the rights of nature in contrast to India's pro-industry government; Sheeba Chhachhi's *The Water Diviner*, an installation exploring the mythologies around water in New Delhi; and Desire Machine Collective's *Trespassers Will Be Prosecuted*, an imaginary forest soundscape that accessed an archaic remembrance of India's rural places.

The symposium "Art, Ecology, Politics," held at the Centre for the Study of Developing Societies in February 2013, advanced these emerging energies. "A new configuration of ecology and politics has emerged in the post-globalisation decades," it stated, "with debates around nuclear power, forests, mining, toxicity, urbanism, and GM crops joining new ways of thinking about water, air, and land. These debates, movements and ecological emergences have also foregrounded an emerging eco-aesthetics. [...] Eco-aesthetics traverses not just the domain of art practice but also of social and political theory—the links between humans and non-human formations, debates on political ecology, and the possibility of alternatives beyond the present."[12] While ecologically concerned art has experienced a surge of interest in the Indian context, the ways it has been approached are also far from homogenous, and its complexity extends to the variable definitions of environmentalism as much as to the aesthetic differences between artistic and filmic positions. The latter are particularly pronounced among the three models I'll focus on here—Sanjay Kak's *Red Ant Dream*, Ravi Agarwal's investigations of the ecology of the Yamuna River running through Delhi, and Amar Kanwar's *The Sovereign Forest*, an installation that returns us to Odisha to explore the traumatic violence of industrial development, and to propose experimental modes of poetic justice—even while each rejects India's current neoliberal ideology.

The Development We Want

Red Ant Dream exposes the violence that accompanies the conflicting narratives of development in India—between those supporting the project of continued modernization and corporate industrialization, and others that both challenge the socio-environmental destruction introduced by that model and propose more just, sustainable forms of life. The red ant of the film's title refers to the Maoist guerrillas who often come from rural villages and Adivasi (Indigenous) communities to join the rebellion and resist India's military-corporate complex. While historically recalling the Telangana Rebellion, the late 1940s peasant uprising modeled on the Chinese Revolution and its agrarian-based socialist reforms, as well as India's pre-independence anticolonial struggles, the movement originated in the Naxalbari uprising in West Bengal in 1967. Emphasizing this long history, the film opens with a written epigraph by Indian socialist revolutionary Bhagat Singh, who stated in 1931: "Let us declare that the state of war does exist and shall exist. The choice of the course, whether bloody or comparatively peaceful, which it should adopt rests with you. Choose whichever you like. But that war shall be incessantly waged." That state of war, as shown in Kak's film, is ongoing today, and the voice of Azad, Communist Party India (Maoist) spokesman, explains why, from the perspective of its contemporary revolutionaries: "Violence is

12 Coinciding with the release of the *Third Text* special issue on art and ecology that I guest-edited, the symposium included the participation of Ravi Agarwal, Sheba Chhachhi, Shuddhabrata Sengupta, and Ravi Sundaram. See "Art, Ecology, Politics: A Roundtable," *CSDS*, accessed November 20, 2015, http://www.csds.in/events/art-ecology-politics-roundtable. Also see the symposium "Reterritorializing Ecologies" held at Khoj International Artists' Workshop in May 2013, in coordination with the Maldives Pavilion of the Venice Biennale, organized by Ravi Agarwal and Khoj, with Navjot Altaf, Amar Kanwar, Vikram Soni, Ravi Sundaram, and Camilla Boemio.

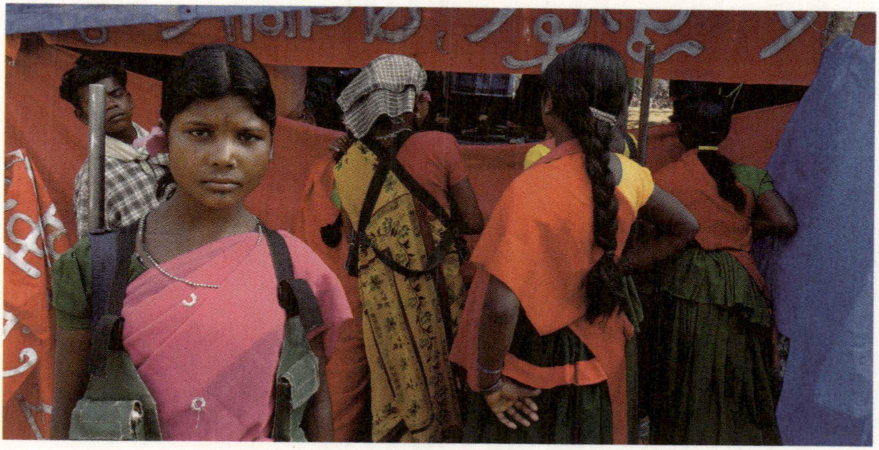

Sanjay Kak, still from *Red Ant Dream*, 2013

a structural feature of our society. It is an inbuilt, inherent characteristic of the existing, unjust, authoritarian, hierarchical, oppressive and rotten society."[13] Under the aegis of the CPI (Maoist), itself formed in 2004 from various leftist armed factions, the current aim of the movement is to contest the elite-serving neoliberal government that largely ignores the majority of the country's underclasses, and to call for a "new democratic revolution" to end India's oppressive caste system and subjugation to multinational corporations.[14] The CPI (Maoist) politburo constitutes the movement's ideological leadership, the PLGA its underground military. Unlike the Zapatistas, who disavowed armed struggle soon after assuming control of their Mexican region in 1994, the PLGA remain locked in

13 On the deadly aspect of the conflict and the broader system in which it is embedded, see Subhabrata Bobby Banerjee, "Necrocapitalism," *Organization Studies* 29, no. 12 (December 2008): 1541–63.

14 Uday Chandra, "The Maoist Movement in Contemporary India," *Social Movement Studies: Journal of Social, Cultural and Political Protest* 13, no. 3 (2013): 1–6. A CPI (Maoist) press release from 2004 reads: "The immediate aim and programme of the Maoist party is to carry on and complete the already ongoing and advancing New Democratic Revolution in India as a part of the world proletarian revolution by overthrowing the semi-colonial, semi-feudal system under the neo-colonial form of indirect rule, exploitation and control. This revolution will remain directed against imperialism, feudalism and comprador bureaucratic capitalism. This revolution will be carried out and completed through armed agrarian revolutionary war, i.e. protracted people's war with the armed seizure of power remaining as its central and principal task, encircling the cities from the countryside and thereby finally capturing them." Central Committee of the Communist Party of India (Maoist), "CPI (ML)(PW) and MCCI – Merged: Communist Party of India (Maoist) Emerged," *BannedThought.net*, October 14, 2004, http://www.bannedthought.net/India/CPI-Maoist-Docs/Statements/PressStatementOnMerger.htm; see also "Founding Documents," *BannedThought.net*, September 2004, http://www.bannedthought.net/India/CPI-Maoist-Docs/#Founding_Documents.

guerrilla-style conflict with India's police, military, and paramilitary forces (including the notorious right-wing government-supported Salwa Judum militia, declared illegal by India's Supreme Court in 2011 owing to its human rights abuses).

In Kak's film, guerrillas speak in detail of the state violence they and their kin face on a regular basis, including punitive rapes and beatings that officers use as intimidation tactics to remove people from their land, making way for corporate mining projects.[15] The situation exemplifies the realities of uneven development, or what David Harvey terms "accumulation by dispossession."[16] As Vandana Shiva reiterates, "'Development' as capital accumulation and the commercialization of the economy for the generation of 'surplus' and profits thus involved the reproduction not merely of a particular form of creation of wealth, but also of the associated creation of poverty and dispossession."[17] *Red Ant Dream* addresses that accumulation by dispossession and resulting uneven development, translating it into its filmic structure. What is the aesthetics of uneven development in Kak's work? Literary historian Upamanyu Pablo Mukherjee discusses what might be considered the literary equivalent, found in Arundhati Roy's prose: "We need to examine the *environment* of uneven development as we try to develop an account of the uneven cultural styles and forms," which are employed to represent and allegorize such inequitable formations.[18] Contesting the assumption that fiction is nonpolitical, Mukherjee argues that Roy's 1997 novel *The God of Small Things* does not displace the political that Roy engages in her nonfiction prose so much as bring it into aesthetic form. Her novel's doomed cross-caste romance is framed by stories of social marginalization and village dispossession, informed by the legacy of colonial servitude and the reality of neocolonial global capitalism. That economic inequality accompanies the disparity of her literary approaches, which draw on both European and Indian styles, modernist magical realist fiction and precolonial modes borrowing from the classical Sanskrit. Such

15 "In the name of development, [corporate-friendly government officials] deprive people of their means of living, throw them out on the streets, force the women into prostitution; then they set up NGOs, and campaign for self-employment and brothel reform centres. Not much money needs to be spent on this: even a tiny percentage of the millions and billions earned through the rampant looting of forest resources and minerals is sufficient to set up the propaganda machinery." Satnama, *Jangalnama: Travels in a Maoist Guerilla Zone*, trans. Vishav Bharti (New Delhi: Penguin Books, 2010), 121.

16 David Harvey, "The 'New' Imperialism: Accumulation by Dispossession," in *Socialist Register 2004: The New Imperial Challenge*, ed. Leo Panitch and Colin Leys (London: Merlin, 2003), 63–87.

17 Shiva, *Staying Alive*, 1.

18 Upamanyu Pablo Mukherjee, "Arundhati Roy: Environment and Uneven Form," in *Postcolonial Green: Environmental Politics and World Narratives*, ed. Bonnie Roos and Alex Hunt (Charlottesville: University of Virginia Press, 2010), 22.

"heteroglossic gestures," according to Mukherjee's Bakhtinian reading, compose an "amalgam of archaic with more contemporary forms," which highlights Roy's attempt to process the disturbing effects of those contradictions and challenge their socially unjust conditions without any easy resolution. "The historical condition of unevenness is felt and lived as a toxic environmental condition," writes Mukherjee, "as the condition of postcoloniality itself."[19] *Red Ant Dream* bears its own heteroglossia, a result of Kak combining film forms—the militant image of Third Cinema, documentary and ethnographic footage of Indigenous cultural rituals, government and Maoist agit-prop, and the speculative voice-over of the filmmaker. These are sequenced so that the film's images can work on their own, as well as enabling other commentators—in the form of audio recordings from the historical archive—to speak for themselves. Allowing these elements to clash without resolution, the film allegorizes unevenness in its formal composition. A contemporary model of the militant image—one that professes sympathy with the plight of the militant and Adivasi dispossessed, inviting audiences to join the struggle—it challenges the viewer to interpret the film's politicizing subjectivity and respond to the conflict over development in India.[20]

Uneven development is specifically addressed in Kak's film through the bauxite-mining dispute in Odisha between the state-military-corporate complex and the largely disenfranchised tribal villagers. The strip mining proposed by corporations like Vedanta would blast away up to one hundred feet of surface material in the Niyamgiri hills, removing all trees and vegetation, and would then, in its efforts to refine the ore into aluminum, stand to abandon hazardous by-products ("externalities") on site, especially "red mud," a highly toxic waste, as is common practice in India. "It is the silent alchemy of ignored externalities that has allowed the aluminium cartel to travel light, scouring the earth for the mineral, carrying only a heavy bludgeon that ensures that deals can be sealed quickly," Kak notes.[21] The tribals who live in these targeted areas, and who resist the corporate takeover of their land (often without advance consultation or informed consent), are labeled as terrorists by the government and subjected to abuse, arrest, repression, and even extrajudicial assassination. Among them

19 Ibid., 24.

20 See Kodwo Eshun and Ros Gray, "The Militant Image: A Ciné-Geography; Editors' Introduction," *Third Text* 25, no. 1 (January 2011): 1–12; and the 2014 film series I curated that included Kak's film, "Specters: A Cinema of Haunting," Museo Nacional Centro de Arte, Reina Sofía, Madrid, http://www.museoreinasofia.es/en/activities/spectres-cinema.

21 Sanjay Kak, "The Bauxite Mountains of Orissa," *Economic & Political Weekly*, September 18, 2010, 32. Also see Padel and Das, *Out of This Earth*, 42.

are the Dongria Kondh, an Indigenous micro-minority of some eight thousand people, who worship their hills as gods. Niyam Dongar, the mountain presided over by the Dongria's Niyam Raja (God of Universal Law), was in fact sold by the government to Vedanta Resources. That decision was contested by the Dongria, assisted by NGOs like Survival International and backed up by the Supreme Court in 2013, who reversed an earlier 2009 decision granting Vedanta rights to the land in what was an unprecedented judgment against the multinational (rendered just after the completion of Kak's film).[22] The Dongria's success came after years of struggle. *Red Ant Dream* shows a tribal member of the Save Niyamgiri movement speaking at a protest, green mountains and a threatening refinery in the background, which Vedanta had prematurely set up before permission was officially granted. He contends that Niyamgiri is under attack and Vedanta will destroy Mother Earth, so the Dongria need to fight to protect it and, by extension, their very existence. "What do they mean by development?" he asks. "We too want development. But when all humans are equal in authority, when all humans are equally respected, when all humans live together in equality, that's the development we too want, the whole world wants, every human wants."

Kak's film, in this regard, refutes the portrayal by mainstream media, which largely supports state-sponsored industry, represents opponents to corporate industrialization as primitives and terrorists, and forsakes any attempt at reasoned analysis. Investigative journalists are frequently banned from the conflict areas—Kak's film replays one alleged interception from a police radio in Chhattisgarh that dramatizes the risks: "If any journalists come by to cover the Naxalites, just get them killed, is that clear?" By challenging this abuse of government power and listening to the personal histories of the guerrillas, Kak's film extends justice and dignity to their struggle against the government's oppression and dehumanization of its opposition, whose political recourse is stymied at every turn by the state's use of military might. "Kak shows the rebels as human beings, not just as faceless insurgents," writes Shuddhabrata Sengupta in an essay on the filmmaker. "In doing so, he compels us to confront the conditions that produce the guerrilla who dances, as much as he asks us to think about the dancer who chooses to bear an automatic rifle," as shown in *Red Ant Dream*.[23]

However, Sengupta criticizes Kak for his "over-identification with the subjects" of his film: "He

22 That said, not all NGOs are operating on the side of the tribals. Some, like Action Aid and its offshoot Action Aid India, receive donations from corporations such as Sterlite (Vedanta's parent company), which sets their pro-industry agenda. In fact, as Kak observes, "NGOs have played a critical part in helping to depoliticise opposition to the neoliberal programme" (Kak, "The Bauxite Mountains of Orissa," 33).

has apparently felt compelled to abdicate his natural questioning stance about his protagonists' political intentions, and the consequences of their politics," evident in his earlier documentaries, such as his treatment of the India-Pakistan territorial conflict in Kashmir in *Jashan-e-Azadi* (2007).[24] It's true that Kak offers no critical accounting for the Maoists' commitment to a "protracted people's war." Nor does he scrutinize the group's rigid hierarchies and controlling militaristic regime, driven by an outdated authoritarian ideology intolerant of detractors. Kak's film has nothing to say either about the evidence that the Maoists have on occasion committed their own human rights abuses against perceived government collaborators, accepted bribes from corporations to protect their operations, and inadvertently encouraged and expanded the state's militarization of the conflict, playing into the hands of the Right. Indeed, *Red Ant Dream* traces a fine line between seeking to comprehend the insurgency and legitimizing its practices. Corroborating Sengupta's point, a further lapse is an implication in the film between conditions in Chhattisgarh and Odisha: one sequence depicts first a guerrilla march through the forests of Chhattisgarh, then a pristine stream in Odisha where a man bathes and celebrates its waters, and finally a Kondh tribal gathering in Lakhpadar, Odisha. The progression suggests that the Maoists are on their way to the Kondh to enlist them in their ranks and militarize their conflict—a dangerous implication should the government take note. Asked about this sequence, Kak responded that it shows merely a potential eventuality, rather than a causal link, connecting the dots between the destructive situation of warfare in Chhattisgarh and the repression of Indigenous tribes in Odisha.[25] The filmmaker has made the same case previously: "The argument of armed insurrection is nibbling at the edges of mineral rich Odisha, an echo of the more bloody exchange already underway in the neighbouring states of Chhattisgarh and Jharkhand, where Maoist cadres have already put a stake in the path of the juggernaut. Will Odisha take that same way?"[26]

According to Kak, the film is not simply pro-Maoist, even though it expresses sympathy for their cause. It's a stance similar to Roy's, with whom Kak has frequently collaborated, and who has been widely criticized (in India especially) for romanticizing the revolutionary movement even though it contains antidemocratic and violent elements and is pursuing what some see as a hopeless militarized conflict that only encourages the state's war

23 Shuddhabrata Sengupta, "A Long March: Sanjay Kak's Cinema of Rebellion," *Caravan*, July 1, 2013, http://www.caravanmagazine.in/arts/long-march.

24 Ibid.

25 Sanjay Kak, interview with the author, New Delhi, February 10, 2014.

26 Kak, "The Bauxite Mountains of Orissa," 34.

machine.[27] The question of whether *Red Ant Dream* endorses the Maoists' tactics, rather than merely acknowledging the legitimacy of their grievances, is not definitively answered by the film—however, it does emphasize that tribal culture remains a crucial resource for sustainable living in an age of ever-increasing environmental crisis. In other words, the Dongria's form of life constitutes not an outdated backwardness to be rejected, but an accomplished form of an alternative development from which we can all learn, especially at a time when the neoliberal model of maldevelopment continually shows itself to be environmentally, socially, and politically devastating.[28] Anthropologist Felix Padel and filmmaker Samarendra Das observe: "India's high state of spiritual and social development is being jettisoned terrifyingly fast in a mad rush to follow the Western path of material development through industrialization. [... But] if anything can save our earth for all of us, it's the uncompromising struggle of these Adivasi activists."[29] *Red Ant Dream* amplifies the Niyamgiri struggle as a test case of how development will be defined globally in the future.

A River Manifesto

A second model of environmental engagement is offered by New Delhi–based artist and activist Ravi Agarwal. His documentary photography connects to his work with Toxics Link, an NGO he founded in 1996. Operating between speculative artistic proposals and environmental policy, he works toward political transformation in local, regional, and national governance in India.[30] Agarwal acknowledges the limits of his NGO's reformist approach within the current political system without proposing systemic alternatives, although it does connect him to the world of governmental policy. His artistic practice builds on this knowledge to consider experimental forms of structural change and radical proposals in the cultural sphere.[31] Distinct from both gallery-bound art, with

27 For reactionary criticism of Roy's position, see the comments posted on Outlookindia.com following her article "Walking with the Comrades." Also see Arundhati Roy, *Broken Republic: Three Essays* (London: Hamish Hamilton, 2011), which contains photographs of Maoists in India by Sanjay Kak. For a sympathetic critical view of the Maoists, see Nirmalangshu Mukherji, *The Maoists in India: Tribals under Siege* (London: Pluto, 2012).

28 Shiva explains how the perception of backwardness (articulated frequently by government and corporate officials) is due to the inappropriate projection of Western measurements of wealth—in relation to the satisfaction of non-vital needs—onto cultures of an "original affluent society," as described by anthropologist Marshall Sahlins. She argues that their "impoverishment lies in the fact that resources which supported their survival were absorbed into the market economy while they themselves were excluded and displaced by it" (Shiva, *Staying Alive*, 12–13).

29 Padel and Das, *Out of This Earth*, xxiv–xxv. "Political struggles of women, peasants and tribals based on ecology in countries like India are far more acute and urgent since they are rooted in the *immediate threat to the options for survival*

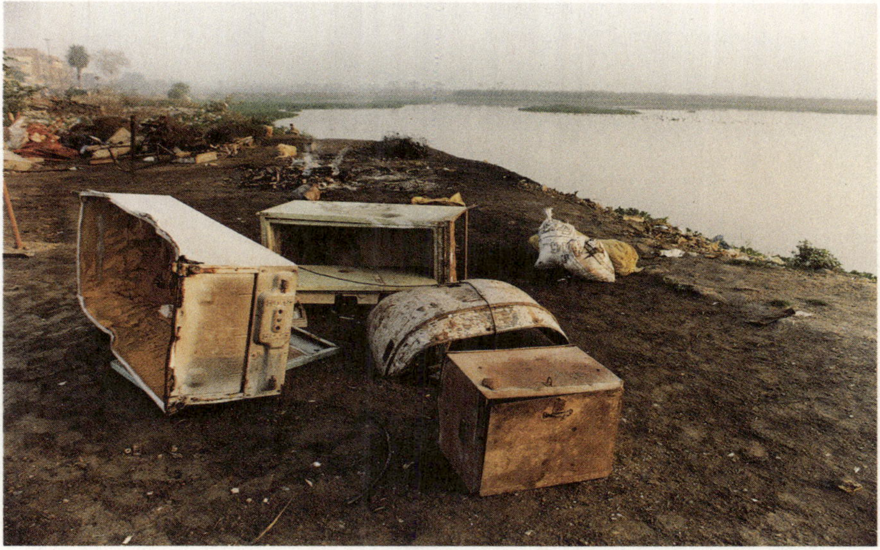

Ravi Agarwal, from the series *Alien Waters*, 2004–6

its often minimal contact to political reality, and policy-making realism, with its lack of speculative invention, Agarwal's model is one of hybrid engagement: art offers ambitious conceptual possibility and the NGO develops political-judicial regulations. Research in each field benefits the other, whether it's the nuts and bolts of political negotiation in Delhi, fieldwork study of river ecologies, or visual approaches to a more theoretical environmentalism. In this regard, his practice also merges diverse areas of investigative journalism, policy research, photography, video, Web and graphic design, political activism, and social organization.

Agarwal's photography investigates a range of socio-environmental issues—the precarious conditions of migrant labor in India, the threat of species extinction (particularly the vulture in the subcontinent), and the political ecology of water. His work has frequently addressed the environmental degradation of the Yamuna River, a tributary of the Ganges that originates in the

for the vast majority of the people, *posed by resource intensive and resource wasteful economic growth* for the benefit of a minority" (Shiva, *Staying Alive*, 9; italics in original).

30 Toxics Link is "a group of people working together for environmental justice and freedom from toxics. We have taken it upon ourselves to collect and share information about the sources and dangers of poisons in our environment and bodies, and about clean and sustainable alternatives for India and the rest of the world" (mission statement on *Toxics Link*, accessed May 30, 2016, http://toxicslink.org).

31 Ravi Agarwal, interview with the author, New Delhi, February 6, 2014.

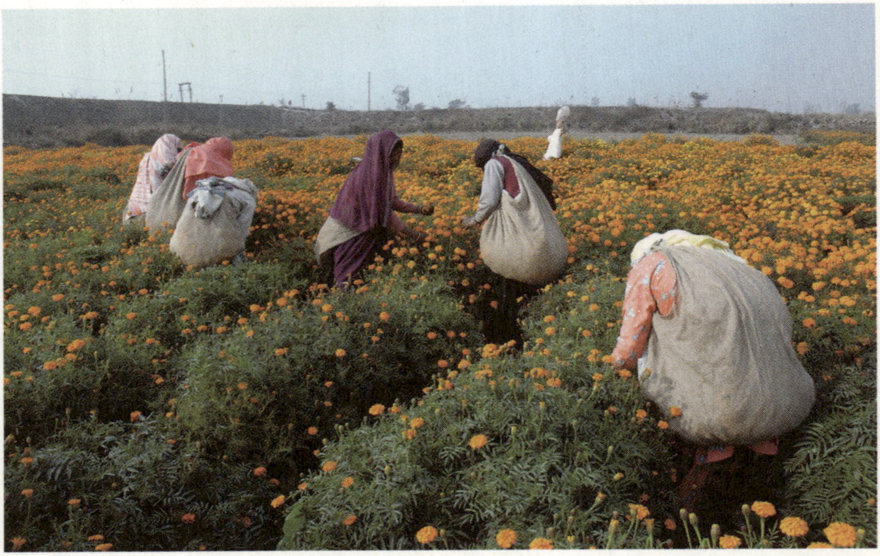

Ravi Agarwal, from the series *Have you seen the flowers on the river?*, 2007

glaciers of the Lower Himalayas and supplies the water needs of Delhi's seventeen million inhabitants, although its source is threatened by global warming. *Have you seen the flowers on the river?* (2007) portrays the northernmost parts of the Yamuna in the city, where the relatively clean water and fertile shores support traditional, small-scale marigold production. Coedited with artist Till Krause, *Yamuna Manifesto* (2013) combines NGO research and documentary photography, describing how the life-sustaining biodiversity of the river is destroyed as it flows through Delhi and becomes a "dead" river into which the city dumps more than 3.8 million liters of untreated sewage every day, which accounts for more than 80 percent of the total pollution of the entire 850-mile length of the waterway.[32] And the photo series *Alien Waters* (2004–6) records the river's environmental condition at different stages as it passes through the city. Buildings are seen in ruins and abandoned stretches of the riverfront appear as unofficial dumping grounds, trash heaps mixing into the river's ecosystem. Rag pickers compete with wild dogs for meager resources, and river gurus attend to their rituals and shrines. Such desecration is no small irony for a river celebrated in Indian mythology

32 See Ravi Agarwal, "Fluid Landscapes," *Seminar*, no. 673 (September 2015): 35; and Ravi Agarwal and Till Krause, eds., *Yamuna Manifesto* (New Delhi: Toxics Link/Project Y, 2013).

for its purifying holy waters; according to the Bhagavata Purana, which recounts life two thousand years ago, "Simply by bathing in the Yamuna, anyone can diminish the reactions of his sinful activities."[33] In the Vedas, the oldest scriptures of Hinduism, the Yamuna is twinned with the Ganges, and exists as source of infinite love and compassion, possessor of power to grant freedom from death, and place of worship for priests to offer prayers to this day.[34]

The research in *Yamuna Manifesto* supports an assortment of visual documents—a selection of Agarwal's photographs of the river with images of Yamuna River projects by other artists, including Atul Bhalla, Sheba Chhachhi, Raqs Media Collective, and Vivan Sundaram. The mixed-media work of Delhi-based artist Chhachhi, for instance, addresses the lost mythology of the river and uses poetic personifications to reanimate its legacy as part of an ecofeminist practice. This visual component, presented in a color folio at the end of the volume, supplements a substantial study of the Yamuna's ecology by environmental sociologist Manoj Misra and engineer and activist Himanshu Thakkar, which forms the bulk of the writing in the book. The authors define the Yamuna as "a hydrological, geomorphic, ecological, biodiversity-rich landscape-level system," which, like all major rivers, provides "a number of social, cultural, environmental and economic services to people and ecosystems all along its watershed."[35] They observe that the Yamuna is suffering from upriver dams, hydropower plants, pollution, the destruction of catchment forests (which retain water for riparian ecologies), and overuse of water, compounded by a nonresponsive state, despite a popular awareness of these problems that emerged in the 1990s. In fact, the deterioration of Delhi's river started in the 1980s, owing to increased land development, so that today, write Misra and Thakkar, the Yamuna is "one of the most polluted rivers in the country," owing to "domestic, agricultural and industrial sources of pollution."[36] Into this mix Agarwal adds the Delhi Development Authority's recent practice of aestheticizing parts of the river in the name of greening its banks; yet here too

33 Krishna Book, chap. 38. See: http://krsnabook.com/ch38.html.

34 "In Indian mythology, the river Yamuna is the daughter of the sun god 'Surya' and his wife Sanjna (consciousness) and is the twin sister of Yama, the god of death. It is believed that Sanjna, when confronted with the luster of Surya, could not keep her eyes open and quivered. [...] The goddess Yamuna is depicted along with Ganga in the sculpture of many Indian temples, often flanking their entrance. Ganga, white as the moon, stands on a *makara* (crocodile). Yamuna is the dark goddess (Kalindi), and she stands on a *kachchappa* (tortoise). [...] In the *Mahabharata*, the Yamuna is a sacred river. [...] It is believed that a bath in the river results in one achieving *moksha* (escaping the cycle of birth and death)." Manoj Misra and Himanshu Thakkar, "Meet the Yamuna," in Agarwal and Krause, *Yamuna Manifesto*, 24. See also Shiva, *Earth Democracy*, 172–73.

35 Misra and Thakkar, "Meet the Yamuna," 11–12.

36 Ibid., 30, 46.

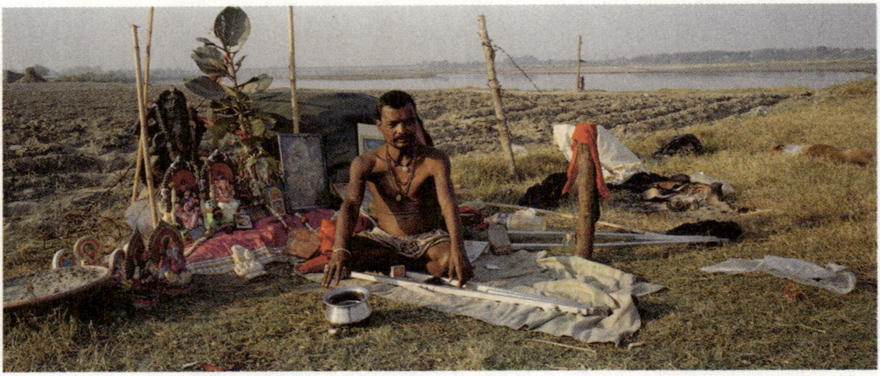

Ravi Agarwal, from the series *Alien Waters*, 2004–6

such designs, rather than serving ecological needs, are a means to displace unwanted populations, as when the Yamuna Pashta colony of over forty thousand people was brutally thrown off their land in 2004 to make way for "Golden Jubilee Park."[37] In 2007, several NGOs, including Toxics Link, formed the Living Yamuna Campaign in the interest of reviving the moribund river, proclaiming: "River: An ecological lifeline for millions (perhaps for the earth itself) or an economic resource for the fortunate or a greedy few?"[38] Their work, part of a larger citizens' movement, led to a new court order in January 2015 challenging development and polluting practices and the failure of state regulatory bodies, wherein the river entered into the debate over the future form of urban development.[39] In *Yamuna Manifesto*, Misra and Thakkar outline proposals for saving the waterway, including developing rainwater harvesting at governmental, commercial, educational, institutional, and industrial levels, enacting groundwater recharge, protecting Yamuna flood plains and catchment areas, improving crop irrigation policy, and implementing pollution control throughout the river's course. They ask, will nature be seen as "a resource, or as a geography to be conquered or even as a landscape to be admired," or will its identity be recognized as part of a "complex web of life" without "being excessively controlled"?[40]

Building on these proposals, Agarwal and Krause state the ambitious conceptual goals of their book, which transcend specific policy measures: "Clearly the real challenge of today is to contest the whole paradigm of 'development' as is currently understood and promoted by the advocates of 'economic growth at all costs.' The need is to redefine development in

37 Agarwal, "Fluid Landscapes," 38.
38 Misra and Thakkar, "Meet the Yamuna," 85.
39 Ravi Agarwal, e-mail to the author, September 10, 2015.
40 Agarwal, "Fluid Landscapes," 38.

terms of wellness of the majority in terms of their economic, health and spiritual well being, rather than as the accumulation of wealth (sometimes obscene in its scale) by a few, with a fond hope (repeatedly disproved historically) that this would trickle down to the masses."[41] Contributing to this transformation, the book project advances a revolution of values, moving from an economic framework where the "institutions of capital, technology and markets, have come to define progress and development," toward the replacement of "economy" with "ecology," so that "new relationships are formed with nature at the centre." That new definition would support the river's ecology, indeed its renewed life as a river (serving animal populations, restoring flood plains, and enjoying a less-interrupted flow), rather than subjecting it to an instrumentalized channeling of human design, whether for aesthetic purposes or industrial uses. Agarwal has written elsewhere: "Human development has to be re-thought with additional values like 'equity' and 'balance,' and not merely monetary ones. 'Enough to satisfy every man's need but not every man's greed,' wrote Gandhi, speaking of the planet's resources.'"[42] Taking that ecological call to heart, Agarwal's analysis opposes the reduction of nature to a "commodity," a thing outside us that satisfies human desires, defined financially and exhausted until it becomes worthless as waste—exactly the fate of the Yamuna as it appears in his images. Yet rather than turning to exemplars of violent struggle against the corporate-military state, Agarwal practices an aesthetic politics that insists on making the condition of the Yamuna River visible, mobilizes energy for its future restoration through his researched investigations, and points toward the radical structural shifts—starting with effective government regulation—necessary to bring about that transformation.

The Sovereign Forest

Amar Kanwar's *The Sovereign Forest* (2012–ongoing) returns us to Odisha, which was captured in a very different way by Kak in *Red Ant Dream*. The conflict over worldviews—between the traditional practice of a sustainable life by subsistence farmers and tribal villagers, and the short-term profit-based extractivism of the neoliberal corporate-state complex—is presented by Kanwar via a mixed-media installation comprising handmade books, photographs, video projections, and a collection of indigenous rice-seed varieties. The elements cross-reference each other, their histories framing the discord in Odisha,

41 Agarwal and Krause, *Yamuna Manifesto*, 92–94.

42 Ravi Agarwal, "Have you seen the flowers on the river? 2007–2011," *Ravi Agarwal*, accessed August 26, 2015, http://www.raviagarwal.com/works.php?workid=4.

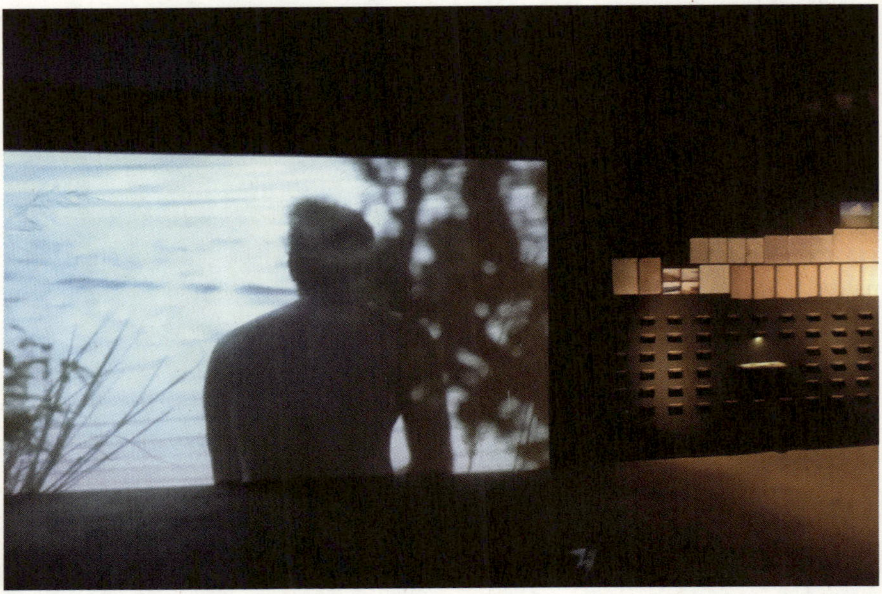

Amar Kanwar, *The Sovereign Forest*, 2012; installation view, Samadrusti, Bhubaneswar, 2014

to form a multisensorial installation whose style and substance distinguish the project from the filmic and photographic work of Kak and Agarwal. More than a straightforward documentary, Kanwar employs poetic allegory to animate a range of affects that aren't addressed by the creative nonfiction of Kak or Agarwal. Presenting tales of corporate socio-environmental devastation (but without directly addressing the guerrilla war of the Naxalites), Kanwar's installation interweaves fact and fiction, producing a ritualized, subjective mediation endowed with speculative-conceptual elements. It investigates epistemologies alternative to Western realist objectivity and its exploitative pragmatism, touching on a post-secular space of Indigenous knowledge and cultural ritual, one appropriate to portraying alternative modes of community building, animist environmentalism, and nonviolent activism. Kanwar explores otherwise undervalued paths beyond the destructive cycle of state-corporate repression and armed insurrection.[43]

Included in *The Sovereign Forest* is *The Prediction* (1991–2012), a large handmade book

43 The project began as Kanwar's contribution to "48°C Public. Art.Ecology," where it comprised four digital color videos with sound, 150 color photographs (stills from Kanwar's videos), forty-nine light boxes with color photographs, and texts. It was situated in a public space, near the Indian Parliament, on a triangular traffic island where a single tree grows.

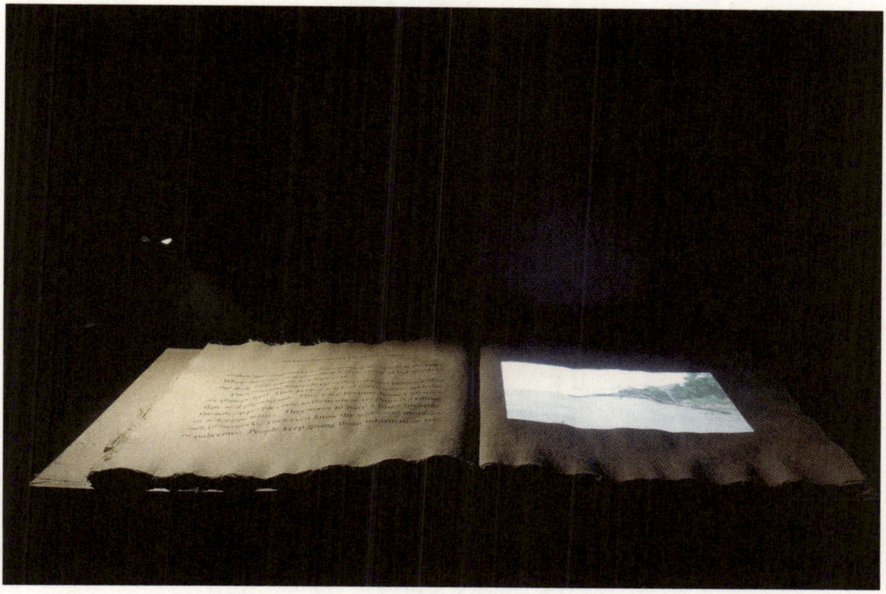

Amar Kanwar, *The Counting Sisters and Other Stories*, 2011; installation view, *The Sovereign Forest*, 2012

with silkscreened banana-fiber pages, presented on a white pedestal, which tells the story of the leftist labor organizer Shankar Guha Niyogi. The leader of the labor-rights group Chhattisgarh Mukti Morcha (CMM) and a proponent of nonviolent activism, Niyogi, we learn from Kanwar's book, knew that he was being targeted for his anti-industry activities. On September 28, 1991, he was shot and killed while asleep. The book's prose, written by Kanwar, explains, "If the next wave of industrialization had to unfold, if the enormous mineral and ecological wealth of Chhattisgarh had to be consumed, if large areas of agricultural, tribal and forest lands had to be acquired then it would be the popular and mass based force of the CMM that would become the greatest obstacle." A group of leading industrialists was convicted of orchestrating the crime, but the rulings were overturned by the Supreme Court in 2005, an example of the collusion in India between corporate and government interests. Kanwar sees Niyogi—whose popular slogan was "Create while you resist!"—as a tragic model of collective activism. "The CMM," he writes in *The Prediction*, "never took to violence and instead created a vital democratic space through perhaps one of the largest mass movements of workers, peasants and tribals in post Independent India." Visitors can freely turn the pages of the book. A video is projected on the blank right-hand sheets, showing portraits of the groups referenced in the text on the left-hand side.

A second book, *The Counting Sisters* (2011), contains a collection of short stories about six elderly women who mourn the mounting dead of their respective villages. Handmade banana-fiber pages are embedded with different materials—a fishing net, a fragment of a cloth garment, rice seeds, a betel leaf, a newspaper. The large tome weaves a tale about these traces, which seem to be pieces of documentary evidence, but of unknown origin, integrated into the book's support structure. "The Counting Sisters sing very well," one page reads. "They rarely sing together though. It is said that when they do sing together, the clouds converge over them. Everyone in the shadow of this momentary twilight cannot but weep as they sing. This weeping often becomes a rhythm to their song." Poetic in their abstraction, the accounts condense the real experience of disappearance at the hands of the state into a poignant mythology of registering loss through this unofficial archive of death. The book presents as well the defiant refusal to forget on behalf of survivors. *The Counting Sisters* and *The Prediction* join five smaller printed volumes in the installation that document protests, police violence, and record the names of Odisha farmers who have committed suicide owing to inescapable debt in recent years—constituting the artist's own running count of the devastating human costs of an increasingly expensive chemical- and transgenic-based agriculture, which is part of the development story that is wreaking havoc across India. And the story is familiar: farmers are trapped in a vicious cycle of debt in order to continue buying expensive GM seeds and paying for their chemical-intensive agriculture, and as the economic burden grows, so does the desperation, ending frequently in the tragedy of suicide (often committed by drinking the pesticide poison that is at the root of the system). Around three hundred thousand Indian farmers have committed suicide since 1995.[44]

At the center of *The Sovereign Forest* is *The Scene of the Crime* (2011), a forty-two-minute large-scale video projection about the murder of a villager, or, more broadly, an elegy to the human-environmental sacrifices of neoliberal development. The circumstances of the death are never fully explained, the names never given; the affective sensibility of its abstractness is heightened by dramatically colored landscape images and ambient sounds. Minimal narration via occasional intertitles describes the widow's mourning. The characters never speak—rather than documentary subjects, they are

44 Vandana Shiva, "Farmers Suicides: What Is Causing Them, and What Can Be Done to Stop the Tragedy?," *Dr Vandana Shiva* (blog), April 24, 2015, http://vandanashiva.com/?p=231.

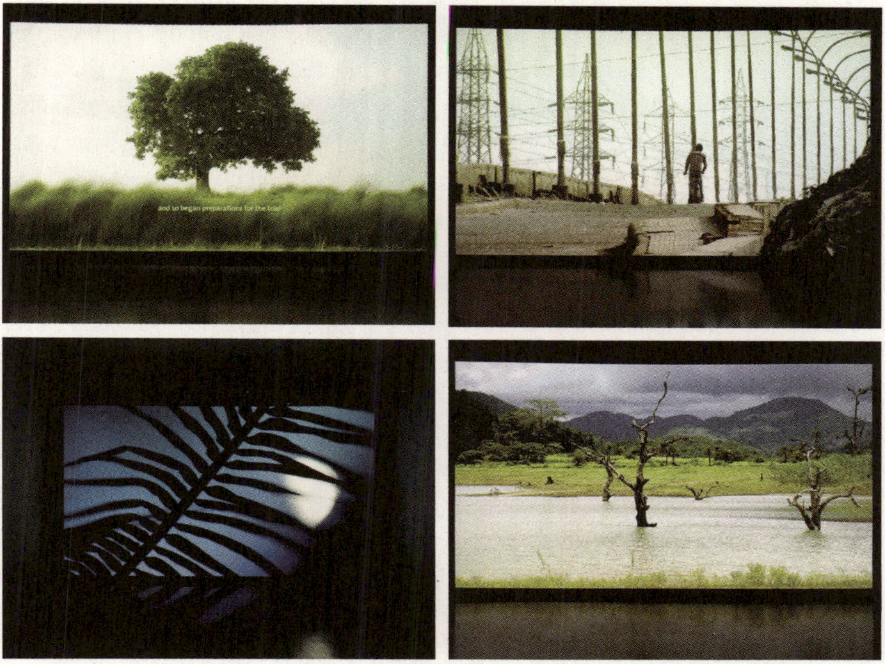

Amar Kanwar, *The Scene of the Crime*, 2011; installation views

allegorical figures representing the all-too-common trauma of a population. Viewers parse the world through the perspective of the female protagonist, whose loss is translated into environmental terms: "There is a map of Kalinga in the corner of her eye," reads one title, "across the fields, past the tree, down the river; she always sees him coming." His absence is felt in the trees, mountains, and streams, which are shown in long-duration fixed-frame shots that imply the scene of the crime in the film's title. A film of yearning for vanished love, its sense of melancholy is heightened by the emotions of injustice—another title reads, "The judge refused to accept the evidence of his murder ... so he is neither dead nor alive." The environment, more than being a sympathetic background or exploitable resource, also plays the role of sentient observer ("The river is the only witness to what she feels"); equally, the film implies that the woman mourns for the environment itself, intertwined as it is with the death of her lover. Blurring the boundaries between nature and culture resonates strongly with Adivasi animism, where the environment figures as the source of life that infuses all being (for the Dongria, natural entities are commonly compared to brothers and sisters, fathers and mothers; though Kanwar's film never makes this reading explicit, nor does it expand upon the gendered implications).[45] The film's visual language here turns speculative, as if asking: What justice remains when the state's bureaucracy impedes victims' access to the courts? What alternatives are there to name a crime outside of the official but biased criminal justice system? And how can we speak of crime, and also of justice, when the lead witnesses are trees, rivers, and mountains?[46] Concluding with an allusion to an imaginary court case, "The Sovereign Forest vs. The Union of India"—not likely to happen in India anytime soon given its current administration, although environmentalists like Vandana Shiva publicly support the universality of rights-of-nature legislation[47]—the film leaves it to viewers to consider how such a lawsuit might establish the forest's sovereignty, and what that might mean for the future protection of nature. At the very least, it would entail a radical philosophical shift away from dominant conceptions of the environment as an instrumentalized source of wealth accumulation, and toward a newfound recognition of tribal rights and belief systems. The film, in this regard, takes on an activist dimension as an artwork, positioned to transform perspectives and invite viewers to play a role in the eventual realization of its visions for socio-environmental justice.[48]

The poetic-allegorical dimensions of *The Scene of Crime* distinguish it from Kanwar's earlier film-essays, such as *Many Faces of Madness* (2000), which also addresses the politics of ecology in Odisha. The nineteen-minute video features landscapes being destroyed by industrialization, as the artist's voice-over denounces the present state of "madness"

45 See Padel and Das, *Out of This Earth*, 141–42. In this regard, Kanwar's work offers the opportunity to move beyond a Western-based "animism," which, in its Latourian framework as elaborated by curator Anselm Franke, critiques the modern divisions between spiritualism and objectivism (a porous relation between subjects and objects as found in "primitives," premoderns, and children, or a rigid separation between those realms as proclaimed in modern science), toward an embrace of Indigenous cosmology as a resource for sustainability. See Anselm Franke, "Much Trouble in the Transportation of Souls, or: The Sudden Disorganization of Boundaries," in *Animism*, ed. Anselm Franke, vol. 1 (Berlin: Sternberg Press, 2010), 34; and for a critique of this Latour-Franke position in relation to Indigenous knowledge and tradition, see Horton and Berlo, "Beyond the Mirror."

46 Kanwar speculates in previous work about the possibility of justice as inscribed in cultural forms, including *The Torn First Papers* (2004–8), which presents poetry as evidence against Burma's dictatorship. See my essay, "Poetic Justice: On the Art of Evidence," in *The Question of Evidence*, ed. Diana Baldon and Daniela Zyman (Vienna: Thyssen-Bornemisza Foundation, 2008), 49–53.

47 See Vandana Shiva's contribution to Ayma et al., *The Rights of Nature*, and her participation in the Global Alliance for the Rights of Nature, http://therightsofnature.org.

48 The end credits of *The Scene of the Crime* state Kanwar's "solidarity with the resistance of local communities in Odisha against Vedanta Alumina, Sterlite Industries, Niyamgiri hills, Vedanta University Project, Sterlite Industries, POSCO, Pohang Iron & Steel Company; Tata Steel & other companies, Kalinga Nagar Industrial Area."

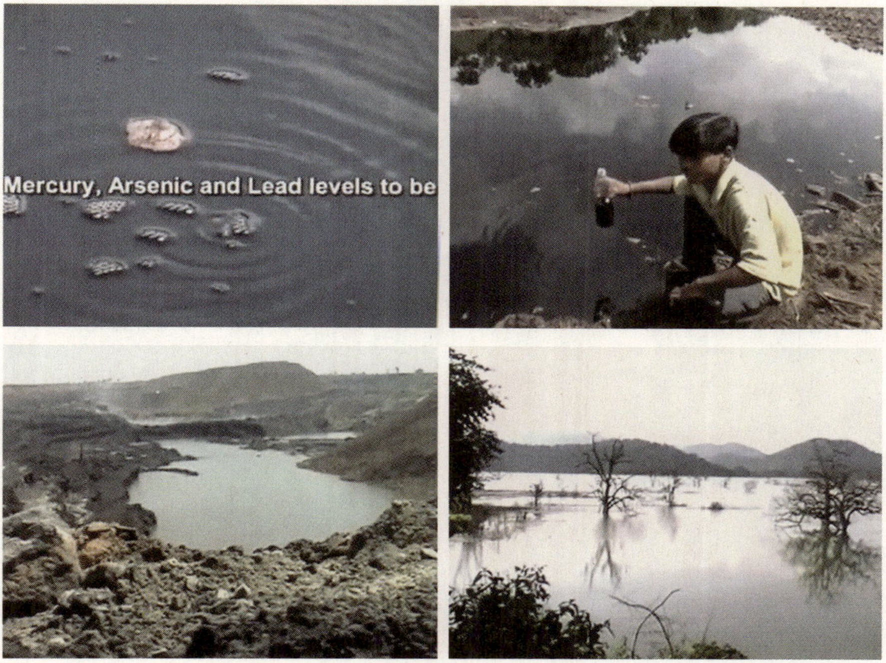

Amar Kanwar, stills from *Many Faces of Madness*, 2000

in which India has become "a nation at war with our own land and water, with our own people," for how else, he asks, "do you describe the state of an animal that begins to eat its own flesh?" Accompanying tracking shots of industrial factories and land development, as well as aerial views of environmental destruction in Odisha, Kanwar's searing commentary points to multiple counts of irrational behavior of India's industrial state: pumping chemical waste into the groundwater so that mercury, arsenic, and lead reach one to seven hundred times the permissible levels; the decimation of forests for timber; mineral extraction that tears up the earth, laying waste to biodiverse ecosystems; the damming of rivers that flood the countryside, displacing millions; the commercial exploitation and privatization of plant life by pharmaceutical companies while 80 percent of Indians depend on traditional systems of medicine; and the destruction of mangrove forests for land development, forests that otherwise protect the coastline from erosion, salinity ingress, and extreme weather events. What else can it be but a form of collective madness, Kanwar asks in the film, when a society

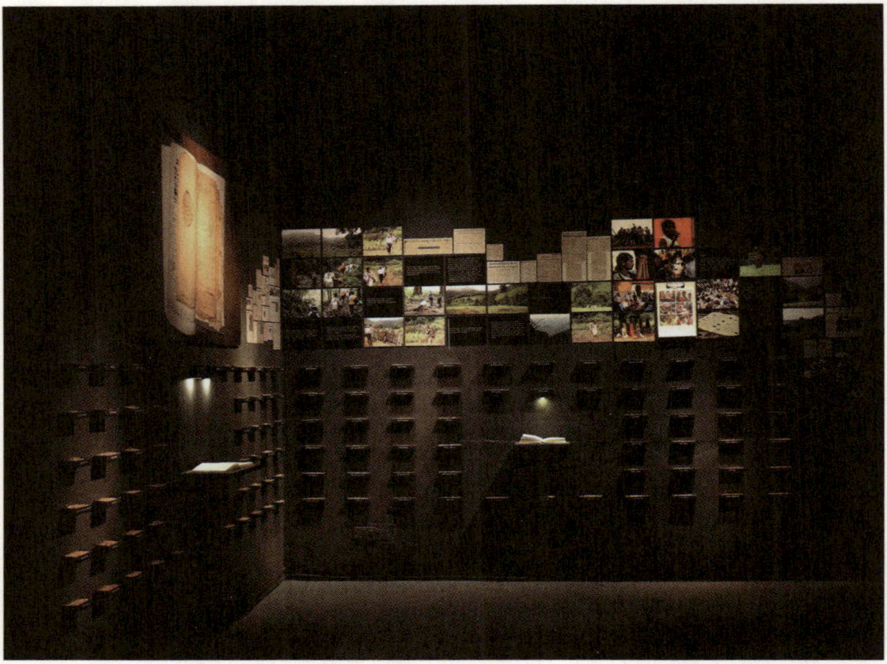

Amar Kanwar, *The Sovereign Forest*, 2012; installation view, Samadrusti, Bhubaneswar, 2014

destroys its own natural home "so that a golden opportunity for economic growth is not missed?"[49]

The Sovereign Forest presents additional evidence of this madness, but notably without the pointed commentary of Kanwar's earlier film. Documents and photographs are displayed in the project's permanent installation at Samadrusti, an independent civic and cultural institution in Bhubaneswar, Odisha—its most compelling version, in my view, owing to the extensive material that is only partially exhibited when the project is shown elsewhere. It's a veritable archive of the human cost of the economic greed that drives government indifference to the plight of India's village and tribal communities. The installation includes numerous "Memorandums of Understanding" between the Indian government and corporations regarding plans to industrialize certain rural areas

49 The American Indian activist Russell Means invoked Indigenous environmentalism in a 1980 speech to likewise contest the economic calculus of late-capitalist development: "In terms of the de-spiritualization of the Universe, the mental process works so that it becomes"—scandalously—"'virtuous' to destroy the planet" (cited in Padel and Das, *Out of This Earth*, 594).

(most often with mining operations, accompanied by refinery, energy, and transportation infrastructure, and port development), all typically approved without public consultation. To contest their prospective displacement, villagers who have lived on and cared for their land over multiple generations are forced to "prove" their ownership—a ruse forcing rural farmers into the state's burdensome bureaucracy. This legalistic entrapment coerces generally under-resourced people to generate innumerable documents, such as decades-old land leases and property maps, copies of which are included in Kanwar's archive. Joined to these elements of legal strife are petitions and protest letters signed with thumbprints by illiterate villagers, as well as media images of objectors who have been killed by paramilitary forces. These are the traces of a continuing and devastating ecologico-political conflict, with further evidence contained in storage boxes in the Bhubaneswar installation—boxes that await further evidence of crimes likely to unfold in the near future. Collecting the traces of socio-environmental destruction, *The Sovereign Forest* also testifies to the ongoing struggle for justice.

Seeds of Nonviolence

The Sovereign Forest has appeared internationally in several art exhibitions—most significantly dOCUMENTA (13), in 2012—but its installation at Samadrusti is part of a long-term engagement with community members in Odisha. Kanwar began visiting the region in the 1990s, researching the destruction and the protests, and, in 2005, helped to set up the institution with Sudhir Pattnaik, its current director. Dedicated to advancing independent cultural and political life in a region where institutions typically serve a particular governmental or political cause, Samadrusti, in addition to housing Kanwar's installation, offers facilities for the production of a biweekly independent news magazine in the local Odia language, covering issues such as land and forest use, forced displacement, and human and labor rights conflicts in the region. It also contains a video-editing studio where local villagers can participate in media-training workshops (Kanwar regularly teaches video production and editing). Additionally, the organization generates *Madhyantara*, a community video series that produces and distributes DVD documentaries by a range of makers, professional and amateur alike, that offer critical portrayals of the extraction industry, the political struggles of local people (as when farmers recently opposed the construction of a Jindal thermal power plant), police violence, and environmental destruction in the area (such as polluted rivers and illegal dumping of waste). Through these activities, Samadrusti supports independent news and citizen-based reporting, intervening in a mediascape otherwise dominated by pro-government and pro-corporate outlets and providing a place for critical learning and discussion. For instance, when members of twelve Dongria Kondh villages were invited by the state in April 2013 to vote on the proposed Vedanta mining project—which they successfully opposed[50]—they also visited Samadrusti in order to view *The Sovereign Forest*.[51] The institution functions as a critical and nonpartisan NGO supported by grassroots initiatives and local community funding in what Pattnaik calls "the colonial state of Odisha."[52] According to him, "Presenting truth has itself become the most radical act on earth today, which even political regimes governed by the best of ideologies fail to encourage."[53]

Kanwar's installation thus assembles the diverse materials of a composite and complex truth, mixing bureaucratic documents, photographic testimony, forensic evidence (in the form of land leases), and cinematic allegories, all presented in a darkened environment. This ritualistic atmosphere endows the presentation with an aura of gravitas, which however is not merely melancholic or fatalistic. *The Sovereign Forest* honors the ongoing resistance, accumulating evidence that strengthens current and future battles for environmental sustainability, tribal rights, and subsistence farming. In this sense, it supports the formation of what Shiva has called "Earth democracy"—comprising a set of principles based on social inclusion, nonviolence, reclaiming the commons, and free access to the earth's resources, defining "an emergent political movement for peace, justice, and sustainability"—and what Pattnaik terms, simply, "life"—that is, a fundamental reverence of the biodiverse elements and self-reproducing cycles of nature, and how they intersect with human culture.[54] It

50 "In August 2013, the Dongria were given the unprecedented opportunity to choose their own future in what became known as India's 'first environmental referendum'. During village consultations, the Dongria expressed their unanimous opposition to Vedanta's mine. The mine was finally blocked by the central government in January 2014." "Dongria Kondh Boycott Indian Elections over Police Harassment," *Survival International*, May 7, 2014, http://www.survivalinternational.org/news/10225.

51 Samadrusti's director Pattnaik spoke about the reception of the installation: "Several visitors have come from the remote areas of the state that are scenes of great crimes, such as Niyamgiri, Kalinganagar, Lower Suktel, and Jagatsinghpur. Each one of them has got excited about *The Sovereign Forest*. None of them needed any interpreter or a resource person to explain anything to them. The happiest moment for me was when a 'semieducated' fighter from the Lower Suktel anti-dam project area told me, 'The most exciting and interesting object in the *The Sovereign Forest* was the Constitution book.'" "Sudhir Pattnaik in Conversation with Amar Kanwar," in *Amar Kanwar: The Sovereign Forest*, ed. Daniela Zyman and Thyssen-Bornemisza Art Contemporary (Berlin: Sternberg Press, 2014), 187.

52 Sudhir Pattnaik, interview with the author, Bhubaneswar, February 13, 2014.

53 "Pattnaik in Conversation with Kanwar," 188. In addition to helping fund Samadrusti, since the late 1990s Kanwar has also financially supported independent journalists covering the conflict in Odisha (Pattnaik, interview with the author, February 13, 2014).

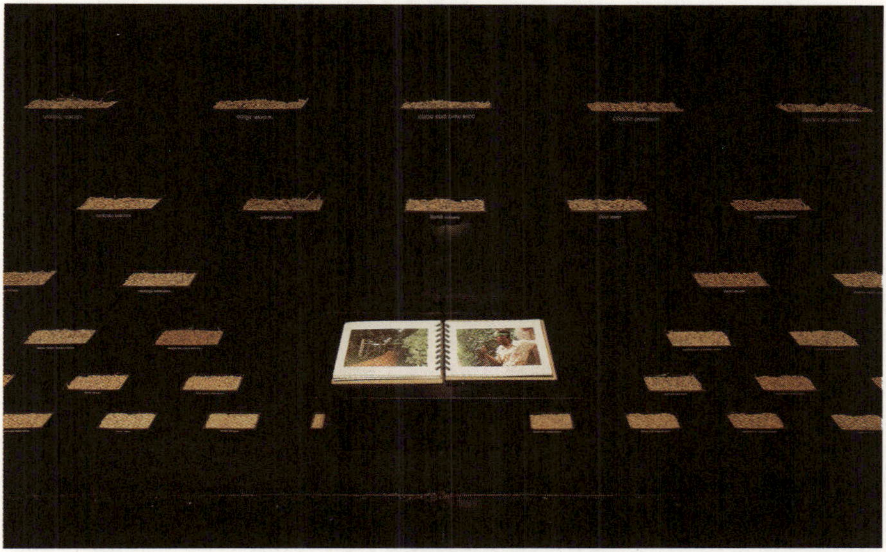

Amar Kanwar, *The Sovereign Forest*, 2012; installation view, dOCUMENTA (13), Kassel

rejects not only the violence driven by the corporatized and militarized state, but also, by implication, the Maoist resistance, and partisan cultural politics such as those of Sanjay Kak and Arundhati Roy. By refusing to romanticize armed struggle, Kanwar's project keeps avenues of nonviolent resistance open. *The Sovereign Forest* joins to that resistance a speculative and nonprogrammatic relation to the political, expanded to an earth democracy that extends agency to the nonhuman and embraces peaceful social mobilization and creative resistance as the only viable responses to environmental and social destruction.

One vital element of *The Sovereign Forest* is most hopeful in this regard: handfuls of 272 seeds of native rice varieties are exhibited in small boxes mounted gridlike on the walls of the exhibition space. Labeled in Odia, each variety's name resonates with local cultural connections to family, life, and the universe—*Debrani* (Sister-in-law), *Basana Bhog* (Food for a dwelling), *Judamari* (Magical diamond), *Chandrakanti* (Girl from the moon), among others, resonating with the cosmopolitics of traditional communities (in contrast to the depersonalized and delocalized names of transgenic rice, such as LLRice60 or LLRice62). The display correlates with *The Seed*

54 Shiva, *Earth Democracy*, 1. Pattnaik explained, "Life is not a 'model' of sustainability" (interview with the author, February 13, 2014).

Book, a small photo-text album commemorating the work of Natbar Sarangi, an elderly organic farmer working thirty-three kilometers from Bhubaneswar. Raised in a family of farmers, Sarangi lived through the Green Revolution and ultimately rejected its GMO-based and chemical-intensive terms in the 1990s.[55] He then returned to the tradition of organic farming of his parents' and grandparents' generations, achieving greater yields through this agriculture that also supports the long-term health and fertility of the soil, and subsequently became an outspoken proponent of its practice. *The Seed Book* relates to Sarangi's recovered traditional knowledge, listing the diverse rice varieties traditionally grown for recipes for both special feasts and common meals. Kanwar's research, presented in the book's text, explains that in Odisha prior to the Green Revolution there were an astounding ten thousand varieties of the traditional paddy seed, with consistently high yields per year, whereas today some twenty "high-yielding" varieties dominate, with harvests that compare poorly to traditional seeds and are dependent on chemical inputs and higher costs, and generally produced and controlled by agribusiness corporations connected to corrupt government officials. Reclaiming and growing 460 traditional rice varieties, some ten thousand years old, Sarangi runs a living seed bank, sharing his seeds with local farmers. For Sarangi, the regime of "liberalization, privatization, globalization" has proved to be nothing but a lie, destroying "Mother Earth" through a false sustainability that is merely greenwashing.[56] The land transcends economic valuation, in Sarangi's experience, which cannot possibly capture the wealth of a cultural heritage and knowledge base used for generations to sustain society and its environment. That heritage is potentially lost forever when we surrender land to destructive industry and conventional agriculture.

Becoming Indigenous

The meaning of development, as we have seen, is anything but self-evident. In the words of Felix Padel and Samarendra Das, "India's high state of spiritual and social development is being jettisoned terrifyingly fast in a mad rush to follow the Western path of material development through industrialisation."[57] Naked capitalist short-term profiteering, unsustainable extractivism, and

55 Sarangi's moment of transformation came upon reading Masanobu Fukuoka's 1978 manifesto for anti-interventionist farming, *The One-Straw Revolution* (Natbar Sarangi, interview with the author, Cuttack, Odisha, February 13, 2014).

56 Natbar Sarangi, "Art and Culture of the Soil and Our Ecological Thoughts" (lecture at the symposium "Art and Ecology: Search for Sustainability," organized by Jagannath Panda, Bhubaneswar, February 12, 2014).

neocolonial land grabs lead to ecocide, poverty creation, and accumulation through dispossession. "In effect, mining companies make their profits by dispossessing the land's indigenous population, pushing the people into worse poverty than anything they faced before."[58] Padel and Das recount tribal activist Dai Singh's appropriate reply to the representative of Sterlite Industries when he visited Odisha in the hopes of swaying local opinion to support industrial development and the supposed benefits of job creation, new tractors, and fat bank accounts: "We cannot eat your money," Singh said.[59]

Tribal culture is based upon its own highly developed approach to ecological sustainability. Far more advanced than the "madness" of industry's wanton destruction of the environment, the Adivasi form of life sees itself as integrated into nature's biodiversity, with mountains, streams, rivers, forests, and fields forming a living ecosystem. Adivasi seasonal festivals revere mountains and rivers—as glimpsed in Kak's film and Kanwar's installation—and celebrate this living relation to their natural surroundings, connecting culturally to natural seasons, the first harvests, sacred hunts, and the sowing of seeds. Taking such a view does not entail romanticizing Indigenous life as a pure expression of ecological harmony. While one can rightly be suspicious of uncritically idealizing Indigenous cultures, the "realist" views presented by critics of such romanticism tend to inadvertently validate ongoing dispossession,[60] and, according to Padel and Das, are simply misguided: "Dismissing a positive view of tribal culture as 'ecological romanticism' serves to justify the ongoing dispossession of Adivasis, which is taking place throughout tribal areas of India on a vast scale. This dispossession is turning people whose cultural norms of sharing and equality are very close to the ideals of communism into an industrial labour-pool of near-slavery."[61] Moreover, these views risk supporting "the mainstream, desacrilised, view of nature," which "is the antithesis of [tribal ecology], reducing everything to economic value, seeing the *sources* of life in terms of *resources*—water, forest, agricultural land and crops, as well as the minerals lying under the earth's surface. Not taking too much from nature, and wasting virtually nothing are at the heart of Adivasi culture."[62]

Adivasi low-impact culture thus offers a model for an environmentally and socially just form of life—a provocation for

57 Padel and Das, *Out of This Earth*, xxv.
58 Ibid., 11.
59 Ibid., 148.
60 See, for instance, Archana Prasad, *Against Ecological Romanticism: Verrier Elwin and the Making of Anti-Modern Tribal Identity* (Delhi: Three Essays Collective, 2003); or Krech, *The Ecological Indian*.
61 Padel and Das, *Out of This Earth*, 69–70.
62 Ibid., 68.

living differently in an era threatened by climate breakdown. Building on anthropologist James Clifford's recent work, "becoming indigenous" proposes a new imperative to live within one's environment in a way that is newly sensitive to relations between the local and the global, and supportive of the integrity of natural biodiversity as well as the politics of equality and social justice.[63] Rather than a proposal for a new exoticism, it asks: How can we invent new ways to be local, low impact, and part of a degrowth economy that are specific to our own circumstances, while avoiding the dangers of provincialism and regional or national prejudice?[64] How might we diversify food production and move away from factory farms as well as its export industry, so as to safeguard our ecosystem? How, in the words of Vandana Shiva, can we contribute to a collective mode of living that "legitimizes the way of knowing and being that creates wealth by enhancing life and diversity, and which delegitimises the knowledge and practice of a culture of death as the basis for capital accumulation"?[65] These are crucial questions that will not be easily solved in the future, though we have all of the resources to address them in the present.

63 James Clifford, *Returns: Becoming Indigenous in the Twenty-First Century* (Cambridge, MA: Harvard University Press, 2013).

64 Ursula Heise outlines these dangers in *Sense of Place and Sense of Planet.*

65 Shiva, *Staying Alive,* 13.

Decolonizing Nature

Chapter 6

Making the World Matter

Instead of this speculative philosophy taught in the schools, we may thus discover a practical philosophy whereby we could know the force and actions of [...] all the bodies in our environment [...] so as to make ourselves as it were the masters and possessors of nature.

—René Descartes, *Discourse on the Method for Conducting One's Reason Well and for Seeking Truth in the Sciences*, 1637

Mastery and possession: these are the master words launched by Descartes at the dawn of the scientific and technological age, when our Western reason went off to conquer the universe.

—Michel Serres, *The Natural Contract*, 1990

Resource overconsumption, corporate landgrabs, widespread environmental degradation, and runaway climate change. Now, almost a quarter century after philosopher of science Michel Serres's discerning book, and nearly five hundred years after Descartes described the terms of an emerging "practical philosophy" that would be the guiding principle of both Western science and colonialism, we are living in a time of ecological tipping points, more than ever conscious of the disastrous global legacy of Enlightenment modernity. Serres argued that the origin of the environmental crisis is located in our fundamental relation to the material world around us: "We dominate and appropriate it [nature]: such is the shared philosophy underlying industrial enterprise as well as so-called disinterested science, which are indistinguishable in this respect. Cartesian mastery brings science's objective violence into line, making it a well-controlled strategy. Our fundamental relationship with objects comes down to war and property."[1] Historically, nature has been treated by humans as a thing to be used, exploited, commercialized, fetishized, and colonized—as many Marxist critics and Indigenous peoples have long realized[2]—so what we need, Serres proposed, is a "natural contract" that will reconceptualize our relation to material objects, environments, and nonhuman life-forms.

Serres's prescient analysis has been given new life in the international artistic project World of Matter, a collaborative platform of diverse practices formed in 2013. Addressing global political ecology, the group operates between institutions, academic disciplines, and nonacademic fields, as well as between the areas of art, architectural research, spatial politics, and visual culture. Comprised of core members Mabe Bethônico, Ursula Biemann, Lonnie van Brummelen and Siebren de Haan, Uwe H. Martin, Helge Mooshammer and Peter Mörtenböck, Emily Eliza Scott, and Paulo Tavares,[3] World of Matter has reanimated Serres's writings—perhaps once considered at the remote ends of speculative philosophy, but currently gathering newfound momentum as climate change has gained greater visibility. His analysis and proposal for a natural contract represent a key conceptual entry point for the projects of this collective.[4] Indeed, their works all function on the dual register of a critical documentary analysis of the present and speculative modeling of alternate worlds, which echoes some of the central terms of Serres's writing. Bringing together ecological research, social justice activism, and environmental

1 Serres, *The Natural Contract*, 32.

2 For instance, as Fredric Jameson wrote in his now-classic 1984 text, "Multinational or consumer capitalism, far from being inconsistent with Marx's great nineteenth-century analysis, constitutes, on the contrary, the purest form of capital yet to have emerged, a prodigious expansion of capital into hitherto uncommodified areas. This purer capitalism of our own time thus eliminates the enclaves of precapitalist organization it had hitherto tolerated and exploited in a tributary way. One is tempted to speak in this connection of a new and historically original penetration and colonization of Nature." "Postmodernism, or the Cultural Logic of Late Capitalism," *New Left Review* 1, no. 146 (July–August 1984): 78. On Marx(ism) and nature, see John Bellamy Foster, *Marx's Ecology: Materialism and Nature* (New York: Monthly Review Press, 2000).

3 These were the members during the developmental phase, from 2011 to 2013. World of Matter thereafter considers itself to be a shifting collective with flexible membership.

4 In fact, various projects of World of Matter members—including Tavares's research video *Non-human Rights* (2012), Scott's audio tour accompanying the 2014 exhibition "World of Matter: On the Global Ecologies of Raw Material," and Van Brummelen and De Haan's notes on their cinematic essay *Monument of Sugar: How to Use Artistic Means to Elude Trade Barriers* (2007)—directly reference Serres's writing. In this chapter I draw on both World of Matter's invocation of Serres and his work directly.

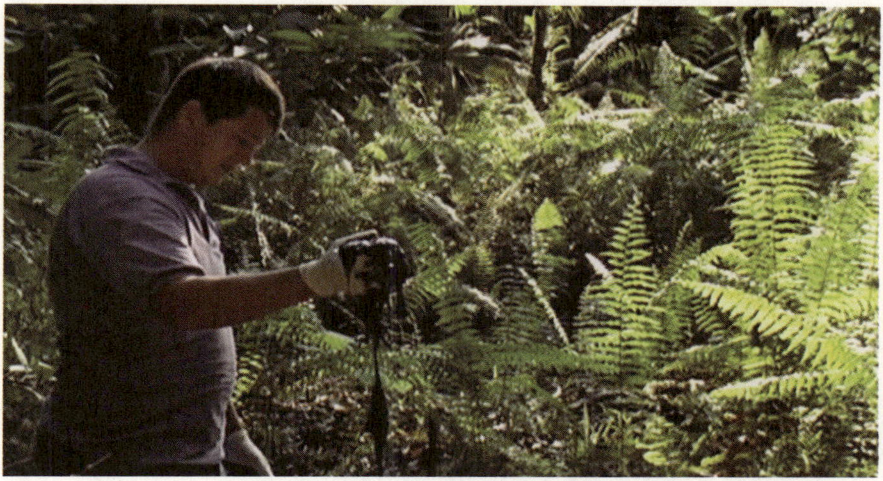

Paulo Tavares, still from *Non-human Rights*, 2012; evidence of spilled Texaco oil in the Ecuadorian Amazon

humanities, and given aesthetic form through video, text-based displays, cartographic analyses, and sculptural and mixed-media installations, their efforts could not be more relevant to our current global crisis.

In a collective statement from 2013, World of Matter explain: "Humans have exhausted virtually all known resource deposits on the planet with heightening efforts geared toward locating yet undiscovered and untapped reserves. Large-scale mining is penetrating ever deeper layers, multinational land grabs are advancing to remote corners, and the race is on for the neocolonial division of the seabed. [...] With growing consciousness about global environmental limits, there is urgent need for new discourses and modes of representation that shift resource-related debates from a market-driven domain to open platforms for engaged and decentralized public discourse."[5] The research of World of Matter answers this imperative and reinvigorates the environmentalist urgency of addressing climate disruption. By doing so it invents new approaches and creative options for living in a world of finite resources.[6] Representing

5 World of Matter, "From Supply Lines to a World That Matters," introduction to *Provisões: Uma conferência visual*, ed. Mabe Bethônico (Belo Horizonte: Instituto Cidades Criativas, 2013), 11. See also World of Matter's portfolio of essays in *Third Text*, no. 120 (January 2013); and its website, www.worldofmatter.net.

6 For corresponding eco-socialist proposals that help contexualize World of Matter's approach to capitalist modernity, see, for example, Williams, *Ecology and Socialism*; Smith, "Green Capitalism"; and Klein, *This Changes Everything*.

a platform for creative speculation, researched analysis, and pioneering projects that explore advanced capitalist relations to the natural environment, and how those relations might be conceived differently, its participants concern themselves with how we might "decolonize nature"—as poignantly expressed in Tavares's *Non-human Rights* (2012)—in ways that resonate, both directly and indirectly, with Serres's writing. In videos, photographs, presentations of material evidence, and texts, their critical documentary work investigates how the current regime of resource colonialism, industrial ecocide, and neoliberal agro-economy is socially and environmentally destructive, historically rooted in paradigms of imperialism that go back centuries, and economically and politically unequal in the distribution of its negative effects, which disproportionately impact the poor and disfranchised in unevenly developed nations.

What would it mean to *decolonize* nature? Colonialism, at its most basic, implies a subject–object relation mediated by power and defined by mastery and appropriation, to reiterate Serres's terms. In the mid-twentieth century, Martinican poet and thinker Aimé Césaire wrote that the colonial relation (as between European colonizers and the Afro-Caribbean colonized) defines the naked assertion of power in the name of economic exploitation, involving manifold techniques of racist domination and cruel dehumanization ("forced labor, intimidation, pressure, the police, taxation, theft, rape, compulsory crops, contempt, mistrust, arrogance, self-complacency, swinishness, brainless elites, degraded masses").[7] More recently, the Cameroonian postcolonial theorist Achille Mbembe has explained how colonialism constitutes multiple forms of violence: an inaugural violence that creates and defines the brutally unequal and racialized terms of colonialism's existence; a second violence that asserts its exclusive power in terms of law, right, and legitimacy; and a third violence that consolidates, spreads, and makes permanent its unquestionable control.[8] European colonialism, in this regard, treated both land and human nature as resources for capitalist industry, subjecting Indigenous peoples to "a complex mix of brute exploitation, paternalistic exhortation and racist disdain."[9] In other words, land and people, nature and the colonized, were subjected to the same Cartesian logic of mastery and appropriation that Serres brings out in his study.[10] Given this (admittedly schematic) overview stretched

7 Aimé Césaire, *Discourse on Colonialism* (1955), trans. Joan Pinkham (New York: Monthly Review Press, 2000), 42.

8 Achille Mbembe, "Of *Commandement*," in *On the Postcolony*, trans. A. M. Berrett (Berkeley: University of California Press, 2001), 25.

9 Adams and Mulligan, introduction to *Decolonizing Nature: Strategies for Conservation in a Post-colonial Era*, 6.

10 No doubt a further implication of this homology is that the colonized tended to be naturalized (i.e., deprived of culture, dehumanized, and relegated to the natural order), while nature was colonized by human industry.

across a half century of anticolonial theory and practice, I propose that to decolonize nature would broadly entail the following: dissolving the subject–object relation in the social and natural environment; ending the conditions of mastery and appropriation that determine the connection between the two; and stopping the multiple levels of violence that enforce these relations. The projects in World of Matter bring us closer to understanding this process of decolonizing nature, beginning with those that present and analyze destructive industrialization and its domination of nature.

War and Property

With *Field: Amazonia* (2012), a photo-essay travelogue published in a World of Matter catalogue, Paulo Tavares recounts his research trip across Brazil, where he investigated the socio-environmental disaster zones of the country's modern history. These include areas of state-supported deforestation, industrial ranch and farm development, and oil exploration from the 1960s to the '80s—all of which feed into subsequent waves of IMF-supported privatization and neoliberal policies implemented in the '90s. In the wake of this development, large sections of the Amazon rain forest, we learn from his project, lie depleted and degraded, and it's become the stage for ongoing conflicts between resource grabs for new global markets and social movements struggling for democratic Indigenous sovereignty and control of local land use.[11] Focusing on agribusiness in the western Brazil state of Mato Grosso, Uwe H. Martin and Frauke Huber's video *Landrush: Frontier Land* (2011–14) portrays the region's commercial farming industry and considers its socio-environmental impacts. Original research footage presents Indigenous activists explaining that such development comes "without limits" and fouls traditional farmlands with chemical pesticides and GMOs, forecasting a dark future of depleted clean-water supplies, which are polluted by these farming practices, and the resulting social conflicts.[12] Placing Brazil in a comparative international perspective, Martin and Huber's video also tracks farming developments in the remote region of Gambela, Ethiopia, where pastoralists have been pushed aside

11 See Paulo Tavares, "Field: Amazonia," in Bethônico, *Provisões*, 72–97. For further accounts of environmental and Indigenous conflicts in the Brazilian Amazon, see Susanna Hecht and Alexander Cockburn, *The Fate of the Forest: Developers, Destroyers, and Defenders of the Amazon*, rev. ed. (Chicago: University of Chicago Press, 2010); Susanna Hecht, *The Scramble for the Amazon and the "Lost Paradise" of Euclides da Cunha* (Chicago: University Of Chicago Press, 2013); A. C. Roosevelt, "The Amazon and the Anthropocene: 13,000 Years of Human Influence in a Tropical Rainforest," *Anthropocene* 4 (December 2013): 69–87; and the reports of Amazon Watch, amazonwatch.org.

12 For an overview of water politics under corporate globalization, see Vandana Shiva, *Water Wars: Privatization, Pollution, and Profit* (Boston: South End Press, 2002).

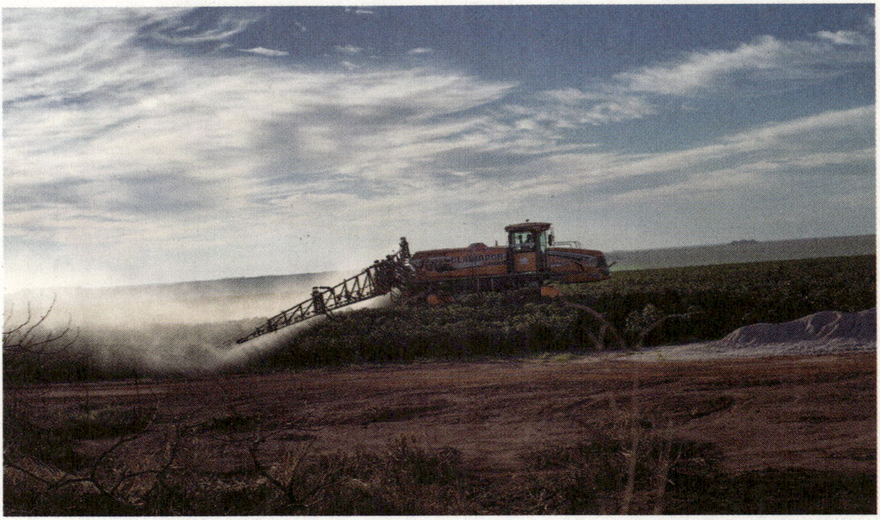

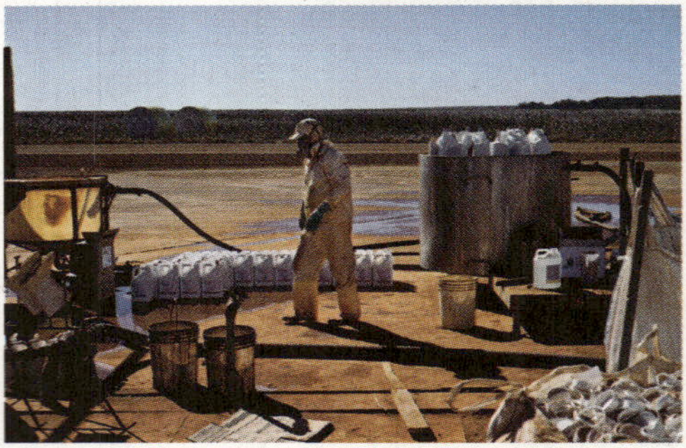

Uwe H. Martin and Frauke Huber, stills from *Landrush: Frontier Land*, 2011–14

by large-scale foreign investors, supporting the country's move to high-tech farming and the corporate enclosure of lands, and sending long-established subsistence and cattle farmers into resettlement programs that significantly disrupt their lives. The video's globally relational vantage point connects disparate geographies that are experiencing similar threats of industrialization and corporate colonization, damaging not only regional ecosystems but also threatening the survival of traditionally self-sufficient communities.

Ursula Biemann's *Deep Weather* (2013) is also exemplary of this sensitivity to relational geographies. The video depicts the exploitation of the Albertan Tar Sands, where corporations have industrialized an area roughly the size of England, mining dirty and hard-to-access hydrocarbons (in the form of bitumen, a heavy black oil that comes mixed with clay, sand, and water). In the process of clearing ancient boreal forests, extraction firms such as ConocoPhillips, Petro-Canada, and ExxonMobil have devastated the biodiversity of this area in northern Canada, bringing ruin to the environments and lives of the First Nations peoples who live nearby (where cases of illness caused by air and water pollution have risen drastically over the last decade). This includes the Chipewyan community, for whom "the land is the essence of the ACFN [Athabasca Chipewyan First Nation] culture, values, and spirituality," and who have filed grievances with Shell for practicing ecocide, and with the Canadian government for reneging on historical treaties and failing to protect the health of Indigenous populations.[13] Aerial shots of the vast oil fields in the Athabasca River region are narrated by Biemann in a whispered voice-over (or rather, a hushed and humbled voice-under) that speculates about the geological impacts of these corporate activities:

> *Day and night they mine the black sediments and boil the Athabasca water to separate the tar from the clay. The toxic fluids collect in lakes where rhythmic explosions keep the birds from bathing in acid. The wildlife has retreated, the traplines are empty, the elders call the spirits, the young ones sing rap songs, and the acid wind's hissing "Evolution isn't fast enough. Mutate!" For a hundred more years, there is enough stuff here for heavy fuel that will bring toxic clouds over the boreal woods and continue to warm and swell the seas. No longer to be witnessed but elsewhere, in equatorial zones.*

One such equatorial zone is depicted in the second half of the video, where the socio-environmental consequences of fossil fuel climate change is seen in such a faraway place as Bangladesh's Ganges Delta. Bringing the camera down to human-scaled ground level, Biemann shows the efforts of a coastal community to construct barriers against the rising seas. The manual labor of the community contrasts sharply with the high-tech infrastructure in Canada. Like Martin and Huber's *Landrush*, the relational geographic analysis at play here connects faraway regions linked by industrialization and its resulting climate disruption. The monumental effort carried out by Bangladeshi collective labor to reinforce embankments and protect against catastrophic submersion is a socio-environmental externality of the oil industry,

13 See Jenna Winton and her report on one of the leading spokespersons of the ACFN, "Eriel Deranger: Fighting the World's Largest Industrial Project, the Alberta Tar Sands," *Cultural Survival*, February 5, 2014, http://www.culturalsurvival.org/news/eriel-deranger-fighting-worlds-largest-industria-project-alberta-tar-sands.

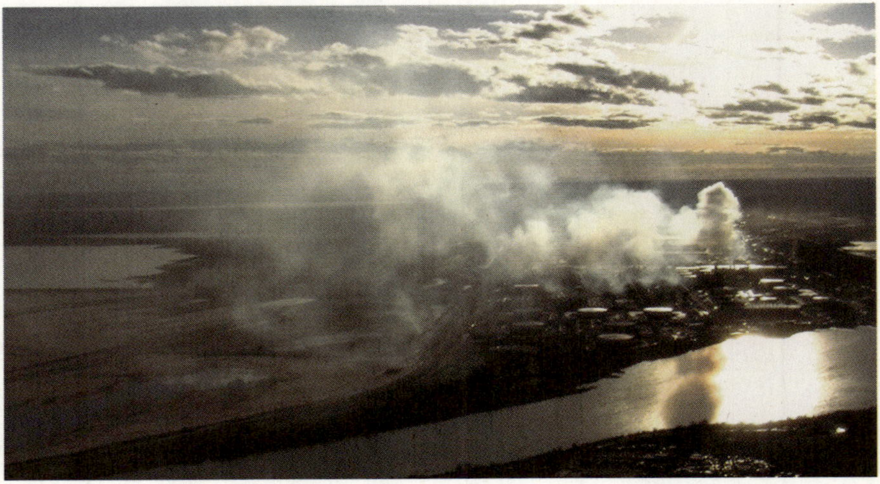

Ursula Biemann, still from *Deep Weather*, 2013

generally disavowed by corporations, including the (recently defeated) conservative and pro-drilling government of Stephen Harper in Canada.

Uwe H. Martin's *White Gold* (2007–14) is a ten-part documentary (each part four to eight minutes long) that compares North–South and East–West geographies under neoliberal globalization by linking agricultural practice, land-use policy, advanced technology, and development economics. One part, "Texas Blues," focuses on a family of cotton growers in Texas who are locked in a cycle of conventional production. They explain how subsidies allow them to stay afloat, and that while organic cotton growing might be viable otherwise, they are nonetheless beholden to this system, which also pushes down prices elsewhere in the world. "Killing Seeds" brings this small-scale cooperative industry into dialogue with agriculture in India, looking at the region of Vidharbha in Maharashtra. There, Indian farmers have received none of the government welfare granted to their US counterparts. Rising expenses of chemical inputs to grow patented GM seeds, mechanized farming technology, and WTO policies that drive down cotton prices have lead to a massive increase in debt, which many farmers tragically answer with suicide (approximately three hundred thousand cases since 1995). The terms of this global system repeat an old colonial power relation, as scientist and activist Vandana Shiva comments in the video. She states that these agribusiness arrangements constitute nothing less than "economic genocide"—ruining farmers and breaking up regional control of seeds ("seed sovereignty"), destroying

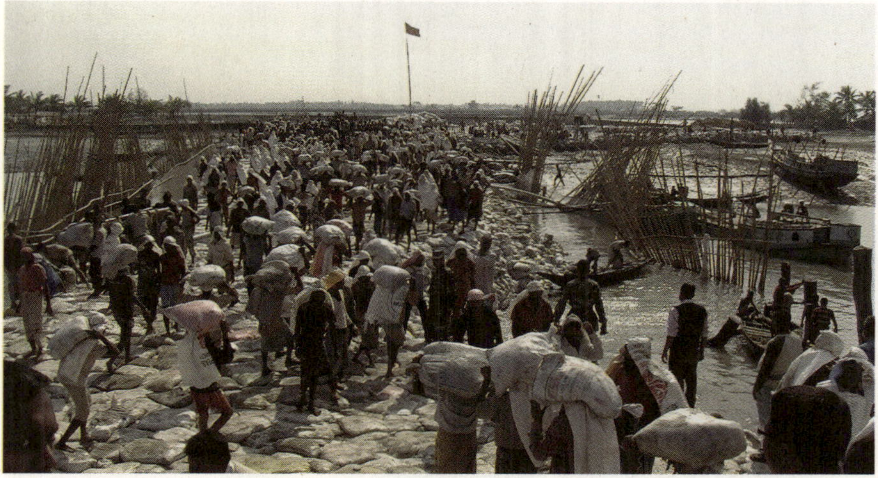

Ursula Biemann, still from *Deep Weather*, 2013

the economic independence of Indian farmers so corporations like Monsanto, a major player in this market, can expand their markets worldwide.

These projects—most freely accessible on the group's extensive website—evidence a collective commitment to investigate and visualize industrial modernity's colonization of nature, including analyses of the energy, extraction, mining, agricultural, and transportation industries. While each work has its own aesthetics, they nonetheless share a common set of approaches. Most notable are the multiple inflections of experimental documentary video: the researched video essay, combining interviews with diverse subjects, sociopolitical analysis and historical investigation (often presented as voice-over or explanatory titles) alongside environmental footage, and politico-ecological philosophical speculation.[14] The latter tendency resonates in particular with recent developments in the philosophies of new materialism and object-oriented ontology, where World of Matter members creatively engage the writing of theorists such as Serres, Bruno Latour, Karen Barad, and Graham Harman, in addition to connecting to the climate-justice activism of figures like Vandana Shiva and formations such as the Landless Workers' Movement in Brazil, fighting for land reform and social justice. The World of Matter participants' approach to ethnography and field research is critical and experimental, involving theatrical reenactments and collaborations (especially in

14 On Biemann's use of the video essay, see my text "Video's Migrant Geography: Ursula Biemann's *Sahara Chronicle*," chap. 8 in *The Migrant Image*, 201–20.

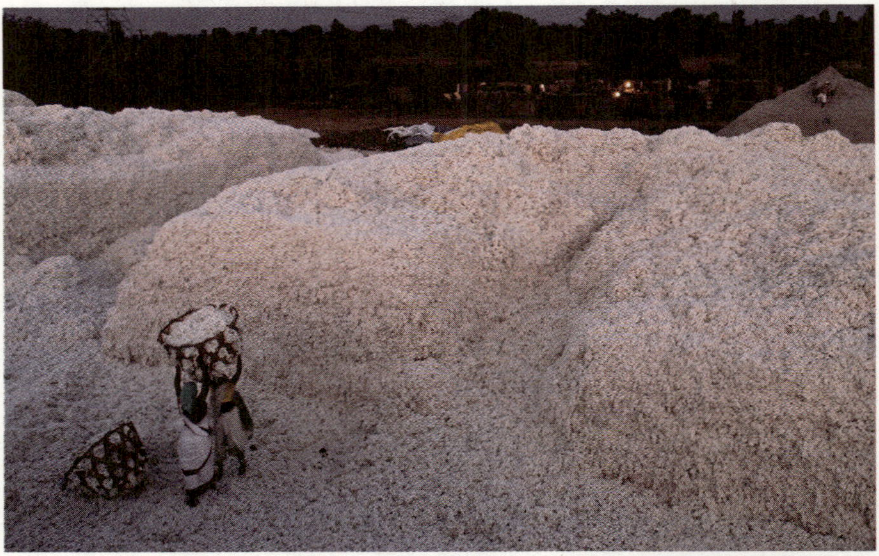

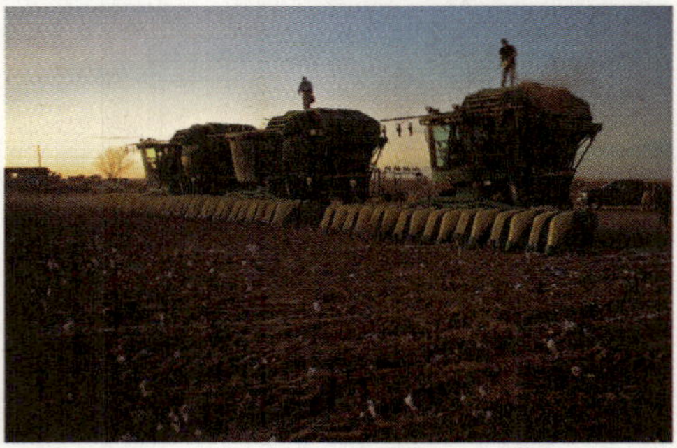

Uwe H. Martin, stills from *White Gold*, 2007–14; above, from "Killing Seeds"; right, from "Texas Blues"

the films of Lonnie van Brummelen and Siebren de Haan, who worked closely with Dutch fisherfolk from Urk for *Episode of the Sea*, 2014).[15] In addition to these various ethnographic and documentary models, the group's work also takes on the form of mixed-media installations, pedagogical presentations (some drawing from the natural sciences), and critical cartographies and diagrams. The interdisciplinary scope of their research bridges geography, chemistry, visual culture, agriculture, political science, and—particularly in the case of Emily Eliza

15 For a recent significant contribution to the discourse on art and ethnography, proposing new ways of considering this connection, see Okwui Enwezor, ed., *Intense Proximity: An Anthology of the Near and the Far* (Paris: Artyls, 2012).

Scott—an ecological art history, contributing to the emerging discipline of environmental humanities.[16] Developing ways to materialize and translate the language of things—ecosystems as much as nonhuman life—and the traces and effects of human activities is also part of experimental forensic practice (which resonates with the conceptual, technological, and practical applications in the Centre for Research Architecture at Goldsmiths).[17] Finally, World of Matter's mode of collective artistic and interdisciplinary research is commonly mediated through constellations of texts, images, and videos that share the imperative to explore how the world *matters*—how it enters into diverse forms of materialization *and* conflicted forms of valuation (not only as war and property, but also, newly configured, as post-anthropocentric and intrinsically valuable within ecosystems).

Limits to Growth 2.0

Questioning the mainstream government policies of "sustainable growth" embedded in an unsustainable neoliberal economy, World of Matter effectively join a history of environmentalism stemming from the "limits to growth" discourse of the 1970s.[18] The year before the 1973 oil crisis, the Club of Rome commissioned the eponymous report, which deployed computer modeling to forecast the effects of growth—chiefly in relation to world population, industrialization, pollution, food, and resources—on the earth's natural systems. It concluded that only by reducing growth could humanity save itself from the collapse of those global systems before the close of the twenty-first century—a warning that was largely ignored at the time in policy-making circles, but has gained new relevance in recent years within the larger context of concerns about industrial modernity's impact on the environment.[19] This "limits" approach was a culmination of the first wave of postwar environmentalism. It was then gradually eclipsed by contrarian voices that stressed emerging models of sustainable development, superseded by the pro-growth "green capitalism" of the '80s and '90s, which ideologically—and falsely—reconciled restoring environmental

16 For more on the environmental humanities, which attempts to link the concerns of fields such as literature, history, anthropology, and art to ecology, and to develop new research methodologies that address this convergence, see the Transatlantic Research Network in Environmental Humanities (environmental-humanities-network.org), and the journal *Environmental Humanities*, which released its first issue in 2012.

17 See, for instance, Forensic Architecture, *Forensis*.

18 See their collectively written statement, "Introduction to the World of Matter Project," in *World of Matter*, ed. Inke Arns (Berlin: Sternberg Press, 2014), 6–7.

19 Meadows et al., "The Limits to Growth"; and Donella H. Meadows, *The Limits to Growth: The 30-Year Update* (White River Junction, VT: Chelsea Green, 2004).

20 For an analysis of the transition from limits-to-growth to green capitalism, see Cooper, *Life as Surplus*.

health and expanding the economy.[20] Now, at the tail end of that eco-economic compromise, corporations commonly advertise green business practices and a sustainable development supported by organizations such as the World Bank and WTO—where economic development, more than anything else, is what is meant to be sustainable. Recent research shows, however, that the Club of Rome's forecasts have turned out to be largely accurate; global society, with its unbridled expansion of population, industrialization, pollution, food production, and resource depletion, is nearing collapse.[21] "The warnings that we received in 1972 from LTG [Limits to Growth]," noted one scientist in 2011, "are becoming increasingly more worrisome as reality seems to be following closely the curves that the LTG scenario had generated."[22]

The logic of mastery and appropriation that Serres identified as the founding episteme of the present ecological crisis, in other words, has only been exacerbated with green capitalist approaches to climate change, where environmental calamity is viewed principally as a market failure and a market opportunity—the solution being to integrate nature (including natural disasters) ever more fully into global financial systems. Carbon trading, for instance, came about because atmospheric pollution was seen to be the result of unregulated externalities and needed to be integrated into economic frameworks—effectively privatizing the air—to redress the problem of global warming. According to the tenets of green capitalism, nature should be valued economically if it is to be protected environmentally.[23] Yet it's now clear that this approach—including initiatives such as carbon taxes, cap-and-trade schemes, and debt-for-nature swaps, and ethical consumerism such as green design, hybrid cars, recycling practices, and biogas—has failed to mitigate the increase of greenhouse gases. In fact, current capitalist society is so destructive that, in the words of environmental activist Bill McKibben, "we're running Genesis backward, decreating," reducing biodiversity substantially and initiating a mass species extinction event (the last one wiping out the dinosaurs sixty-five million years ago).[24] As economic historian Richard Smith puts it, "For all the green initiatives, corporate business practices have changed little—or the little they've changed has had no great

21 Graham Turner, *Is Global Collapse Imminent? An Updated Comparison of "The Limits to Growth" with Historical Data*, MSSI Research Paper no. 4 (Melbourne: Melbourne Sustainable Society Institute, University of Melbourne, 2014).

22 Ugo Bardi, *The Limits to Growth Revisited* (New York: Springer, 2011), 3.

23 See Paul Hawken, Amory Lovins, and L. Hunter Lovins, *Natural Capitalism: Creating the Next Industrial Revolution* (Boston: Little, Brown and Company, 1999); Brown, *Eco-Economy;* and Porritt, *Capitalism as if the World Matters*.

24 McKibben, *Eaarth*, 29. On biodiversity loss, see Kolbert, *The Sixth Extinction;* Thom van Dooren, *Flight Ways: Life and Loss at the Edge of Extinction* (New York: Columbia University Press, 2014); and the Extinction Studies Working Group, http://extinctionstudies.org.

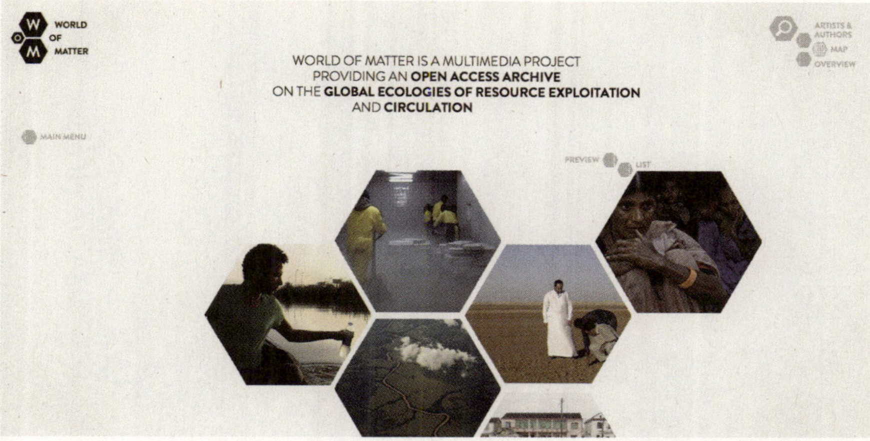

Screenshot of the World of Matter website, 2016

effect" in combating the causes of climate change.[25] With increased environmental devastation, green capitalism has only brought us closer to irreversible catastrophe.[26]

Few cultural practitioners address climate change from outside the hegemony of green capitalism—that World of Matter *does*, refusing to propose solutions to climate change that endorse the neoliberal market, is testimony to its radical practice. Connecting anticapitalist degrowth to social justice, and exchanging top-down governance for democratic participation in the formation of climate justice policy and grassroots activism, especially in the Global South, the group reinvents a limits-to-growth discourse, one shed of both the Club of Rome's neo-Malthusianism—where limiting population growth, especially in the developing world, forms the central priority of climate action—and Northern provincialism. Most importantly, World of Matter addresses ecology and questions of sustainability beyond the contradictions of free-market capitalism and its financialization of nature. Their transnational reach also conceives new modes of social organization, linking social movements, networked activism, and online communities in search of alternative "resource ecologies."[27] Exemplary is the group's website, which (as of April 2016) includes: *Earth Poison* (2014), artist and writer Nabil Ahmed's video-based project exploring arsenic's environmental and political violence in the Bengal Delta; *Chernobyl: Sounds*

25 Smith, "Green Capitalism."

26 On the potential future convergence of eco-catastrophe, systems collapse, societal breakdown, and rampant militarism, see Parenti, *Tropic of Chaos*.

27 See Helge Mooshammer and Peter Mörtenböck, "Of Multi-directional Forces: Interdependencies between Material, Social, and Other Resources," in Bethônico, *Provisões*, 99–125.

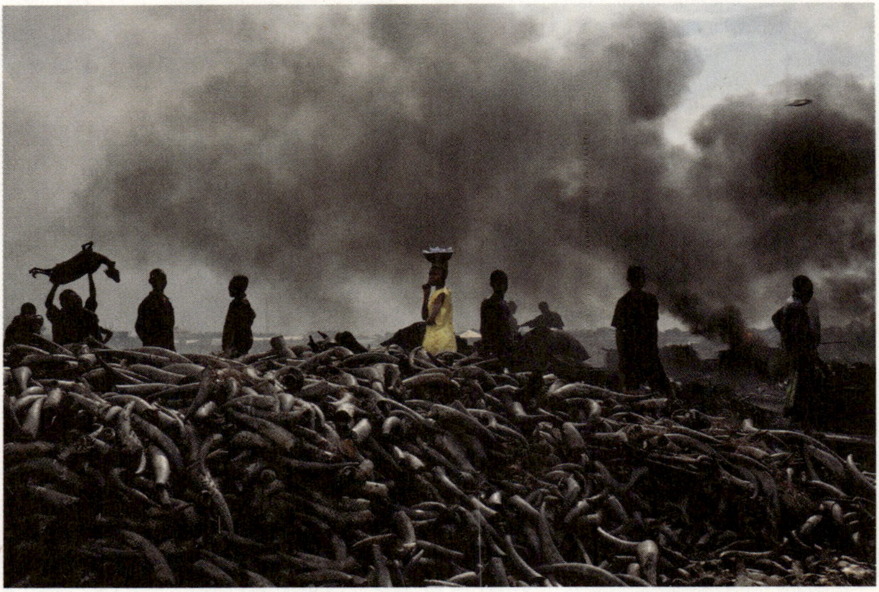

Ed Kashi, *Curse of the Black Gold*, 2008

of Contamination (2014), sound artist Peter Cusack's investigation of post-nuclear-disaster soundscapes; *Curse of the Black Gold* (2008), photojournalist Ed Kashi's documentation of oil-industry pollution in the Niger Delta; and *White Oil* (2013), artist Judy Price's examination of the geopolitics of Israeli neocolonial resource extraction in the quarries of occupied Palestinian territories. Just as its online content transcends the enclosure of the art-institutional space, the group's varied research moves beyond the exclusivity of specialist debate or discipline hierarchy and brings diverse voices—artists, activists, students, industrial laborers, agricultural workers, scientists, academics—into the discussion and deliberation of the politics of ecology. Consequently, their work proposes a new media ecology as much as a collaborative and transdisciplinary social practice. As Emily Eliza Scott notes, World of Matter intends to contribute to an "ecological knowledge commons," a free production of shared knowledge that remains open, collective, and widely accessible, pitched against corporate-governmental surveillance and proprietary control of the Internet.[28] Their globalized research methodology represents an expanded platform with which to address a fundamental element of political ecology—to carry out, in Bruno Latour's words, "the progressive composition of a common world."[29]

By exploring the political, social, and economic dimensions of land use around the globe, with specific attention to the Global South, World of Matter overcome a central limitation of other environmentally concerned artistic research that tends to focus on the developed North (as with the Center for Land Use Interpretation and Critical Art Ensemble).[30] World of Matter's areas of concern align with postcolonial critiques of the ecology of affluence, which focuses on environmental commitments in developed nations, such as conservationism, organic products, and recycling, rather than on social justice, alleviating poverty, and combating corporate ecocide in the non-West.[31] World of Matter takes into account conditions under postcolonial globalization—something it shares with Platform in London and Sarai in Delhi, environmental, artistic, and political formations of which there are still too few. With these priorities in mind, they explore the new possibilities of the "commons," uniting resource ecologies, knowledge-based systems, collective labor practices, and circumstances of natural environments, while remaining attentive to modalities and histories of social inequality and conflict around the world that mark the uneven developments under neoliberalism.[32]

The postcolonial, global scope points as well to the *social ecology* in World of Matter's collective practice—the correlation between the exploitation of people and environments—evidenced in its portrayal of precarious communities: women miners in Brazil (in Mabe Bethônico's *Mineral Invisibility*, 2008–ongoing); former subsistence farmers in Egypt driven out of business by government-favored monoculture (Biemann's *Egyptian Chemistry*, 2012); debt-saddled small-scale farmers in an oppressive climate of agribusiness in India (Martin's *White Gold*); a Dutch fishing community struggling with increased global competition and the threatened viability of their

28 "Collaborative research platforms such as World of Matter enact the concept that knowledge is an inherently sustainable resource. Moreover, they point to the vital connection between *commons* as a shared good (whether material or immaterial) and *common-ing* as an act or process." Emily Eliza Scott, "Wandering Subjects: Ecological Knowledge Commons," in Arns, *World of Matter*, 175.

29 See Latour, *Politics of Nature*, 18. For Latour, by replacing "matters of fact" with "matters of concern," certainty with contingency, and well-defined essences with entangled hybrids, scientific discourse is opened to a newly inclusive community of participants and stakeholders that proposes a new ecology of politics, which holds unprecedented democratic potential (ibid., 24–25).

30 As referenced by Emily Eliza Scott in "Relational Research: On Building Ecological Knowledge Commons," in Bethônico, *Provisões*, 258–83; although my analysis draws some differences between World of Matter and the collectives she identifies as important precursors (including CLUI).

31 For further critical exploration of the ecology of affluence and the environmentalism of the poor, see Ramachandra Guha and Joan Martinez-Alier, *Varieties of Environmentalism: Essays North and South* (London: Routledge, 1997), xxi.

32 For more on commoning practices, see Linebaugh, *Stop, Thief!* On globalization and uneven development, see Harvey, *Spaces of Global Capitalism*; Smith, *Uneven Development*; and Martinez-Alier, *The Environmentalism of the Poor.*

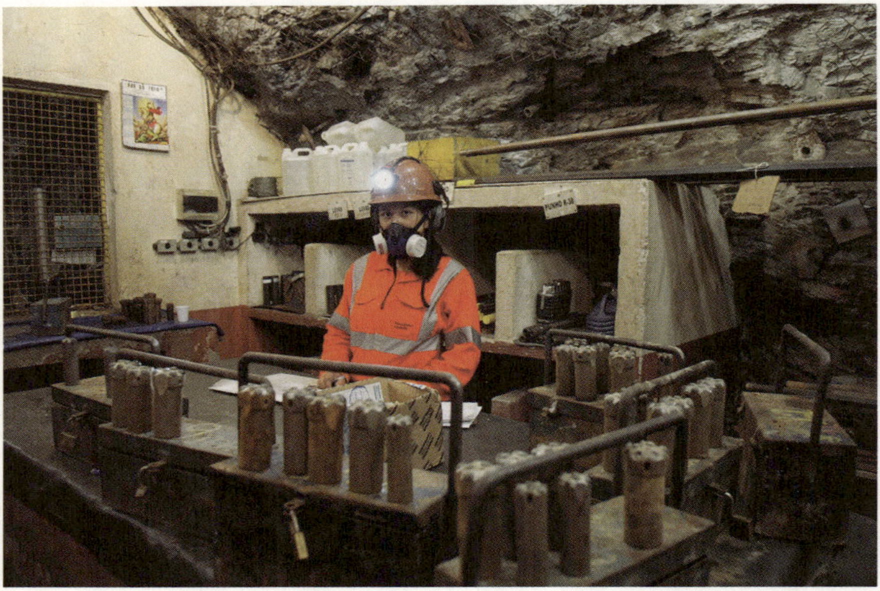

Mabe Bethônico, *Mineral Invisibility*, 2008–ongoing

regional economy and identity (Van Brummelen and De Haan's *Episode of the Sea*). Representing the devastating results of global agricultural policies and industrialization on those often with the least means to resist, the group shows how the capitalist economy, and its ideology of possessive individualism, is in fact *not* intrinsic to humanity. As evoked by Martin in *White Gold*, this emancipatory process begins, for example, by reclaiming the "seed commons"—that is, nature's regenerative fertility, which, for Vandana Shiva, must not be privatized, patented, or commodified. Shiva proposes this commons as the basis of a "living democracy" and a "planetary citizenship" posed against global capitalism's genocidal economy (her own organization, Navdanya, pursues this by protecting food heritage in India).[33]

The effects of the current economy correlate with what Rob Nixon terms the "slow violence" inflicted on the disenfranchised—the protracted temporal effects and accretive material circumstances of oil industry devastation on rain forests and deltas, or the economic demolition of subsistence farmers caused by corporate agriculture's

33 See Shiva, *Earth Democracy*; and Navdanya International, *Terra Viva: Our Soil, Our Commons, Our Future* (Florence: Stampa Tipografia Fabri, 2015), http://www.navdanyainternational.it/attachments/article/202/Manifesto%20English.pdf. Also relevant here is Amar Kanwar's *The Sovereign Forest*, as discussed in chapter 5.

war of attrition. The social ecology made evident by World of Matter indicates how repairing ecological destruction necessitates rectifying social violence and inequality as a mode of decolonization.[34] But one must first understand the causes and effects of such violence, and herein lies the importance of the group's research and representation of forms of life that are often invisible—kept so, at times, by corporate and governmental design. With *Mineral Invisibility*, Bethônico presents research into the conditions of women miners in Minas Gerais, Brazil, via documentary video and photo-essays, and thereby unravels one such area of institutionalized invisibility. Her construction of new archives of documentation focusing on women laborers' experiences aims to enable public debate of the negative environmental impact of the mining industry. As well, it contributes to the campaign for workers' rights and gender equality—subjects that couldn't be addressed previously because the documentation hadn't been publicly accessible owing to the mining companies' resistance to transparency. The case is similar with World of Matter's research on subsistence farmers in India, Brazil's landless farmers, and the Shuar and Sarayaku peoples in the Ecuadorian Amazon, all variously impacted by corporate industry (whether industrial agriculture, palm-oil plantations, or mineral extraction), but typically underrepresented in global mainstream media. Corporate practice is also researched, as in Huber and Martin's *Landrush*, which includes interviews with several agribusiness representatives, including a commercial farmer in Brazil who uses chemical pesticides and fertilizers and an operator of a large-scale pig production farm; and *White Gold*, which presents a biotechnologist in a Texas university who argues in favor of his research on GM cotton, and a Brazilian grower who came to Sudan at the government's invitation to help develop greater efficiency in agricultural production. Investigating the intersection of economic, social, and ecological injustice, World of Matter's research extends to interview subjects who articulate their own concerns from different sides of the issues. The videos ultimately leave it open to viewers to form independent positions and political opinions on how the world does matter and—perhaps more importantly—might matter differently.

34 "Economic, ethnic, cultural, and gender conflicts, among many others, lie at the core of the most serious ecological dislocations we face today." Murray Bookchin, "What Is Social Ecology?," in *Environmental Philosophy: From Animal Rights to Radical Ecology*, ed. Michael E. Zimmerman (Englewood Cliffs, NJ: Prentice Hall, 1993), 93.

Nonhuman Agency

Extending representation to social groups in diverse regions forms only one part of World of Matter's conceptual objective. Important for generating participation of disenfranchised communities in debates around land use, this social ecology often nonetheless remains anthropocentric. Going beyond this limitation, World of Matter also seeks to investigate modes of collective composition that extend beyond human agents alone (the group has no direct relation to "deep ecology," however, which attempts to bypass anthropocentrism to the point of excluding the human altogether, and in extreme cases is criticized for misanthropy).[35] Drawing on thinkers like Latour, Félix Guattari, and Manuel DeLanda, the project conceptualizes and materializes a radically inclusive sociability, positing what Mooshammer and Mörtenböck term a new "cooperative of things" (resonating with the terms of Latour's actor-network theory). This new grouping surpasses positioning humans as sole acting agents or the exclusive subjects of political processes and legal standing. As such, World of Matter proposes decolonizing nature by recalibrating the commonality of which Latour speaks.

Which returns us to the debate over the value of nature and the nature of value. How *does* the world matter, and how does the very definition of the world depend on competing systems of valuation? As we have seen, there are different forms of valuation—some economic, others intrinsic, some ecological, others founded in religious practice—the diversity of which, including their sometimes complex interaction, is normally covered up by the financial myopia of neoliberalism. One model that World of Matter develops comes from the interdisciplinary field of science and technology studies (connecting particularly to the work of Donna Haraway, Anna Tsing, and Karen Barad), which investigates the politico-environmental value of physical and geological systems, where ecology itself represents an interactive (or even, intra-active) field of nonhuman forces. Independent of human meaning, intentionality, and causality, things possess their own circuitry, modes of reproduction, and mutually formed chemistries—but how to track, translate, and understand them outside of anthropocentric priorities? Broadly, the participants' experimental research evidences a transition in this regard from considering nature as a resource to what they term an "aesthetic-philosophical arena." Relating, for instance, to the intra-actions between chemical particles or neutrons, as

35 For a canonical critique of deep ecology, see Murray Bookchin, "Social Ecology versus Deep Ecology: A Challenge for the Ecology Movement," *Green Perspectives: Newsletter of the Green Program Project*, nos. 4/5 (Summer 1987): 1–23. For an overview of deep ecology, see: J. Edward de Steiguer, "Arne Naess and the Deep Ecology Movement," in *The Origins of Modern Environmental Thought* (Tucson: University of Arizona Press, 2006), 185–202.

developed by Barad, this arena proposes a field of value defined within nature, operating beyond market-based assumptions or financial imperatives.[36] Researchers are increasingly probing the world beyond the human, a world that also impacts human culture and politics. As political theorist Jane Bennett observes, resonating with Serres, "modern selves are feeling increasingly entangled, cosmically, biotechnically, medially, virally, pharmacologically, with nonhuman nature. Nature has always mixed it up with self and society, but lately"—owing to anthropogenic climate change, for instance—"this comingling has intensified and become harder to ignore."[37] World of Matter explores nature's realm beyond the conventional anthropocentric gaze, as well as its comingling with culture and technology.

Consider Ursula Biemann's *Egyptian Chemistry*, which tracks the transformation of water in Egypt through large-scale geo-engineering projects, aquaculture biology and industry, and the recent revolutionary politics of the Arab Spring. The video and mixed-media installation engages a post-anthropocentric methodology that draws on new materialism and speculative realism as well as environmental science and chemistry. It demonstrates an aesthetic sensitivity to the agency of objects, both beyond and intertwined with human systems. In her related photo-essay, Biemann describes the Nile as a "hybrid interactive system that has always been at once organic, technological, and social," though traditionally its value has been directed toward primarily human benefit. "The question is," Biemann asks, "how we can conceive of reality indifferent to humans."[38] *Egyptian Chemistry* explains how the World Bank and IMF, in conjunction with US- and EU-driven economic policies, guided President Mubarak's government in the 1990s to move Egypt increasingly toward an export-based agro-industrial economy by funding large-scale monoculture farms (with many leading food and farming corporations owned by Egyptian MPs and military officers). The result sapped funds from small-scale farmers, who were denied their traditional state subsidies even while the interest rates of village bank loans rose dramatically. A number of farmers, including the peasant-farmer and activist Shahinda Maklad, are interviewed in Biemann's video. We learn that local food production was depleted, leading to food scarcity, urbanization, unemployment, and

36 See World of Matter, "From Supply Lines to a World That Matters," 11.

37 Bennett, *Vibrant Matter*, 115.

38 Ursula Biemann, "Egyptian Chemistry," in Bethônico, *Provisões*, 31–35. There is also a connection here to "hybrids" (systems that mix politics, science, technology, and nature) as theorized in Latour, *We Have Never Been Modern*; and "hyperobjects" (assemblages, such as climate change, that extend over vast spaces and temporalities) as discussed by Timothy Morton in *Hyperobjects: Philosophy and Ecology after the End of the World* (Minneapolis: University of Minnesota Press, 2013).

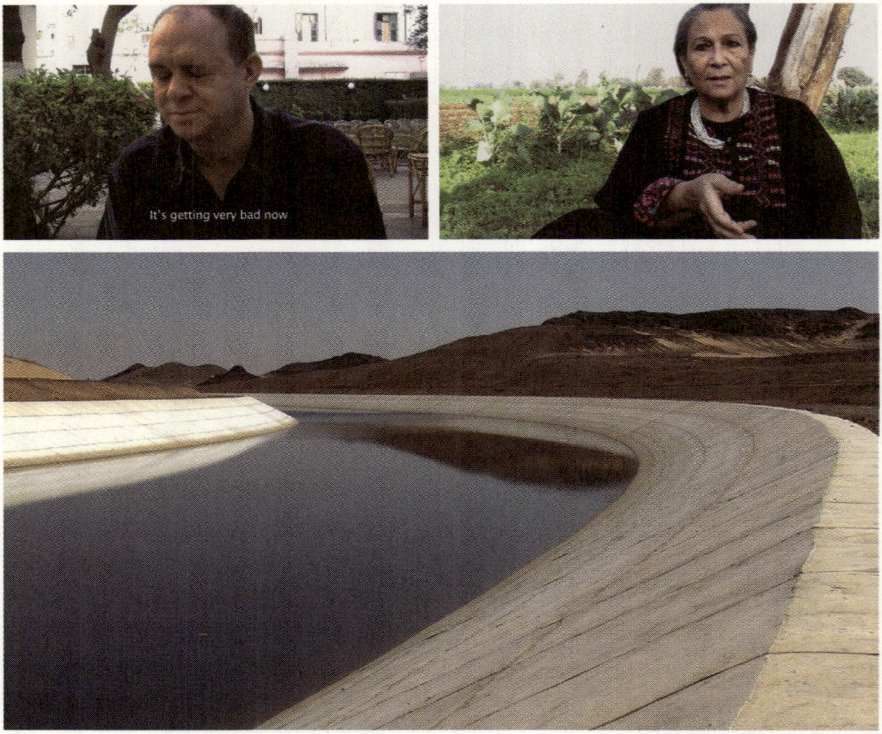

Ursula Biemann, stills from *Egyptian Chemistry*, 2012

social conflict—a familiar cycle under neoliberalism (also mapped in Tavares's *Non-human Rights*, Martin's *White Gold*, and Martin and Huber's *Landrush*).[39] Biemann shows how Mubarak adopted the logic of the dominant global economy that privileges corporate profits over local needs.

Shifting resources away from small-scale farmers and toward export-oriented industrial agriculture, his government inadvertently threw multitudes into urbanization and precarious labor, expanding slum-like conditions in Cairo and fueling the rebellious energies that erupted in early 2011 and

39 On the logic of corporate neoliberalism—which favors deregulated trade, privatization of industries, and minimization of social welfare spending—plus a discussion of meaningful alternatives, see Cavanagh and Mander, *Alternatives to Economic Globalization*. Also see Klein, *The Shock Doctrine*: "This book is a challenge to the central and most cherished claim in the official story—that the triumph of deregulated capitalism has been born of freedom, that unfettered free markets go hand in hand with democracy. Instead, I will show that this fundamentalist form of capitalism has consistently been midwifed by the most brutal forms of coercion, inflicted on the collective body politic as well as on countless individual bodies" (16).

eventually brought down Mubarak. Her video thereby outlines a network of relations, a "cooperative of things" comprising water politics, hydraulic energy systems, the damming of the Nile, fish ecologies, nitrate industries, and social revolution, each impacted by neoliberal policy, which, with some degree of irony, ended up destroying that system's very basis of political legitimacy (although the revolution remains repressed and unfinished under the terms of the post-Mubarak military government).

In Biemann's model, nature is never idealized as isolated or pure, separate from human activity, and neither does it figure as an object to be instrumentalized or financially speculated upon. Rather, *Egyptian Chemistry* moves us toward a dynamics of causality and "inter-agential becoming," in Barad's terms, where all things are formed in mutually constitutive relations to other things, even down to the atomic level studied by quantum physics.[40] Biemann's focus on such hybrid Earth objects is shared by World of Matter member Elaine Gan, whose *Rice Child (Stirrings)* (2011–ongoing) comprises a wall-sized map of rice production, charting the global history of rice's cultivation and biotechnological modification. Her project historicizes four periods of rice production in which diverse varieties emerged through shifting human, environmental, and technological relations: informal exchange, colonial invasions, monocrop economies, and futures markets.[41] The dispersed consequences of the human-nature assemblage envisaged in Biemann's *Egyptian Chemistry* similarly posits a human-nonhuman multicausal network, linking Egypt's military government, the Nile River, damming technology, subsistence farmers, tilapia fish, and migrant laborers. The piece explains the complexity of geopolitics (including Mubarak's downfall) by distributing agency beyond strictly conceived anthropocentric causality.[42] Indeed, human systems bear an unintentional agency, to be precise, in her project, as when the Aswan Dam altered the biology of the Nile, inadvertently favoring fish who thrived in the stilled waters, like the tilapia, which demonstrates what Biemann calls chemistry's "ontology of internal relations"—natural objects' mutual networks

40 On "intra-agential becoming," where the being and meaning of things is contingent upon their relation to other things in perpetual formation, see Karen Barad, *Meeting the Universe Halfway: Quantum Physics and the Entanglement of Matter and Meaning* (Durham, NC: Duke University Press, 2007).

41 See Elaine Gan, "Mapping Rice/Mapping Time," in Arns, *World of Matter*, 152–57.

42 "The tendency to define social problems as moral failures, exclusively the doing of individual or collective human agents (and the implicit assumption that we are in charge of nature) prevented us from discerning the real locus of agency—the assemblage of human and nonhuman actants—and attempting to alter the configuration of that human-nonhuman assemblage." Jane Bennett, in Loenhart, "Vibrant Matter, Zero Landscape."

that exist beyond anthropocentric epistemologies or determinations.[43] Matter here is endowed with political implications that are ultimately beyond human control: Egypt's state agricultural policy introduced a new material and organic environment via neoliberal policy shifts and geo-engineering projects, which in turn accidentally created the social conditions that culminated in profound socio-political transformation. Biemann brings visibility to the political ecology of that networked causality, dispersed agency, and multiple effects within and beyond the human.

In a revealing segment of *Egyptian Chemistry*, titled "Speculative Realism, Object-Oriented Ontology: Tahrir Square," Biemann interviews the philosopher Graham Harman at the American University in Cairo, where he is based. He discusses his critique of traditional philosophy, which, insofar as it remains generally locked into questions of epistemology, tends to give priority to considerations of how humans access the world, rather than exploring the world itself. To bring politics into the equation, he notes, would only further corrupt his ontological methodology, instrumentalizing its philosophical imperatives, which, for him, would reinforce precisely the "correlationist" approach to the world that reaffirms human-centric knowledge—according to which the being of something is inextricable from the thinking that represents it.[44] During the interview in the university's courtyard, the Egyptian military in nearby Tahrir Square was dispersing an anti-Mubarak demonstration with tear gas, and the affected air, wafting into the interview, interrupts Harman's anti-correlationist account. With Harman's eyes watering from the crowd-control measures of the Arab Spring unfolding just outside his secluded academic space, the scene dramatizes how the depoliticization of philosophy practiced by speculative realism problematically, even impossibly, disregards the unavoidable correlations between politics and object-oriented ontology, which ultimately share the same environment. It is precisely these interlocked phenomena that Biemann explores. Her incisiveness ultimately sets her work apart from speculative realism, relating river ecologies to neoliberal policy, geo-engineering, land use, and political revolution.

43 Biemann, "Egyptian Chemistry," 49. For more on the "ontological turn" in contemporary philosophy, see Coole and Frost, *New Materialisms*; and Bryant, Harman, and Srnicek, *The Speculative Turn*.

44 Correlationism is "the idea according to which we only ever have access to the correlation between thinking and being, and never to either term considered apart from the other." Quentin Meillassoux, *After Finitude: An Essay on the Necessity of Contingency*, trans. Ray Brassier (London: Continuum, 2008), 5.

Rights of Nature

Biemann's sensitivity to material agents compliments the philosophical implications of radical new laws that institutionalize the "rights of nature," a global juridico-political development to which World of Matter is also attentive. Most directly, Paolo Tavares investigates this discourse in *Non-human Rights*, a video project exploring eco-centric legality that revalues and thereby redefines nature in ways that exceed the framework of not only anthropocentric epistemologies but modern capitalism itself. Tavares finds a case study and conceptual resource for natural jurisprudence in Indigenous rights claims in Latin America, particularly in Amazonia.[45] Tavares's theoretical point of departure is Serres's observation, in *The Natural Contract*, that after centuries of abuse by human civilization, the earth is no longer in a position to be ignored: "Global history enters nature; global nature enters history: this is something utterly new in philosophy."[46] Serres's point is driven home by the recent legal revolution in Bolivia and Ecuador, whose governments have rewritten their constitutions and legal codes in the last decade in order to extend rights to nonhuman life-forms and environmental objects: "Nature or Pachamama [...] has the right to exist, persist, maintain and regenerate its vital cycles, structure, functions and its processes in evolution," declares article 71 of Ecuador's 2008 constitution. Apart from granting inalienable rights to the environment and animals, this innovative legislature allows Ecuadorian citizens to bring lawsuits against anyone who violates these laws, making the country's constitution, according to one proponent, "the most progressive in the world."[47] The judicial system dissolves conceptual boundaries between matter and life, human and nonhuman subjects, agents and resources. As Tavares notes, in his video's intertitles, this legal transformation represents nothing less than a "radically new universalism." A further way to conceive a post-anthropocentric commonality, the result attempts to legally realize the "decolonization of nature" after centuries of domination.

But can the legal system, which is often directed toward the hegemonic interests of a powerful minority (including in contemporary Ecuador), be redirected to effectively serve the formerly disenfranchised? Fiction writer and political theorist China Miéville observes: "The attempt to replace war and inequality with [just] law is not

45 This transformation in legality (also called "wild law") is in fact occurring internationally. See, for instance, the Nonhuman Rights Project, a US civil rights organization dedicated to establishing rights for species other than human, nonhumanrightsproject.org); Cullinan, *Wild Law*; and Burdon, *Exploring Wild Law*.

46 Serres, *The Natural Contract*, 4.

47 A claim made by environmental activist Zoe Tryon, cited in Clare Kendall, "A New Law of Nature," *Guardian*, September 24, 2008, http://www.theguardian.com/environment/2008/sep/24/equador.conservation.

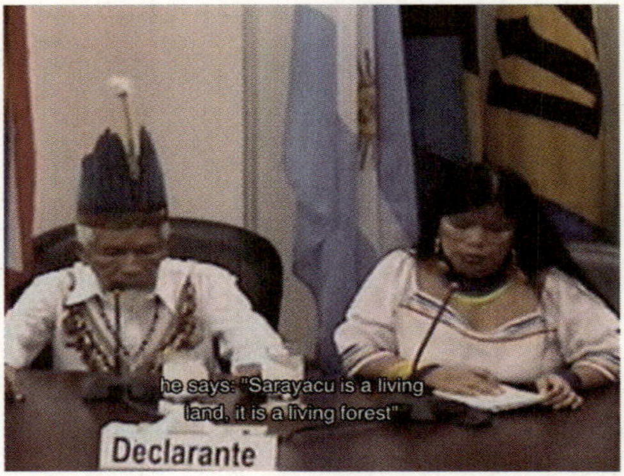

Paulo Tavares, still from *Non-human Rights*, 2012

merely utopian but is precisely self-defeating. A world structured around international law cannot but be one of imperialist violence. The chaotic and bloody world around us is the rule of law."[48] Yet rights-of-nature discourse moves toward a legal formulation that refuses to equate law as such with injustice. Such rights could be called idealistic on the international level; at least, until they are enforced. At present there's no international body to implement these regulations and hold offenders accountable in criminal or civil courts, even though proponents of this legal shift, led by Bolivia and supported by Ecuador, Venezuela, and several Caribbean nations, made proposals in 2011 for the UN to recognize universal rights of nature (which still remains under consideration).[49] And even Ecuadorian communities that have drawn on the new rights-of-nature legislation to support claims against states and corporations have run into obstacles given corruption, the vagueness of the wording of the amendments, and, perhaps most significantly, the ambivalence of President Rafael Correa, who has both supported rights of nature in principle and yet sponsored further drilling projects, as in Yasuní National Park, in order to alleviate the country's

48 China Miéville, *Between Equal Rights: A Marxist Theory of International Law* (London: Pluto, 2006), 319.

49 Steven Edwards, "UN Document Would Give 'Mother Earth' Same Rights as Humans," *Common Dreams*, April 13, 2011, http://www.commondreams.org/news/2011/04/ 13/un-document-would-give-mother-earth-same-rights-humans. Also see the Global Alliance for the Rights of Nature, therightsofnature.org.

50 When the international community failed to match the promised $3.6 billion, according to a 2007 agreement, in exchange for Ecuador keeping Yasuní oil in the ground and preventing deforestation, Correa controversially annulled the agreement in 2013. See Mary Elizabeth Whittemore, "The Problem of Enforcing Nature's Rights under Ecuador's Constitution: Why the 2008 Environmental Amendments Have No Bite," *Pacific Rim Law & Policy Journal* 20, no. 3 (June 2011): 559–691; and see the video documentation for "Global Climate Justice Today," a series of talks I organized

international debt and develop the nation's economy.[50] Nevertheless, the tide is turning, with growing social activism supporting international adoption of the rights of nature in the name of environmental justice—when over thirty thousand gathered in Cochabamba, Bolivia, in 2010, at President Evo Morales's invitation, to demand rights for Mother Earth; or in 2014, when the UN held a conference in Geneva over the proposed universal declaration on the rights of nature; and when the European Citizens' Initiative developed plans in 2014 to lobby the European Commission to support biocentric legality.[51] Perhaps in the near future we will see the vision of Serres realized, when natural objects become legal subjects, no longer existing as mere material for industry, commerce, and economic growth: "Law [of the past] tries to limit abusive parasitism among men but does not speak of this same action on things. If objects themselves become legal subjects, then all scales tend toward equilibrium."[52]

Tavares contextualizes this development in *Non-human Rights* by referring to deforestation and environmental despoliation in the Ecuadorian Amazon, where farmers and Indigenous communities have successfully sued the state and fossil fuel corporations over the destruction carried out by oil companies such as Texaco (merged into Chevron in 2001), which operated in Ecuador's Lago Agrio region between the 1960s and '90s, leaving billions of gallons of toxic petrochemical waste pooled over two hundred square kilometers in the rain forest during those three decades.[53] "It is genocide in the Ecuadorian Amazon," argues activist Donald Moncayo in the video, echoing Shiva's indictment of corporate ecocide in the Indian countryside, as Tavares's handheld camera shows decades-old sludge

through the Center for Creative Ecologies, UC Santa Cruz, October 13–27, 2015—featuring Valentin Lopez, Flora Lu, Néstor L. Silva, Leila Salazar-Lopez, Andy Szasz, and Paulo Tavares—which investigated the current meanings of climate justice for communities from California to the Ecuadorian Amazon, https://creativeecologies.ucsc.edu/global-climate-justice-today.

51 See Terisa Turner, "From Cochabamba, a New Internationale and Manifesto for Mother Earth," *Capitalism Nature Socialism* 21, no. 3 (2010): 56–74; Alex Latta, "Matter, Politics and the Sacred: Insurgent Ecologies of Citizenship," *Cultural Geographies* 21, no. 3 (July 2014): 323–41; Mari Margil, "Building an International Movement for Rights of Nature," in *Wild Law: In Practice*, ed. Michelle Maloney and Peter Burdon (New York: Routledge, 2014), 177–89; "Report of Last Year Conference in United Nations, December 2014: A Universal Declaration of Rights of Nature?," *OSI Geneva Forum*, accessed December 18, 2015, http://www.osi-genevaforum.org/Conference-of-December-2014-in-United-Nations.html; and "European Citizens Initiative for the Rights of Nature," *International Centre for Wholistic Law*, accessed December 18, 2015, http://www.wholistic-law.org/european-citizens-intiative-for-the-righs-of-nature.

52 Serres, *The Natural Contract*, 37; cited in Tavares, "On the Earth-Object," in *Savage Objects*, ed. Godofredo Pereira (Lisbon: INCM, 2012), 228.

53 On the case of the Indigenous community of the Sarayaku, see Tavares's project *Against the State* (2012–14), http://www.paulotavares.net/NHR/AS.html.

on the forest floor.[54] The situation in Ecuador motivated a class-action lawsuit of at least thirty thousand victims in 1993, leading to a remarkable trial (joined by thousands of Ecuadorian campesino and Indigenous peoples, including the Siona, Secoya, Cofán, Waorani, and Kichwa) that continues to this day (although Chevron has challenged the trial at every turn).[55] As such, Ecuador functions as a legal laboratory for the rights of nature, which approximates the natural contract that Serres called for more than twenty years ago.

Alberto Acosta, a politician and former president of the assembly responsible for writing the 2008 constitution, is also interviewed in the video. He explains that Ecuador's recent legal changes originated with the political and human rights struggles of the country's Indigenous peoples in the 1990s. Acosta's interview is intercut with TV footage of several of these protests in Quito, where hundreds of Indigenous peoples demonstrated while accompanied by intimidating military forces. The connection between social and natural rights is affirmed by Luis Macas, a Quechua politician, scholar, and founding member of the Confederation of Indigenous Nationalities of Ecuador. In the video, he states that when these past struggles for collective rights in relation to ancestral lands are taken to their logical conclusion, protecting the biodiverse environments that tribal life depends on for regeneration, they cannot but reaffirm the rights of nature. Nonhuman legal agency extends in this case from Indigenous rights claims (and it is not surprising, then, that this legal revolution has been pioneered in Ecuador, with at least eight major communities of Indigenous peoples, spread across thirteen hectares of the country's tropical rain forest in the Amazon basin, who have been particularly active in this struggle).

Many Amerindian cosmologies in fact recognize a shared subjecthood among all living things (and even some inanimate ones), which also finds a certain affinity with Serres's call for a natural contract (though he doesn't discuss Indigenous philosophy, his frame of reference being largely Eurocentric).[56] Such developments, of course, are not

54 See the work of the environmental lawyer Polly Higgins, who argues that creating a law against ecocide is the necessary complement to natural-rights legislation, as it extends the force of governance to Earth law and the rights of nature, making ecocide an international crime on the same scale as genocide, http://eradicatingecocide.com.

55 See the overview of the case, "Chevron's Chernobyl in the Amazon," *Amazon Watch*, accessed November 26, 2015, http://amazonwatch.org/work/chevron.

56 See Viveiros de Castro, "Perspectivism and Multinaturalism," 36–75. Viveiros de Castro argues that the anthropomorphic projection of legal subjectivity onto nonhumans is far from a reassertion of an anthropocentric logic, and that the former can actually contest the latter. Common to Andean Amerindian belief is the recognition that human personhood extends to the animal world, where humans exist in animal guise. Such a metaphysical sharing of personhood is qualitatively different from the anthropocentrism of Western cos-

limited to the Ecuadorian context, and the commitment to rights of nature remains a priority for many social movements worldwide fighting against green capitalism. In Rio de Janeiro in 2012, the Kari-Oca II Declaration was signed by over five hundred aboriginal groups from various countries. "We see the goals of UNCSD Rio+20, the 'Green Economy,' and its premise that the world can only 'save' nature by commodifying its life-giving and life-sustaining capacities as a continuation of the colonialism that Indigenous Peoples and our Mother Earth have faced and resisted for 520 years," it reads.[57] In contrast, the declaration calls for a newfound respect for Mother Earth: "We need to fundamentally reorient production and consumption based on human needs rather than for the boundless accumulation of profit for a few. Society must take collective control of productive resources to meet the needs of sustainable social development and avoid overproduction, overconsumption and overexploitation of people and nature which are inevitable under the prevailing monopoly capitalist system. We must focus on sustainable communities based on indigenous knowledge, not on capitalist development."

Significantly, the declaration uses the original Indigenous word *Pachamama* (as does the Ecuadorian constitution), referring to the goddess long worshiped in the Andean region. Originating in the Quechua and Aymara languages, Pachamama literally translates as "World Mother," and conceptualizes the source of all life. This choice of terminology, as Macas explains, reaffirms native understandings of a common world infused with interconnected life, inseparable from human culture, which is itself inextricable from nature.[58] The video also includes an interview with the activist Esperanza Martínez, member of the NGO Acción Ecológica in Quito,

mopolitics, which grounds human exception precisely against the animal world. On the animism of stone in Andean Amerindian culture, see Carolyn Dean, *A Culture of Stone: Inka Perspectives on Rock* (Durham, NC: Duke University Press, 2010).

57 The meeting corresponded to the UN Conference on Sustainable Development, generally seen by environmental activists as one more failed attempt by global governance to introduce effective solutions to avert climate change, and echoed the spirit of the first World Conference of Indigenous Peoples on Territories, Environment and Development, in 1992, where the first Kari-Oca Declaration supporting Indigenous rights was signed.

58 On Pachamama reverence in Latin America, see Vincenta Mamani-Bernabé, "Spirituality and the Pachamama in the Andean Aymara Worldview," *Earth Stewardship: Linking Ecology and Ethics in Theory and Practice*, ed. Ricardo Rozzi et al. (New York: Springer, 2015), 65–76. Perhaps Morton's emphasis on ecology without nature could be reconciled with Indigenous Pachamama discourse that extends rights to nature, as both uses of the term "nature" reject the conventional understanding of nature as distinct from human society. The difference however is that Indigenous activists refuse to surrender the term nature. See Morton, *Ecology without Nature*. On Amerindian approaches to nature and culture (fundamentally different from European colonial models in that human culture is located inextricably in nature), see Viveiros de Castro, "Perspectivism and Multinaturalism." Also see Kohn, *How Forests Think*.

explaining that Pachamama discourse constitutes a process of "opening to diversity," building an episteme in which multiple worlds coexist, countervailing the hegemony of Western modernity's domineering and appropriative relation to nature. The discourse opens onto "multinaturalism," which, as Brazilian anthropologist Eduardo Viveiros de Castro writes, designates the Amerindian belief system that recognizes nonhuman perspectives and opens nature to a fundamental multiplicity. Distinct from multiculturalism, which implies multiple perspectives on a self-same nature, multinaturalism asserts that human and nonhuman epistemologies—or ways of seeing—are continuous, but that the object of their gazes is itself different, insofar as nature is a site of diverse ontological becoming (what may be blood to us may be beer to a jaguar). "Amazonian multinaturalism affirms not so much a variety of natures as the naturalness of variation—variation *as* nature," Viveiros de Castro notes.[59] The multinaturalist system decenters human sovereignty over the environment by acknowledging the perspectives of other beings and diversifying the ontology of nature—an apt way of describing the politico-ecological significance of *Non-human Rights*. The Ecuadorian case and its representation in Tavares's work form part of a growing international movement for an eco-centric legal paradigm, thus moving beyond the market-defined and property-based relation to the environment that has dominated Western law in the past. In its place is the site of nature-as-variation that recognizes multiple agents and participants, including the non-human, as part of a newfound universality of political commonality, which may as yet exert a legal power to forcefully defend the environment in the near future.

Mapping Globalization

In tracking the many connections between the disparate geographical studies of World of Matter, is it possible to arrive at a planetary overview? Indeed, as Emily Eliza Scott asks, in her audio guide for the 2014 "World of Matter" exhibition: "How to picture globalization—including its complex networks and dizzying temporalities—in a way that does not generalize or flatten? In a way that attends to the hyper-local while keeping larger geopolitical and Earth systems in view? That considers how global forces hit the ground, unfolding and mutating as they interact with particular contexts?"[60] Mooshammer and Mörtenböck's wall-sized map of the globe, *A World of Matter* (2014), offers one approach to these questions, charting the maritime and overland trade routes worldwide. Modeled after

59 Eduardo Viveiros de Castro, "Multinaturalism," in *Cannibal Metaphysics*, ed. Peter Skafish (Minneapolis: Univocal, 2014), 74.

60 Scott, audio guide for "World of Matter."

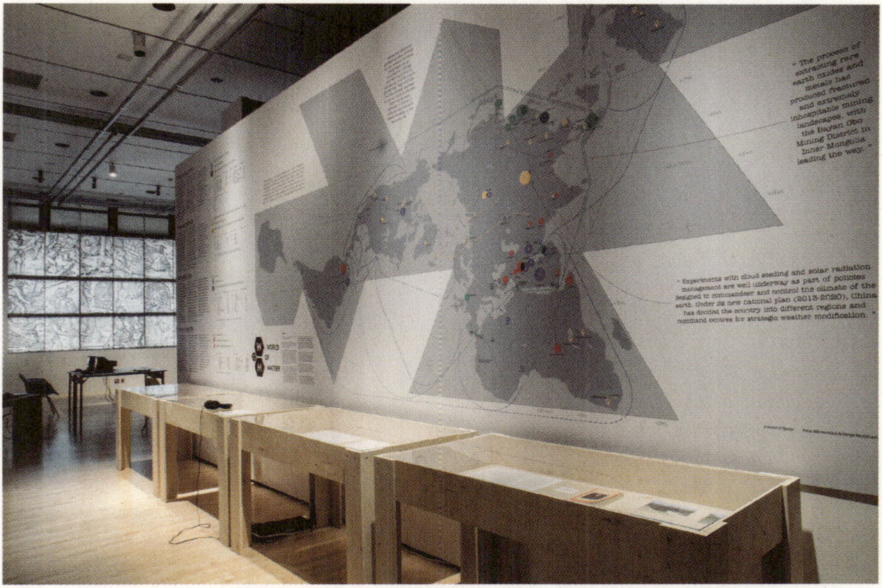

Helge Mooshammer and Peter Mörtenböck, *A World of Matter*, 2014

Buckminster Fuller's Dymaxion Map from 1954, which connects all continents as a single landmass in one ocean in accurately scaled size, the expansive cartography notes the sites of rare earth metals and oil deposits, the congested choke points of trade, transportation routes and immigration and customs controls. Reproducing the research of the Social and Spatial Inequalities group at the University of Sheffield and of complex-systems theorist Mark Newman at the University of Michigan, additional diagrams visualize the world's "economic center of gravity," calculated by translating regional GDPs into the respective cartographic sizes of nation-state shapes. The map thereby identifies the correspondence between national wealth and ecological footprint of countries such as the United States, EU member states, China, and India, whose relatively weighted shapes balloon outward, while lower-GDP areas of Africa and Latin America dwindle to mere slivers, revealing a system of eco-economic and politico-environmental disparity. In the map's textual annotations, Mooshammer and Mörtenböck observe that resources function as "a mechanism aimed at the manipulation of social and political climates, the regulation of civic anxieties and the creation of order based on narratives of technological mastery and environmental control"—familiar terms that once again resonate with the perspective of Serres.

Moving beyond the visualization of economic and environmental dynamics, the map's text also calls for "intervening in the geopolitical circuits of value production via the development of a democratic politics." To do so, it is imperative to invent a new and different "ecological capital" that would definancialize nature, which, reiterating the conclusions of much of World of Matter's research, correlates a new ecological understanding with a new political economy—a political ecology that posits the environment's sustainability as a source of intrinsic value. As environmental depletion and destruction become increasingly visible, we will surely encounter a greater stimulus to imagine alternative worlds—similar to those envisioned in rights-of-nature discourse—which transcend the logic of mastery and appropriation that have colonized nature since the Enlightenment. As we have seen, environmental and social devastation have already inspired a new type of contract inaugurating an age founded on the universalism of rights-bearing subjects, and it is this very movement that World of Matter advances.

Gardening against the Apocalypse

Chapter 7

The Case of dOCUMENTA (13)

"We are told that we live in a state of permanent crisis, a state of emergency and thus of exception," wrote Carolyn Christov-Bakargiev in her main curatorial statement for dOCUMENTA (13).[1] Calling to mind the endless wars in the Middle East, the retraction of civil liberties worldwide, and the generalized conditions of emergency law theorized, for instance, by Giorgio Agamben as the contemporary "state of exception," and by Paul Virilio as "pure war," this recognition could seem to set the stage for an engaged presentation of agit-prop political art. Joined by a supportive team of curatorial agents,[2] the director of this most ambitious of international exhibitions chose, however, to respond to the state of crisis with a marked prevalence of artist-rendered gardens. Overgrown with experimental planters, creative landscapes, and installations relating variously to horticulture, farming, and natural life-forms, the 2012 iteration of documenta, the high-profile exhibition that occurs every five years in Kassel, Germany, was the most "green" yet. However, the show's implicit linkage of gardening and political emergency produced not so much a clear approach to exceptional conditions as it did a series of conceptual challenges and unresolved contradictions, which, intentionally or not, demonstrated a state of crisis in terms of how ecology is addressed within the artistic realm.

1 Carolyn Christov-Bakargiev, dOCUMENTA (13) press release, October 25, 2010. The letter is published as the third "notebook" in the series dOCUMENTA (13): 100 Notes—100 Thoughts.

2 The curatorial team's "agents" included Leeza Ahmady, Ayreen Anastas and Rene Gabri, Sofía Hernández Chong Cuy, Sunjung Kim, Koyo Kouoh, Joasia Krysa, Marta Kuzma, Raimundas Malašauskas, Chus Martínez, Lívia Páldi, Hetti Perkins, Eva Scharrer, Kitty Scott, and Andrea Viliani.

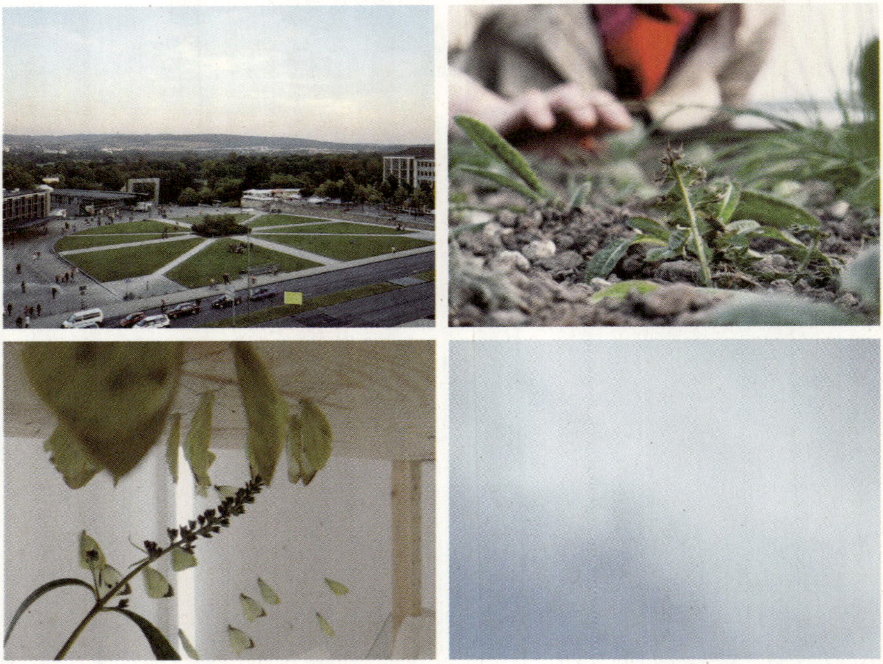

Kristina Buch, *The Lover*, 2012

The many models of garden-as-art, all created for the 2012 show, included: Kristina Buch's *The Lover*, an open-air butterfly habitat installed in front of Kassel's Staatstheater, a central location in the exhibition, which comprised approximately three thousand plants ideal for the insect. The artist bred forty-five different butterfly species in her temporary Kassel apartment, over three thousand insects in total; as they hatched she delivered them at dawn to her garden installation. Acknowledging that it's impossible to enclose such bug life in the wild, Buch pointed to the infinite nature of her garden project: "Inherent in the work is the fact that you cannot really contain or control it. You can't own it. By nature it's boundless and ephemeral."[3] Christian Philipp Müller's *Swiss Chard Ferry, The Russians Aren't Going to Make It across the Fulda River Anymore* presented a group of small barges floating on a canal in Karlsaue Park, each filled with sixty edible varieties of the leafy vegetable.

3 Kristina Buch, as cited in Aimee Walleston, "Kristina Buch's Constant Garden," *Art in America*, June 26, 2012, http://www.artinamericamagazine.com/news-features/news/kristina-buch-documenta-13. The only remnants of the butterfly breeding were the empty chrysalides, which were exhibited in a vitrine in the nearby documenta-Halle.

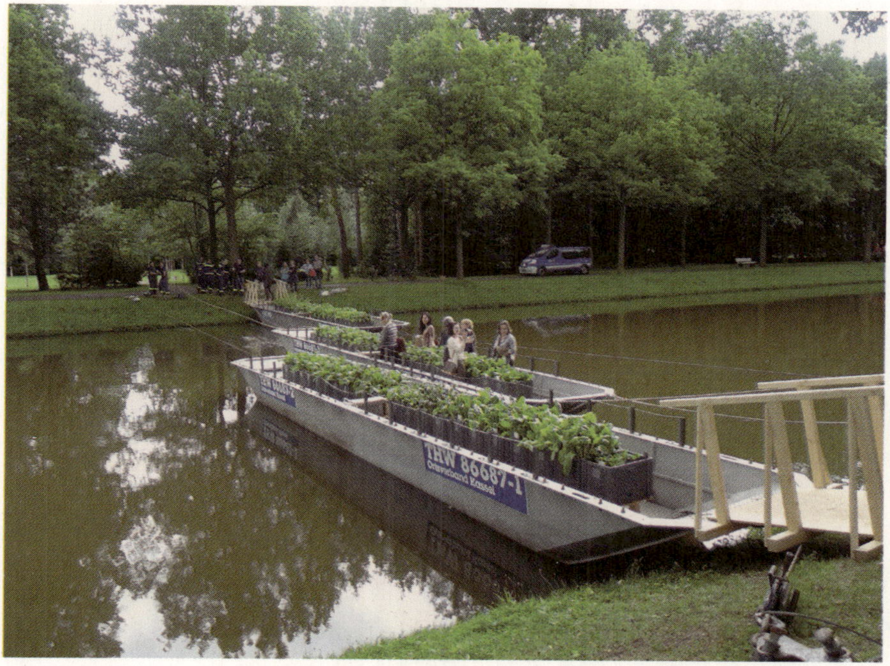

Christian Philipp Müller, *Swiss Chard Ferry, The Russians Aren't Going to Make It across the Fulda River Anymore*, 2012

Müller realized his project in cooperation with the University of Kassel's Department of Organic Agricultural Sciences, and drew on various seed banks worldwide. The Cold War–era pontoons were borrowed from the German Technical Relief Organization—an infrastructure of post-disaster relief aid, calling to mind an emergency situation plagued by food scarcity. And Song Dong's *Doing Nothing Garden*, centrally located on the lawn in front of the Orangerie, comprised a six-meter-high accumulation of rubble and organic refuse, which, without further artistic or agricultural intervention, sprouted grass and flowers and displayed neon signs that read "Doing" and "Nothing" in Chinese. The entropic site dramatized Song's Tao-like maxim: "That left undone goes undone in vain; that which is done is done still in vain; that done in vain must still be done."[4] These were admittedly only a small selection of the many "green" projects presented in the extensive exhibition;

4 Quoted in Einar Engström, "Song Dong and Yin Xiuzhen: The Way of Chopsticks III," *Leap*, October 23, 2011, http://leapleapleap.com/2011/10/song-dong-yin-xiuzhen-the-way-of-chopsticks-iii.

nonetheless, they indicate a tacit but sustained commitment to investigating artist-directed creative ecologies in the era of environmental crisis. But to what end?

To some, gardens might seem irrelevant in addressing our world of crises and emergencies, the specific circumstances of which Christov-Bakargiev neglected to identify. But in fact they represent, and might be seen to respond to, the most urgent of global conflicts: the financialization of nature by agricultural and pharmaceutical corporations enforcing use of their patented genetically modified seeds; greenhouse gas emissions from a monoculture- and export-based agribusiness reliant on chemical fertilizers and fossil-fueled transportation industries; and the destruction of unions and small-scale farms displaced by large-scale mechanized agricultural production.[5] In these different cases, life itself—from biological organisms to human labor—has become increasingly subjected to capitalist ownership, exploitation, manipulation, and ruin. Yet these various crises weren't addressed by the curatorial team in their catalogue essays or press releases.[6] Instead, a series of general statements described the show's concerns, including the subjects of "composite ontologies that generate paradoxical conditions of contemporary life and artistic production," "human life and other forms of life facing multispecies entangled histories," and "the specificity of being an artist and the non-specificity of artistic practice."[7] Consequently, without precise contextualization, the biotic artworks risked becoming mere embellishments to Karlsaue Park's eighteenth-century Baroque landscaping. Case in point was Claire Pentecost's vertical gardens, which, sprouting a range of edible vegetables, adorned the front grounds of the Ottoneum natural history museum (located next to the exhibition's main venue, the Fridericianum). For her contribution, the Chicago-based artist, collaborating with designer and philanthropist Ben Friton of the urban gardening nonprofit Can YA Love, created a series of structures concerning soil as a medium of organic life and its relation to the urban context. "Can soil be distinguished from real estate?" she asked. "If people can make soil from organic waste but they have no land, what are the options for growing food in limited space?" Answering these questions, Pentecost's proposals took

5 "The globalization of agricultural systems over recent decades is likely to have been one of the most important causes of overall increases in greenhouse gas emissions," owing to their energy-intensive, high-emissions model of industrial agriculture and reliance on international transportation. Steven Shrybman, *Trade, Agriculture, and Climate Change: How Agricultural Trade Policies Fuel Climate Change* (Minneapolis: Institute for Agriculture and Trade Policy, 2000), 1; cited in Klein, *This Changes Everything*, 78.

6 See core agent Chus Martínez's tellingly titled notebook, *Unexpress the Expressible*, dOCUMENTA (13): 100 Notes—100 Thoughts, no. 75 (Ostfildern: Hatje Cantz, 2012).

7 See "dOCUMENTA (13) Announces Curatorial Team and Process," *dOCUMENTA (13)*, October 29, 2010, http://d13.documenta.de/#/press/news-archive/press-single-view/?tx_ttnews[tt_news]=75&cHash=bc6b812c82b2c6c9da56c83a4f8d867d.

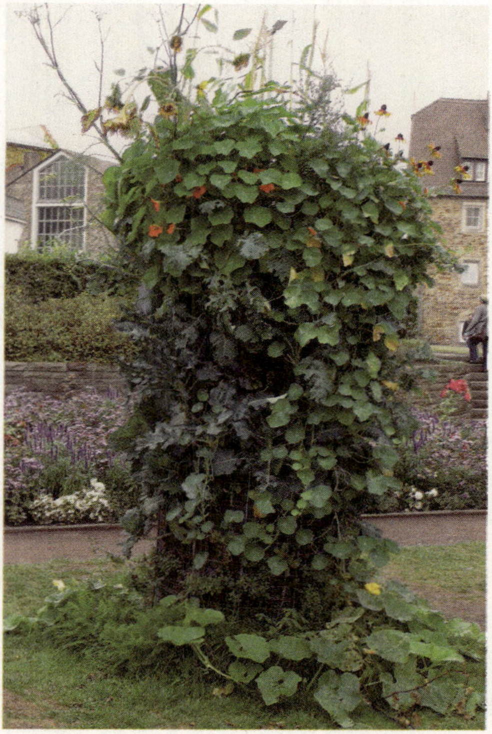

Claire Pentecost, *soil-erg* (growing systems), 2012

the form of pillar-like vertical planters made out of metal mesh, "simple and inexpensive and easily adapted to dense urban spaces."[8] However, placed in front of the natural history museum, far from a dense urban space, the eight-foot-high towers packed with dirt and plants appeared to be extensions of the museum's lush landscaped exterior, as if her project were merely decorative sculpture composed of organic aesthetics. Far from evident was the radical nature of her proposals, meant as prototypes for self-sufficient food production in land-poor urban areas, based on conceptually delinking arable land from commercial property—that is, unless one were familiar with the artist's politico-ecological commitments.[9]

8 Claire Pentecost, "soil-erg," accessed September 15, 2015, http://www.publicamateur.org/?p=85. Also see Claire Pentecost, *Notes from Underground*, dOCUMENTA (13): 100 Notes—100 Thoughts, no. 61 (Ostfildern: Hatje Cantz, 2012).

9 Pentecost's prototypes, in my view, are not of the restorative eco-aesthetic variety, as they are directed toward crisis situations in public space. As sites of political antagonism, they function as interventions into concretized cities and their food deserts, but are hardly redemptive or reparative in a definitive or simplistic way, as is sometimes proposed as the goal of eco-aesthetics, especially in landscape design or community participation.

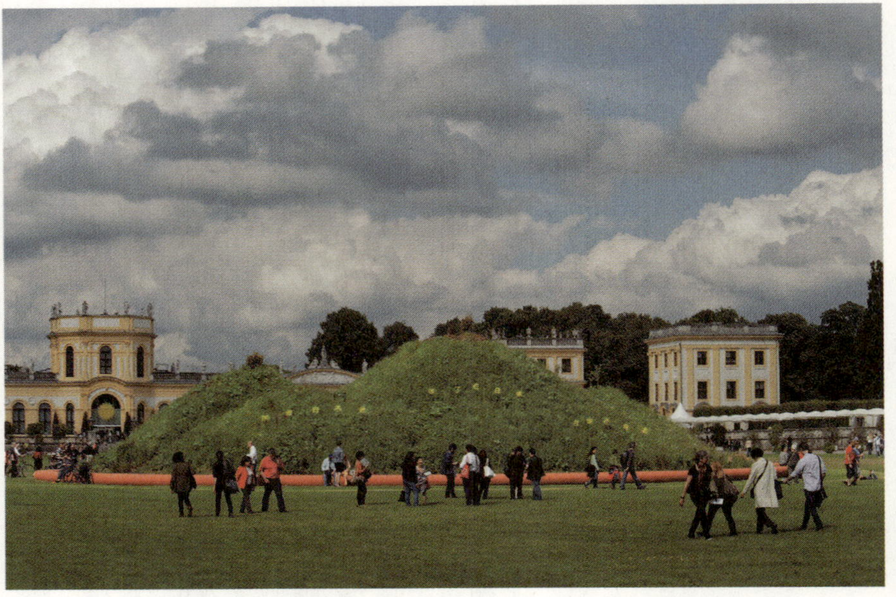

Song Dong, *Doing Nothing Garden*, 2010–12

Varieties of Political Ecology

Described as "an exhibition without a concept" by Christov-Bakargiev in the run-up to the show—in order to allow inclusions to stand on their own, visitors were told—the curators effectively outsourced the show's conceptualization to its impossibly extensive, and sometimes internally conflicted, "100 Notebooks."[10] While this overwhelming panoply provided little immediate service to visitors at the exhibition, the publications do open up fertile territory for considering the pressing environmental matters raised, among the many other topics. The series assembles essays by a range of artists and theorists, including some relating to the ecological, which suggest numerous productive, if competing, ways to approach

10 The number 100 plays off the exhibition's traditional hundred-day run. The notebooks were published individually and then together as one volume with additional material after the exhibition ended, as *The Book of Books* (Ostfildern: Hatje Cantz, 2012). On Christov-Bakargiev's stated absence of one curatorial concept, see Martin Conrads, "Of Dogs and Humans: Documenta 13 in Kassel," trans. Chris Cave, *Goethe Institute*, June 2012, http://www.goethe.de/ins/cn/en/lp/kul/mag/bku/9556034.html. An e-flux announcement sent out by the exhibition after it had ended added this (non)clarification: "An exhibition could be thought of as a pre-reflexive consciousness, a qualitative duration of consciousness without itself" (September 8, 2012). Also see Terry Smith, "Carolyn Christov-Bakargiev: On Not Having an Idea: dOCUMENTA (13)," in *Talking Contemporary Curating* (New York: Independent Curators International, 2015), 37–68.

the gardens and, more broadly, the treatment of the environment in the exhibition. For instance, Donna Haraway's contribution, *SF: Speculative Fabulation and String Figures*, develops the terms of a techno-organic hybrid aesthetics, building on her well-known work on cyborgs, which finds inspiration in the science of gene research and bioengineering. For Haraway, "SF" proposes multiple meanings—"speculative fabulation, speculative feminism, science fiction, science fact, science fantasy."[11] Each, like the intertwinements of "string figure" games to which the author also alludes, represents a bridge between categories in ways reminiscent of her cyborg, "a creature of social reality as well as a creature of fiction" that prefigures a world transcending the oppressive binaries of modernity (male-female, culture-nature, subject-object, technology-biology, etc.).[12] Haraway's contribution was not merely theoretical; her penchant for post-binary multiplicity was also discernable in the exhibition's spatial dispersion—with more than fifty locations comprising a rhizomatic geography throughout Karlsaue Park—and in the show's thematic diffusion, where a hundred approaches eclipsed any single reigning theme (in addition, Haraway served as a member of the exhibition's "honorary advisory committee").[13] Her influence was also felt in the "natureculture" and "intra-actional" aspects of the "becoming with" ontology of the gardens—all terms of Haraway's (although not used by the curators)—suggesting hyphenated mediums that both organize and provide socio-aesthetic support systems for human life, a theoretical framework that significantly opens up the conceptual potential of the artists' work with gardens.

Yet mobilizing Haraway's insights as a model for environmental aesthetics proves tricky in this context, especially when placed in relation to the more overtly political garden practices in the exhibition. Providing one such example, the collective And And And embraced an anticapitalist, organic localism, with several garden kiosks selling regional food and produce on the exhibition grounds during the length of the show. The initiative, run by artists Ayreen Anastas and Rene Gabri, formed part of the

11 Donna Haraway, *SF: Speculative Fabulation and String Figures*, dOCUMENTA (13): 100 Notes—100 Thoughts, no. 33 (Ostfildern: Hatje Cantz, 2012), 4.

12 "A cyborg is a cybernetic organism, a hybrid of machine and organism, a creature of social reality as well as a creature of fiction. Social reality is lived social relations, our most important critical constructions, a world-changing fiction. [...] Contemporary science fiction is full of cyborgs—creatures simultaneously animal and machine, who populate worlds ambiguously natural and crafted. Modern medicine is also full of cyborgs." Donna Haraway, *Simians, Cyborgs and Women: The Reinvention of Nature* (London: Free Association, 1991), 149–50.

13 For the exhibition, Tue Greenfort created *The Worldly House*, a mixed-media archival installation in Karlsaue Park inspired by Haraway's writings. The exhibition also expanded to Kabul, Cairo, and Banff, aspects that extend beyond the scope of this analysis.

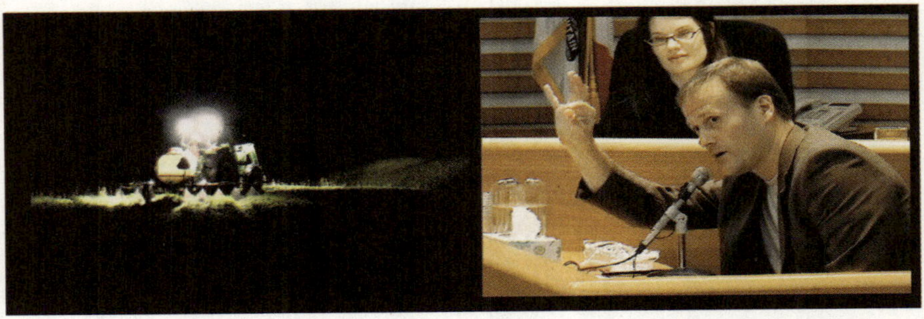

Stills from *The Monsanto Hearings*, 2012; dir. Sarah Kanouse and Sarah Lewison

dOCUMENTA (13) core research team, and in that capacity investigated the notions of the commons and noncapitalist living in gatherings and seminars across the world over the two years preceding the exhibition—from participation in the US Social Forum in Detroit to workshops in Tunis; Yerevan, Armenia; and Buenos Aires. Exemplary was "Event 13," when, acting in alliance with the Compass of the Midwest Radical Culture Corridor (a collective of fourteen artists, including Claire Pentecost, based in the US heartland), they held public hearings on the practices of Monsanto—in Illinois on January 28, 2012, and in Iowa on April 21, 2012. The creative modeling of legal theater outlined how Monsanto produced 20 percent of US corn in 2011, 85 percent of which was GM, and critically examined the corporation's harmful effects, both socioeconomic and environmental. At the beginning of the inquiry, one of the presiding judges explained, "We are here to consider not just violations of statutory or common law, but violations of the laws of nature, of ethics, of humanitarian principles, of environmental principles, and of the precautionary principle. [...] In this courtroom, by mixing together both claims and claimants in one proceeding, we are doing law that is impossible"—that is, in conventional legal courts. "We are bringing together consumers and farmers, human concerns and the pleas of the voiceless, the politically silenced and the interests of nonhumans as well." The video that documents the hearings shows diverse witnesses, including local farmers and animal impersonators, taking the stand and describing the injurious ecological effects of Monsanto's products (such as Roundup herbicide, designed to be used with GM crops), including their devastating impact on the migrating Monarch butterfly and local ladybug populations. "Pesticide is homicide," declares one organic farmer, linking the poisoning of nature to a deadly act against animals and humans alike.[14]

In addition to supporting such off-site events, And And And organized an open experimental public program in a large workshop space near the back of the Kassel train station during the length of the exhibition, inviting artists, activists, farmers, students, thinkers, residents, and visitors to participate in daily public discussions.[15] Their program addressed diverse philosophical, political, pedagogical, and aesthetic matters of concern, "grounded in a conviction that, today, all fields of human activity must critically re-examine the values, assumptions, and modalities of doing."[16] More specifically, the group attempted to realize a process of "militant joyful collective research into non-capitalist life," revolving around "commoning in Kassel," to ask, "What is it that we are capable of sharing and can we construct a common space or a common time for thinking about common concerns?"[17]

The political ecology of this work—though not unrelated to Haraway's approach to SF and her emphasis on the speculative, fictional, and fantastic—is perhaps most directly connected to the practice of Indian environmental activist Vandana Shiva, another of the exhibition's notebook authors, known for her activism against the commercial patenting of seeds and plant life in India by corporations like Monstanto and Syngenta. Haraway also opposes the patenting of life-forms (as commodified GMOs in agribusiness and the pharmaceutical industries), but her techno-feminist sci-fi aesthetic does not ultimately fit with Shiva's alter-globalization climate-justice activism, leading to a conflict of ecological visions.[18] As Shiva writes, in *The Corporate Control of Life*, "Living organisms, unlike machines, organize themselves. Because of

14 For the hour-long documentary, directed by Sarah Kanouse and Sarah Lewison, excerpting moments from the hearings, see "Monsanto Hearings," *Compass*, accessed September 28, 2015, http://midwestcompass.org/monsanto-hearings.

15 However, for those who weren't physically present, the meetings' proceedings are largely inaccessible, relayed via short online descriptions on the group's website (andandand.org), with few archival transcripts and little video documentation.

16 See "About And ... And ... And," *dOCUMENTA (13)*, accessed December 3, 2015, http://d13.documenta.de/#programs/the-kassel-programs/and-and-and/about-and-and-and.

17 "Commoning in Kassel," *dOCUMENTA (13)*, accessed December 3, 2015, http://d13.documenta.de/#/programs/the-kassel-programs/and-and-and/commoning-in-kassel; "A Militant Joyful Collective Research into Non-capitalist Life," *dOCUMENTA (13)*, accessed December 3, 2015, http://d13.documenta.de/#en/programs/the-kassel-programs/and-and-and/a-militant-joyful-collective-research-into-non-capitalist-life. Also see Anastas and Gabri's investigation of the commons as part of their project at The Showroom in London: "common(s) are ideas, language, seeds, air, water, the earth under our feet, the spaces and cultures we collectively produce each and every day, the forests, the seas, the trees and all that bares and gives life. indeed common(s) are the premise of life. they are the ecology of practices and complex entities which conjoin the many forms of life on the planet." "Some Preliminary Notes for London," *Commoning Times*, accessed December 3, 2015, http://commoningtimes.org/london.

18 See Donna J. Haraway, *Modest_Witness@Second_Millennium.FemaleMan_Meets_OncoMouse: Feminism and Technoscience* (New York: Routledge, 1997), 62.

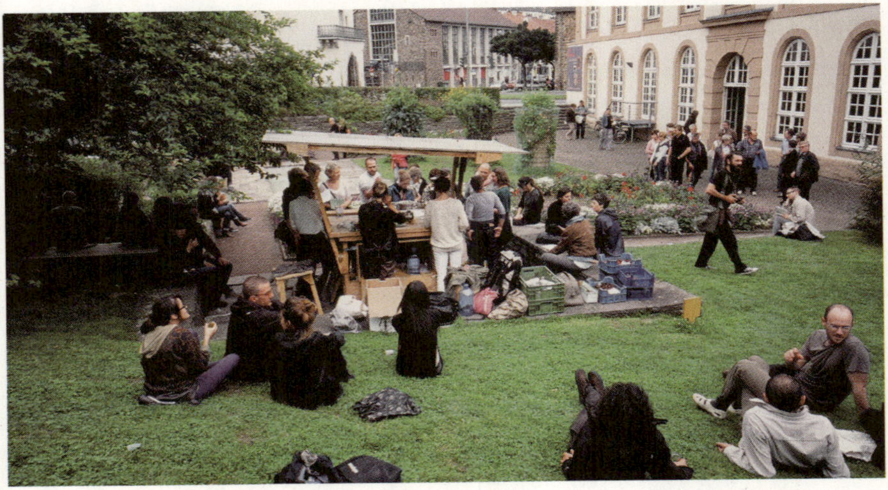

And And And, *Non-capitalist Tea Garden*, 2012

this capacity, they cannot be treated as simply 'biotechnological inventions,' 'gene constructs,' or 'products of the mind,'" terms that are used to justify their commercial patenting as human creations.[19] Challenging this logic, and condemning the corporate "biopiracy" of indigenous culture and resources, Shiva emphasizes the fight to protect the legal sovereignty of noncommercialized knowledge, and the free and universal access to the life processes of humanity's shared heritage, such as regenerative seeds, clean water, and fertile land. These views resonate with the queries of And And And, particularly where they speculate about a radically different, postcapitalist world: "Can we imagine addressing these questions of our basic necessity for sustainable food production without arguing for a necessary shift in priorities which through contemporary capitalism define sustainability first and foremost through the lens of profit?"[20]

19 Shiva, *The Corporate Control of Life*, 7. Between 2008 and 2010, some 261 patents were filed related to growing "climate-ready" crops, involving seeds able to ostensibly withstand extreme weather conditions—close to 80 percent of these patents were controlled by six agribusiness giants (DuPont, BASF, Monsanto, Syngenta, Bayer, and Dow). "Who Will Control the Green Economy?," *ETC Group*, November 1, 2011, 23; http://www.etcgroup.org/content/who-will-control-green-economy-0.

20 "Food," accessed December 3, 2015, *dOCUMENTA (13)*, http://d13.documenta.de/#en/programs/the-kassel-programs/and-and-and/food. The artistic-activist platform 16 Beaver Group, based in New York (including And And And members Anastas and Gabri, who were involved in Occupy Wall Street as well) have also investigated the question of the ecological politics of food in the aftermath of documenta. See, for instance, their workshop, "Food Sovereignty, Housing Activism, and Climate Justice within a Common(s) Horizon," *16 Beaver*, September 16, 2014, http://16beavergroup.org/mondays/2014/09/16/thursday-09-18-14-food-sovereignty-housing-activism-and-climate-justice-within-a-commons-horizon.

Conversely, Haraway's model, as instantiated by the cyborg, "does not dream of community on the model of the organic family," and "would not recognize the Garden of Eden," as s/he is "wary of holism, but needy for connection."[21] For Haraway, writing more with speculative theoretical intent than with activist purpose, the "lively area of transgenic research worldwide"—giving rise to such hybrids as "the tomato with a gene from the cold-sea-bottom-living flounder, which codes for a protein that slows freezing"[22]—inspires visions of new forms of emancipation from essentialist identities and cultural-ontological purities that are socially oppressive and conceptually simplistic. She has also voiced a suspicion of activist positions that oppose corporate science with the values of the local and organic: "I cannot help but hear in the biotechnology debates the unintended tones of fear of the alien and suspicion of the mixed. In the appeal to intrinsic natures, I hear mystification of kind and purity akin to the doctrines of white racial hegemony and U.S. national integrity and purpose."[23] Yet with Shiva's politics in mind, Haraway's enthusiasm for GMOs conjures a philosophical commitment that may unintentionally align with corporate practices, like Monsanto's global threat to small farmers, biodiversity, and human health.[24] The Spanish philosopher Alicia Puleo points out that Haraway would rather be a cyborg than a goddess, the latter implying an essentialist and organicist form of ecofeminism—whereas Shiva would prefer being a sacred cow than a mad cow, the latter produced by technobiological farming practices (a risk of Haraway's eschewal of organicism).[25] While "radical constructivism [as in Haraway] has been a tool for emancipation from prejudice," Puleo writes, "it

21 Haraway, *Simians, Cyborgs and Women*, 151.

22 Haraway, *Modest_Witness*, 88.

23 Ibid., 61. For a recent (Haraway-indebted) critique of both Shiva's neo-humanism and the perceived dangers of organicism, see Braidotti, *The Posthuman*, esp. 49, 101.

24 On the dangers of GM foods to human health, the environment, regulatory practice, and democracy, see Jeffrey M. Smith, *Seeds of Deception: Exposing Corporate and Government Lies about the Safety of Genetically Engineered Food* (Totnes: Green, 2004); Marie-Monique Robin, *The World According to Monsanto: Pollution, Corruption, and the Control of the World's Food Supply* (New York: New Press, 2010), as well as Robin's 2008 film of the same name; Kevin Zeese and Margaret Flowers, "The Growing Global Challenge to Monsanto's Monopolistic Greed," *Truthout*, May 22, 2013, http://www.truth-out.org/opinion/item/16516-the-growing-global-challenge-to-monsantos-monopolistic-greed; and "Former Pro-GMO Scientist Speaks Out on the Real Dangers of Genetically Engineered Food," *Food Revolution Network*, June 2, 2013, http://gmosummit.org/former-pro-gmo-scientist. One major problem with such biotechnology is the lack of independent rigorous evaluation of the public health and environmental impacts of GMOs, especially with the FDA typically colluding with corporate interests and fast-tracking the approval of experimental applications.

25 See Alicia H. Puleo, "From Cyborgs to Organic Model and Back: Old and New Paradoxes of Gender and Hybridity," *Comparative Critical Studies* 9, no. 3 (2012): 358; citing Haraway, "A Cyborg Manifesto," 181; and Vandana Shiva, "Mad Cows and Sacred Cows," in *Stolen Harvest: The Hijacking of the Global Food Supply* (Cambridge, MA: South End Press, 1999).

may become a sophisticated license to domination," particularly when directed by the interest of biogenetic capitalism; in this case, constructivism functions as "the cultural corollary of neoliberal productivism."[26]

Disowning Life

There was consequently a profound divergence within the discourse on the garden in dOCUMENTA (13)—between Haraway's post-human constructivist approach to biotechnological hybridity as a model of creative liberation on the one hand, and, on the other, Shiva's postcolonial commitment to ecological justice opposed to corporate property claims on organic resources pilfered from local communities in the Global South. While the exhibition tacitly raised this very conundrum by including these divergent voices in its notebooks, the clash of positions—which concerns increasingly volatile global conflicts over food production, capitalist agro-economy, and the status of the natural world (whether financialized or ecologized)—was never explicitly engaged in the exhibition's framework. As a result, Christov-Bakargiev's project risked a (non)-position of uncommitted theoretical pluralism, a tendency familiar in the liberal milieu of contemporary art, eager to allude to crises and emergencies—even to aestheticize them—but taking no clear stand in relation to them.

Not that it didn't have the chance. There was no better place to address this debate between the respective political ecologies represented by Haraway and Shiva than during "On Seeds and Multispecies Intra-action: Disowning Life," a two-day public conference taking as its starting point, in the words of the press release, "dOCUMENTA (13)'s ecological perspective, building on a global alliance between different forms of research and knowledges that is actively being developed in a variety of fields."[27] While both Shiva and Haraway participated as two of the key speakers in this conference (albeit on different days, and Haraway via Skype), there wasn't any discussion that addressed the relations and conflicts between their disparate approaches or public consideration of the larger stakes of their positions. Rather, the two were presented, but without any attempt at relating them, or negotiating their respective differences and implied conflicts. Although the exhibition can be credited with opening up a politico-ecological artistic discourse to confront visitors with these differing positions, it was also exemplary of the failure to take a stand about the very problems it

26 Puleo, "From Cyborgs to Organic Model," 359, 362.

27 For archival videos, see "On Seeds and Multispecies Intra-action: Disowning Life," *dOCUMENTA (13)*, accessed December 3, 2015, http://d13.documenta.de/#/programs/the-kassel-programs/congresses-lectures-seminars/on-seeds-and-multi species-intra-action-disowning-life.

raised—as if knowledge production releases us from any ethico-political responsibilities, or from assuming such responsibility at the curatorial level.

To take a position would demand critiquing the political economy of sci-fi aesthetics (of the kind Haraway supports) in relation to social and climate justice activism (of the kind Shiva advocates).[28] The garden practices of dOCUMENTA (13) should not be dismissed, only critically considered within the exhibition's discourses by exploring the intersection of art and ecology at this crucial moment in exhibition making. For artistic gardens, like Buch's butterfly habitat *The Lover*, offer an aesthetic imaginary of being-together that displaces the human subject from a position of masterful sovereignty, which resonates with Haraway's work on companion species, post-anthropocentric sociability, and distributive agency (as pollinators, the insects are integral to the biodiverse web of life on which humans depend, and Buch proposes that relationality as a source of love, rather than one of profit or exploitation).[29] Similarly, Müller's *Swiss Chard Ferry* provides a way of conceiving an experimental interdisciplinarity between art and organic agroecology, corresponding to Shiva's support for the sharing of non-GM seeds and the strengthening of a newfound ecological commons, as well as to Haraway's call for a new "techno-scientific democracy" built upon cultural-scientific collaboration, according to which wartime technology becomes relief-aid infrastructure, buttressing what Haraway calls our "response-ability."[30] Likewise, Song's *Doing Nothing Garden* invites a speculative modeling of interspecies relationality between humans and biotic life, which transforms the gardener into a nonintervening witness to nature's self-organizing capacity, connecting variously to Haraway's becoming-with ethics and Shiva's understanding of the importance of nonhuman organic processes.

Building on Haraway's post-humanism theories *and* Shiva's postcolonial politics, theorist Rosi Braidotti—offering one productive synthetic model outside the framework of this documenta—advocates a "zoe-centered egalitarianism," an equality that reaches beyond the human, which both bridges the theoretical divide and provides a further way to understand these artistic-garden models. At its core is a post-anthropocentric turn, which figures as "a materialist, secular, grounded and unsentimental

28 For inspiring examples of political eco-criticism, see Ashley Dawson, "Biohazard: The Catastrophic Temporality of Green Capitalism," *Social Text* 31, no. 1 (Spring 2013): 63–81; and Nixon, *Slow Violence*.

29 See, for instance, Donna Haraway, *The Companion Species Manifesto: Dogs, People, and Significant Otherness* (Chicago: Prickly Paradigm, 2003).

30 Haraway, *Modest_Witness*, 95; and Donna Haraway, "Anthropocene, Capitalocene, Plantationocene, Chthulucene: Making Kin," *Environmental Humanities* 6 (2015): 164, n17.

response to the opportunistic trans-species commodification of Life that is the logic of advanced capitalism."[31] For Braidotti, this "becoming-Earth" movement offers a "new transversal alliance across species and among posthuman subjects [which] opens up unexpected possibilities for the recomposition of communities, for the very idea of humanity and for ethical forms of belonging."[32] dOCUMENTA (13), in this regard, significantly raised the stakes for what it means today for an art exhibition to include ecological practices as art, and not just as models of radical gardening.[33] These activist-artistic practices also figure as forms of social engagement, collective mobilization in public space, and ambitious proposals for a different natural-cultural world today, as well as the reinvention of contemporary art.[34] The curatorial discourse unfortunately displaced the crucial political and economic differences between speculative theory and environmental activism, and failed to address how they might be creatively connected; instead, it opted for a seemingly conflict-free aestheticization of nature without a clear sense of the important and specific stakes of these theoretical positions or their relation to the artistic selections in the show.

The End of the World

Rather than curatorially addressing these conflicts (and their negative consequences), dOCUMENTA (13) included several artists who posed related questions in work created for the exhibition: How do futurist imaginings of corporate biotechnology correlate with current political struggles over land use, energy policy, and GMOs? How might we represent a world facing environmental catastrophe, a post-human landscape, a mass extinction event? And what is the political economy of postapocalyptic aesthetics? In fact, this documenta contained numerous visions of dystopian futures after an eco-catastrophe, which the exhibition's experimental gardens seemed so intent on forestalling. Consider "News from Nowhere" by South Korean

31 Braidotti, *The Posthuman*, 60.

32 Ibid., 103.

33 For further literature on radical gardening, see Annette Giesecke and Naomi Jacobs, eds., *The Good Gardener? Nature, Humanity, and the Garden* (London: Artifice books on architecture, 2014); McKay, *Radical Gardening*; David Tracey, *Guerrilla Gardening: A Manualfesto* (Gabriola Island, BC: New Society Publishers, 2007); Kenneth I. Helphand, *Defiant Gardens: Making Gardens in Wartime* (San Antonio, TX: Trinity University Press, 2006); and Wilson and Weinberg, *Avant Gardening*.

34 For further discussion of farming-as-art, see Spaid, *Green Acres*, 14–43. Spaid argues that such a category has operated since the 1960s in multiple ways: to engage issues of place; make art pragmatic by producing things people need; offer a platform for survivalist individualism; enrich modes of community engagement; reject farming as a simple means to an end by reinventing it as an aesthetic space; provide a creative and experimental path toward self-sufficiency and radical democracy; and release farming from market mechanisms.

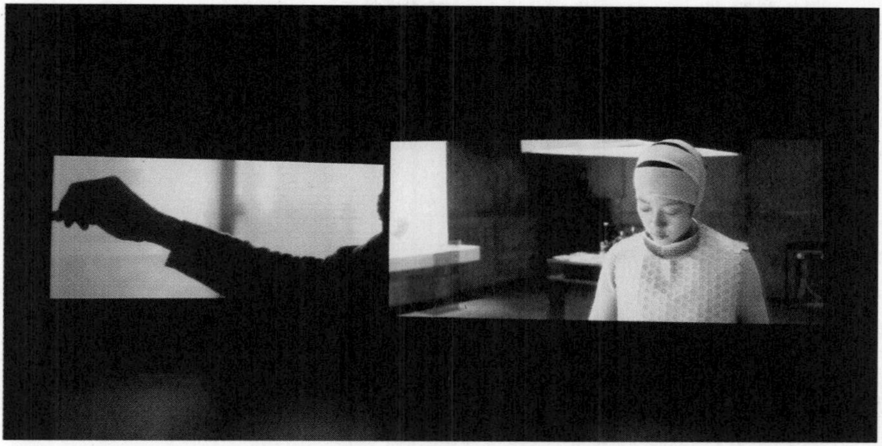

Moon Kyungwon and Jeon Joonho, *El Fin del Mundo*, 2012; installation view, "News from Nowhere"

artists Moon Kyungwon and Jeon Joonho. A model of postapocalyptic science fiction, the project comprises the video *El Fin del Mundo* (*The End of the World*), a mixed-media installation, and a collaborative research publication, building an iconography of genetic engineering and biotechnology (gone awry) that resonates with Haraway's cyborg futurism and represents a further approach to considering relations between science, ecology, and advanced capitalism in contemporary art.

Inspired by socialist craftsman William Morris's eponymous 1890 tale of a future agrarian worker society, Moon and Jeon's "News from Nowhere" visualizes a disastrous time to come when humanity, owing to a series of unspecified major climate changes, is reduced to an endangered species living in a contaminated biosphere, whose survivors must reconsider their philosophies of life.[35] Referencing utopian socialism and science fiction alike, the installation's subject is set on a late twenty-first-century earth permeated with radioactivity and hazardous waste, where raised sea levels necessitate floating settlements and the (imaginary) corporate giant Tempus rules over all. Those seeking citizenship in this dystopian corporatocracy, including the female protagonist of *El Fin del Mundo*, are obliged to collect material samples in the surrounding

35 Morris's *News from Nowhere* begins with the narrator returning home from a meeting of the Socialist League and falling asleep to wake up in a future world where society is organized around the common ownership and democratic control of the means of production. The agrarian culture has no system of authority, money, legal courts, prisons, or class system—only the shared pleasure in work and nature.

irradiated exterior and test them back at the laboratory. The subjects don't realize that they are actually being used as living research specimens exposed to atmospheric contamination for the benefit of corporate science. The film is presented on two screens, one showing the woman's journey into the toxic environment, the other depicting a male character—unnamed, they are played by well-known South Korean actors Yim Soojung and Lee Jungjae—living during the time of the catastrophic event, which is shown occurring in a sudden flash of light, as if from a nuclear explosion, outside his apartment window. Their two stories intertwine across time—in one sequence, the female figure wanders into the very place where the man had lived; the apartment lies abandoned, though viewers have no sense just how much time has passed since the catastrophe. As she retreats back to her laboratory to catalogue and examine specimens from the environment, she is shown meditating on her existential situation. "My life was never again the same. Now I can dream of a new world. My future will reflect this," she intones. The accompanying archival installation *Voice of Metanoia* assembles an array of related futuristic products, such as clothes and tools created in collaboration with other artists, designers, and architects, presented as if they are from the fictional Tempus corporation. The book project is similarly collaborative: the architecture group MVRDV designed a residence for a future world that had flooded due to global warming; the design firm TAKRAM modeled a water bottle capable of operating as an additional organ in the human body to conserve water; and fashion designers

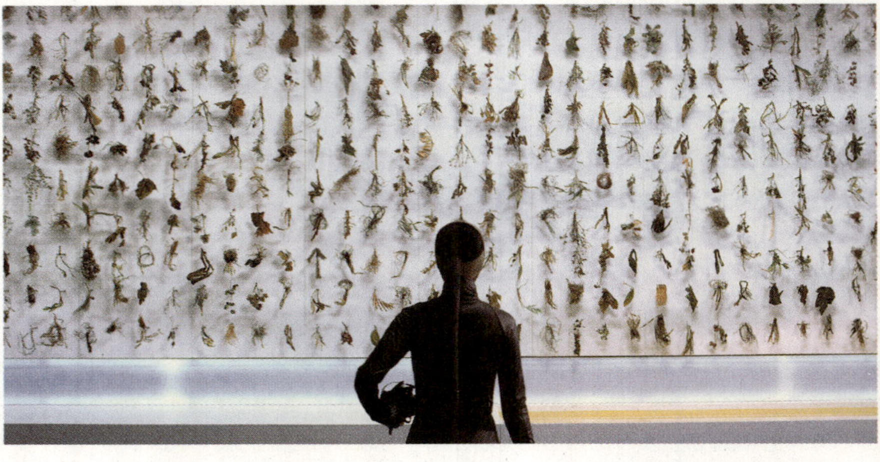

Moon Kyungwon and Jeon Joonho, still from *El Fin del Mundo,* 2012

Kosuke Tsumura and Kuho created a survivalist uniform to protect against harsh environmental conditions. While several contributions to the book project reflect on the 2011 Fukushima Daiichi nuclear disaster, it was not directly referenced in the artists' installation.[36]

The mixed-media documenta installation made apparent the risk of a sci-fi poetics that merely aestheticizes crisis: it establishes little political traction in the present. Much like the speculative fabulation of so many pop-culture blockbusters, the piece sidesteps critical environmental knowledge in favor of a generalized eco-catastrophic context, opting for visual gratification, even fatalistically dwelling in the morbid enjoyment of imagining future horrors. We have the privilege of witnessing the time to come but can do nothing to stop it from happening. Indeed, the project merely pays lip service to the failures of the present without identifying the causes of—or better, providing alternatives to—the "major climate changes" that serve as its fiction's generic foundation. As a result, we are invited to enjoy our own future demise aesthetically. The film and installation's corporate-scientific social order, technological redemption, and the imagery of a transfigured posthuman cyborg body construct a dystopian imaginary within our otherwise calamitous circumstances. Indeed, as Naomi Klein argues, such pop apocalypticism "is so much a part of our culture that we think all we're capable of doing is becoming like societies portrayed in *Snowpiercer*, *Elysium*, or *The Hunger Games*. It's actually not controversial to say this is where we are headed. The question is, can we imagine another way of responding to crisis other than one of deepening inequality, brutal disaster capitalism and mangled techno-fixes, because that seems to be where people agree we're headed."[37] In this regard, our contemporary catastrophism—related to both climate breakdown and nuclear meltdown—follows an earlier period of nuclear Cold War "exterminism," defined in 1980 by Marxist historian E. P. Thompson

36 See, in particular, the essay of Korean literature and political scholar Joe Jeonghwan, "Between Cognitive Capitalism & Disaster Capitalism: Fukushima," in *News from Nowhere: A Platform for the Future & Introspection of the Present*, ed. Moon Kyungwon and Jeon Joonho (Seoul: Workroom Press, 2012), 42–59; and architect Toyo Ito's proposals for post-Fukushima construction, "Home for All: The Restoration of Publicness & a Great Transformation of Architecture," in ibid., 60–119.

37 See Tarleton, "Interview: Naomi Klein Breaks a Taboo." Also see Antony Loewenstein, *Disaster Capitalism: Making a Killing out of Catastrophe* (London: Verso Books, 2015). For a contrary position, consider Wall Street's crass catastrophism, as exemplified in James Altucher and Douglas R. Sease, *The Wall Street Journal Guide to Investing in the Apocalypse: Make Money by Seeing Opportunity Where Others See Peril* (New York: HarperCollins Publishers, 2011). On biogenetic capitalism's attempts to turn life itself into an economic growth model without limits, based on a principal of neoliberal catastrophism that depends on complexity theory, see Melinda Cooper, "Life beyond the Limits: Inventing the Bioeconomy," in *Life as Surplus*, 15–50.

as the irrational logic of the military-industrial society, where the preoccupation with the horrors of an always-impending nuclear war became a diversionary tactic, driven by competing ideological systems invoking the end of human civilization, and perpetuating war as a means to legitimate the oppressive rule of governing regimes: "With each effort to dominate the other, [exterminism] calls into being an equivalent counter-force. It is a non-dialectical contradiction, a state of absolute antagonism, in which both powers grow through confrontation, and which can only be resolved by mutual extermination."[38] Of course, nuclear-war exterminism differs from contemporary eco-catastrophism. The former depends on a different calculus of agency and temporality, with a threat that can be abated via political regime change. Our current situation, however, is being gradually realized through a dispersed and impersonal anthropogenic causality driven by the capitalist logic of corporate growth. Ours is a catastrophism that seemingly comes about by simply participating in everyday life.

The World without Us

Can we imagine an equitable way of positively responding to crisis, as Klein asks? If so, what would its artistic corollary be? Thompson had looked for an internationalism that would "embody, in its thought, in its exchanges, in its gestures, and in its symbolic expressions, the imperatives of human ecological survival."[39] Similarly, Klein states that we need to get over our cultural addiction of imagining apocalyptic scenarios in favor of engaging with the deathly politics of corporate globalization today in order to invent a hopeful future.[40] One such countermodel, presented at dOCUMENTA (13), was offered with the Otolith Group's *The Radiant*, which focuses on the real corporate-science complex and its disastrous failure in the present, an actual scenario nonetheless worthy of science fiction.[41] The

38 Edward Thompson, "Notes on Exterminism, the Last Stage of Civilization," *New Left Review* 1, no. 121 (May–June 1980): 26. For more on the contemporary politics of catastrophism, see Lilley et al., *Catastrophism*.

39 Thompson, "Notes on Exterminism," 30.

40 Klein elaborates on the comprehensive solutions for system change—reverse privatization, decarbonize energy systems, support sustainable transportation, relocalize economies, scale back overconsumption, initiate long-term planning, honor climate debt to the Global South, reduce influence of corporations on political process, and reinvent democracy. She struggles against the resigned conclusion that "changing the earth's climate in ways that will be chaotic and disastrous is easier to accept than the prospect of changing the fundamental, growth-based, profit-seeking logic of capitalism" (*This Changes Everything*, 89).

41 For more on the corporate-science complex, see Alan P. Rudy et al., *Universities in the Age of Corporate Science: The UC Berkeley-Novartis Controversy* (Philadelphia: Temple University Press, 2007), which reviews the growing collaboration between industry and academia, using the case study of the plant and microbial biology department at UC Berkeley and its multimillion-dollar ties to Novartis, the international pharmaceutical and agricultural conglomerate.

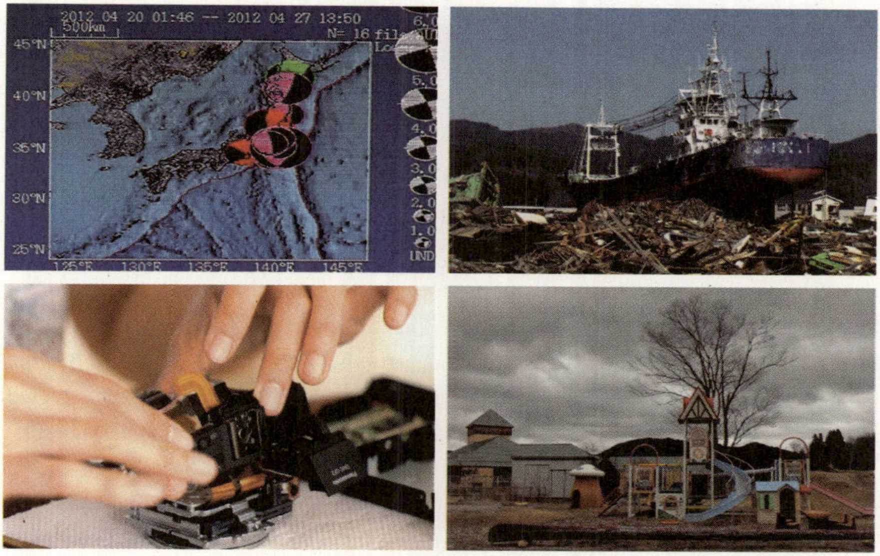

The Otolith Group, stills from *The Radiant*, 2012

film, about an hour in length, takes its point of departure as March 11, 2011, when the Tohoku earthquake off the coast of Japan triggered a tsunami that left more than fifteen thousand people dead and caused the catastrophic meltdown at the Fukushima Daiichi nuclear power plant, which continues to contaminate the land, air, and sea (the effects of radiation will stretch over thousands, even millions of years).[42] Mixing historical and contemporary TV reports about the triple catastrophe, as well as interview footage with scientists, activists, and local residents, the film joins the erstwhile promise of nuclear energy from the plant's postwar construction (from 1966 to 1971) to the future threat of a contaminated global earth, forming an explosive equation that opens critical rifts in our forsaken present. Resonating with the premise of *El Fin del Mundo*, but all the more scary for its documentary realness and contemporary reference, *The Radiant* depicts evacuated Japanese villages and the irradiated natural environment within the contamination zone (stretching approximately thirty kilometers around the plant). Among the affected areas is Tomioka, a village about four kilometers from the Fukushima power station, where rice and vegetable farming was commonly practiced by its sixteen thousand residents prior to the nuclear meltdown. Now more than one hundred thousand of the region's

42 On the prolonged temporality of radiation, see Nixon, "Slow Violence, Neoliberalism, and the Environmental Picaresque," in *Slow Violence*, 45–68.

former inhabitants live in a state of long-term displacement, accompanied by the traumatic memory of their sudden evacuation; they can visit their contaminated homes safely for only a few hours per month.[43] As *The Radiant* shows (reminiscent of the toxic milieu of *El Fin del Mundo*), the exclusion zone also functions as an experimental laboratory in which elderly volunteers—including Nobuyoshi Ito, an interviewed farmer, among those called "abandoned people" by antinuclear activists—willingly expose themselves as self-described "guinea pigs" to what the Otolith Group terms "the necropolitics of radiation." That order designates a governmentality of death administered by TEPCO (Tokyo Electric Power Company) in collusion with Japan's political elites, and more broadly the global nuclear regime promoted by the International Atomic Energy Agency, whose policies place human and environmental health at extreme risk.[44] The volunteers believe that they will die of old age before experiencing the carcinogenic results of exposure; yet they take this risk as test subjects to prepare all for a future of generally elevated radiation levels. Elements of this necropolitics of radiation are glimpsed in *The Radiant*—from governmental policy to local sacrificial volunteerism, from corporate malpractice to the colonization and destruction of nature.

In the video, the abandoned landscape within the containment zone appears deathly quiet, suffused only with the sounds of birds and insects in playgrounds and streets strangely empty of human activity. These images and sounds emerge without explanatory voice-over, inviting the viewer's speculations: What do we make of a world suddenly evacuated of humanity? For Slavoj Žižek, such a "pure disembodied gaze observing our own absence"—like the protracted fixed-frame shots in *The Radiant*—"is the fundamental subjective position of fantasy: to be reduced to a gaze observing the world in the condition of the subject's non-existence."[45] Yet here it is not a matter of subjective make-believe, but an objective reality that inspires a phantasmic prefiguration of human extinction. Or rather, it's a blurring of temporalities and spaces, present and future, Fukushima and the planet, depicting a "zombie ecosystem," in the words of ecologist Roger Bradbury—a zone that is "neither dead nor truly alive in any functional sense," which points to

43 Dorothy Parvaz, "Life in Fukushima Radioactive Exclusion Zones," *Al Jazeera*, March 4, 2014, http://www.aljazeera.com/indepth/features/2014/03/looking-signs-life-near-fukushima-2014346489521261.html.

44 For an additional reading on Fukushima's necropolitical condition, see Jeonghwan, "Between Cognitive Capitalism." According to Klein, "Nuclear is a heavy industrial technology, based on extraction, run in a corporatist manner, with long ties to the military-industrial complex" (*This Changes Everything*, 57).

45 Slavoj Žižek, *Living in the End Times* (London: Verso Books, 2010), 80.

46 Bradbury uses the term "zombie ecosystem" to describe the condition of coral reefs, in his op-ed, "A World without Coral Reefs," *New York Times*, July 13, 2012, http://www.nytimes.com/2012/07/14/opinion/a-world-without-coral-reefs.html.

an environment that is on "a trajectory to collapse."[46] *The Radiant*'s post-human terrain also confronts the post-anthropocentric condition as considered by such speculative realists as Ray Brassier, who writes, reminiscent of Žižek, of a "mind-independent reality, which, despite the presumptions of human narcissism, is indifferent to our existence and oblivious to the 'values' and 'meanings' which we would drape over it in order to make it more hospitable."[47] Indeed, such an environment indifferent to humans, in all of its eeriness, appears to be exactly the one that we witness in *The Radiant*.[48]

Also eerie is how radiation permeates the area, which *The Radiant* attempts to visualize.[49] In one sequence, a rural forested landscape is seen in grainy black-and-white shots. These infrared images are taken with a special camera capable of recording electromagnetic radiation as luminescence, which emanates from the grid powered by the Fukushima plant. The video shows light produced by nuclear energy that is normally not visible, even while radiation functions as an imperceptible actor in its midst, suffusing the atmosphere. It thereby evokes the nonhuman agency of radiation, an agency encoded in the Japanese characters for "landscape," which, as Japanese photographer Chihiro Minato explains in the video, translate literally as "scenery of the wind," a phrase that captures movement and immateriality rather than the stability and groundedness of the English terminology. When coupled with the invisibilities of radiation, the mythopoetic resonance of the scenery also, as Minato speculates, prefigures the potential future divinity of radioactivity, as if we are witnessing the birth of a new religion.

How, *The Radiant* asks, does radiation suffuse, disrupt, and alter the scenery of the wind? While investigating how to visualize radiation, the artists discovered that infrared cameras lack the filter that prevents the registration of infrared energy in regular cameras (electromagnetic radiation with larger wavelengths than those of light visible to human perception). This realization led to a scene in the film where a young female scientist, at the Otolith Group's invitation, attempts to manually modify a regular camera so that it can visually register

47 Ray Brassier, preface to *Nihil Unbound: Enlightenment and Extinction* (Basingstoke: Palgrave Macmillan, 2007), xi. Quentin Meillassoux also writes on "the great outdoors, the absolute outside," as a realm of being "which was not relative to us, and which was given as indifferent to its own givenness to be what it is, existing in itself regardless of whether we are thinking of it or not." *After Finitude: An Essay on the Necessity of Contingency*, trans. Ray Brassier (New York: Continuum, 2008), 7.

48 The conceptual and aesthetic investigation of "eerie" landscapes, eerie in the sense that they evoke a metaphysical realm beyond the human (distinct from the anthropocentric "uncanny"), is also shared and developed by artistic colleagues, and sometimes Otolith Group collaborators, Mark Fisher and Justin Barton, particularly their audio projects *On Vanishing Land* (2013), and *londonunderlondon* (2006). See my review, "Mark Fisher and Jason Barton: *On Vanishing Land*," *Artforum*, September 2013, 204.

49 This paragraph has benefitted from the author's e-mail correspondence with Kodwo Eshun, April 2013.

infrared energy. The passage dramatizes the mechanism of the camera's inner apparatus, uncovering the hidden technology that was used to shoot some of its footage, and which, in the future, might be able to capture the irradiated scenery of the wind. In this regard, *The Radiant* offers a meditation on the technology to visualize radiation, which is only "seen" using a nonhuman technological eye that records a world invisible to the human eye.[50]

The agency of radiation and an inhospitable world-without-us—do such meditations lead to an irredeemable nihilism? In his 2007 book *Nihil Unbound: Enlightenment and Extinction*, Ray Brassier attempts to comprehend the consequences of the Enlightenment's disenchantment of the world through reason, yet refuses to defend against the threat of nihilism by safeguarding the experience of meaning. Rather than understanding nihilism as the heroic conquering of metaphysical thought, or as an act of empty negativity that represents a "calamitous diminishment" of the world's significance deprived of human values—as Nietzsche and Heidegger do—Brassier uses nihilism as a "speculative opportunity" to consider the meaning of extinction when no one will be around to think it.[51] Nihilism thus provides a chance to posit a new non-anthropocentric ontology of things: for Brassier, the world-without-us is based on an irreducible "gap between conceptual identity and non-conceptual difference—between what our concept of the object is and what the object is in itself."[52] Cognizant of that gap, Brassier's reading of nihilism allows us "to understand the meaninglessness of existence, truths about the world" that are not comprehensible as narrative, in a way that rejects "our psychological need for stories that unfold from beginning, through crisis, to ultimate resolution."[53] That said, it is striking that Brassier's book makes no reference to the current ecological or financial crisis; *Nihil Unbound* was, after all, written as scientists suggest that we entering the earth's sixth mass extinction event, following the last one sixty-five million years ago that wiped out approximately 80 percent of all species. Brassier's position remains philosophically abstract. However, we know that climate change, environmental destruction, habitat loss, and the spread of industrial activity worldwide have depleted the earth of half its

50 For an interesting comparison, see Shimpei Takeda, "Trace—Cameraless Records of Radioactive Contamination," in Ellsworth and Kruse, *Making the Geologic Now*, 206–13. Takeda's artistic project is "to capture the current state of Japan directly, by exposing photo-sensitive material to traces of radiation emitted from contaminated particles" (ibid., 206).

51 Brassier, preface to *Nihil Unbound*, xi.

52 See Ray Brassier, "Concepts and Objects," in Bryant, Harman, and Srnicek, *The Speculative Turn*, 55.

53 Ray Brassier, "I am a nihilist because I still believe in truth: Ray Brassier Interviewed by Marcin Rychter," *Kronos*, February 2011, http://www.kronos.org.pl/index.php?23151% 2C896.

wildlife in the last forty years.[54] This threatening statistic poses the question of what a world would be like without biodiversity, and, as we depend on that biodiversity for our very survival, ultimately without us. This question has us look at the earth in the way of speculative realism—that is, without putting ourselves at its center, as sovereign agents gazing over an infinite supply of exploitable resources.[55] *The Radiant* presses us to go beyond Brassier's reluctance to locate his extinction theory in current ecological terms. In this regard, the Otolith Group's film joins current geopolitics to an otherwise dehistoricized and depoliticized speculative realism, or rather mobilizes the ecological and political potential of that philosophy to reflect on the conditions of the environmental crisis. Steve Shaviro addresses this as well when he theorizes "a registration on the intimate, subjective level—of the cosmic, deflationary truth of planetary extinction" (in relation to Lars von Trier's 2011 film *Melancholia*).[56] In distinction to that model, the Otolith Group's film is at once speculatively inventive and actually embedded in the reality of a political ecology defined by a state-corporate system, and its social sacrifice zones, which is contributing to the very momentum around the present extinction event. As such, *The Radiant* raises the ironic implications of the Anthropocene—just as human beings come to be recognized as the central drivers of the earth's current geological epoch, they are also becoming agents of their own destruction. (Will the Anthropocene then name a geological epoch when no humans will be around to think it?)[57]

Negative Utopianism

In addition to the Otolith Group's film, posthuman nuclear environments are further thematized in contemporary speculative photography and video works, where they cross and blur temporalities, uncovering hidden pockets of futurity in the present. As with *The Radiant*, they seize that speculative opportunity of which Brassier speaks. Consider the image complex surrounding disaster zones such as Chernobyl (to say nothing of the visual records of the World War II bombings of Hiroshima and Nagasaki, and those of the experimental laboratory of the Marshall Islands, where residents were

54 See the WWF press release, "Half of Global Wildlife Lost, Says New WWF Report," *World Wildlife Fund*, September 30, 2014, http://www.worldwildlife.org/press-releases/half-of-global-wildlife-lost-says-new-wwf-report.

55 For comparison, see Alan Weisman's speculative experiment that considers what would happen to our material environment—architecture, cities, plastics, nuclear plants, the atmosphere—were contemporary humans to suddenly and permanently disappear. Weisman, *The World without Us*.

56 Steve Shaviro, "*Melancholia*, or, The Romantic Anti-Sublime," *Sequence* 1, no. 1 (2012): 8.

57 For a critical analysis of the Anthropocene thesis, see my book *Against the Anthropocene*.

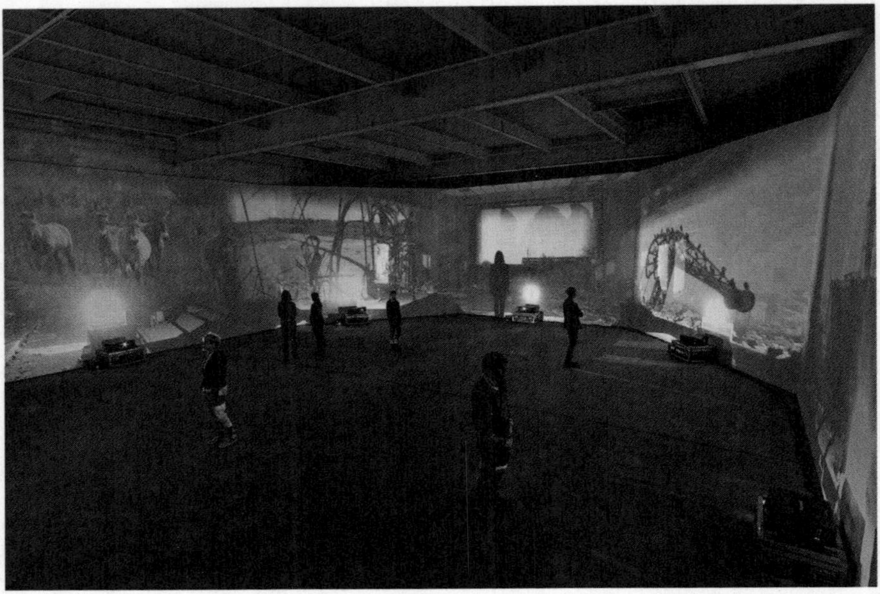

Diana Thater, *Chernobyl*, 2012

studied by the US military for the effects of radioactive fallout from nuclear tests between 1946 and 1958). Diana Thater's video installation *Chernobyl* (2011), for instance, shows haunting images of Prypiat, a city near the reactor in northwestern Ukraine, founded in 1970 for nearly fifty thousand workers and their families and now lying abandoned after the plant's meltdown in 1986. Thater's scenery presents an architecture of sudden abandonment, the aftermath of disaster, where nature and animals—altered genetically in as-yet-unknown ways by radiation exposure—reclaim formerly human spaces. *Chernobyl*'s imagery and staged technology, with projectors and wires lying haphazard on the floor, present a denaturalized nature emptied of human life (except viewers), constituting a further instance of a zombie ecosystem in partial collapse. Or take Jane and Louise Wilson's *The Toxic Camera* (2012), a video that investigates the circumstances of Soviet filmmaker Vladimir Shevchenko's recordings of Chernobyl in the days after the accident that resulted in his own film *Chronicle of Difficult Weeks* (1986). He had produced footage that was marked with static interference from radiation; radiation rendered "visible," that is, via the obfuscations in his imagery—what artist and theorist Susan Schuppli has called "an act of radiological recording, whereby the radical imprint of disaster was inscribed directly

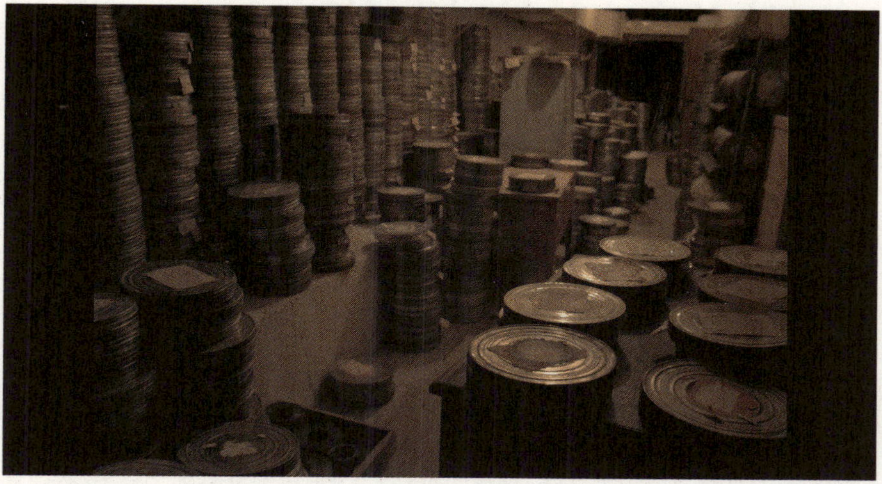

Jane and Louise Wilson, still from *The Toxic Camera*, 2012

into the emulsion of the film as decaying particles moved through the exterior casing of the movie camera."[58] Shevchenko's camera was so contaminated that it had to be buried on the outskirts of Kiev, and the filmmaker died the same year due to the radiation exposure. Prypiat will take twenty-four thousand years to recover from radioactive danger. These works relate the uninhabitable spaces of nuclear contamination to the limitations of technologies of perception. Still, their forlorn context, a zone of sacrifice dedicated to our own nuclear gods, can't suppress the desire to visualize its conditions—a contemporary death drive to know what the aftermath of human life looks like. If this presents a world-without-us, then it is because no subject should really be around to think it.[59] The nausea and profound alienation that such a vision provokes is none other than the affective response to the scene of environmental catastrophe.

The Radiant further entangles the futuristic gardens of the post-human in the political conflicts of the present, implicating us in the necropolitics of radiation. Consider the video's now-famous appropriated footage of the pointing man—the Fukushima worker who pointed his index finger directly at a security camera for ten minutes just after

58 Susan Schuppli, "The Most Dangerous Film in the World," in *Tickle Your Catastrophe! Imagining Catastrophe in Art, Architecture and Philosophy*, ed. Dominiek Hoens et al. (Ghent: Academia Press, 2011), 127. Schuppli also contributed to the script of the Wilsons' film.

59 Philosopher Eugene Thacker differentiates between the world-for-us ("the world in which we live"), the world-in-itself ("the world as it exists apart from us"), and the world-without-us (a "spectral and speculative world" that exists "at the limits of our thought"). Thacker, *In the Dust of This Planet*, 4–5.

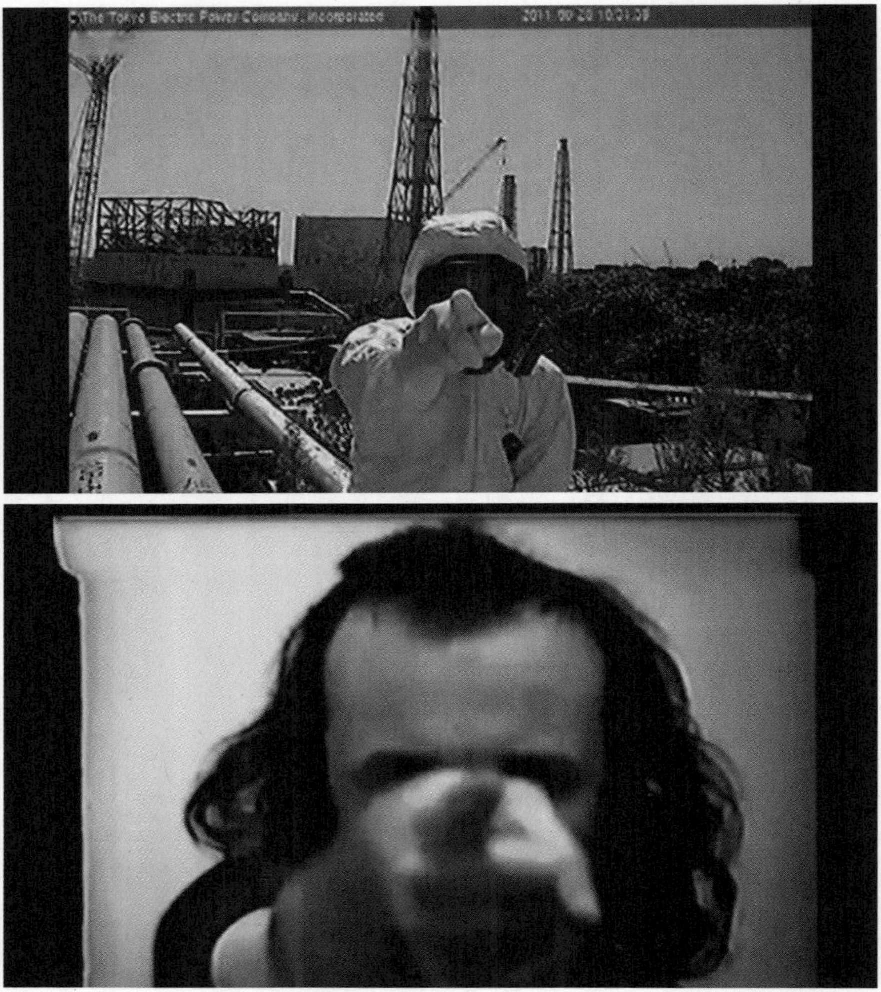

The Otolith Group, stills from *The Radiant*, 2012

its meltdown. This sequence is more than a protest act to articulate workers' grievances (regarding poor labor conditions, and the lack of insurance and contracts) against the TEPCO management, as the twenty-nine-year-old worker, Kota Takeuchi, explained later on his blog.[60] The inclusion of the footage in the film suggests that if the pointing man's video went viral on the Internet in the days after the meltdown, then it

60 See the blog of Kota Takeuchi, http://pointatfuku1cam.nobody.jp/e.html.

did so because that resonant gesture unleashed an explosively charged index of the meeting point of the present and future, when the origins of the potential coming catastrophe of mass extinction are seen to be firmly rooted in our own world, not in sci-fi speculation. And by referencing Vito Acconci's video *Centers* (1971)—as Takeuchi, also an artist, did on his blog—the Otolith Group retools video art's "aesthetics of narcissism" (as Rosalind Krauss once wrote of Acconci's self-referential video) as a defiant sign of popular accusation against a nuclear necropower.[61]

The Radiant exemplifies, finally, what Fredric Jameson has described as a "negative" utopianism, "transforming our own present into the determinate past of something yet to come."[62] Negative utopianism can mean two things here: First, it suggests a critical image that captures the catastrophe of the present utopianism (of nuclear energy, for example, and its necropolitics of radiation), by highlighting its failures and portraying its negativity as apocalyptic ecocide. Second, it articulates the potential for a new imagination once the false utopianisms of the present have been cleared away (along the lines of what Jameson calls "anti-anti-utopianism"—the rejection of those capitalist-realist arguments that contend that utopian thinking is impossible, irresponsible, and escapist, which ends up reasserting the status quo by denying the imagination of other possible worlds). Rather than giving itself over to the sci-fi seductions of a future biotechnology, this work finds the future preordained in the conditions of our present. In this sense, the future intimated by *The Radiant* works like a mechanism to make the present different than it normally appears, thereby sparking a political energy to resist what is already occurring, the desire to challenge contemporary nuclear destruction. The film shows protesters contesting Japan's irresponsible and media-spun response to the disaster—especially given the government's decision (in cahoots with TEPCO) to distribute irradiated soil throughout the country, destroying control groups of forensic samples, to shield itself against future liability lawsuits by victims of radiation-caused illnesses, as discussed in the film by journalist May Shigenobu.[63] Ending on this note, the Otolith

61 Rosalind Krauss, "Video: The Aesthetics of Narcissism," *October*, no. 1 (Spring 1976): 50–64.

62 Fredric Jameson, *Archaeologies of the Future: The Desire Called Utopia and Other Science Fictions* (London: Verso Books, 2005), 288.

63 Shigenobu is the daughter of Japanese Red Army member Fusako Shigenobu and a Palestinian who was allegedly a former head of the Popular Front for the Liberation of Palestine (whose identity remains secret to this day for political reasons)—indicating a fascinating political trajectory that lies behind *The Radiant*. For more on Fukushima's political situation, see Satoko Oka Norimatsu, "Fukushima and Okinawa: The 'Abandoned People,' and Civic Empowerment," *Truthout*, November 28, 2011, http://www.truth-out.org/news/item/5210:fukushima-and-okinawa-the-%E2%80%9Cabandoned-people%E2%80%9D-and-civic-empowerment.

Group seizes the speculative opportunity of an environment in the clutches of extinction to reveal contours of our own necropolitical regime. While it provides witness to a world-without-us, haunting in its eerie calm, the video's own antinuclear activism also amplifies the agency of political resistance.[64]

Occupy Curating

dOCUMENTA (13)'s "concept-less" exhibition, as we've seen, tended more toward the hybrid aesthetics of sci-fi than political engagement, even while it included voices that insist on politicizing ecology. Its curators missed the opportunity to explicitly address and position the exhibition within the philosophical and political controversies surrounding the status of life today (even as the massive resource consumption of the show's production and operation contradicted its green rhetoric).[65] What would be the ramifications of taking seriously the ecological insights of—and most importantly conflicts between—Haraway and Shiva at the level of curating? Is it easier to imagine the end of the world than the end of the unsustainable mega-exhibition? How can future documentas take into account the externalities of their production—their carbon footprint and exploitation of fossil-fuel-based resources? And in recognizing this crisis situation, how might future shows work critically within that framework, acknowledging its contradictions openly, if not overcoming them practically?

In the present age of crises and emergencies, we need bold proposals, not fuzzy non-concepts. Consider the symbolic weight if such a high-profile exhibition determined that it is simply environmentally unviable and calling itself off, or doing something sustainable in its place. Such an alternative has yet to be invented, even though we have recent precedents that have glimpsed it. One modest proposal was offered on the front lawn of the Fridericianum during dOCUMENTA (13): a tent city of the Occupy movement, part of the global anticapitalist uprising that

64 In February 2016, after nearly fifteen thousand Fukushima residents repeatedly filed a complaint with the courts, the former CEO and two former executives of TEPCO were indicted for negligence over the Fukushima disaster. The case is currently pending.

65 In his review of the show, Julian Stallabrass wrote: "The strapline, 'A Sustainable Exhibition', the use of Karlsaue and the inclusion of gardening pieces may lead the casual viewer to think of this as a 'green' production. Yet, of course, the increasingly event-driven character of the art world contributes to environmental despoliation. Artists, curators, critics, gallerists and buyers are flown to venues across four continents. Objects of shipped by air and massively heavy piles of scrap metal are displaced. VIPs travel to Kassel by helicopter and private jet. Ordinary viewers travel long distances for the latest unique, but also standard, art-world mega-event. There is nothing green about any of this, and the curatorial moves to evoke environmental issues, like the green hue of the BP logo, are an insulting camouflage." "Radical Camouflage at Documenta 13," *New Left Review*, no. 77 (September–October 2012): 132.

began in 2011. It was a token inclusion for sure (insofar as it was welcomed by the show's organizers), no match for a mega-exhibition, but one figuring as an alternative paradigm of a localist formation with a minimal ecological footprint, inclusively participatory, anti-elitist, and committed to degrowth and recycling, without admission costs or traveling far distances. As such, the Occupy movement offered a largely unacknowledged radical alternative in the shadow of dOCUMENTA (13), mostly invisible to the conventional art world. If taken seriously as a model, however, it would transform the contemporary art exhibition into something largely unrecognizable from today's perspective.[66] Against the exhibition's curatorial position of nonengagement, such ecological imperatives must be taken up in forceful, ambitious proposals, so that emergency conditions are not simply invoked at a distance, through artworks, representation, or discourse[67]—that is, even while dOCUMENTA (13) remains significant for opening paths to explore the biopolitics of nature in its current guise, including the mixed economies of food production, experimental gardens, and environmental governance in the age of nuclear threat and catastrophic climate breakdown. These questions lie at the heart of contemporary debates over what kind of world we want to live in, how it will be organized, and what role art might play to imagine, represent, and realize it. With each passing day, the stakes of those debates only continue to grow more momentous.

66 For a recent attempt to conceptualize this transformation, see McKee, *Strike Art*. For McKee, the Occupy movement figures as transitive verb, complex noun, truth event, and reinvented form of contemporary art, drawing together "the aesthetic dimension of activism that emphasizes the importance of the sensuous, embodied experiences of sight, sound, and touch in the staging of nongovernmental political claims and the forging of movement imaginaries relative to the media assemblages within which political action is inscribed" (39–40).

67 In this regard, artist and curator Artur Żmijewski's 2012 Berlin Biennale could be taken as another example, one that did more to integrate the local iteration of the Occupy movement into its venue and operations, even though the exhibition was far from centrally engaged with ecological matters. Not surprisingly, the initiative was largely panned by mainstream art criticism, and conventional art-seeking visitors were left dissatisfied. For two complex, critical, and constructive views of this biennial occupation and its possibilities from an activist perspective, as well as a critique of the mainstream art world's limited understanding of politics as represented in the responses to the project, see Gavin Grindon, "Protest Camps and White Cubes," *Gavin Grindon* (blog), September 28, 2012, http://gavingrindon.net/?p=172; and Noah Fischer, "Agency in a Zoo: The Occupy Movement's Strategic Expansion to Art Institutions," *Field*, no. 2 (Winter 2015), http://field-journal.com/issue-2/fischer.

Ways Forward

To Be Continued ...

While finishing work on this book, I woke up one morning to two pieces of disturbing news. One article reported that around 1,500 sea-lion pups, starved and near death, had recently washed up on California beaches, the unprecedented event overwhelming animal rescuers.[1] Another was an op-ed stating that California, which experienced its driest month in January 2015 since record keeping began, in 1895, had approximately one year left in its water reservoirs. What's more, the state lacked any contingency plan or long-term strategic vision for how to confront its current four-years-and-running drought.[2] The two calamities, of course, are related—anthropogenic climate change has warmed the oceans to record-breaking temperatures and disrupted the sea lions' food supply, weakening the animals and making them prone to pneumonia, parasites, and exhaustion. And that same climate breakdown has altered the atmospheric conditions affecting North America's West Coast, leading to disastrous dryness, the depletion of river basins, and the emptying of aquifers.[3] The news comes as another morsel of the media's daily diet of eco-pessimism, exemplifying our collective psychosis of denial. Government representatives seem to be waiting for the wave of a magic wand

1 Jack Healy, "Starving Sea Lions Washing Ashore by the Hundreds in California," *New York Times*, March 12, 2015, http://www.nytimes.com/2015/03/13/us/starving-sea-lions-washing-ashore-by-the-hundreds-in-california.html?_r=0.

2 Jay Famiglietti, "California Has about One Year of Water Stored: Will You Ration Now?," *Los Angeles Times*, March 12, 2015, http://www.latimes.com/opinion/op-ed/la-oe-famiglietti-drought-california-20150313-story.html.

3 See Justin Gilligsaug, "California Drought Is Made Worse by Global Warming, Scientists Say," *New York Times*, August 20, 2015, http://www.nytimes.com/2015/08/21/science/climate-change-intensifies-california-drought-scientists-say.html?_r=0.

to rescue them from any need to critically address our growth-obsessed and unsustainable ways of life (although California Governor Jerry Brown has recently enacted some important policy shifts toward conservation). In the meantime, most are doing nothing. The news hit home for me since I had recently moved with my family from London to take up a new position at the University of California, Santa Cruz. It has given me renewed motivation to consider, in light of the preceding chapters, what the path forward might be, and how we can turn these depressing circumstances into urgently needed creative responses, from the cultural realm as well.

So what is to be done, given the state of ecological crisis that we face—global warming, environmental degradation, dirty extractivism, destruction of biodiversity, species extinction, acidification of the oceans, desertification, colonization of nature, and corporate control of life? This book's chapters, dedicated to various art and activism in diverse and relational geographical contexts, make clear that there is no single solution or sole approach to our ecological predicament. Indeed, multiple paths are required—targeting industrial, state, and corporate practices and policies, as well as inventing alternatives for sustainable living. There are also hybrid artistic-activist models that bring the critical and creative together. Another thing is clear: given the situation, we cannot afford to be complacent with the status quo, for we're running out of time. As we tumble down the slope toward civilizational collapse, hopes for techno-fixes or geo-engineering solutions appear as misplaced as ever; indeed, as Naomi Klein argues, proponents of such an approach call for "a doubling down on exactly the kind of reckless, short-term thinking that got us into this mess."[4] Moreover, current government proposals tend to support corporate, military, and engineering responses to climate change, which reaffirm the very power of technocrats and government officials, while consigning the rest of us to the catastrophic futures envisioned in so many Hollywood apocalypse films. The imperative for something different is called for by political ecology, which insists on thinking environmental concerns in relation to the political, economic, and social structures that mediate them, all of which require comprehensive analysis.

One such proposal is the "Great Transition," a Marshall Plan–scale approach to the environmental crisis involving "managed degrowth" and immediate decarbonization to put a stop to climate-changing emissions. Pioneered by the Tellus Institute, a Boston-based nonprofit research and science policy organization, it's not a technocratic solution; the transition necessitates a multifaceted move away from the liberal-capitalist investment in possessions and development and toward a new imperative to consume less. It entails "changing how much energy we actually use: how often we drive, how often we fly, whether our food has to be flown to get to us, whether the goods we buy are built to last or to be replaced in two years, how large our homes are."[5] Yet rather than another form of ethical consumerism—inadequate for putting the burden on individuals rather than corporations and governments—this new politics of energy will require effective democratic policy and global governance.[6] If we act now, as the London-based New Economics Foundation argues, we stand to save trillions of dollars by addressing future environmental crises before they unfold. And "by sharing our resources more equally, by building better communities and a better society and by safeguarding the natural environment, we can focus on the things that really matter and achieve genuine and lasting progress with higher levels of well being."[7] Such a *just* transition includes several elements: a revaluation of production (so environmentally healthy things are cheaper than destructive things), the redistribution of wealth to achieve greater equality (including proposals for universal economic benefits, and greater corporate and inheritance tax), the shortening of the workweek to facilitate degrowth,[8] and the creation of "economic democracy" by sharing ownership via cooperatives and worker-owned collectives. It also comprises de-globalization using the concept of subsidiarity, whereby decisions are localized and made by the communities impacted most directly to redefine efficiency by considering ecological impacts on towns, rural areas, and cities; reskilling production to support regional agriculture and green manufacturing, finance, and governance; creating new tax structures that disincentivize harmful environmental production and consumption and short-term speculation; and forming a new "ecology of finance" that stresses environmentally friendly investment, institutions, and cooperative interdependency (rather than competition) between countries in relation to trade and transportation.[9]

This transition entails, for Naomi Klein, a move toward renewable energy sources (solar, wind, thermal, wave), in addition to "cheap public transit and clean

4 Klein, *This Changes Everything*, 58.

5 Ibid., 89. See Raskin et al., *Great Transition*; also Spratt et al., *The Great Transition*.

6 "There is virtually no governmental policy which is aimed at changing the way we produce, incentivizing farmers for low energy farming, or how we consume, incentivizing consumption of local and seasonal food. [...] There are incentives to drive more efficient cars, but very little is done to discourage car dependent settlement patterns." Rebecca Willis and Nick Eyre, *Demanding Less: Why We Need a New Politics of Energy* (London: Green Alliance, 2011), 9, 26.

7 Spratt et al., *The Great Transition*, 4.

8 John Stutz of the Tellus Institute proposes that the number of hours of paid labor could be substantially lowered for a workweek of three to four days, introduced gradually over a period of decades, which could offset much of the emissions growth projected through 2030 while improving quality of life. John Stutz, *Climate Change, Development and the Three-Day Week* (Boston: Tellus Institute, 2008), 4–5.

light rail accessible to all; affordable, energy-efficient housing along those transit lines; cities planned for high-density living; bike lanes in which riders aren't asked to risk their lives to get to work; land management that discourages sprawl and encourages local, low-energy forms of agriculture; urban design that clusters essential services like schools and health care along transit routes and in pedestrian-friendly areas; programs that require manufacturers to be responsible for the electronic waste they produce, and to radically reduce built-in redundancies and obsolescences."[10] The goal would also include job growth in green sectors such as mass public transit, renewable energy, and ecosystem restoration. The demand for a universal basic income is part of the Great Transition as well—a steady pay granted to all unconditionally and without qualifications. The proposal is supported by groups like Basic Income Earth Network and many Green Parties worldwide as a catalyst for abolishing poverty, a human right, and a mechanism of ecological sustainability.[11]

There are many options for moving forward, and no doubt it will take the power of social movements composed of engaged citizens, creative practitioners, local communities, and Indigenous activists to realize these alternatives and get governments to act. It will require regional engagements and transnational alliances to bring about the necessary reinvention of politics, policy, and global governance—effectively a worldwide transformation, even revolution.[12] While the transition is eminently doable, these ideas will inevitably strike some as idealist. But a dismissive reflex overlooks the fact that the truly irresponsible thinking today is accepting the assumption that we can simply continue down the same path forever, or that we can't do anything to change our direction. Another irresponsible reaction is to think our current hegemonic system of neoliberal capitalism, which is responsible for the problems in the first place, will provide the solution—the era Jason Moore and Donna Haraway designate as the "Capitalocene," in contrast to using the problematically human-centered and generic Anthropocene.[13]

The current unsustainable state of affairs cannot continue—for reasons that are ecological as much as political and economic—and this is equally true in the

9 In addition to Spratt et al., *The Great Transition*, see also the recommendations in Cavanagh and Mander, *Alternatives to Economic Globalization*.

10 Klein, *This Changes Everything*, 91.

11 See the website of BIEN (Basic Income Earth Network), http://www.basicincome.org.

12 See David Graeber, "How Change Happens," chap. 4 in *The Democracy Project: A History, a Crisis, a Movement* (London: Penguin Books, 2013), 208–70.

13 See Jason W. Moore, "The Capitalocene, Part I: On the Nature & Origins of Our Ecological Crisis," *Jason W. Moore*, 2014, http://www.jasonwmoore.com/uploads/The_Capitalocene_Part_I_June_2014.pdf; and Haraway, "Anthropocene, Capitalocene, Plantationocene, Chthulucene," 161.

cultural realm. How can current forms of production, exhibition, distribution, marketing, transportation, and travel continue in their present forms given their carbon footprints, part of the neoliberal growth regime driving climate change? In this sense, political ecology provides a new imperative for us all to join with social movements and mobilize art for its creative speculation, alternative models, critical analysis, political investigation, and conceptual insight. How, we must ask, can artistic activity contribute to and expand the activist imaginary, infusing protests, demonstrations, and direct action campaigns with creativity and effective poetics, building on social and political engagement at multiple levels, from the local to transnational? How can the arts work toward and realize a transitional culture, joining ecological sustainability and social justice, in the widest sense of these terms?[14]

One effect of such ecological sensitivity is a newly infused demand for cultural activism, defined as a preemptively transformative approach to habits and behaviors, conceptual thinking and practical solutions, institutions and modes of governance, aesthetics and politics. Of course, twentieth-century avant-gardes represent a long history of diverse (and uneven) relations to social and political movements, which potentially enriches contemporary engagements with the politics of representation and the representation of politics, providing diverse aesthetic innovations, social models of collectivization, experimental exhibition and distribution practice, institutional critique, and creative ways of addressing spectatorship and perception.[15] Political ecology, comprising an integral element of some of these artistic developments with origins that go back to 1960s environmental art, as we've seen over the course of this book, only adds to the contemporary momentum of aesthetic engagements, charged further with ever-new scientific research and growing environmental knowledge, and propelled with the recent energy of global movements and protests against

14 The imperative implied here contradicts the idea of "duty-free art" in a world of corporate globalization, an art of autonomy and freedom that repeats an outmoded liberal conceit, a new articulation of autonomy that appears, in my view, as a problematic embrace of accelerationism: "The idea of duty-free art has one major advantage over the nation-state cultural model: duty-free art ought to have no duty—no duty to perform, to represent, to teach, to embody value. It should not be indebted to anyone, nor serve a cause or a master, nor be a means to anything." Hito Steyerl, "Duty-Free Art," *e-flux journal*, no. 63 (March 2015): 10. Conversely, I argue that our current ecological crisis introduces a new imperative for art's ethico-political duty.

15 Among the most provocative of recent literature, see Blake Stimson and Gregory Sholette, eds., *Collectivism after Modernism: The Art of Social Imagination after 1945* (Minneapolis: University of Minnesota Press, 2007); Feher, Krikorian, and McKee, *Nongovernmental Politics;* Claire Bishop, *Artificial Hells: Participatory Art and the Politics of Spectatorship* (London: Verso Books, 2012); Thompson, *Living as Form;* Flood and Grindon, *Disobedient Objects;* Nixon, *Slow Violence;* McKee, *Strike Art;* and Hickey, *A Guidebook of Alternative Nows.*

neoliberalism.[16] This activist culture, broadly speaking, is motivated by a wide-ranging commitment to nongovernmental politics—a commitment "not to be governed *thusly*," as Michel Feher writes, where "looking at the political field from the perspective of its nongovernmental dimension arguably undermines the notion that there should ever be an end to politics."[17] The conflicts of politics, in this light, will never be resolved, and not simply given the general governmental failure to address climate change (as evidenced particularly by the UN COP meetings, including most recently COP21 in Paris).[18] We—the diverse agents of a growing opposition to governmental and corporate environmental inertia, a we that refuses to be governed *thusly*—have a massive challenge before us. That challenge involves wresting legitimacy from an unjust state-corporate apparatus—unjust for causing inequality, social exclusions, and disastrous ecological practices—and forming alliances with social movements beyond the strictly environmentalist (such as Black Lives Matter or innumerable Indigenous movements) who are resisting the subjugation and exclusion enforced by militarized police defending the power of the corporate state. It entails both remaking a compromised public space into a place for diverse and active publics, and transforming a government-surveilled and corporate-dominated digital sphere into a newly democratic commons.[19] Eco-activist Bill McKibben wrote recently: "The richest industry in human history [oil] wants to keep on their current path for a few more years, even if it means dragging the whole planet over a cliff. [...] Their power lies in money and the political favour it can buy; our power lies in movement-building, and the political fear it can instill. They know they're in a tough spot so they're spending like crazy. [...] We've therefore got to organise like crazy."[20]

Considering what should be done in the cultural sector, we stand to learn from how scientists have been engaging with politics—especially those who are

16 See Yates McKee, "Art after Occupy: Climate Justice, BDS and Beyond," *Waging Nonviolence*, July 30, 2014, http://wagingnonviolence.org/feature/art-after-occupy/; McKee, *Strike Art*; and Demos, "Playful Protesters."

17 Michel Feher, "The Governed in Politics," in Feher, Krikorian, and McKee, *Nongovernmental Politics*, 14, 26. Also see McLagan and McKee, *Sensible Politics*.

18 Many analysts see the corporate-dominated COP21 agreement as inadequate, owing to both the nonbinding nature of the commitments and the fact that the national promises of reductions fall below the emissions cutbacks necessary to keep global warming below two degrees Celsius. See Deschamps and Mychalejko, "Did World Leaders Sign a 'Death Warrant'"; Oliver Milman, "James Hansen, Father of Climate Change Awareness, Calls Paris Talks 'A Fraud,'" *Guardian*, December 12, 2015, http://www.theguardian.com/environment/2015/dec/12/james-hansen-climate-change-paris-talks-fraud; and Tokar, "Paris Climate Conference Designed to Fail?"

19 On such a political project, see Judith Butler, "Bodies in Alliance and the Politics of the Street," *European Institute for Progressive Cultural Policies*, September 2011, http://www.eipcp.net/transversal/1011/butler/en.

20 Bill McKibben, "Pressure Is Growing: A Relentless Climate

rejecting the neutrality of empirical observation, and turning instead to activism in an effort to turn their research into public-policy advocacy. Scientists like James Hansen and Kevin Anderson, to name some of the best known, are joining protesters and civil-disobedience campaigns, even getting arrested for their cause. In 2012, twenty-one past laureates of the prestigious environmentalist Blue Planet Prize, a group that includes Hansen (former Director of NASA Goddard Institute for Space Studies) and Gro Harlem Brundtland (former Prime Minister of Norway), authored a landmark report. "In the face of an absolutely unprecedented emergency, society has no choice but to take dramatic action to avert a collapse of civilization," it stated. "Either we will change our ways and build an entirely new kind of global society, or they will be changed for us."[21] Why should artists, curators, scholars, writers, and students—equally citizens and agents in the reproduction of this world and the creation of its future—be any different? A Great Transition will likely entail civil disobedience in public life, as it has for these scientist-activists, in order to press for changes in government composition, structure, and policy. Besides, "there isn't a non-civil disobedience route here," contends Anderson. "You either disobey the current civil structures or orders that we have to say you shouldn't get in the way of fracking or whatever development for that matter," or you resign yourself to the catastrophic route forward.[22] For Anderson, deputy director of the Tyndall Centre for Climate Change Research, "silence is an advocacy for the status quo," and those scientists who think of themselves as the least engaged, are inadvertently among the most political.[23] The cultural sphere can claim no exception. To cling to some outdated notion of artistic autonomy, individualist creative freedom, or transgressive and free avant-garde identity, divorced from any duty or responsibility for environmental considerations, is to advocate, intentionally or not, for the status quo of neoliberal exceptionalism and its destructive ecocide.

Movement Is Starting to Win Big, Unprecedented Victories around the World, Victories Which Are Quickly Reshaping the Consensus View," *Guardian*, March 9, 2015, http://www.theguardian.com/environment/2015/mar/09/climate-fight-wont-wait-for-paris-vive-la-resistance.

21 Gro Harlem Brundtland et al., *Environment and Development Challenges: The Imperative to Act* (Tokyo: Asahi Glass Foundation, 2012), 7; cited in Klein, *This Changes Everything*, 22. The Blue Planet Prize was established by the Asahi Glass Foundation in 1992, the year of the Rio Earth Summit, and recognizes outstanding contributions to solving global environmental problems.

22 "Professor Kevin Anderson on Shale Gas, Civil Disobedience and Barton Moss #Manchester #climate," *Manchester Climate Monthly*, December 17, 2013, http://manchesterclimatemonthly.net/2013/12/17/professor-kevin-anderson-on-shale-gas-civil-disobedience-and-barton-moss-manchester-climate.

23 "Professor Kevin Anderson on Science, Silence and 'Neutrality' #Manchester #climate," *Manchester Climate Monthly*, December 23, 2013, http://manchesterclimatemonthly.net/2013/12/23/professor-kevin-anderson-on-science-silence-and-neutrality-manchester-climate.

The activist imperative, however, risks falling into forms of emergency protocols that bypass critical thinking, restrict options, and abdicate agency by delegating decision-making power to scientists, governments, NGOs, or transnational organizations such as NATO, the EU, and the UN. Such a course could introduce an ecological state of exception driven by a climate of fear, itself antidemocratic and antipolitical, obviating critical analysis and economic justice, and leading to more militarized borders, xenophobic nationalism, and human rights violations, targeting growing numbers of (climate) refugees, on a massive scale.[24] Giorgio Agamben adapts Walter Benjamin on World War II for our post-9/11 militarized present when he writes, "The voluntary creation of a permanent state of emergency (though perhaps not declared in the technical sense) has become one of the essential practices of contemporary states, including so-called democratic ones."[25] If so, then we need an altogether different state of emergency that will reclaim democratic practice in the face of environmental challenges—one that is more inclusive in political deliberation, direct action, and social movements, and that invents new institutions freed of corporate interests, built on critical dissensus and democratic decision-making.

For one instructive model of what the Great Transition might mean within the cultural realm, consider again the work of the Laboratory of Insurrectionary Imagination (Labofii). Their argument for the necessary unification of ethics and aesthetics informs their ten-years-and-running no-fly policy (especially striking in a European context of deregulated budget airlines whose flights are usually cheaper than train travel). It also informs their activist-artistic experiment with collective living in Brittany, France, and their opposition to corporate (and particularly fossil-fuel corporate) sponsorship of cultural events. In late 2014, the group was invited to participate in the 2015 Donaufestival in Krems, Austria, a two-week festival of contemporary art, film,

24 On these risks, see Craig Calhoun, "A World of Emergencies: Fear, Intervention, and the Limits of Cosmopolitan Order," *Canadian Review of Sociology and Anthropology* 41, no. 4 (November 2004): 373–95; Didier Fassin and Mariella Pandolfi, eds., *Contemporary States of Emergency: The Politics of Military and Humanitarian Interventions* (New York: Zone Books, 2010); Alex Gourevitch, "Environmentalism—Long Live the Politics of Fear," *Public Culture* 22, no. 3 (Fall 2010): 411–24; and Jeff Goodell, "The Pentagon & Climate Change: How Deniers Put National Security at Risk," *Rolling Stone*, February 12, 2015, http://www.rollingstone.com/politics/news/the-pentagon-climate-change-how-climate-deniers-put-national-security-at-risk-20150212. "'It's not a question of what the military can do for climate change,' says one former Pentagon official. 'It's what climate change will do to the military and its mission.' It's a scary notion, but that's where we are headed. In the end, it doesn't matter how many climate-adaptation road maps the Pentagon puts out. We are now committed to a future of disorder and conflict—one in which today's emergencies will always interrupt tomorrow's plans" (ibid.).

25 Giorgio Agamben, *State of Exception*, trans. Kevin Attell (Chicago: University of Chicago Press, 2005), 2.

music, and theater that proposed to radically remake the current world. The group saw, however, that the festival's sponsors included Vienna International Airport, the Austrian power company EVN (which owns coal-fired power stations and distributes gas across Europe), and Raiffeisen (Austria's largest bank, which funds oil refineries in Russia and helps finance exports from Siberian coal mines). Labofii felt they could respond only by declining the invitation with an open letter. Rather than view such corporate sponsorship as a model of philanthropic leadership in the arts, Labofii claims that it represents a form of "anesthesia" that numbs us to the reality of the destructive functions of capitalist culture, where "the arts are supporting their lie that they care about anything other than making profits even though it means annihilating the life support systems of this planet."[26]

In this regard, Labofii are extending the mission of Liberate Tate, the artistic-activist collective that has attempted in recent years to free the major London art institution from BP's sponsorship (John Jordan and Isa Frémeaux of Labofii were also involved in the formation of Liberate Tate in 2010). They see this funding as culturally sanctioning the viability of petro-capitalism, according to which "every exhibition at Tate and other oil-sponsored public cultural institutions is part of the creation of climate chaos through the construction of a social licence to operate for oil companies." As such, the museum "makes visitors complicit in the ecological destruction of its corporate partners."[27] Labofii's open letter similarly demands we desist from all projects, institutions, exhibitions, and festivals funded by the oil industry. Rather than limiting their activity to eco-institutional critique, the group continues their long-standing commitment to creative activism against corporate globalization, building alternatives that support sustainable collective living and political engagement in the present. They join environmental, social, and political dimensions in the reinvented practices of everyday life, which becomes the very site of an expanded zone of aesthetic creativity. In other words, alterations and experimentations at the everyday scale of consumption, transportation, and energy use combine with the political commitment of activist

26 The Laboratory of Insurrectionary Imagination (Jordan and Isa Frémeaux), "An Open Letter in the Dark"; all Labofii citations in the conclusion are from this text. Also see my text, "Between Rebel Creativity and Reification: For and Against Visual Activism," *Journal of Visual Culture* 15, vol. 1 (April 2016): 85–102.

27 Liberate Tate, in Steven Lam et al., "Art, Ecology and Institutions: A Conversation with Artists and Curators," *Third Text* 27, no. 1 (January 2013): 143. Also see their website, http://www.liberatetate.org.uk; as well as the related work of the New York–based collective Not an Alternative, http://notanalternative.org/collections/the-natural-history-museum-grand-opening. In March 2016, Tate announced that it would end a twenty-six-year practice of accepting BP sponsorship, in large part the result of activist campaigns.

practices that militate for structural change at local, regional, and global governmental levels—all of which proposes an expanded notion of what art can be today.

But what of the counterpositions in the art world? Labofii explain:

> *Many of our artists and intellectual friends fly from biennial to festival, from one city to another to make "radical culture". It's all part of the "rights" of the hyper mobile cultural class, a global generation that that has been uprooted from any material place, ripped from local communities, distanced from contexts where they might have some agency in transforming the material world. It suits the status quo that the radical thinkers and makers don't have a territory, belong to nowhere and float in an abstract vapid world where no solution is graspable, where radical thinking has no anchor in action.*

Against this state of affairs, the group observes (with reference to John Berger) that to have a positive effect on a place, you have to know it well and spend time there, and this process of localization, according to some, such as permaculture farmers, can take hundreds of years and more. To ground their argument, Labofii point to research of the Tyndall Centre, which states that UK residents must slash their CO_2 emissions by roughly 90 percent by 2050 to stop runaway climate breakdown and fairly redistribute the global production of greenhouse gases. According to their calculations, a transatlantic roundtrip flight would use up someone's entire carbon allowance for the year, with none remaining for eating, Internet use, electricity, or other transportation. We must learn to live differently.

But what about international festivals and mega-exhibitions, whose infrastructure relies on fossil fuels? Isn't it important to hold these events, especially when they raise the alarm over the threat of climate change? No, according to Labofii. "Such logic seems absurd to us: do we really want to continue the survival of the international art world at the expense of the survival of our species on this planet. Or do we want an art world that provides models for other ways of living and behaving in this one?" Ultimately, artistic practice for Labofii is about creating viable and sustainable alternatives to the current collusion between culture and petro-capitalism. They assert a radical Marxist ecology for the goal of art: "*to remove the ability of the rich to steal from the poor and dismantle the ability of the powerful to destroy our biosphere.* The role of art for us is to make this process as creative, desirable and effective as possible—to stop the war of money against life in the most beautiful way possible." Art, in this regard, opens a radical imagination, one that is possible in few other spaces—radical for its structural critique of art's political economy, and for its experimental creativity in inventing and practicing noncapitalist, environmentally holistic, and socially democratic modes of living. Labofii's withdrawal from institutions funded by fossil-fuel industry represents an inspiring example of activism that could be adapted appropriately to other locales across the world.

Other options present themselves as well for how we might contest the status quo of environmental inaction and the threat of climate disaster. What might be appropriate in relation to organic farming in rural India, as we've seen in the work of Amar Kanwar, will inevitably be different from what's appropriate in the urban context of London, as proposed in the utopian schemata of Nils Norman. Similarly, the anti-NAFTA ecology of the Zapatistas, set within Mexico's corrupt military-state neoliberalism, will contrast with the Indigenous and environmental imperatives of contesting oil drilling in Alaska's Chukchi Sea, as represented in the work of Subhankar Banerjee. And there is more than one way to deal with the ethics of sponsorship. Naomi Klein acknowledges that "no one's hands are clean," and that even some of the top foundations that support the environmental movement (including the Environmental Defense Fund and the Natural Resources Defense Council, with which she's been involved) are linked to fossil-fuel investments (for instance, owning stocks in Shell and BP). Yet that hasn't stopped her from mobilizing those funds for her own purposes, including support in writing her recent book.[28] For many others, the battle to be fought will similarly occur from within compromised cultural and research institutions. From within these contradictory situations, where most of us find ourselves, we can only continue working to support and catalyze change, including commitments to the reduction of one's carbon footprint as a first step forward.

The Occupy movement opened up a radical imagination of environmental and financial activism on a global scale, and its impacts are still being felt, its work far from finished. It moreover taught us not to restrict ourselves to the creation of autonomous spaces alone, but to direct them toward the occupation of institutions, as political theorists Mark Fisher and Chantal Mouffe, among others, have recently advocated. It is imperative, in other words, to practice immanent critique and not simply build separate spaces (as in the exodus-based models of Italian autonomism, or in varieties of Occupy).[29] The political parties

28 Klein, *This Changes Everything*, 198.

29 These points were made in Chantal Mouffe, Gavin Grindon, and Mark Fisher, "Art and Radical Democracy after Occupy" (seminar discussion, Center for the Study of Contemporary Art, University College London, December 7, 2013, orga-

of Podemos in Spain and Syriza in Greece offer hope here (despite recent setbacks), as do progressive Latin American activist organizations and Indigenous movements in Bolivia and Ecuador, which stand as leading examples of "occupations" of institutions, some governmental, that are realizing alternatives to Western ideologies of development, liberalism, and economics. In other words, such movements demonstrate the effectiveness of multi-sited interventions that are both top-down and bottom-up, as Mouffe has pointed out,[30] giving rise to an intersectionalist politics that insistently links movements and political concerns in diverse alliances, as with *buen vivir* (the collective, environmentalist Andean-Amazonian culture of "living well") in South America, global rights-of-nature movements, climate-justice activism, and local, urban, and rural practices of ecological sustainability. Different levels and scales of engagement are already connected to diverse disciplines, institutions, and communities, all working together toward changing the paradigm, moving toward environmental livability, greater economic equality, and social justice.[31] As Mouffe writes, "The building of a new hegemony implies the creation of a 'chain of equivalence' among the diversity of democratic struggles, old and new, in order to form a 'collective will', a 'we' of the radical democratic forces."[32] This new composition must come together to struggle for a Great Transition.

To make this happen will require the critical production and sharing of knowledge, resistance to flattening aesthetic diversity, and the invention of sustainable models that don't threaten the viability of the whole, whether economically or ecologically, socially or institutionally. One way is to translate ecological values—including subsidiarity, the precautionary principle, and maintaining the ecosystem—into all fields of practice (including artistic), asserting a new biocentric imperative for living,

nized by T. J. Demos and Tom Snow). For a counterexample of creating spaces of political possibility outside state governments, see Holloway, *Change the World without Taking Power*.

30 See Chantal Mouffe, *Agonistics: Thinking the World Politically* (London: Verso Books, 2013).

31 See, for instance, the Portland-based organization Resistance Ecology and their definition of ecological intersectionality: "a movement that is multi-layered, unified, diverse and intersectional. We must understand that social, economic, cultural, environmental, historical, and political factors operate together in complex and intersecting ways. Accordingly, animal and ecological activists need to adopt an approach of solidarity organizing and coalition building. We must build supportive relationships with a broad spectrum of social and political struggle." Resistance Ecology's Facebook page, accessed December 15, 2015, https://www.facebook.com/Resistanceecologyconference/info/?tab=page_info. For the African American and feminist origins of the term and its later adoption within political ecology discourse, see Anna Kaijser and Annica Kronsell, "Climate Change through the Lens of Intersectionality," *Environmental Politics* 23, no. 3 (October 2014): 417–33.

32 Chantal Mouffe, *On the Political* (London: Routledge, 2005), 53.

producing, and consuming. Addressing the local is exemplary of what anthropologist James Clifford calls "becoming indigenous"—learning to live within a place consciously, paying attention to its specific nature ecologically and politically as much as socially and economically, promoting environmental health, and supporting a local politics of justice and equality.[33] Toward the end of his life, Howard Zinn observed that the problem isn't with civil disobedience, but with civil *obedience*—an obedience premised on forgetting the significance of democratic direct-action campaigns in the histories of decolonization, independence movements, the abolition of slavery and Apartheid, and civil, worker, women's, and gay rights. All of these struggles, at various times, had to trespass, set up blockades and protests, and transgress laws of eviction, all in defense of justice within and beyond existing unjust laws. Keeping safely within legal procedure in times of injustice is ultimately unconscionable, unethical, and wrong, and, with the very viability of life at stake, it's evident that we have entered another such period today. Alongside Zinn, I would argue that without civil disobedience, democracy doesn't exist.[34] Today we confront an equally urgent challenge—either a near future of climate catastrophe, or one of just transition, the former achieved by doing nothing, the latter realized through sustainable democracy and the creation of an alternate future. The choice is (still) ours to make. In no way should art be exempt from the imperative to confront this choice. Indeed, the cultural sphere should fight to recognize the value of its creative resources in constructing a different form of life, decolonizing nature within and beyond the human, even while we recognize that art as

33 Clifford, *Returns: Becoming Indigenous*. For one recent inspired example of art and ecological writing, see Lippard, *Undermining*. For an argument in support of "eco-cosmopolitanism," or "environmental world citizenship," as an alternative to nationality and to parochial formations in US environmentalism and bioregionalism, see Heise, *Sense of Place and Sense of Planet*. Even though Heise argues that "a wide variety of both natural and cultural places and processes are connected and shape each other around the world" (21), I feel the book goes too far in dismissing localist engagements. As well, global disconnectedness is more often than not idealized in the art world, and thus a cosmopolitical localism offers an important route forward—as does Clifford's "becoming indigenous," that is, an anti-essentialist becoming neither complete nor divorced from global forces. Moreover, this does not deny Heise's point that "identities are at their core made up of mixtures, fragments, and dispersed allegiances to diverse communities, cultures, and places—or that precisely these mixtures might be crucial for constituting 'identities' politically as 'subjects'" (43). Granted, "there is nothing in the idea of localism itself," Heise argues, "that guarantees its connection with the grassroots-democratic and egalitarian politics that many environmentalists envision when they advocate place-based communities" (48); however, globalism offers no such guarantee either, and risks mirroring destructive free-trade policies and ravaging corporate neoliberal practice.

34 See Howard Zinn, *Disobedience and Democracy: Nine Fallacies on Law and Order* (Cambridge, MA: South End Press, 2002). For additional arguments regarding civil disobedience in our political present, see David Graeber, *Direct Action: An Ethnography* (Oakland: AK Press, 2009).

such offers no automatic or guaranteed redemption. The practices that have brought together aesthetics, ethics, and political ecology allow us to glimpse the beauty of living otherwise.

Acknowledgments

Over the last few years of my attempts to think through the connections between contemporary art, activism, and political ecology, I have encountered and relied on the heartening support, generosity, and friendship of countless people. The innumerable enriching conversations, subtle forms of encouragement, and affirmative argumentation can hardly be adequately recognized here. These figures include the many artists, practitioners, and thinkers whose work I discuss in these pages, colleagues in diverse scholarly fields and institutions, hosts and supporters in museum and publishing contexts, and many family members and friends. The insights that came out of these many dialogues and relationships facilitated and improved my research and writing enormously, even if I've also resisted advice at various times, doubtlessly to my own peril!

Many thanks to Nils Norman for the many lunches and conversations in London, for the informative walk around his edible garden in Utrecht, and for his friendship over the years, and to Emily Pethick for her institutional support on behalf of the Showroom, one of London's leading independent cultural spaces, which has generously hosted rewarding discussions of my work. During the ten years I was based in the United Kingdom, many additional friends, comrades, and colleagues—including Sarah James, Kodwo Eshun, Anjalika Sagar, John Akomfrah, Lina Gopaul, David Lawson, Oreet Ashery, Alex Farquharson, Anna Colin, Karen Mirza, Brad Butler, Eyal Weizman, Ros Gray, Nabil Ahmed, Shela Sheikh, Anthony Downey, Antigoni Memou, Steve Edwards, Gail Day, Stephen Wilson, Irit Rogoff, Luke Skrebowski, Gavin Grindon, Anthony Gardner, Judy Price, Carey Young, and Corinne Silva—created the vibrant intellectual environment in which my ideas took hold and grew. I'm indebted to my former colleagues at the Center for the Study of Contemporary Art at University College London—Briony Fer, Tamar Garb, and Stephanie Schwartz among them—for years of support and critical discussions.

I've shared many fruitful conversations with Tue Greenfort about ecological matters of concern; with Lise Autogena on her Thames-based houseboat; and with Amy Balkin, until recently mostly at a distance, though now happily just up the road in San Francisco. Subhankar Banerjee has been continually engaging, and I've appreciated the many back-and-forths about the rights of nature and environmental justice, in addition to his modeling of what it means to be a committed public intellectual. Gratitude goes to Francesco Manacorda, who commissioned my essay "The Politics of Sustainability" for his 2009 exhibition "Radical Nature" at London's Barbican, inadvertently catalyzing the beginning of this research project.

While in Mexico, Eduardo Abaroa and Ana Maria Sanchez generously supported my research, organizing a SOMA residency in Mexico City in November 2013 to my benefit. Thanks also to Catalina Lozano for conversations about Mexican political ecology; to Cuauhtémoc Medina and Daniel Montero at the Museo Universitario Arte Contemporáneo for productive meetings and inviting me to present my work to an audience there; to Marcela Armas and Gilberto Esparza for their time considering their respective projects; and to Minerva Cuevas for a guided walking tour of Mexico City's historic downtown, and for the introduction to grilled crickets and mescal, which provided an unparalleled context in which to confer about her art. Alessandro Zagato and Natalia Arcos, of Grupo Investigación en Arte y Politica (GIAP), generously discussed their work, and also that of the Zapatistas, with me in Mexico City; and Maria Thereza Alves has been consistently forthcoming in answering my numerous queries, and facilitating my research by putting me in touch with Genaro Amaro Altamirano, who warmly received me at the Museo Comunitario del Valle de Xico.

In India, I enjoyed many conversations with Ravi Agarwal, including one during an eye-opening driving tour of New Delhi's Yamuna River; Sanjay Kak kindly volunteered his time to discuss his film *Red Ant Dream*; and Jeebesh Bagchi, Monica Narula, and Shuddhabrata Sengupta, of Raqs Media Collective and Sarai, spoke at length with me about the complexities of their practice. Ravi Sundaram helped organize a symposium where we collectively examined visual culture and environment in Delhi. And Pooja Sood, of Khoj International Artists' Association, tirelessly facilitated my research at each request, including generously putting me up at Khoj's residency in

Khirki Village. Much appreciation to Anand Patwardhan for moving discussions of his films at Tate Modern, and to Gayatri Sinha of the Critical Collective, Roobina Karode, and Saloni Mathur for hosting a presentation of my work at the Kiran Nadar Museum of Art in Delhi. Many thanks also to Amar Kanwar, who joined me on a trip to Bhubaneswar to visit and talk about his installation of *The Sovereign Forest* there, and to Sudhir Pattnaik, director of Samadrusti, for his insightful critical observations.

The Otolith Group—specifically Kodwo Eshun and Anjalika Sagar—have been long-standing and consistent interlocutors and great friends, deeply appreciated at each turn, as well as makers of inspiring artworks and organizers of endlessly stimulating discourse in London; I thank them both for their engagements. Much appreciation also goes to the members of World of Matter, who have been ongoing partners in dialogue over the last few years, and particularly to Ursula Biemann and Emily Eliza Scott for many discussions of experimental ecologies and for their critical work. Many thanks to John Jordan and Isabelle Frémeaux, as well as to the collective members of la r.O.n.c.e, for hosting my visit to their space in Brittany, and for the many conversations about their inspiring project. *Merci bien* as well to Léonore Bonaccini and Xavier Fourt of Bureau d'Études for their hospitality during my visit to their experiment in La Mhotte, and for provocative considerations of "interspecies communism."

I greatly appreciate the generosity of Ashley Dawson, Sarah James, and Yates McKee for reading sections of the manuscript. As well, there are many friends and colleagues whose warm invitations to present my research, and thoughtful consideration of it through lively critical debate, has significantly benefitted this project, among them: Ursula Frohne in Cologne; Sofía Hernández Chong Cuy in Caracas; Jennifer Teets in Vilnius; Daniel Quiles and Béatrice Joyeux-Prunel in Paris; Michaela Crimmin, Jennifer Walden, Andrew Patrizio, and Gabo Guzzo in London; Jakob Ladegaard in Aarhus; Henk Slager, Jan Kaila, Terike Haapoja, Hanna Husberg, and Laura McLean in Venice, at different times; Bo Zheng in Shanghai; WHW in Zagreb; Eric de Bruyn, Rachel Esner, Sven Lütticken, and Kitty Zijlmans in Leiden; Katherine Carl in New York; Boris Buden, Maria Hlavajova, and Simon Sheikh in Utrecht; Heidi Bale Amundsen and Gerd Elise Mørland in Oslo; Alexander Streitberger, Brianne Cohen, and Hilde van Gelder in Belgium; and Inke Arns in Berlin. In addition, sincere thanks are owed to Alex Farquharson, Irene Aristizabal, and Janna Graham at Nottingham Contemporary for collaborating on and cocurating the 2015 show "Rights of Nature: Art and Ecology in the Americas," which informs my research here. Jean Fisher was an important critical converser in the accompanying conference's preparation.

Since moving to UC Santa Cruz in 2015, I've gained many more perceptive interlocutors, including new friends and inspiring colleagues such as Jennifer González, Albert Narath, Jim Clifford, Donna Haraway, Flora Lu, Andy Szasz, Anna Tsing, Karen Barad, Rick Flores, John Weber, Rachel Nelson, and the many collaborators of my emergent Center for Creative Ecologies. I look forward to growing this network further in the future. In addition, Helen and Newton Harrison have provided many provocative conversations about things politico-ecological, including their work's ambitious objectives, which warrant more extensive examination than I've provided here.

In London I received a Leverhulme Research Fellowship from 2013 to 2014, which facilitated my research in giving me time away from teaching to substantially develop this project. Some of the material contained herein has been published in earlier versions elsewhere: chapter 1 appeared as "The Politics of Sustainability: Art and Ecology," in *Radical Nature: Art and Architecture for a Changing Planet, 1969–2009*, edited by Francesco Manacorda and Ariella Yedgar (Barbican Art Gallery, 2009); chapter 3 as "The Post-Natural Condition: Art after Nature," *Artforum*, April 2012; chapter 6 as "Decolonizing Nature: Making the World Matter," in *World of Matter*, edited by Inke Arns (Sternberg Press and Hartware MedienKunstVerein, 2014); and chapter 7 as "Gardens beyond Eden: Bio-aesthetics, Eco-Futurism, and Dystopia at dOCUMENTA (13)," *Brooklyn Rail*, October 2012. These essays have been significantly revised for this book.

Enormous appreciation is extended to the team at Sternberg Press—to Caroline Schneider for her continuing support of my work; to Louisa Nyman for her help with image acquisition; and to editor Max Bach for his incisive interventions in the text, which have substantially improved the book—as well as to Miriam Rech for the beautiful book design.

Finally, my most heartfelt thanks to Joy Schendledecker and Zoë and Leila Demos, for their generosity, tolerance, and encouragement, and for the innumerable everyday things that make my work possible. It is to them that I dedicate this book.

Index

Image Credits

Chapter 1
The Art and Politics of Sustainability

p. 32
Helen Mayer Harrison and Newton Harrison, *Greenhouse Britain, Green House Britain First Sketch, 2006: Where the loss of land due to ocean rise is first expressed*, 2006. Detail of map. Ink and oil on vinyl. Each 78 1/2 x 46 in. Photo: Hermann Feldhaus. Courtesy of Ronald Feldman Fine Arts, New York.

p. 39
Alan Sonfist, *Time Landscape New York City*, 1965–present. 45 x 200 ft. Courtesy of the Alan Sonfist Studio.

p. 41
Helen Mayer Harrison and Newton Harrison, *Portable Orchard: Survival Piece #5*, 1972–73. Twelve hexagonal redwood boxes four feet in diameter, three feet deep, planted with assorted citrus trees, topped by hexagonal redwood light boxes. Dimensions variable. Courtesy of Ronald Feldman Fine Arts, New York.

p. 47
Hans Christoph Carl Haacke, *Rhine-Water Purification Plant*, 1972. Glass and acrylic containers, pump, polluted Rhine water, tubing filters, chemicals, goldfish, drainage to garden. Installation view, Museum Haus Lange, Krefeld. © VG Bild-Kunst, Bonn.

p. 49
Dan Graham, *TV Camera/Monitor Performance*, 1970. Performance with television camera and monitor. Performed at Nova Scotia College of Art and Design. Courtesy of Dan Graham.

p. 51
Pulsa Group, *Automation House Installation*, 1971. Video projectors, plants, loudspeakers, analog digital control system, etc. Installation view. Automation House, New York. Courtesy of Pulsa Group.

p. 56
SUPERFLEX, *Supergas*, Tanzania, 1997. Created in collaboration with the Tanzanian nongovernmental organization SURUDE (Sustainable Rural Development). Photo: SUPERFLEX. Courtesy of the artists.

p. 57
Henrik Håkansson, *Fallen Forest*, 2006. Wood, steel, soil, metal halide lights, plants. Installation view, "A travers bois pour trouver la forêt," Palais de Tokyo, Paris, 2006. Courtesy of the artist; Galleria Franco Noero, Turin; and the Modern Institute, Glasgow. © PDT/Kleinefenn, 2006.

p. 59
Tue Greenfort, *Diffuse Einträge*, 2007. Modified manure-spreading machine, 100 liter tank filled with iron(III)-chloride, water fountain. Courtesy of the artist and Johann König, Berlin.

pp. 60–61
Nils Norman, *Ideal City, Research/Play Sector*, 2005. Mural size vinyl print. Courtesy of the artist.

p. 62
Nils Norman, *Geocruiser*, 2003. Mixed media. Installation outside Peckham Library, London. Courtesy of the artist.

Chapter 2
Climates of Displacement

pp. 66–67
Guillaume Collanges, Coral reef in the Maldives, 2005. © Guillaume Collanges/Picturetank/Agentur Focus.

p. 69
Laurent Weyl, Funafuti Atoll, Fongafale Island, Tuvalu, during a tsunami, 2006. © Laurent Weyl/Picturetank/Agentur Focus.

p. 71
Josephine Starrs and Leon Cmielewski, *SOS*, 2013. Digital print. Courtesy of the artists.

p. 74
Underwater cabinet meeting, Maldives, October 17, 2009. © Mohammed Seeneen/AP Photo/picture alliance.

p. 83
Caleb Larsen, *Land Grab*, 2008. Diptych. Courtesy of the artist.

pp. 86–87
Subhankar Banerjee, *Caribou Migration II*, 2002. Digital photograph from the series "Oil and the Caribou." Courtesy of the artist.

p. 88
Subhankar Banerjee, *At the Corral III—Ilya Golikov, Nikolayev Matvey and Osenina Dariya Mikhailevna*, 2007. Digital photograph from the series "Even and the Climate." Courtesy of the artist.

pp. 90–91
Subhankar Banerjee, *Caribou Tracks on Coal Seams II*, 2006. Digital photograph from the series "Coal and the Caribou." Courtesy of the artist.

p. 92
Center for Land Use Interpretation, from the series *The Trans-Alaska Pipeline*, 2008. Photo: CLUI. Courtesy of CLUI/Morgan Cowles Archive.

p. 94
Senator Barbara Boxer on C-SPAN, March 19, 2003, with Subjankar Banerjee's photograph *Polar Bear on Bernard Harbor, Barter Island*, 2001. Television still. Courtesy of the artist.

p. 95
Political advertisement in the *New York Times*, November 2005. Subhankar Banerjee, *Caribou Migration I*, 2002. Digital photograph from the series "Oil and the Caribou." Courtesy of the artist.

Chapter 3
The Post-natural Condition

p. 102
Lise Autogena and Joshua Portway, *Black Shoals Stock Market Planetarium*, 2004. Real-time data visualization of the financial markets. Nikolaj Copenhagen Art Centre and Copenhagen Stock Exchange, 2004. Photo: Nikolaj Copenhagen Contemporary Art Centre. Courtesy of the artists.

p. 103
Lise Autogena and Joshua Portway, *Black Shoals Stock Market Planetarium*, 2001. Real-time data visualization of the financial markets—an ecology of artificial life-forms feed off the light of the stars (real-time trading). Installation view, Tate Britain, London. Photo: Lise Autogena and Joshua Portway. Courtesy of the artists.

p. 107
Amy Balkin, *Public Smog over Los Angeles*, 2004. Courtesy of the artist.

p. 108
Amy Balkin, *Public Smog*, 2004. Excel spreadsheet of NOX purchase. Courtesy of the artist.

p. 111
Amy Balkin, *Public Smog*, 2015. Screenshot, http://www.publicsmog.org. Courtesy of the artist.

p. 113
Tue Greenfort, *Exceeding 2 Degrees*, 2007. Thermo hydrograph (meteorological instrument), coffee table, Malaysian rubber wood, glass, human hair, plastic membrane, *Stern Review* quotes, A4 photocopy, photograph, climate diagram, certificate, map. Installation view, "Still Life: Art, Ecology and the Politics of Change," 8th Sharjah Biennial, Sharjah Art Museum, Sharjah, 2007. Photo: Tue Greenfort. Courtesy of the artist and Johann König, Berlin.

p. 118
Critical Art Ensemble, *Free Range Grain*, 2003–4. Courtesy of Critical Art Ensemble (CAE).

p. 121
Nils Norman, *Edible Park*, 2010. Collaboration with Permacultuur Centrum Den Haag. Courtesy of the artist.

p. 125
Reclaim the Streets, M41 Party, July 13, 1996. Photo: Julia Guest. Courtesy of the photographer.

pp. 127, 128, 129
La r.O.n.c.e., ca. 2012. Photos: John Jordan. Courtesy of la r.O.n.c.e.

Chapter 4
¡Ya basta!

p. 134
Minerva Cuevas, *Seascape*, 2012. Oil on compressed wood board covered in chapopote, 102 x 92.5 cm. Photo: Estudio Michel Zabé. Courtesy of the artist and kurimanzutto, Mexico City.

p. 135
Minerva Cuevas, *Serie hidrocarburos*, 2007. Multimedia installation, variable dimensions. Photo: Estudio Michel Zabé. Courtesy of the artist and kurimanzutto, Mexico City.

p. 137
Minerva Cuevas, *Del Montte*, 2003. Acrylic paint on wall, black-and-white research scheme on paper, 100 relabeled tomato cans (English), scheme: 90 x 60 cm, mural: 500 x 600 cm. Courtesy of the artist and kurimanzutto, Mexico City.

p. 139, above
Marcela Armas, *Occupation: Sound Action for Car Space with Seven Car Horns*, 2007. Photo: Gilberto Esparza. Courtesy of the artist.

p. 139, below
Marcela Armas, *Obstruction with Two-Stroke Engine: Two Motorcycles, Gasoline, Plastic Container, Gas Combustion*, 2009. Courtesy of the artist.

p. 141, above
Helen Escobedo, *Negro basura, negro mañana*, 1991. Inorganic rubbish covered with thin iron mesh and gray acrylic paint. Photo: Helen Escobedo. Courtesy of Beatriz Escobedo.

p. 141, below
Gustav Metzger, *Project Stockholm, June (Phase 1)*, 1972/2007. Scaffolding, polythene sheets, 120 cars. Installation view, behind Sharjah Expo Centre. Commissioned and produced by Sharjah Art Foundation. Photo: Peter Reidlinger. Courtesy of the Sharjah Art Foundation. © Gustav Metzger.

p. 147
Gilberto Esparza, *Plantas Nómadas*, 2008–13. Autonomous robot, microbial fuel cells, live plants, polluted water. Photo: Gilberto Esparza. Courtesy of the artist. www.plantasnomadas.com

p. 149
SUPERFLEX, *Supergas*, Mexico, 2014. Photo: SUPERFLEX. Courtesy of the artists.

p. 151
Pedro Reyes, *Palas por Pistolas*, 2008. © Pedro Reyes. Courtesy of Lisson Gallery.

p. 155, left
Grupo de Investigación en Arte y Política (GIAP), *The Farewell of Subcomandante Marcos*,

2014. Photo: Alessandro Zagato. Courtesy of GIAP (Alessandro Zagato and Natalia Arcos).

p. 155, right
Grupo de Investigación en Arte y Política (GIAP), *Mural in La Realidad*, 2014. Photo: Alessandro Zagato. Courtesy of GIAP (Alessandro Zagato and Natalia Arcos).

p. 156
Grupo de Investigación en Arte y Política (GIAP), Zapatista farmers practicing agroecology, 2014–15. Photos: Oleg Myasoedov. Courtesy of GIAP (Alessandro Zagato and Natalia Arcos).

pp. 157, 158
Maria Thereza Alves, *Return of a Lake*, 2012. Installation views, dOCUMENTA (13), Kassel, 2012. Photos: Mikula Lüllwitz. Courtesy of the artist.

p. 161
Diego Rivera, *The Great City of Tenochtitlán*, 1945. Detail of mural, Patio Corridor, Mexico City, National Palace, 4.92 x 9.71 m. © 2016. Photo Art Resource/Bob Schalkwijk/Scala, Florence/Banco de Mexico Diego Rivera Frida Kahlo Museums Trust/VG Bild-Kunst, Bonn 2016.

p. 163
Museo Comunitario del Valle de Xico, 2013. Exterior and interior views. Photos: T. J. Demos. Courtesy of the author.

Chapter 5
Many Faces of Madness

pp. 168, 175
Sanjay Kak, *Red Ant Dream*, 2013. Film stills. Color, English, 120 min. Courtesy of the artist.

p. 181
Ravi Agarwal, *Alien Waters*, 2004–6. Color photograph from a series. Courtesy of the artist.

p. 182
Ravi Agarwal, *Have you seen the flowers on the river?*, 2007. Color photograph from a series. Courtesy of the artist.

p. 184
Ravi Agarwal, *Alien Waters*, 2004–6. Color photograph from a series. Courtesy of the artist.

p. 186
Amar Kanwar, *The Sovereign Forest*, 2012. Installation view, Samadrusti, Bhubaneswar, Odisha, 2014. Courtesy of the artist and Marian Goodman Gallery, New York/Paris.

p. 187
Amar Kanwar, *Counting Sisters and Other Stories*, 2011. Silk-screened, handmade banana-fiber-paper book and color HD video projection, 40 min. From *The Sovereign Forest*, 2012. Courtesy of the artist and Marian Goodman Gallery, New York/Paris.

p. 189
Amar Kanwar, *The Scene of the Crime*, 2011. Video stills. HD video, color, sound, 42 min. Installation views from *The Sovereign Forest*, 2012. Courtesy of the artist and Marian Goodman Gallery, New York/Paris.

p. 191
Amar Kanwar, *Many Faces of Madness*, 2000. Video stills. Color, English, 19 min. Produced by the Foundation for Ecological Security, Anand, Gujarat, India. Courtesy of the artist.

p. 192
Amar Kanwar, *The Sovereign Forest*, 2012. Installation view, Samadrusti, Bhubaneswar, Odisha, 2014. Courtesy of the artist and Marian Goodman Gallery, New York/Paris.

p. 195
Amar Kanwar, *The Sovereign Forest*, 2012. 272 varieties of indigenous, organic rice seeds, in labeled seed storage containers. Installation view, dOCUMENTA (13), Kassel, 2012. Courtesy of the artist and Marian Goodman Gallery, New York/Paris.

Chapter 6
Decolonizing Nature

p. 201
Paulo Tavares, *Non-human Rights*, 2012. Video still. Color, 45 min. Courtesy of the artist.

p. 204
Uwe H. Martin and Frauke Huber, *Landrush: Frontier Land*, 2011–14. Video stills. Courtesy of the artists.

pp. 206, 207
Ursula Biemann, *Deep Weather*, 2013. Video stills. Color, 9 min. Courtesy of the artist.

p. 208, above
Uwe H. Martin, *White Gold—Killing Seeds*, 2007–14. Video still. Courtesy of the artist.

p. 208, below
Uwe H. Martin, *White Gold—Texas Blues*, 2007–14. Video still. Courtesy of the artist.

p. 212
Ed Kashi, *Curse of the Black Gold*, 2008. Digital image. Courtesy of Ed Kashi/VII.

p. 214
Mabe Bethônico, Women miner in Minas Gerais, Brazil; from *Mineral Invisibility*, 2008–ongoing. Images produced for donation to the International Labour Office, Geneva. Collection: Museum of Public Concerns. Courtesy of the artist.

p. 218
Ursula Biemann, *Egyptian Chemistry*, 2012. Video stills. Courtesy of the artist.

p. 222
Paulo Tavares, *Non-human Rights*, 2012. Video still. Color, 45 min. Courtesy of the artist.

p. 227
Helge Mooshammer and Peter Mörtenböck, *A World of Matter*, 2014. Installation view. Courtesy of James Gallery, New York, and the artists.

Chapter 7
Gardening against the Apocalypse

p. 230
Kristina Buch, *The Lover*, 2012. Garden with 180 species of plants and 40 species of butterflies. Installation views, dOCUMENTA (13), Kassel, 2012. Courtesy of the artist.

p. 231
Christian Philipp Müller, *Swiss Chard Ferry, The Russians Aren't Going to Make It across the Fulda River Anymore*, 2012. Sixty varieties of chard planted on six barges, floating in the Karlsaue, Kassel. Installation view, dOCUMENTA (13), Kassel, 2012. Photo: Christian Philipp Müller. Courtesy of the artist.

p. 233
Claire Pentecost, *soil-erg* (growing systems), 2012. Installation view, dOCUMENTA (13), Kassel, 2012. Created in collaboration with Can YA Love. Photo: Claire Pentecost. Courtesy of the artist.

p. 234
Song Dong, *Doing Nothing Garden*, 2010–12. Daily-life rubbish and building rubbish with plants and neon signs, 7 x 32.3 x 23.5 m. Installation view, dOCUMENTA (13), Kassel, 2012. Sponsored by Uli Sigg and Pace Gallery Beijing. © Song Dong. Courtesy of Pace Beijing.

p. 236
Sarah Kanouse and Sarah Lewison, *The Monsanto Hearings*, 2012. Video stills. 58 min. Courtesy of the directors.

p. 238
And And And, *Non-capitalist Tea Garden*, 2012. Installation view, dOCUMENTA (13), Kassel, 2012. Courtesy of the artists.

p. 243
Moon Kyungwon and Jeon Joonho, *El Fin del Mundo*, 2012. Two-channel HD film, 13:35 min. Installation view, "News from Nowhere," dOCUMENTA (13), Kassel, 2012. Courtesy of the artists and GALLERY HYUNDAI.

p. 244
Moon Kyungwon and Jeon Joonho, *El Fin del Mundo*, 2012. Still. Two-channel HD film, 13:35 min. Courtesy of the artists and GALLERY HYUNDAI.

p. 247
The Otolith Group, *The Radiant*, 2012. Film stills. © The Otolith Group. Courtesy of the artists.

p. 252
Diana Thater, *Chernobyl*, 2011. Installation view, David Zwirner, New York, 2012. Six projectors, six media players, and Lee filters. Courtesy of David Zwirner, New York/London.

p. 253
Jane and Louise Wilson, *The Toxic Camera*, 2012. Still. © Jane and Louise Wilson/VG Bild-Kunst, Bonn 2016. Courtesy of 303 Gallery, New York.

p. 254
The Otolith Group, *The Radiant*, 2012. Film stills. © The Otolith Group. Courtesy of the artists. Including a still from Vito Acconci, *Centers*, 1971. © VG Bild-Kunst, Bonn 2016.

Author Biography

T. J. Demos is a professor in the History of Art and Visual Culture Department, University of California, Santa Cruz, and founder and director of its Center for Creative Ecologies. He is the author of *The Migrant Image: The Art and Politics of Documentary during Global Crisis* (Duke University Press, 2013)—winner of the College Art Association's 2014 Frank Jewett Mather Award—and *Return to the Postcolony: Specters of Colonialism in Contemporary Art* (Sternberg Press, 2013). Demos cocurated "Rights of Nature: Art and Ecology in the Americas," Nottingham Contemporary (2015), and organized "Specters: A Ciné-Politics of Haunting," Museo Reina Sofía, Madrid (2014). His book *Against the Anthropocene: Visual Culture and Environment Today* is forthcoming from Sternberg Press.

T. J. Demos
Decolonizing Nature
Contemporary Art and the Politics of Ecology

Published by Sternberg Press

Editor: Max Bach
Proofreading: Michael Runyan
Image research: Louisa Nyman
Printing: Tallinn Book Printers, Estonia

Design by Miriam Rech, Berlin

Cover image: Lise Autogena and Joshua Portway, *Black Shoals Stock Market Planetarium*, 2001. Real-time data visualization of the financial markets. The first stars in the planetarium. Photo © Lise Autogena and Joshua Portway. Courtesy of the artists.

ISBN 978-3-95679-094-2

First published 2016, reprinted 2024

Distributed by The MIT Press, Art Data, Idea Books, and Les presses du réel

Sternberg Press
71–75 Shelton Street
London WC2H 9JQ
www.sternberg-press.com